Violent Land

Violent Land

Single Men and Social Disorder from the Frontier to the Inner City

David T. Courtwright

Harvard University Press
Cambridge, Massachusetts
London, England

First Harvard University Press paperback edition, 1998

Library of Congress Cataloging-in-Publication Data

Courtwright, David T., 1952–
 Violent land : single men and social disorder from the frontier to
the inner city / David T. Courtwright.
  p. cm.
 Includes bibliographical references and index.
 ISBN 0-674-27870-4 (cloth)
 ISBN 0-674-27871-2 (pbk.)
 1. Violence—United States—History. 2. Single men—United
States—History. 3. Sex distribution (Demography)—United States—
History. I. Title.
HN90.V5C68 1996
303.6'0973—dc20   96-9277

In memory of my parents, Betty and Bob Courtwright

Acknowledgments

This book is an interdisciplinary explanation of the historical pattern of American violence and disorder. It was researched and written with financial support from the American Council of Learned Societies, the University of Hartford, the University of Connecticut Health Center, and the University of North Florida. I have depended no less crucially on the advice, criticism, and support of colleagues in my own and other disciplines. Among those to whom I am indebted are Jim Baumohl, Bill Brayfield, James Dabb Jr., Don Des Jarlais, Roger Desmond, Linda Foley, Dean Gerstein, Kermit Hall, Sam Kimball, Roger McGrath, Bob Massey, Pat Plumlee, Joseph Pleck, Dan Schafer, Wes Shrum, and James Q. Wilson.

The help of librarians and archivists was crucial to my endeavor. Many thanks to the staffs of the Beinecke and Sterling Libraries at Yale, the Newberry Library, the Libraries of the Universities of Chicago and North Carolina, the University of Connecticut Health Center, and the Library of Congress. Librarians at the University of Hartford's Mortensen Library, especially Ann Maio and Jean Prescott, rendered continuing service. So did the faculty and staff of the University of North Florida's Carpenter Library, particularly Eileen Brady, Kathy Cohen, Alisa Craddock, Geraldine Collins, Mary Davis, Andrew Farkas, Joan Foley, David Green, Bruce Latimer, Paul Mosley, Sarah Philips, Joan Pickett, Peggy Pruett, Barbara Tuck, and Felicia Williams. My wife Shelby Miller again demonstrated the wisdom of historians' marrying librarians.

Eugene Albertson and Patricia Berry helped me gather quantitative information, as did Constanze Roman, who also read an early version of the manuscript. Janice Fluegel and Michael Hoffman scrutinized a later version. John Morrell and Teresa St. John helped me with figures and maps. My colleagues Donna Mohr and Bill Wilson lent statistical advice. Marianne Roberts assisted with the word processing. Angela von der Lippe and Camille Smith helped me to revise and polish the manuscript.

I want to extend special thanks to Edmund Morgan, Sterling Professor Emeritus of Yale University, with whom I studied in 1983–1984 under a Mellon Visiting Faculty Fellowship. My training as a graduate student in the 1970s, working with Harold Hyman, Allen Matusow, Martin Wiener, and Thomas Haskell—exceptional scholars to whom I also owe a large debt—had led me to focus on the nineteenth and twentieth centuries. When I began studying the literature of early American social history with Morgan I saw it with fresh eyes. The thing that struck me most forcibly was the difference between the orderly, family-centered life of seventeenth-century New England and that of the Chesapeake colonies, roisterous bachelor societies where the chief preoccupation seemed to be men quarreling with and exploiting other men. This contrast, which I have here simplified, gave rise to a question: was the violence and disorder attendant to male societies peculiar to the early Chesapeake or was it an important and recurring theme in subsequent American history? What follows constitutes an extended affirmative answer, based on a variety of sources. I do not know whether Professor Morgan or any of the other people I have acknowledged fully approve of my answer, but I am nevertheless deeply grateful for the assistance they rendered me on my historical odyssey.

Contents

Illustrations

Following page 182

Bound for Potter's Field: the morgue, New York City, 23 February 1895. From the Social Reform Papers of John James McCook [hereafter SRP], the Antiquarian and Landmarks Society, Inc., Hartford, Connecticut

"Just a Common Drunk": Fourth Precinct Station House, Oak Street, New York City, 22 February 1895, 11:15 P.M. SRP

Mail-order gun, 1908. From Sears, Roebuck and Company's Catalogue no. 117

Illustrated letter from boot camp. Letter from Jack Whalen to Betty Brown, 30 October 1943, collection of the author

"Two Pike County Arrivals." Frederic Remington illustration for *Century Magazine*, 1890

"The Used-Up Man." Caricature from Alonzo Delano's *Pen Knife Sketches*, 1853. Library of Congress

"Judge Lynch," California, 1848, as imagined by Stanley Berkeley in 1905. Library of Congress

Miners and recently arrived immigrants sleeping in the sawdust of a saloon in Leadville, Colorado, circa 1880. Library of Congress

"Here lies poor Jack; his race is run," by C. M. Russell, 1901. Library of Congress

A trader offers a Plains Indian a bottle of whiskey. From *Leslie's Illustrated Weekly*, 23 September 1871. Library of Congress

Rabbit hunters on the Kansas prairie. Photograph, half of an Underwood and Underwood stereograph, probably from around 1900. California Museum of Photography, Keystone-Mast Collection, University of California, Riverside

"The Danites." Undated cartoon. Library of Congress

Julia Etta Parkerson Reynolds, Alvin Reynolds, and their son, William, in 1883. Kansas State Historical Society

Anti-Chinese cartoon. From the *Wasp*, a San Francisco newspaper, 1876

Lumberjacks' bunk house, Minnesota. Library of Congress

"Riding the Rods" as demonstrated by Providence Bob and Philadelphia Shorty on 5 December 1894. SRP

"A Timber Lesson." From Josiah Flynt Willard, *Tramping with Tramps* (1899)

John James McCook presiding over his Trinity College Classroom. SRP

William "Roving Bill" Aspinwall, 8 June 1893. SRP

The Billy Goat saloon, 153 Park Row, East Side, New York City, 22 February 1895. SRP

Anti-saloon cartoon, 1911.

Wedding photograph taken 18 March 1944 for Yeoman Second Class Paul W. Heinz of the USS Ranger. Serial A3781-2, Roman B. J. Kwasniewski photographs, 1907–1947, MS collection 19, U. Manuscript Collections, Golda Meir Library, U. of Wisconsin-Milwaukee. Used with permission

California gunfighters, circa 1970. From Bill Owens, *Suburbia* (1972). Used with permission

Despair of an old head, Red Hook, Brooklyn. From Eugene Richards, *Cocaine True, Cocaine Blue* (1994). Used with permission

Street portrait, North Philadelphia. From Eugene Richards, *Cocaine True, Cocaine Blue* (1994). Used with permission

Inmates watching television at the Detention Center of St. Johns County, Florida, 1994. Photo by M. Jack Luedke, *Florida Times-Union*. Used with permission

Michael Bell, new frontiersman, on trial for first-degree murder. Photo by M. Jack Luedke, *Florida Times-Union*. Used with permission

Figures

INTRODUCTION

The Historical Pattern

> There is a tendency, in any analysis of violence, to look
> upon it in one of two ways: as a deviation from the past
> *or* as a continuation from it.
>
> —Bill Buford, *Among the Thugs*

Violence and disorder constitute the primal problem of American history, the dark reverse of its coin of freedom and abundance. American society, or at any rate a conspicuous part of it, has been tumultuous from the very beginning of European colonization. Seventeenth-century Virginia was a disorderly place, though the Massachusetts Bay Colony was not. Violence in America has long manifested this uneven quality. Some regions, such as the South and the frontier and the urban ghettos, have experienced very high levels of violence and disorder, while others, such as rural New England or Mormon Utah, have been far more tranquil places.

In this book I examine three related questions about the historical pattern of American violence and disorder: Who has been responsible for it? Why, relative to other western nations, has there been so much of it? And why has it been so unevenly distributed?

Note that I ask these questions about violence and disorder, not about "crime." By violence I mean acts of direct physical aggression like beatings, shootings, stabbings, and lynchings, which, depending on the circumstances, may or may not be deemed criminal offenses. By disorder I mean acts of theft and destruction like looting or vandalism, as well as misconduct like drunkenness, drug abuse, and reckless driving—essentially, any irresponsible behavior that entails the unwarranted taking or destruction of property or causes preventable injury or premature death. While crime overlaps with disorder, and is often a useful index of it, the two are not synonymous. A drunk lost in a blizzard is as dead as one killed fighting a policeman, though the former may have broken no law or suffered no arrest. Much violent and disorderly behavior in American history has either been legal or ignored by authorities; in some cases, such as bounties for Indian scalps or election-day binges, it has been encouraged. To focus exclusively on crime and criminal justice is to surrender too much of what has actually made American history so bloody. Therefore I shall look broadly, and with an interdisciplinary spirit, at all types of violence and disorder.

Taking the last question first, why have violence and disorder in American history been so unevenly distributed, with some places relatively safe and peaceful and others the opposite? The disparities may seem, at first glance, to be a product of America's pluralism and diversity of social environments. Perhaps New England was less violent because the Pilgrims and Puritans, devoutly religious people, originally settled there. Perhaps southern and western communities were more violent because the presence of slaves and Indians aroused fear in white inhabitants and prompted them to carry guns. These sorts of explanations are plausible, and indeed go a long way toward accounting for the regional and ethnic peculiarities of American violence and disorder. They are not, however, the whole story.

Anyone who looks closely at the underside of American history will find mostly young and single men. They have accounted for far and away the largest share of homicides, riots, drug dealing, and the like. This pattern is common to all societies. But the American experience with young, single men has been unusually bad because, until recently, the country has had a higher proportion of them in its population than the European, African, and Asian nations from which its immigrants came.

America's violent history was played out with a bad hand of cards dealt from a stacked demographic deck. As an immigrant society America experienced a more or less continuous influx of youthful male workers, resulting in a population with more men than women for every year prior to 1946. In a monogamous society, many of these surplus young men could not marry. Insofar as young, single men are any society's most troublesome and unruly citizens, America had a built-in tendency toward violence and disorder.

The demographic tendency was heightened by cultural and social influences. American men, especially southerners and frontiersmen, were contemptuous of other races and touchy about personal honor, which they were inclined to defend by violent means. American men drank a great deal of hard liquor and grew up in cultures that equated drunkenness with obstreperousness. American men, particularly those of the lower classes, resisted attempts at religious conversion and the feminized style of life associated with it. They often took their recreation with other men in bibulous places of commercialized vice, such as gambling halls and saloons, thereby multiplying the opportunities for violent conflict. The guns and knives they carried increased the likelihood that such conflicts would have fatal results. When killings did occur the police and courts were often unable or indisposed to deal effectively with them.

This mixture of demographic, cultural, and social characteristics guaranteed that American society would experience unusually high levels of violence and disorder, but not that American society would be uniformly violent and disorderly. These troublesome elements—the surplus of young men, widespread bachelorhood, sensitivity about honor, racial hostility, heavy drinking, religious indifference, group indulgence in vice, ubiquitous armament, and inadequate law enforcement—were concentrated on the frontier. An expanding subnation of immigrants within a larger nation of immigrants, the frontier was, at least as far as white Americans were concerned, the most youthful and masculine region of the country and, consequently, the one most prone to violence and disorder.[1]

The frontier was the principal arena of single male brutality in American history. Tens of thousands of drunken and disorderly white frontiersmen perished prematurely, as did countless native and animal inhabitants whose territory they despoiled. Nor is the carnage entirely in the past. Insofar as the frontier experience has become a foundation of the national self-image—that is, insofar as Americans continue to think a manly man is someone with a gun and an attitude—it continues to influence the amount and type of violence in the United States, as well as our collective response to it.

Frontier violence was, however, a transient and self-limiting phenomenon. The single men who sought their fortunes along the frontier either died off or returned home or drifted elsewhere or eventually married, usually to young brides who had numerous children of both genders, thereby evening out the population and eliminating its statistical tendency toward higher levels of violence and disorder. This process of demographic adjustment also occurred within immigrant groups, which initially tended to have more men than women. The passage of time balanced the numbers of men and women both regionally and ethnically, unless, as in the special case of Chinese immigrant laborers, the government enacted laws that made family formation difficult.

To be sure, not all of America's surplus men were to be found in frontier or western districts. From the end of the Civil War through the Great Depression a floating army of itinerant workers, variously known as tramps, hobos, navvies, shanty boys, and bindle stiffs, moved about the country seeking work in construction sites, lumber camps, canneries, threshing crews, and other places where temporary or seasonal jobs were available. Migratory work, while often dangerous, provided men with experiences and wages they would not have otherwise had. The problem was the purposes to which these wages were often put. Money that might have gone into savings and family formation was dissipated in saloons, poker games, and brothels. Bachelor workers led a life of alternating work and spree until they finally either got out, burned out, landed in jail, or ended beneath the dissecting knife on the coroner's slab.

Such a life was not simply the result of individual weakness. It was fostered by vice purveyors and unscrupulous employers who understood the usefulness of a mobile, self-enslaved male work force. But it was anathema to Evangelical Protestants and

Progressives, who counterattacked with reforms like prohibition, designed to break the cycle of male vice and the personal and social ills that stemmed from it.

It was ultimately economic and technological change that cut most deeply into the ranks of the floating army. Agricultural mechanization, the growth of jobs in cities, and the automobile, which permitted family-based commuting, reduced the number of itinerant single male workers. At the same time the overall male surplus was disappearing, due to shifts in immigration patterns and the fact that women's life expectancy was improving more rapidly than men's.

With a balanced population and a prosperous industrial economy, post–World War II America experienced a sustained marriage boom. The two popular images of the 1950s—that it was the decade when Americans settled down to raise their children in safety and plenty and that it was a decade of conformity—were both rooted in the postwar marital efflorescence. Families were about procreation and social control, control of the parents as much as the children. Postwar American parents worked hard, paid off their mortgages, sacrificed for their children. Church attendance went up, violent crime went down. It looked as if America's built-in tendency toward violence and disorder, the excesses of excess men, had finally run its troubled course.

Then came the 1960s and 1970s, the decades of the youthful baby boomers, the sexual revolution, and a sustained rise in violent crime and drug abuse. It was not simply that there were more young and therefore trouble-prone men in the population, though that was true enough. It was that more of these men were avoiding, delaying, or terminating marriages. Overall, the number of American men living alone roughly doubled between 1960 and 1983, an unprecedented change for prosperous times and one that undoubtedly contributed to the upsurge of violence and disorder.

Though marriage and conventional family life were becoming less common among young men, sexual intercourse was not. The result, despite widespread contraception, abortion, and a decline in fertility, was a huge increase in the percentage of children who were illegitimate and raised in fatherless families. Another feature of the post-1960 social terrain, the much higher frequency of divorce, also increased the number of poorly supervised, poorly socialized, and just plain poor children. Though these problems were national in scope, they were most severe in black America, particularly in the urban ghettos. By the early 1990s there were black neighborhoods, which sociologists began calling hyperghettos, in which two-thirds or more of the families were headed by single mothers and three-quarters of all births were illegitimate.

Growing up without a father, and growing into anomic lives with no regular family life of their own, young men in these circumstances were in a sense twice single, and a good deal more than twice as likely to become involved in shoot-outs or run afoul of the law. Their family instability was compounded by, and in many ways originated in, the everyday realities of ghetto life: social isolation, skewed demography, and the ubiquity of guns, alcohol, drugs, and vice. These problems made the white frontier boom towns of the nineteenth century into violent hot spots, and they did the same for late-twentieth-century black ghettos. In fact, except for the apparent paradox that the ratio of men to women is low in the inner city while it was high on the nonagricultural frontier, there is an important sense in which ghettos are the raw frontiers of modern American life, the primary arenas in which the recurrent problem of youthful male violence continues to be played out.

Like any historian I bring a set of convictions to my work. The most basic of these, that peace and order are good and violence and disorder are bad, is, in the Burkean sense of the term, conservative. I understand—more to the point, I feel—that the events described in this book constitute a vast tragedy of spoiled and severed lives.

My explanation for this collective tragedy is not, however, conservative in a conventional political sense, and is certainly not emotional. It instead emphasizes the interplay of large biological, demographic, cultural, social, and economic forces. Explaining mass historical phenomena without drawing upon empirical research from other fields is an impossible task, rather like exploring a cave without a light. Social historians cannot find explanatory "laws" in history—that is the fallacy of historicism—but we can borrow laws in the form of empirically tested generalizations to better understand how and why things happened in the past. Conversely, social science generalizations based on current data must be tested against, and seen in the context of, events occurring over a longer span of time. A grant, a computer, and six variables spanning the last decade are not enough to comprehend American violence and disorder. Like so many problems in so many disciplines, this one requires historical knowledge and perspective for a full understanding.

Among the disciplines whose findings I have used to illuminate the dark side of American life are anthropology, biology, criminology, demography, epidemiology, psychology, sociobiology, and sociology. Borrowing from two of these, biology and sociobiology, is apt to be controversial. The idea that human behavior is shaped by an underlying animal nature determined by millions of years of evolution is roughly as popular among contemporary historians as it is among Baptists. For political and ideological reasons, large and important elements of the profession have ignored or declared anathema the Darwinian renaissance taking place in the rest of the social scientific world.

That is unfortunate, for an evolutionary perspective can yield new insights into the history of American violence and disorder, especially into the behavior of young men, where the problem has always been centered. To borrow an image from the anthropologist Adam Kuper, human history is like a clock with three hands. The sweep hand tracks what the French call the history of events, the passing wars, coups, booms and busts that make headlines and fill the pages of most narratives. The minute hand corresponds to the long-term changes, the gradual, less-noticed but profoundly important cultural adaptations that take many generations to effect. The hour hand, which historians largely ignore, is the evolution of human beings as a species. But anyone who wants to know exactly what time it is needs to know the position of all three hands.

The same criticism can be turned against the Darwinophiles. Evolution cannot explain everything any more than the hour hand of the clock can alone tell the exact time. This book is not—and no study of violence should be—a reductive exercise in historical sociobiology. Rather, it is an attempt to show that biological *and* sociocultural explanations, usually regarded as so much oil and water, can be blended together to provide a more comprehensive explanation of social and historical events. Though my primary concern is explaining the historical pattern of American violence and disorder, I write with a sense that the methodological stakes are high. If a combined approach centered on gender works in the American case, then perhaps those who seek to explain the destructive behavior of our species elsewhere will elaborate the culture-learning model with some biological borrowing of their own.

Finally, I write with the conviction that historians who make use of empirical generalizations ought to do so in plain English in a narrative salted with the experiences of real people. Although I have drawn on statistical literature and bolstered my argument at key points with statistics, I have tried to avoid what William Cronon has called the twin evils of quantitative analysis—boredom and mystification. This has meant, among other things, using letters, diaries, memoirs, biographies, literature, interviews, movies, photographs, cartoons, and sketches to provide stories, insights, and illustrative material. Except for the first two chapters, in which I review the scientific and social scientific literature, the book is a straightforward social historical narrative. It proceeds in roughly chronological fashion, looks at a variety of ethnic and racial groups, and has a thematic beginning, middle, and end. The beginning focuses on violence and disorder among youthful, unattached men as a migratory and demographic anomaly most commonly found in nonagricultural frontier regions; the middle on the near-eclipse of this phenomenon during the first half of the twentieth century; the end on its troubling reappearance as an intractable feature of ghetto life in the late twentieth century.

ONE

Biological and Demographic Roots

I begin with a simple argument, an argument that can be stated in the form of a statistical syllogism. Young men are prone to violence and disorder; America attracted unusually large numbers of young men; therefore America, or at any rate that part of it to which the surplus young men gravitated, was a more violent and disorderly place. Wherever and whenever young men have appeared in disproportionate numbers, there has been a disproportionate likelihood of trouble.

Few would doubt that young men are prone to violence and disorder. Given the choice, on an unfamiliar street, of walking past a knot of eighteen-year-old boys or an assortment of men, women, and children, most of us would choose the latter course. We know, both intuitively and experientially, that the odds of being insulted, jostled, robbed, or worse lie with the young men, not with the "normal" group of passersby. This is, to be sure, a prejudice, but not an unreasonable one. Young men's affinity for trouble is a real phenomenon. This is especially true of young American men, who are statistically among the most dangerous people on earth. The more interesting and controversial question is why this is so.

This question can be broken down into two parts: Why are young men generally prone to violence and disorder, and why

9

have young men in America been particularly so? In this chapter I consider the first part of the question, looking at the violent and disorderly tendencies of young men as a statistical and biological phenomenon, rooted in the evolutionary history and biochemistry of the human species.

Men's Problematic Behavior

The male proclivity for violent and disorderly behavior is most readily apparent in criminal statistics, an imperfect but useful index of who did what to whom. Historians have reconstructed criminal statistics for selected American communities, colonies, and states in the seventeenth through nineteenth centuries; statisticians have compiled them for the nation as a whole in the twentieth century. Whether local or national, historical or contemporary, fragmentary or complete, these statistics tell the same story about gender and crime.

American men led women in nearly every category of crime as far back as 1636. The only exceptions were sex-related offenses like prostitution or the killing of illegitimate newborns, and these were not entirely exceptions, for their underlying cause was men's carnal use of women. The preponderance of male criminality has been observed in all regions and periods of American history, from Massachusetts to the Carolinas to California, from the colonial to the early national to the Progressive era. Drunkenness, assault, and property crime were overwhelmingly male endeavors, as were lethal acts against self and others. In nineteenth-century Philadelphia men were four to five times as likely as women to do away with themselves and more than ten times as likely to be accused of murder. They were also more than five times as likely to die accidental deaths, partly a reflection of their affinity for drink and reckless behavior.[1]

Drunken men who survived their misadventures often wound up in jail. Sober men did too, or at any rate they did so far more often than women. The finding of a study of Oakland, California, police records for 1872–1910 is typical: nine men arrested for every woman. "These differences are so great," the authors comment, "that they *must* reflect behavior. Women broke fewer laws, created fewer disturbances, than men."[2]

National statistics point to the same conclusion. Eighty-nine percent of those imprisoned for homicide in the United States in 1890 were men; ditto 88 percent of the homicide arrests recorded in this century. Male involvement in capital murder has been even greater. More than 98 percent of the convicts sent to Death Row have been men, a statistic that has remained practically unchanged since 1880, when it was first noted. Serial killing and mass murder, the most spectacular forms of homicide, have been virtual male monopolies.[3]

Those who have lived by the gun have often died by it. In the twentieth century American men have been four times more likely than women to be murder victims and between two and three times more likely to commit suicide, most often by pulling a trigger. The male-female ratio in the other leading category of violent deaths, accidents, has ranged from two-to-one among older adults to five-to-one among younger ones. Because accidental or homicidal death often conceals a self-destructive impulse—manifested by driving recklessly or picking a fight with a deadly antagonist—the male tendency toward self-annihilation may well be greater than suicide statistics alone would suggest.[4]

American men have continued to dominate crimes of property as well as those of violence. Arrests of women for serious property offenses like robbery and burglary gradually rose from 1934 to 1994 but remained below 10 or 11 percent of the total. Because violent and serious property crimes are most likely to lead to incarceration, the number of female inmates has also been low, averaging only 5 percent of those received in state and federal prisons and reformatories during the period 1910–1982.[5]

The low percentage of female prisoners could reflect a tendency to suspect, arrest, convict, and imprison men rather than women. However, survey research suggests that higher male arrest and imprisonment rates are not simply artifacts of prejudice. When guaranteed anonymity, men more often admit to having shot, stabbed, or seriously injured another person. They more often confess to alcohol, drug, and gambling addictions, as well as to lying, cheating, stealing, bribery, and tax evasion. In one survey the sole disreputable activity in which women exceeded men was surreptitiously checking on a spouse or lover.[6]

They had reason to check. Sex research dating back to Alfred Kinsey's work in the 1940s and 1950s has consistently shown a higher incidence of extramarital and premarital sexual activity among males, and nothing in the historical record suggests otherwise for earlier periods. American men report fantasizing more about sex, having more varied fantasies, and acting on their fantasies more often than women do. Whether or not men's sex drives are stronger and more central to their identities, as some researchers believe, they are certainly more apt to get men in trouble. Incest and pedophilia are largely male offenses, as are patronizing prostitutes and purchasing pornography. So is rape, although it is a crime of violence as well as sexual impulse.[7]

The consistent pattern of higher male rates of socially disruptive behavior throughout American history suggests that such behavior is rooted in biological differences between men and women. Suggests, but does not prove. The pattern might be due to a peculiarity of American society or culture, some quirk of the national character. When we look elsewhere, however, we discover that the male penchant for violent, disorderly, and sexually compulsive behavior is hardly an exclusively American trait. It can be observed throughout history, across cultures, and among different primate species.

The pioneering European social scientists and statisticians of the nineteenth century were among the first to systematically document the male tendency for violent and disorderly conduct. Lambert A. J. Quetelet, who analyzed French and Belgian records from the 1820s and 1830s, discovered that men were more than four times as often accused of any crime as women, the ratio increasing in proportion to the violence and seriousness of the offense. Francis Neison noticed virtually the same pattern in English criminal statistics from the 1830s and 1840s. Emile Durkheim, in his study of suicide, found that men were three to four times more likely than women to kill themselves in every European nation for which information was available. European historians have been able to trace the record of violent death back further—to the thirteenth century in the case of England, where nine out of ten murderers were male, as were eight of ten of their victims. Male-on-male is still far and away the commonest variety of murder in contemporary European societies; likewise North America, South America, Africa, Asia, and the Pacific.[8]

Social statistics are sketchy or nonexistent for most tribal societies, but anthropologists who have used ethnographic reports to make cross-cultural comparisons have found men to be the more aggressive, sexually active, and less responsible gender. Tribal men also report dreaming about sex, death, and weapons more often than women. Male violence has been a fact of hunter-gatherer life for a long time. Male skeletons exhibit more clubbing and stabbing wounds than female skeletons and are wounded more often on the left side, suggesting a right-handed opponent attacking from the front. The earliest known victim was a Neanderthal man apparently stabbed in the chest fifty thousand years ago. Among primate species, the earliest fossil evidence of gender-differentiated aggression—longer male canine teeth for threatening or attacking rivals—is fifty million years old.[9]

Age and Male Behavior

Male behavior is most likely to be socially problematic in the late teens and twenties. This is the age range in which American men have been likeliest to kill or be killed;[10] to set fires, filibuster, riot, vandalize, rob, and steal;[11] and to abuse alcohol and other drugs.[12] These are also the years in which reckless and intoxicated driving most frequently claim the lives of men. Young women die too, often as hapless passengers of negligent male drivers.[13]

The surest way to reduce crime, remarks the psychologist David T. Lykken, would be to put all able-bodied males between the ages of twelve and twenty-eight into cryogenic sleep. He has a point. Though the median age of arrest is subject to historical variation (it has gone down in the United States in the last century), the arrest bulge invariably occurs in the teens and twenties and declines rapidly from the thirties on. Figure 1.1 shows the rate of criminal offenders by age and gender for England and Wales in the years 1842–1844. Figure 1.2 shows the arrest rate by age and gender for the United States in 1990. The two societies could hardly be more different: one industrial-

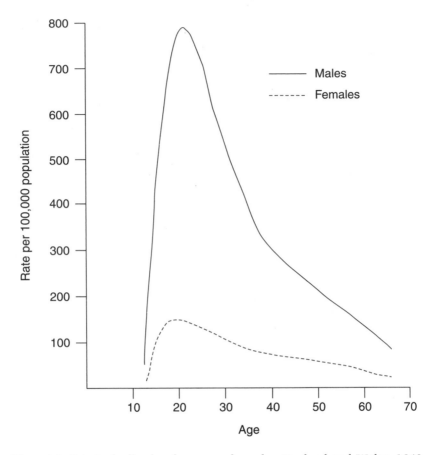

Figure 1.1 Criminal offenders by age and gender, England and Wales, 1842–1844. Based on data from F. G. P. Neison, *Contributions to Vital Statistics* . . ., 3rd ed. (London, 1857), 303–304, as plotted by Travis Hirschi and Michael Gottfredson, "Age and the Explanation of Crime," *AJS* 89 (1983): 556.

izing, racially homogeneous, and thinly policed; the other postindustrial, pluralistic, and heavily policed. Yet the shape of the curves is similar, with the highest levels for men (and women) in the teens and twenties. All societies, from Sweden to Samoa, manifest the same basic pattern. "Crime everywhere and throughout history is disproportionately a young man's pursuit," sum up Richard J. Herrnstein and James Q. Wilson. "Nowhere have older persons been as criminal as younger ones." It follows that any society or community with a surfeit of young

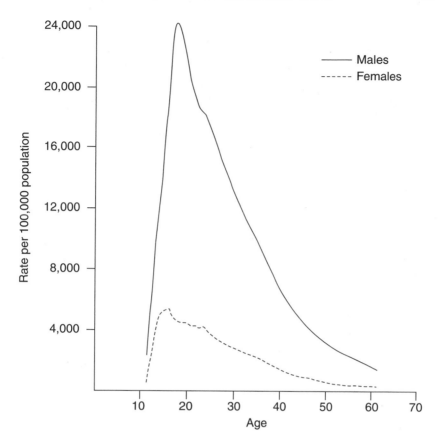

Figure 1.2 Arrests by age and gender, United States, 1990. Based on U.S. Department of Justice, *Uniform Crime Reports, 1990* (1991), 186–189, and U.S. Bureau of the Census, *1990 Census of Population: General Population Characteristics, United States* (1992), 17.

men will have, other things being equal, a built-in tendency toward a higher level of crime.[14]

Evolution, Aggression, and Sexuality

Crime, a social construct, is not identical with aggression, a cluster of behaviors that involve intimidation of or taking from others by threat or deed. Nevertheless, crime and aggression are connected both logically (taking life and property is often illegal) and empirically, insofar as criminologists have shown that aggressive personalities are more likely to run afoul of the law. The fact that men, on average, are more aggressive than women goes a long way toward explaining why men engage in more law-breaking and socially disruptive behavior. So does the more impulsive male sex drive, which helps to explain men's greater involvement in rape, pornography, and other illicit sexual practices.[15]

But why are men more aggressive and sexually impulsive? Evolutionary biologists from Charles Darwin on have stressed reproductive asymmetry. Women have a finite number of eggs and, because of the long period from conception to weaning, must invest a large amount of time and energy in their offspring. Men, who produce billions of sperm, invest little time and energy in reproduction. A man who has intercourse with many women in the course of a month can conceive many children, but in the same interval a woman can become pregnant only once. Quality rather than quantity of partners is the best reproductive strategy for females, though not for males, who increase the chances of passing on their genes through intercourse with multiple partners.

This is where aggression comes into play. Over the millennia human males, like males of all mammalian species, have competed for access to the finite reproductive capacity of females. Those who were predisposed to aggressive behavior, and who thereby intimidated or eliminated their rivals, were able to sire more offspring and pass on more genes, including those which favored aggression. This phenomenon can be observed in many animal and human societies. Dominant males inseminate females; successful warriors and potentates often have many wives and concubines.

It may be objected that aggression should be selected *against* because it increases the prospect of early death. In fact, aggression does lead to a shortened life span. Women die violent deaths less often than men. Castrated males live longer than those who are not castrated. But, in the Darwinian scheme of things, the longevity of an individual organism does not matter as much as its reproductive success. A trait penalized by *natural* selection can win out by *sexual* selection. Males who fight hard, mate often, and die young have a greater genetic influence on posterity than passive males who seldom mate and yet live a long time.

Prowess and risk-taking in hunting pay similar reproductive dividends. Successful hunters in tribal societies frequently have more wives than unsuccessful ones. Though they increase their own chances of sudden death, aggressive hunters and warriors enhance both their own reproductive prospects and the fitness of the group by increasing the food supply and driving away competitors. Because hunting and war-making entail cooperation, traits like the ability to lead and plan are also selected for, not just raw aggression. Men kill one another as individuals, but they also kill one another and other species through concerted action in hierarchical groups.[16]

The more pronounced male sex drive, like aggression, is a consequence of reproductive asymmetry. Women do not require sexual arousal to conceive. Men do. As the anthropologist Donald Symons points out, selection favored the male tendency to be aroused sexually by the sight of females. Other things being equal, men who were easily and frequently aroused mated more often, thereby increasing the species' tendency toward male concupiscence. Because women necessarily invest more in reproduction, they are more circumspect about intercourse and, in any case, do not require sexual arousal to conceive and pass on their genes. These differences, magnified by selection over thousands of generations, explain biologically the greater male preoccupation with sexuality.[17]

But if selection favors more aggressive and highly sexed males, why hasn't evolution produced a completely violent, rut-and-run gender? Why do men love and nurture women and children? Why, in other words, do families exist?

One answer is that sexual selection is not entirely in the hands of men. Women (or, in traditional societies, their parents or guardians) generally do the choosing, and they do so on the basis of something more than toughness and virility. They look for the ability and willingness to make a long-term commitment to support children, a responsibility that women would otherwise face alone. Courtship is the process by which male capabilities and intentions are vetted. Men with the means and disposition to share in the task of raising a family are favored because they are more likely to be approved by prospective spouses and their relatives.[18] Men who commit to family life also enjoy nutritional and emotional advantages not available to bachelors, whom they typically outlive. The male evolutionary legacy is thus paradoxical: aggression and sexual drivenness on the one hand, love and nurture on the other. Both sets of traits have been selected for; both are present in varying degrees in every man's genes. Social arrangements and cultural rules influence which set of traits predominates.

Listening to Steroids

The evolutionary account of male aggressiveness and sexuality fits well with paleontological, ethological, anthropological, and historical evidence. It is consistent with a growing body of genetic research showing that personality traits, like eye or hair color, can be inherited.[19] And yet it cannot be directly tested, for we have no way of recreating the circumstances of the distant human past.

We can, however, establish the hormonal basis of differences between males and females, especially the role played by testosterone. Initially, the human fetus is sexually undifferentiated. Physical differences do not occur until minute genetic differences trigger the development of testes or ovaries. The former produce testosterone, which in turn organizes the development of the fetus's genitals and central nervous system. Testosterone is why boys are born boys, and why they later become men. In the absence of testosterone the fetus will develop into a female, nature's "default" body plan.

At the onset of puberty the testes flood the body with testosterone, raising blood levels to as much as twenty times those of women and prepubertal boys. This surge of testosterone in young men has *anabolic* effects, including increased muscle mass and bone density, as well as *androgenic* effects, including hairier bodies, deeper voices, and, what is of concern here, increased libido, impulsiveness, and aggressiveness.[20]

We know that testosterone is causally related to these changes because its presence or absence is easily manipulated. Castrated human males, even castrated criminals, lose interest in sex and fighting. All mammals react in the same way, which is why ranchers, herders, and farmers often clip the testicles of their bulls, stallions, and other livestock. Gelded animals, like gelded humans, are more manageable. But when testosterone is artificially replaced in castrated man or beast its androgenic effects soon reappear, proving that the hormone, not the missing gonad, is responsible for the physical and behavioral changes.[21]

The level of testosterone is a heritable trait subject to environmental modification, typically increasing with gains in status and declining with losses. A study of the Harvard wrestling team found that the victors had significantly higher testosterone levels ten minutes after their matches than the vanquished. Winning tennis players, students graduating from medical school, and successful skydivers react to victory or achievement the same way, with elevated testosterone levels.[22]

Statistical analyses which have controlled for variables like race and education have shown a significant link between higher levels of testosterone and verbal and physical aggression, drug and alcohol abuse, and violent offenses. Adolescents with high levels of the hormone are more prone to juvenile delinquency and to more serious and violent crimes later in life, particularly if they lack education, jobs, and spouses and are uninvolved in organized, prosocial groups. The effects of testosterone in humans are socially mediated. Married, college-educated males who have high serum testosterone levels are one thing; unattached, alienated drifters with abnormally high levels are quite another. Testosterone anomalies, in short, appear to be most dangerous among the least socialized men.[23]

Testosterone has masculinizing effects on females as well as males. Testicular grafts in hens will produce the comb and wattles of a cock. Human females exposed in the womb to synthetic androgenic hormones exhibit greater aggressiveness and other conventionally masculine traits later in life. Female-to-male transsexuals treated with these drugs show greater proneness to anger.[24] Those who say that gender is constructed are speaking a biological and a social truth. Hormonal manipulation and socialization are both powerful means of influencing male and female behavior.

The steroid scandal underscores this point. Steroids, synthetic drugs that mimic testosterone, were tested clinically in 1937 and were reportedly used by German troops during World War II to enhance strength and aggressiveness. Steroid "doping" spread among athletes and weight lifters after the war, and today the drugs are commonly, if illegally, used in sports and body-building circles. The temptation is enormous: a male athlete can add as much as forty pounds of lean muscle in one year. Female athletes and body builders also use steroids to bulk up. They frequently experience masculinizing effects, among them growth of facial and body hair, deepening of the voice, enlargement of the clitoris, and increased libido and aggressiveness. Emotional effects reported by male athletes include increased aggressiveness, energy, explosiveness, self-regard, hostility toward others, tolerance of pain, and supercharged libido. Steroid use in male athletes is a chemical exaggeration of the hormonal changes experienced naturally by young men, with predictably exaggerated results: more sex, more violence, and more death.[25]

There are dissenting voices. The strength of the correlation between steroid use and violence has been questioned. Some researchers suspect that it is not steroid use alone but its interaction with alcohol that is especially dangerous. And there is certainly more to the biology of human aggression than testosterone and its synthetic equivalents. Neurotransmitters like dopamine, norepinephrine, serotonin, and GABA (the levels of which can likewise be affected by alcohol and drug use) are part of the complex neurochemical story that is only beginning to be unraveled.[26] Even so, it seems beyond question that testosterone plays a gender-linked role in human aggression. It is also undeniable that its anabolic effects increase the potential for injury. Better to be hit by a boy weighing 70 pounds than a teenager weighing 140 pounds—or a galoot who has bulked up to 240 on steroids.

Young men, in short, are biologically primed for deeds that may have been reproductively advantageous in the distant past but are problematic in societies that have come to value disciplined competence over raw aggression. Not only are young men hormonally inclined to violent and socially forbidden behavior, they have a greater capacity for it. They can hit hard, run fast, break down doors, and climb in through windows. Though the conventions of the mystery drama invite us to think of crime as something carefully planned and rationally motivated, the thefts and outrages of everyday life are most often the opportunistic acts of young men impulsive or undisciplined enough to break the law and strong or quick enough to get away with it. Street crime is a young man's game. After the age of thirty both physical capacity and sexual drive begin a slow but sustained decline, another important reason why middle-aged and older men are less likely to be arrested for crimes like assault, robbery, and rape.

The decline of criminal involvement with increasing age is also partly attributable to the "selecting out" factor. The most reckless men, the James Deans and Sid Viciouses of the world, die young. In their graves they trouble no one, least of all the other members of their birth cohort as criminologists follow them through their forties, fifties, and so on. Not only do men lose physical capacity and sexual drive as they age, they lose their wildest contemporaries and companions. This too makes a difference.

So does individual character. While human behavior may be predictable in the aggregate, each person's actions are ultimately uncertain and indeterminate. "Individuals vary," Sherlock Holmes observed to Dr. Watson in *The Sign of Four*, "but percentages remain constant." The same is true of statistical generalizations about age and gender, which are best thought of as distributions around a mean. They do not determine individual destinies, nor do they lack exceptions. There have been continent young men of irenic temperament, just as there have been older men and women of opposite bent. Such exceptions do not disprove the generalizations, however, because the generalizations themselves are of a probabilistic nature.

American Population Imbalance

Statistically, then, we may say that violent and disorderly behavior occurs most frequently among men, particularly among men in adolescence and young adulthood. As it happened, America had both a surplus of men and an unusually large percentage of young people during its first three centuries.

Countries with high birth rates have youthful populations, as the most casual inspection of the world's developing nations will attest. America, which had a phenomenally high birth rate during its developing years, was no exception. Endowed with a relative abundance of land and natural resources, the mainland colonists married young and raised large numbers of children, who in turn married and raised large numbers of children, producing a continuous baby boom. That boom, combined with the fact that most colonists did not live past sixty, kept the median age of the population—sixteen years in the eighteenth century—very low. Family limitation by native-born Protestants slowed the boom somewhat during the nineteenth century, but America in 1900 was still a youthful nation, with a median age of only twenty-three years.[27]

It was also, relative to Europe, a disproportionately male nation. It was born that way. From Sir Walter Raleigh's attempted settlement of Roanoke Island in 1585 to the formal declaration of American independence in 1776, the British mainland colonies always had a surfeit of men. In 1608 Jamestown was home to but two women—as good a reason as any why the settlement had such a disastrous early history. Although the demographic imbalance of early Jamestown was extreme, the seventeenth-century colonial male surplus was both sizable and persistent, particularly in the South, where a continuing influx of servants, convicts, and slaves kept the population predominantly young and male.[28]

The colonial population achieved a more normal balance in the course of the eighteenth century. By 1790 the gender ratio (the number of males per 100 females) stood at just under 104 for the white population of the United States. The national gender ratio remained in the 102–105 range for most of the nineteenth century, peaked at 106 in 1910, and thereafter began to decline. It was not until 1946, however, that the country finally acquired a female majority. That female surplus, largely a product of changing immigration patterns and the widening difference in life expectancy between men and women, has been a fact of American life ever since.[29]

European nations developed and sustained female majorities much earlier than the United States. Most of them, in fact, had female surpluses during the entire period of America's colonization and development as an independent nation. The primary reason was migration. Forced or voluntary, American immigrants were heavily male. The proportion of men to women among transported convicts was four to one; among slaves, imported legally or otherwise, upwards of two to one. The proportion among indentured servants, the largest group of colonial immigrants, was three to one during the seventeenth century, increasing to nine to one during the eighteenth.[30]

The nineteenth-century successors to the indentured servants, Chinese laborers indebted for their passage, had the most unbalanced gender ratios of all. In 1890 there were twenty-seven Chinese men for every Chinese woman in the United States: "more monks than rice porridge," as they described the situation. Women were at such a premium that Chinese laborers were said to line up for a block and pay an ounce of gold merely to gaze upon a famous courtesan's face.[31]

Nineteenth-century European immigrants who came without legal or financial obligations were far more likely to come in familial groups, but even among them there was a surplus of prime-age male workers. Only post-famine Ireland, where economic and marital prospects for young rural women were particularly bleak, furnished more female than male immigrants, and then only by a small margin. Male majorities were the norm for immigrants, and they helped to keep the national gender ratio well above parity.[32]

The differences between European and American gender ratios that grew out of migration were magnified by the effects of warfare. With the single exception of white southerners during the Civil War, Americans, unlike Europeans, never suffered catastrophic military losses. It is true that intermittent warfare against the Indians and the French from 1675 to 1760 made widows of many New England women, and that both the American Revolution and the Civil War produced appreciable casualties relative to the total population. Yet these sacrifices were small compared to those made by European nations. France lost a million soldiers during the Revolutionary and

Napoleonic wars and more than a million in World War I. During World War II the Soviet Union, Poland, Germany, and Yugoslavia each suffered more deaths than the United States endured in its entire military history from the Revolution to Vietnam. Because most of the casualties were male, the gender ratios of European nations were noticeably lower after major conflicts. The first Soviet census taken after World War II, in 1959, counted nearly 21 million more women than men. That year there were only 82 men for every 100 Soviet women, compared to 98 men for every 100 women in the United States.[33]

Warfare may well have been more important for its indirect than for its direct effect on the American gender ratio. During the Revolution, the Civil War, and World War I immigration, which would ordinarily have been 60 to 70 percent male, fell off precipitously. The Civil War reduced immigration by half a million, World War I by three million or more. In time of war European nations were reluctant to permit emigration, above all the emigration of young men. One can even think of the maritime impressment that bedeviled the young republic during the Napoleonic wars as a type of enforced reverse migration, brought about by the Royal Navy's ability to siphon off American sailors into its depleted and desertion-prone crews. The impressment of several thousand men into British service did not significantly reduce the overall American surplus, however. Supernumerary males remained a peculiarity of American life throughout the early nineteenth century and beyond.[34]

Circumstances thus conspired to endow America with an abundance of young men. From the standpoint of economic growth this was undoubtedly a good thing. Young adult males have an enormous potential for labor, especially when the labor in question requires vigorous physical exertion. The developing nation needed field hands and stevedores and ironworkers. The demand was initially met by the sellers of servants and convicts and slaves, who received higher prices for male workers than for female, and later by wave after wave of voluntary male immigrants.[35]

The problem, from the standpoint of social control, was that young men who worked hard also lived and played hard, often to the point of causing serious violence and disorder. Endocrine research, bolstered by historical, criminological, and cross-cultural studies, suggests that this tendency is universal and that it has a biological basis. But not that the problematic behavior of young men is biologically determined, for their innate potential for trouble is everywhere mediated by cultural norms and contained, however imperfectly, by social institutions.

TWO

Cultural and Social Roots

If, for biological reasons, young men are more inclined to violence and disorder, and if America had more than its share of young men, it follows that American life had a built-in tendency toward violence and disorder. It also follows that, the higher the ratio of men to women in a given community or region, the stronger this tendency would be. While these arguments make both intuitive and statistical sense, they are only the beginning of an explanation, not a complete one. American violence was not simply a gunfight at the XY corral. Indeed, nothing in human social life is simply the consequence of any genetic trait.

Consider height. The genetic trait for height (the genotype) is influenced by environmental factors such as health and diet, which partially determine the actual height obtained (the phenotype). Men have a genetic tendency toward greater average height than women, but phenotypical differences in stature also depend on who gets the most nourishing food or who does the stoop labor. Scientists and social scientists who are convinced, as I am, that heredity plays a role in human behavior are sometimes accused of biological determinism (or worse), but in fact the modern biological synthesis recognizes no dichotomy between nature and nurture. Biological systems are always and everywhere *open* systems in which innate and environmental influences continuously interact with one another.[1]

The environment also shapes culture, each society's rules for appropriate behavior. Cultures specify what is forbidden, tolerated, expected, admired. Cultures evolve and reproduce themselves, thanks to our ability to reason and learn. Their evolution leads to cultural differences, though biology enforces some common denominators, such as the incest taboo. The legacy of evolution—young men's neurochemical tendency toward and physical capacity for aggression—requires that all societies implement rules to constrain their behavior, as well as to devise means of channeling it in constructive, nurturing ways. The latter task is so universally important that Margaret Mead called it "the recurrent problem of civilization."[2]

The international homicide statistics in Figure 2.1 show that some societies are considerably more adept than others at civilizing young men. In the mid-1980s the homicide rate for American males aged fifteen through twenty-four was more than four times that of its nearest rival, Scotland, and seventy-three times that of Austria. Great differences could also be found within the United States. The rate of homicide for young white men in California was more than eleven times that of Minnesota. In every nation and state men more frequently committed murder than women—that is the biological constant—but the ratio of male-to-female killers varied, as did the total number of killings. In societies with high murder rates the difference is generally accounted for by an unusually large number of young men killing other young men. Certainly this is true of the United States. The American homicide rate is high not because of psychopathic sprees or an epidemic of spousal jealousy but primarily because so many young men kill other, usually unrelated, young men.[3]

What, then, are the cultural and social factors that explain the variation in criminal or other socially disruptive behaviors, especially those involving young men? The literature on this question is vast. One can, however, extract from it six generalizations that are most relevant to explaining the historical pattern of American violence and disorder.

Honor

The first of these generalizations is that cultures or subcultures in which men are sensitive about honor have much higher levels

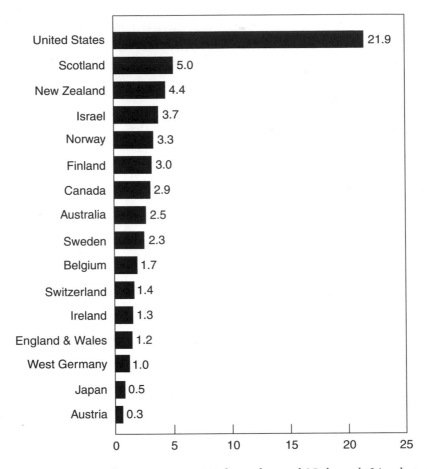

Figure 2.1 Homicide rates per 100,000 for males aged 15 through 24, selected nations, 1986 or 1987. Adapted from Lois A. Fingerhut and Joel C. Kleinman, "International and Interstate Comparisons of Homicides among Young Males," *JAMA* 263 (1990): 3293.

of violence. Honor (or "primal honor," as it is sometimes called) has been succinctly defined as a system of beliefs in which a man has exactly as much worth as others confer upon him. Good opinion is won or lost by the way he handles himself in conflicts. To fail to respond to a challenge or insult is to lose face and therefore surrender self-esteem. In such circumstances insult is intolerable. The approved response is direct action, preferably action that displays physical courage, such as dueling. Aggressive displays outside the immediate community—bagging the most game, slaying the most enemies—are also useful means of achieving, maintaining, or repairing one's standing in the eyes of others. Cultures which stress honor stress male competitiveness.[4]

The violent defense of masculine honor was most common in the South and along the frontier, where it characterized the behavior of both aboriginal and immigrant inhabitants. Indian cultures, though diverse, typically stressed the imperatives of honor and vengeance. In this white frontiersmen were no different. Nor was the similarity accidental, for honor cultures typically flourish in remote rural areas where the state is weak or its rationalizing minions are held in contempt. "Never . . . sue anybody for slander or assault or battery," Andrew Jackson's mother admonished her son. "Always settle them cases yourself." He did, and so did thousands of other like-minded southerners and frontiersmen who resolved their conflicts with pistols and Bowie knives and gouging fingernails. Their vengeful code was epitomized by a Colorado grave marker: "He called Bill Smith a liar." The same epitaph might well have served as a courtroom defense. The cultural preference for violent defense of personal honor was reinforced by a legal system that made it unusually easy to justify killing an opponent.[5]

The historian Frederick Jackson Turner is famous for the thesis that the frontier environment shaped the character of Americans who migrated there, making them tough, self-reliant individualists. More recently historians and cultural geographers have concluded that Turner had the right idea, that environment shapes culture, but that he was looking in the wrong place. He should have been looking at the cultures from which the settlers came. In the seventeenth and eighteenth centuries the whites who settled along the middle and southern frontiers were often immigrants, or descendants of immigrants, from the hard-scrabble periphery of Northern and Western Europe. Among them were Finns, Scots-Irish, Scottish Lowlanders, and various English border clans that had been warring since the time of Duncan and Macbeth. Gaelic-speaking Highlanders also poured into the Carolina backcountry, which one emigrant boasted would "soon be a new Scotland." Relative to other Europeans, people from these fringe lands were *already* individualistic, violent, honor-conscious, and impatient of the yoke of church and state. Preexisting cultural tendencies thus heightened the potential for disorder inherent in America's male population, or at any rate the part of it that settled along the southern and midlands frontier.[6]

So, in a roundabout way, did slavery. Southern slaveowners like Faulkner's Thomas Sutpen were hardened to violence, for violence was at the core of the slave system and was continuously employed to maintain it. Few adult southerners escaped seeing slaves cursed, whipped, hunted, or even killed. Slave executions and lynchings were public events witnessed by all ages. Brutalized slaves were an ever-present reminder that brute power counted in human affairs and that defeat entailed a terrible price.[7]

The intertwined strains of honor and violence in the white South influenced African-American culture, reinforcing tendencies that had deeper African roots. Blacks had originally come from West African tribal cultures which were both heroic and violent. The warrior was an admired figure; raiding and slave-taking were facts of life. Though the plantation system discouraged fighting in the quarters, southern blacks had ample opportunity to observe whites dispatching one another in affairs of honor. After emancipation they did likewise, killing one another over provocations as petty as those that embroiled white southerners. Postbellum black society, like white southern or frontier society, was contaminated by historical fallout from a culture of honor. The fallout seems to have had a long half-life, for the South, the West, and the black ghettos remain the country's most violent places in the late twentieth century. To this day most ghetto homicides are about disrespect, retaliation, and revenge, traditional honor-culture motives that nineteenth-century southerners and frontiersmen would have understood.[8]

Racism

In addition to touchiness about honor, ghetto violence is clearly a product of racial discrimination, as is the ghetto itself. Throughout American history racism has exacerbated violence and disorder in three distinct ways: by inspiring and rationalizing interracial attacks; by blocking intermarriage and family formation; and by impoverishing, isolating, and socially marginalizing minority groups.

Racism is a subset of ethnocentrism, the tendency to favor genetically, socially, and culturally similar in-groups over alien out-groups. Edward O. Wilson has argued that selection favored those humans who were quickest to recognize, fear, hate, and drive away or kill strangers, thereby securing a margin of safety for themselves and their kin. It does appear that ethnocentrism, or at least xenophobia, is in some degree biologically programmed. Infants as young as three months will smile and coo at a parent or caretaker but abruptly cry when confronted by a stranger. Later in life people may learn to suppress their ethnocentric feelings by heeding the counsel of toleration, much the same way they learn to regulate other impulses. Or they may learn to intensify these feelings by internalizing discriminatory laws and customs, listening to demagogic tirades, fighting in bitter wars, or by any of a hundred other actions. That is, the intensity and lethality of ethnocentric behavior, including racism, are products of specific social, cultural, and historical circumstances.[9]

Ethnocentrism is not an either/or proposition. There are degrees of otherness which can be thought of as expanding circles surrounding each self. People are typically closest to those who are related by blood or marriage and/or those who share their ethnicity (national, racial, or tribal), language, religion, ideology, class, neighborhood, occupation, or workplace. They are furthest from those who share none of these things. Some out-groups may seem so utterly alien, so removed from the observer's self-identity, that they seem less than fully human. They may in fact be regarded as another species.[10]

The more alien the out-group, the easier it is to exploit or kill its members. That is, after all, what humans have long done to animals, rendering them beasts of burden or slaughtering them for flesh and sport. People regarded as beastlike have been treated accordingly, and have repaid their persecutors in kind when given the opportunity. The white depredations against Indians (and Indian depredations against whites) are the most notorious examples of this, although the pluralistic nature of American society has furnished many opportunities for and instances of interracial ferocity, especially on the frontier, the most ethnically diverse region and cockpit of racial conflict for the first three centuries of American history.

The strong ethnocentrism and racial antipathies of Anglo-Americans have indirectly contributed to violence and disorder by discouraging intermarriage. Many population groups, including whites migrating toward the frontier, had unequal numbers of men and women, making intermarriage a seemingly natural expedient. But Anglo-American racism trumped demographic logic to a degree unusual in the western hemisphere, resulting in a complex of discriminatory laws and personal decisions that retarded marriage and family formation, delayed the balancing of the population, and, insofar as families restrained and disciplined their members' behavior, weakened the foundation of social control.

Finally, by blocking opportunities for employment and consigning minorities to impoverished and vice-ridden ghettos, racism has increased the amount of violence and disorder in those communities, particularly among their male inhabitants and above all among economically marginalized black men. Once valued and exploited as slaves, many freedmen and their sons and grandsons could not find regular employment after emancipation and drifted into a life of idleness and insobriety in the segregated quarters of cities and towns. The cultural sensitivity about honor they shared with other southerners was dangerous enough in itself, but when combined with unemployment, frustration, and drink it made for a truly explosive mix.[11]

Alcohol

As this last observation suggests, violence and disorder are more likely if men drink alcohol, especially if they drink heavily and in circumstances or cultures that favor aggressive behavior when drinking. That alcohol is associated with mayhem is as well documented as any finding in the social sciences. One particularly compelling type of evidence comes from so-called natural experiments, in which events like annual fluctuations in wine production or a military ban on drinking (such as the one imposed on U.S. troops during the Gulf War) temporarily constrict the supply of alcohol. Crime invariably decreases.[12]

Less certain is how drinking triggers violence. Alcohol impairs judgment, and impaired judgment can lead to an accident or a clumsy offense or, more subtly, to misinterpretation of another person's behavior as insulting, threatening, or sexually inviting. A drunken misstep can be fatal, particularly in a packed bar or in an honor culture. Drunkenness can also invite attack if an intoxicated person is viewed as an easy mark or if a woman who drinks is perceived as a more suitable target for sexual assault. Drunkenness may even provide an excuse for violence, because the drinker knows in advance that his actions are more likely to be tolerated or excused because of intoxication. That is, a decision to engage in violence may "cause" drinking, rather than the other way around.[13]

Some investigators think that alcohol produces hormonal or other neurochemical changes consistent with heightened aggressiveness, but these are not yet well understood or agreed upon, and there is other evidence that alcohol, despite its "Dutch courage" reputation, does not cause aggression in a direct fashion. Experiments have shown that subjects who believed they were drinking alcohol when in fact they were not behaved more aggressively than subjects who actually received alcohol but who had been led to believe otherwise. These curious effects occur because people learn to associate drinking with certain types of behaviors, among them obstreperousness. About half the world's cultures expect and approve of men's becoming loud, angry, abusive, argumentative, and physically belligerent when they drink. In one culture, that of the Mexican Tzeltal, drunken wife beating is so routine that it is mentioned in the wedding ceremony.[14]

Heavy and aggressive male drinking, like sensitivity about honor, has been concentrated in subcultures or regions. The wettest place was the frontier, which from the colonial period on had a high ratio of men to women and of taverns to population. American frontiersmen came, in the main, from cultures in which men drank a great deal of hard liquor and were expected to be boastful and rowdy as a consequence. "Everywhere on the frontier," comments the historian Robert Utley, "nearly all men drank nearly all the time, which made nearly all men more or less drunk most of the time. Drink enhanced self-importance, impaired judgment, generated heedless courage, and encouraged unreasoning resort to violence." This description is hyperbolic, but not by much. Frontier drunkenness was indeed widespread and, if newspaper accounts are accurate, involved in about half of all homicides and a good deal more than half of all assaults and brawls.[15]

These fights often took place in saloons, gender-segregated institutions of sociality and vice that flourished on the frontier and in nineteenth-century cities. Saloons brought drinking men together, and group drinking tends to be heavier than solitary drinking, the cliché about the dangers of the latter notwithstanding. Saloons multiplied occasions of conflict, both because of the imperative of guarding one's honor before other men and because of the presence of gambling, prostitution, prizefighting, and other activities which inspired drunken competition and arguments. The opportunity to extract patrons' wages drew gamblers, pimps, and their ilk to the saloons, usually with the knowledge and connivance of the proprietor. Vice added armed and hardened criminals to the already dangerous mix of inebriated men, ensuring that the saloon would be the historical epicenter of American violence and disorder.[16]

Religion

Devout Americans hated saloons. Appropriately so, for the more religious people are, the less likely they are to tolerate disorderly behavior in themselves or others. Self-discipline is at the heart of intense religious experience. Iron-willed puritans can be found among committed believers in all religions, but in the American case the most numerically and politically important group has been the Evangelical Protestants. The Evangelical outlook, instilled in children from infancy, is predicated on self-denial, on subordination of the individual will to that of God. Observing God's injunctions against anger, lust, fornication, and intemperance commits believers to an unending struggle against the temptations of the world and the deepest impulses of their animal nature. Observing the Gospel message of evangelization commits them to struggle against these same impulses in other people.[17]

Evangelicals have not always succeeded in reining in the self, nor have they necessarily been pacific. In some contexts, as when disciplining their children, they have shown themselves quite capable of violence.[18] They have sometimes persecuted those of different beliefs, though sectarian strife is one form of violence that has been mercifully rare in American history, in part due to constitutional guarantees of religious freedom. Because of this absence of holy wars, and because of the circumspection born of conscience, the net effect of Evangelical Protestantism and of religious belief generally has been to enhance the American social order and to diminish criminal violence.

Evangelical Protestants and other deeply religious people have been, and still are, less likely to be found in circumstances—gambling halls, saloons, other people's beds—that lead to trouble involving the police. They have been less likely to do away with themselves, owing to the religious injunction against suicide and to their close involvement with family, church, and community life. When dealing with strangers, they have been more likely to be helpful, cooperative, and friendly. Religious people, sums up the sociologist Christopher Ellison, are nice people.[19]

The religious revivals of the nineteenth century transformed America into one of the most churchgoing nations in the world. Between 1780 and 1860 the number of Christian congregations increased from about 2,500 to 52,000, a rate of growth nearly three times that of the general population.[20] Millions of born-again Americans found Jesus, renounced Satan, took the pledge. This poses an interesting question. If Americans were becoming so religious, and if religious belief militates against crime and vice, why did America remain such a violent and disorderly society?

The short answer is that spiritual enthusiasm was unevenly distributed throughout the population. Historians of American religion have consistently found that married women were the most faithful churchgoers, young single men the least faithful. Religion was to disorder as money was to poverty: those who needed it most had the least to draw upon. Religious indiffer-

ence was especially widespread on the frontier, the region with
the most bachelors and the fewest churches. "Veritable hea-
thens," summed up Olaus Duus, a Norwegian pastor writing
from Minnesota in 1857, describing what he considered to be
the largest American frontier denomination. "A man among
them never hears much practical discussions about religion," a
diarist observed of the Rocky Mountain miners, adding that
their lives were "wild" and "restless." "Ninety per cent of them
[cowpunchers] was infidels," remarked another memoirist, innocent of both grammar and theology.[21]

Itinerant preachers tried to rectify the situation, traveling
thousands of miles to spread the Gospel message along the
backwoods frontier and beyond. They sometimes encountered
open hostility, everything from dogs in church to ugly threats.
Peter Cartwright, a Methodist circuit rider, recalled several camp
meetings interrupted by cursing, jeering rowdies. Most of the
interlopers were drunken riffraff, but on one occasion they were
led by haughty young men sporting whips and fine clothes.[22]

This is not surprising. Conceptions of appropriate masculine
behavior were class- as well as culture-specific. The model of the
Christian gentleman was most acceptable to middle-class American men, who were on the whole more inclined to join religious
worship than to scoff at it. It was least acceptable to young men
from the lower and upper reaches of society, who thought
religion suspect and unmanly. A recurring theme in American
religious history was the conflict between a feminized and middle-class Evangelical Protestantism and the masculinized culture
of excess found most often among the genteel and rough manual
laborers. The tippling, dueling gentleman was as much a sinner
to the Evangelicals as the saloon brawler. If the brawler in
question happened to be a foreigner or a Catholic, so much the
worse. The rambunctious, drunken behavior of Irish working-
men was a continuing scandal to middle-class Protestants, an
important source of both nativism and the prohibitionist impulse. By the late nineteenth century traditional Evangelical
efforts at temperance and conversion were being superseded by
campaigns to suppress saloon-going, intoxication, and other
lower-class and immigrant vices thought to be ruinous of the
social order and destructive of individual souls.[23]

Anti-vice campaigns were unnecessary in communities that were already religiously disciplined and homogeneous. Puritans, Quakers, Amish, Mennonites, Dunkards, Hutterites, and other devout Protestant groups periodically hived off to establish agrarian communities of exceptional order and stability, places where people loved God and neighbor, tended their fields and orchards, and left the latch string out.[24]

Mormon Utah, though predicated on a different theology, was an equally untroubled place. One utopian village in the southeastern portion of the territory was actually called Orderville. It prospered until 1885, when the federal government, which had better things to do, prosecuted and imprisoned its leaders for plural marriages. In Salt Lake City, the principal Mormon settlement, the only observable vice was associated with the army and its non-Mormon followers at a nearby camp. Travelers, including those hostile to Mormon beliefs, uniformly described the city as prosperous and well planned and its citizens as hard working and virtuous.[25] Collectively, the religious colonies were the most dramatic example of the power of religious conviction to squelch disorderly behavior. Perhaps that is why, collectively, young single men wanted nothing to do with them.

Men and Families

Most young men, however, were interested in the prospect of marriage, which leads to the fifth generalization, that families constrain violent and disorderly male behavior. This is true both of families of origin, in which men are born and socialized, and of families of procreation, which they form to raise their own children. "All government originates in families," Noah Webster once observed, and he was right.[26] Parents set and enforce limits, but their most important role is modeling pro-social behavior: how to control aggression, defer gratification, work diligently, and care for dependents.

Historically, these tasks of discipline and socialization were shared by surrogate parents who supervised apprentices, servants, and farm workers. In exchange for their labor, master and mistress provided food, shelter, correction, instruction, and sometimes wages that would prepare their youthful charges to establish themselves and begin their own families. However, the decay of the apprenticeship system in the years from the Revolution to the Civil War and the gradual disappearance of live-in workers eliminated this traditional method of controlling and educating the young. The responsibility thereupon reverted to the nuclear family, augmented by schools, churches, the YMCA, and other ancillary social institutions.[27]

Parents, natural or surrogate, can ruin children by cruelty, neglect, incompetence, and bad example. Not all parents are responsible, nor do they all inculcate responsible behavior. Even so, it is better on average to grow up in an intact, two-parent family than in a single-parent family or with no parents at all. Children who are abandoned or illegitimate, or who lack a parent for reasons of death, separation, or divorce, are statistically more prone to delinquency, truancy, dropping out, unemployment, illness, injury, drug abuse, theft, and violent crime. Negative effects are most apparent in adolescent boys who, lacking fatherly control and guidance, are socialized by default in hypermasculine, countervalue families like gangs.[28]

Children who experience family disruption are less likely to become or to stay married as adults. This fact has important implications for the social order, because families of procreation, like families of origin, constrain behavior. Married men, as Emile Durkheim pointed out, are subject to salutary discipline.[29] Monogamy controls and focuses their sexual energy; children make them mindful of the example they set; the material needs of their families encourage regular work habits and self-sacrifice. Above all, married men lack the sense of expendability that plagues bachelor communities, in which the prospective loss of life, whether one's own or another's, is often regarded lightly.

A story told by Rebecca Burlend, a Yorkshire immigrant who settled with her husband and five young children in Illinois in the early 1830s, illustrates this principle. One day Burlend's husband discovered that a tall stranger was letting his horses feed in their corn:

> My husband remonstrated with him on the injustice of such behaviour, and persevered in his attempt to drive [the horses] out; at which the person, whose name was Brevet . . . struck him a

blow on the forehead with his fist, and threatened further violence if he did not allow them to remain. Seeing that physical force was the only available argument, my husband began to prepare for resistance; but calling to mind the situation of his family, and not knowing what perfidy might be resorted to, he wisely concluded to leave the man and his horses where they were. I mention this circumstance principally to shew how much we were indebted to an over-ruling Providence for the preservation of my husband's life on this occasion. We afterwards learned that Brevet . . . declared he would have stabbed my partner with a large dirk which he always carried with him, if he had resisted. In a short time afterwards he left the neighborhood, dreaded and detested by all who knew him.

We may not know the role of Providence in this encounter, but the role of family seems clear. Brevet, a drifter with little to lose, behaved aggressively. Burlend, who had no wish to leave a widow with five children, backed down. It is a drama that has been repeated many times. "I took things that I wouldn't have took before that from any man on earth," recalled the Montana cowboy "Teddy Blue" Abbott, explaining why he gave up fighting after becoming engaged. "Simply because of the fear of losing her. I was afraid . . . I might kill a man and have to go to jail or leave the country, and I wouldn't run the risk." Abbott also gave up drinking and chewing tobacco, settled down, raised a family, and went from $40-a-month cowpuncher to owner of a 2,000-acre ranch.[30]

Married men are also likelier to be cleaner, better nourished, and healthier because they have wives, and often daughters, who customarily attend to laundry, cooking, nursing, and other hygienic tasks. In societies with a systematic division of labor, where marriage is the accepted way by which adult men gain the fruits of women's work, the bachelor is at a serious disadvantage. He is, as the anthropologist Claude Lévi-Strauss pointed out, "really only half a human being" and frequently observed in an unclean and disheveled state. "He that hath not got a Wife," declared Ben Franklin's Poor Richard, "is not yet a Compleat Man."[31]

Here is the prejudice against single men distilled into a single sentence. We usually think of discrimination in American his-

tory as centering on race, ethnicity, and gender, but in fact many
of the deepest and most unthinking prejudices have involved
marital status, to the point of incivility to the unmarried dead.
Single men have at times been forced to live in segregated
neighborhoods and dormitories. Like blacks, they have had their
own restaurants and railroad cars. They have been assigned
lower priority for scarce medical resources and have been operated on without benefit of anesthesia.[32] They have consistently
earned less and have paid for their singleness through double
poll taxes, higher land prices, steeper insurance rates, less generous credit, longer prison terms, and less compensation for
job-related disabilities. In hard times they have been laid off
before married men and in dangerous ones they have been
placed in the front lines.[33] On occasion the exposure to danger
has been voluntary, as when a Montana cowboy offered to
break the meanest broncs to spare his married employer the risk.
As with all prejudices, roles and expectations have a way of
becoming internalized. Social marginality reinforces single
men's sense of superfluity and contributes to the risk-taking and
psychology of expendability found in bachelor groups.[34]

Social scientists and statisticians have been investigating the
fortunes of single and married men for over a century and a half.
They have found consistently—to my knowledge without exception—that single men have been more likely than married ones to
be homeless, unemployed, poor, in trouble with the law, or in
prison. In 1890, when national statistics on the marital status of
convicts first became available, 29 percent of all prisoners were
married, compared to 52 percent of the male population over the
age of fourteen. By 1974 the gap had widened in both directions:
only 21 percent of male jail inmates were married, compared to
about 64 percent of the over-fourteen population.[35]

This pattern is consistent with the high arrest rates for men in
their teens and early twenties. Though physical and hormonal
changes are partly responsible, this is also the age range in which
men are typically between households. Leaving or having already left their families of origin, they have not yet entered the
self-disciplinary regimes of their own families of procreation.

Men who have become stuck in or who have reverted to this
single state have been much more prone to violent and disor-

derly behavior. They have more often killed themselves and others; more often suffered venereal disease, insanity, alcoholism, and drug dependency; and more often succumbed to illnesses, like tuberculosis, associated with malnutrition and squalor. Consequently their lives have been shorter. In New York State in the early twentieth century, unmarried men who had survived to age 20 could expect to live a total of only 43.6 years compared to 60 for those who were married.[36] Although life expectancies for both groups have since increased, there is still a significant mortality gap between married and unmarried men.

This gap is partly due to the selective nature of courtship. Men who are undisciplined, unattractive, obnoxious, impoverished, inebriated, or otherwise socially or physically impaired find it harder to acquire spouses. These same traits may result in shorter lives or trouble with the law. Several studies have shown, however, that marriage has a protective effect independent of the selection factor.[37] Marriage imparts a sense of identity, self-worth, and mastery that translates into greater resistance to mental and physical illness. The behavior of married men is more circumspect and healthful, especially if children are also present.

In short, though the purpose of marriage is family formation, one of its chief effects is male social control. The controlling effect works on two generations, fathers and sons, present and future. That is why society-wide family decline always has long-term consequences. Unmarried men may be more erratic and vulnerable than married ones, but they are not necessarily more continent. If they conceive male children out of wedlock the chances are good that their biological sons will be poor and undersocialized and will have trouble establishing families of their own.

Armed Men in Groups

Men who, for whatever reason, are not married generally find themselves in the company of other unmarried men, brought together by the collective nature of their work or recreation. This gives rise to one last generalization: men in groups make for trouble, especially if they are armed and loosely disciplined. People think and act differently in groups than when they are alone; they also think and act differently as a group's age, social class, and gender mix changes. Men who congregate with other men tend to be more sensitive about status and reputation. Even if they are not intoxicated with drink or enraged by insult, they instinctively test one another, probing for signs of weakness. Declining peer challenges can lead to ostracism; accepting them often leads to fighting.

Male jostling goes on in any society. What is peculiar to America is the frequent addition of firearms to the equation. Between 1899 and 1993 no fewer than 223 million civilian firearms were available for sale in the United States, including 77 million handguns. This understates the number of guns actually available, because federal records do not include military weapons, firearms made before 1899, or illegally manufactured or smuggled weapons. Add in the zip guns, the military surplus, and the attic pieces and there may well have been one firearm for every person living in the country in 1993.[38]

Widespread gun ownership does not automatically mean widespread violent crime. Most Swiss households have guns, because most Swiss men serve in the militia. Yet the Swiss male homicide rate is quite low (Figure 2.1). There is also some evidence that gun ownership deters burglars and robbers, who fear getting shot by an irate victim more than they fear the long arm of the law.[39]

The real problem is that when men carry firearms, above all concealed handguns, fights can quickly turn into homicides. A good many murders are simply "successful" aggravated assaults, the result not necessarily expected or planned. Guns that are more forgiving of bad marksmanship—revolvers, repeaters, and automatics—have compounded the problem and increased the prospect of bystander injury. Revolvers first made their appearance in the 1830s and became commonplace after the Civil War, when the country was awash with military pistols. Men, especially southerners, carried pistols as part of their daily apparel. Concealed guns were so common in Kentucky after the Civil War that when a gentleman ordered a pair of pants the tailor automatically inserted a pistol pocket. In the late nineteenth and early twentieth centuries mail-order suppliers got into the act, furnishing weapons, from cheap revolvers to twenty-shot automatics, to anyone who could fill out a form and pay a few dollars. The real merchants of death, it turned out, were reputable American firms. Sears was doing a $3 million annual business in revolvers before the company finally ended its sales.[40]

By the 1920s, if not before, it was apparent that the unusually high American homicide rate was connected with the easy availability and lax control of guns. England, which strictly regulated guns through the Firearms Acts, had few shooting deaths and a homicide rate a tenth that of the United States. Moreover, individual states with the highest percentages of firearms slayings in the period 1924–1926 also had the highest overall rates of homicide, the correlation being +.61. Whatever its deterrent effect on theft may have been, the American habit of gun-toting was significant because it often turned ordinary disputes, usually flare-ups between men, into extraordinary and fatal crimes.[41]

That is, if the crimes were recognized and treated as such. On the frontier murderous brawls were often unprosecuted and served to enhance the reputation of the victor. Someone who had "killed his man" acquired instant standing. The more he killed, the bigger his reputation. Reputations could also be lost. The fastest way to do so, apart from cowardice, was to fail to partake of the masculine vices in the presence of other men. To refuse a drink was to insult the man who offered it. The incorrigibly abstemious were sometimes forced to learn better manners at the point of a gun.[42] Disreputable, lower-class males, men of no account in the middle-class world of family and church, exercised much greater influence in bachelor communities like bunkhouses and mining camps. They both tempted and punished, for to fail to emulate their vices was to fail, in their own terms, to be a man.

This least-common-denominator effect has been a more widespread and important force in American society than generally recognized, particularly in times of mobilization and conscription. "The army is the worst place in the world to learn bad habbits of all kinds," a Michigan private confided to his brother in 1863; "there is several men in this Regt when they enlisted they were nice respectable men and belonged to the Church of God, but now where are they? they are ruined men." The twentieth-century inversion of Victorian standards and values— the increasing popularity of cigarettes, alcohol, gambling, swearing, promiscuous sex, and other vices previously confined to the underworld—was due in no small measure to the military experience of millions of American men. Lower-class men set the social tone in the boot camps and barracks, leading respectable recruits and draftees to acquire vices (and sometimes diseases) they took back to civilian life.[43]

The classic example of the barracks effect was the late Richard Nixon. A devout Quaker when he went into the Navy, Nixon proceeded to learn to drink, smoke cigars, play poker, and swear, well, like a sailor. The famous expletives deleted of the Watergate tapes—mainly "damn," "hell," "Christ," "Goddam," and "crap," with an occasional "shit" or "asshole"—were vestiges of Navy bull-session talk, grafted by the accident of military service onto what had originally been a very different vocabulary.[44]

The armed forces offer important clues to the behavior and disorderly potential of armed, unmarried men in groups. Historically the American military has brought together young men and prepared them, technically and psychologically, to kill their enemies. "On the last day of training before leaving for Vietnam," recalled one marine,

> We were ushered into a clearing where a staff sergeant stood holding a rabbit. He stroked and petted it. As soon as we were all seated, with no word of explanation, he crushed its head with a rock and proceeded to actually skin and disembowel the animal with his bare hands and teeth while showering the entrails on us. As we left the clearing he stood there with fur all around his mouth and blood running down his throat. The intended message was that one was going into a war and civilization and all its emotional vestiges must be left behind.[45]

Intended messages can have unintended consequences. Armed forces foment male violence to serve the ends of state violence, but in doing so they create a social monster, a large group of aggressive youth in a supermasculine environment dominated by unmarried, lower-class men. To control the monster in peacetime, as well as to maintain discipline during battle, armed forces require elaborate rules and strict punishments— the system of rank and command, drill instructors, courts-martial, and so forth. George Armstrong Custer, who was more anxious to keep his men from drink than from massed Indian warriors, went so far as to impound their pay until they were away from the whiskey-peddling sutlers. Unspent greenbacks were found blowing among the corpses at the Little Big Horn.[46]

At best, disciplinary and preventive measures keep soldiers' behavior within manageable limits. Armed forces partially isolate and contain the disorderly potential of their recruits, but they do not eliminate it, as the long history of military vice and criminality attests. When wars wind down and troops become inactive, demoralized or dispersed, trouble always follows. General George Washington complained, with odd exactitude, that seven-elevenths of his troops were close to mutiny at the end of the Revolutionary War. He had to post extra guards to keep them from rioting and insulting their officers. Violent, disorderly, and drunken soldiers were a constant problem during Florida's Seminole Wars, especially during lulls in the fighting or at the end of campaigns. Similar excesses occurred in the last stages of the Mexican War, prompting a disgusted quartermaster's wife to declare "an inactive army . . . a perfect hotbed of evil." Frontier garrison duty—lonely, boring, dispiriting work that drove men to drink, vandalism, desertion, and suicide—was no better. "My experience has taught me," cautioned an officer stationed in Texas in 1856, "to recommend no young man to enter the service." The officer's name was Robert E. Lee.[47]

The end of the Civil War gave rise to an especially large crime wave. Violent offenses rose by nearly 60 percent in New York City in 1865, an increase attributed to "the rough material turned loose upon society by the close of the war and the breaking up of armies." Two-thirds of all those committed to northern state prisons in 1866 were veterans. Crime was sufficiently brisk in Massachusetts to require construction of a new state penitentiary. It was even worse in the South, where emancipation cheapened black life and bitterness inspired racial depredations. A thousand freedmen were killed in Texas be-

tween 1865 and 1868, many by angry veterans and for reasons
no better than spite.[48]

The armed forces, in other words, have acted throughout
American history as a giant sponge. In times of mobilization and
combat they have absorbed the most dangerous elements of society; in times of demobilization and peace they have discharged
them and their acquired vices, lethal skills, and war-surplus guns
back into society. If, as after World War II, most of the young
veterans returned to families or formed new ones, the effects of
mass discharge were mitigated. If, however, a sizable number of
veterans either did not marry or divorced their spouses, as after
the Vietnam War, the negative effects of military service could be
of a more serious and long-lasting character.

Violence and disorder occur most often in groups of armed,
touchy, bigoted, intoxicated, undisciplined, unparented, unmarried, and irreligious young men. For the first three centuries of
American history, groups of such men were found primarily
along the frontier, a shifting region that, apart from its farming
and religious communities, had a deserved reputation for violence and disorder. It also had more than its share of single
young men who migrated there in sufficient numbers to produce an abnormal population structure. How and why this ab-
normality occurred, and with what exceptions, is the subject to
which we now turn.

THREE

The Geography of Gender

Outside of Indian domains, America had a surplus of men from the earliest colonial settlements until just after the end of World War II. It was not just the arithmetical fact of the surplus that mattered; it was how the extra men were distributed. If they had been spread evenly across space and time—if, for example, every community's gender ratio had stabilized at about 105 men for every 100 women—the surplus probably would not have counted for much. Under those circumstances it would have been comparatively easy to attach the supernumerary males to existing families and to keep them from congregating in large groups. Such, however, was not the case.

Men to the Frontier

The surplus men drifted, as if caught in an inexorable current, toward the frontier. Women, especially widows, more often stayed in settled regions or moved to cities. This tendency was apparent everywhere in the colonies by the second half of the eighteenth century and continued throughout the nineteenth. Massachusetts is a prime example. In 1765 the gender ratios for whites sixteen and older in the two oldest coastal counties, Plymouth and Suffolk, were respectively 88 and 87.[1] In the more recently settled Berkshire County, on the colony's western border, the gender ratio for whites sixteen and older was 114. "You know that new towns have usually more males than females," Daniel Webster wrote to a friend in 1802, "and old commercial towns the reverse . . . When I resided at Exeter I thought petticoats would overrun the nation." Later in the nineteenth century, as the frontier moved to the Mississippi River and beyond, Massachusetts was left with more and more women. In 1865 the state's governor, John A. Andrew, actually called for state assistance to relocate unmarried young women, "who are wanted for teachers, and for every other appropriate as well as domestic employment in the remote West, but who are leading anxious and aimless lives in New England." The legislature rejected this scheme as unnecessary and impracticable.[2]

Massachusetts and other eastern states developed surpluses of women primarily because large numbers of young men moved toward the frontier. Frederick Jackson Turner celebrated them as refugees from capitalism, venturesome souls who refused to accept inferior wages and subordinate positions in the new industrial order.[3] In this he was largely mistaken. The key force, which antedated both the commercial and industrial revolutions, was the exponential growth of America's youthful population.

Male migrants were typically losers in a natal lottery. They had poor parents or were crowded out of a comfortable inheritance by too many siblings. This was especially true of New England, where two centuries of rapid population growth inevitably outstripped the supply of good land. Population pressure also came to play a role in the middle and southern colonies, as did exhaustion of the soil and the concentration of coastal lands in the hands of a planter elite.

A farmer's son with little prospect of inheritance essentially had four choices. He could learn a trade, join the army, go to sea, or take advantage of the land and labor opportunities along the frontier. These were not necessarily exclusive options. A few men like Samuel Clemens managed eventually to try all four. Clemens was in his youth a journeyman printer, a soldier, and a prospector; he knew the water as a river pilot and later as a travel writer. It is no accident that his mature literary works are filled with descriptions of masculine groups and subcultures.

Those who were compelled by economic or family circumstances to pursue one of these four courses of action were often unmarried and in their late teens or twenties when they made their choice. Those among them who were engaged or already married, and who decided to migrate permanently, naturally made plans to bring their fiancées or wives and children with them. But they often preceded their families to the new site, spending a year or so girdling trees, building shelters, and keeping a watchful eye for hostile Indians. The Connecticut emigrants who in 1769 began settling "Wyoming," the disputed region along the Susquehanna River in northeastern Pennsylvania variously claimed by Connecticut, Pennsylvania, and the Indians, went as a kind of armed expeditionary force. In May 1772 there were only five white women in Wilkes Barre compared to about 130 men. By the late 1770s, however, the settlement had become normal in both a demographic and social sense. There were prosperous family farms, schoolhouses, and Sabbath days observed with customary strictness.[4]

The men-first, families-later pattern of settlement was common along the great agricultural frontier stretching from the Appalachians to the eastern reaches of the Great Plains. George Carroll, an Iowa pioneer, recalled that there were only half a dozen or so families in the Cedar Rapids area when he arrived. "The larger portion of the inhabitants," he remembered, "were men who had come on in advance of their families to secure their claims and erect some kind of a shelter for them when they came." Married men with families sometimes brought their older sons and hired help with them, collecting their wives and younger children later. Engaged men who returned to their fiancées during the winter or bachelors who went back East in search of a bride would tack a sign on the door to warn off claim-jumpers: "Gone to get a wife."[5]

Fetching wives and families, or going back to find a bride, was less practical in the Far West. Distance and slow transportation made back-and-forth migration difficult before the completion of the transcontinental railroad in 1869. Married men who traveled along the Oregon Trail and other routes generally had to take their families with them or endure a long period of separation. The most typical overland immigrant, however, was a young single man. This fact is readily explained by the region's climate and labor demand. The prevailing lack of rain west of the ninety-eighth meridian (rainfall is abundant only in the Pacific Northwest) discouraged family farming and therefore family migration. The nature of the Far Western economy encouraged the migration of young, unattached men. They were well suited for mining, lumbering, trapping, construction, freight hauling, cattle driving, and other occupations that required itinerancy and physical strength.

Work on the Far Western frontier was dangerous and exhausting. "Many a fine, spruce young clerk coming to California with golden dreams of wealth before him has proved, to his sorrow, that the crowbar is heavier than the pen," cautioned an advice book for prospective emigrants. The forty-niner Richard Ness once hired a man to help him mine in California's Yuba River region. The man lasted ten minutes in the July sun. One reason so many European and Asian peasants were brought to work on frontier mining and construction projects was that they were inured to hard work and capable of sustained physical labor. The mountain excavations of the Chinese are the most famous instance of this, though determined workers of Irish, Italian, and several other nationalities could be found toiling throughout the Far West. The importation of masculine labor from around the world made it the country's most ethnically diverse region, an immigrant nation within a nation of immigrants. In 1870 roughly a third of the population in California was foreign-born; in Idaho and Arizona, more than half.[6]

Women to the City

American women were not inclined toward such jobs, nor were they expected or usually permitted to take them. Many also disliked the prospect of a difficult journey to the frontier and the hardships and isolation of the new country where the chores were more burdensome, the neighbors few, and old friends but a yearning memory. Their apprehensions were magnified by personal correspondence ("none can imagine the suffering that many women underwent in or during the transit"); by memoirists who warned of rattlesnakes and dysenteric death; and by the conventional wisdom of writers like Hinton Helper, who declared that no woman he met in Gold Rush California was willing to make the place her permanent abode. George Napheys, the author of a popular advice book for women, drew his readers' attention to the oversupply of men along the frontier. This was due, he said, to the disinclination of women to emigrate and to the fact that women were "unfitted for the hardships of pioneer life."[7]

Napheys was wrong about women's ability to endure hardships. Thousands of stoic pioneer wives accompanied or followed their husbands westward; their achievements and sacrifices are embedded in the national legend. Without their skilled and patient toil the western lands could not have been permanently settled by Americans of European descent. The "gone to get a wife" signs were more than statements of marital intent. They were admissions that the primitive farms and towns were incomplete and untenable without women and their labor.

Napheys was right, however, about the reluctance of women to migrate. Most women, single or married, wanted nothing to do with the frontier and tried to stay away from it altogether. The wife of David How, a Massachusetts Revolutionary War veteran who aspired to become a frontier farmer, was adamant in her refusal to move into the wilderness. How was forced to give up the New Hampshire land he had already purchased and partially cleared and to open a currier's shop instead. In 1847 Elizabeth Dixon Smith wrote in her Oregon Trail diary of a woman who refused to proceed farther and set fire to her husband's wagon. He put out the flames and then flogged her. Harriet Paddleford Goodnow, the wife of a Kansas emigrant, dreaded the Plains Indians and the climate about equally. When her husband settled there in 1855, she stayed at home in Maine, necessitating a long-distance shuttle marriage of fifteen years.[8]

Other women agreed to venture forth but were so appalled by what they found that they departed for home—with or without their spouses. One Colorado woman, who lived with her husband at a remote way station near Denver, decided she had had enough and resolved to board a stage eastward bound for civilization. An army officer warned her that the stage would almost certainly be attacked by Indians. The woman replied that she had been living in fear all summer, that she was sure to be murdered by Indians if she stayed, and that she might as well die on the stage. As events transpired, she very nearly did.[9]

It was not simply that women were repulsed by the adversity and isolation of frontier life. The economic opportunities open to them were to be found, by and large, in cities and towns. Young women could work in domestic service, in mills, or, later, in offices. Older women and widows could support themselves by operating restaurants or boarding houses. Farm wives who outlived their husbands often sold or rented their properties and went elsewhere, unless they had a son prepared to take over the operation. Women moving to urban areas thus formed a countercurrent to the predominantly male movement toward the rural west. The city, as historian David Potter remarked, was the frontier for American women.[10]

The inevitable result was that cities, except for those dominated by heavy industries like steel, began developing female surpluses. "There are large communities in the East where there is an excess of women," observed the reformer Mary Livermore in 1883. "It is very evident in such communities that there will be large numbers of unmarried women, unless the surplusage of women should emigrate,—Heaven only knows where,—or Utah should be re-enacted in New England."[11]

Black women were in the same predicament. In southern cities before the Civil War female slaves outnumbered male by as much as 50 percent. Free black women outnumbered free men by 25 percent or more. White residents used large numbers of black women as maids, cooks, laundresses, nurses, and seamstresses both before and after the abolition of slavery. As late as 1930 Natchez, Mississippi, was home to 4,194 black women and 2,965 black men, giving it a black gender ratio of only 71. The ratio of *employed* black men to women was doubtless even lower. The difficulty that black men had in securing urban jobs made family formation (and hence socialization) difficult; it also contributed to the rise of a frustrated male counterculture given to petty crime, intoxication, and intraracial violence.[12]

The drift of women to cities was by no means peculiar to America. It has been observed in other societies widely separated by time and place and culture, so much so that it seems a near constant of social history. What was different about the American experience was the presence of a large and continuously expanding frontier which was simultaneously drawing men *out* of cities. The result was a persistent (though never absolute) gender polarization of the population. This polarization had two separate but overlapping dimensions, east-to-west and urban-to-rural. In the West women were not only scarcer than in the East, they were also more concentrated in cities and towns.[13]

More Boys than Girls

The male surplus along the frontier was not solely the result of adult migration. It was also caused, to a lesser degree, by an excess of male children. Historical demographers who have studied nineteenth-century census records have found small but persistent regional differences in gender ratios for children under fifteen years. Rural and agricultural areas nearest the frontier had higher-than-average numbers of male children, eastern urban and industrial areas the reverse. Some have speculated that this difference was due to the greater economic value of boys to farm families. Because girls were less valuable as agricultural laborers, they were less well cared for and hence perished at a higher rate. In cities and commercial areas, where job opportunities for female children were equal or superior to those for males, there was no economic reason to neglect girls or to do anything else that would directly or indirectly cause their deaths.[14]

This is an intriguing hypothesis. If passive female infanticide was widespread, it would help explain the concentration of young men and related social problems. It would also revolutionize the way we think about life and death on the frontier. Is it possible that the deadliest behavior actually took place in sod houses rather than saloons and that it was motivated by cold economic calculation rather than hot-headed passion?

The answer is almost certainly no. Parental behavior toward children was unlikely to have been dictated solely by the value of future labor, unless one dismisses religious conviction out of hand. Protestant Americans who believed in God's stern judgment would not have withheld food or medicine from an unregenerate daughter of tender years. If they had done so it would surely have been remarked by observers, as it has been in societies where such practices are common.[15] Yet no anecdotal, journalistic, or legal testimony suggests that economically motivated neglect of girls occurred in the rural and frontier regions of nineteenth-century America.

What the evidence does show is that parents valued the farm labor of both boys and girls. Pioneer immigrants praised the usefulness of children without reference to gender, emphasizing their helpfulness in gathering wood, hauling water, planting and harvesting crops, picking cotton, minding siblings, and doing sundry other chores. They also stressed the cheapness and abundance of food. Too many mouths to feed could not have been a motive for neglecting daughters, as it often was in peasant societies. "Children are no burden but a great help to their parents," summed up Elise Amalie Waerenskjold, a Norwegian who lived in Texas from 1847 until her death in 1895.[16]

The mystery remains, however. If the neglect of female children did not cause the higher-than-average number of male children reported in western censuses, then what did?

One possibility is that more boys were born in frontier and rural districts than in eastern and urban areas. Different races and classes produce different ratios of male to female births. Whites have more male offspring than blacks; wealthy parents have more than poor. The differences in gender ratios by race and class probably reflect differences in levels of nutrition and physical well-being, healthy women being more likely to bear male offspring than unhealthy ones. Coital patterns also seem to have a bearing, with young males who engage in frequent intercourse more likely to produce sons. Male frontier migrants were typically white and young and vigorous. Those among them who were married and engaged in farming had every incentive to produce children and so may be presumed to have had frequent intercourse. They and their spouses had ample food and a reasonably good material standard of living. All of these factors would have increased the frequency of male births.[17]

If more male children were born in remote rural areas, more of them also survived. Boys were more vulnerable than girls to infectious diseases and, prior to the twentieth century, urban populations suffered more from infectious diseases than rural populations. City boys were more often exposed to diseases like measles and diarrhea than country boys, and they died from them more often than city girls, whose natural immune responses were stronger.[18]

It is also likely that remote rural areas had more boys simply because more boys moved there. A farmer living on a small eastern farm with many sons had a problem and an opportunity. The problem was that his landholdings were apt to be too small to divide among his heirs. The opportunity was that his sons could provide the labor to help him in the arduous task of clearing virgin land.[19] There was, in other words, a double incentive for families with many sons to migrate toward the frontier.

Some boys went without families. They set out on their own like Huckleberry Finn or traveled in "orphan trains" organized by aid societies. These benevolent enterprises relocated about 200,000 men, women, and especially children from eastern slums to rural and western areas from the 1850s through the 1920s. About 60 percent of the transported children were male.[20]

There are thus three independent explanations for the larger number of male children found on or near the frontier: more of them were born there, more of them survived there, and more of them moved there. It is important to keep in mind, however, that the presence of extra boys under the age of fifteen was not the principal reason why the *overall* frontier gender ratio was imbalanced. That imbalance was due, first and foremost, to the presence of young adult male migrants.

Variations in Gender Ratios

Not all frontier populations were dominated by men. Different mixes of immigrants produced different degrees of gender imbalance along the frontier. This point cannot be emphasized too strongly. Some regions had heavy male surpluses that lasted for a comparatively long time, others did not.

The experiences of seventeenth-century Massachusetts and Virginia provide, as they so often do in American history, an instructive contrast. Massachusetts had more men than women during its first decade, but the imbalance was modest and quickly disappeared as wives joined their husbands and began bearing large numbers of children. Puritan society in America was orderly and family-centered from its inception. Bachelors were distrusted and assigned to established households to keep them out of trouble. The repeated attempts to repress Thomas Morton's Merry Mount, a bacchanalian trading post complete with maypole and willing Indians, are a vivid reminder of the Puritan determination to check the sexuality of single men. Virginia, of which the Puritans likewise had a low opinion, was another turbulent bachelor society. The census of 1625 showed a gender ratio of 333, with the bulk of unmarried men between the ages of sixteen and twenty-nine. The gender imbalance of Virginia, and the Chesapeake region generally, persisted into the eighteenth century.[21]

It is useful to think of the demography of subsequent American frontiers as resembling the Massachusetts type, the Virginia type, or something in between. Figure 3.1 shows examples from the nineteenth century. The age and gender distributions are based on census lists compiled shortly after the first influx of permanent white settlers into each area. The population of Richardson County, in the southeastern corner of Nebraska, was only slightly abnormal: 55 percent male in 1860, with children present in substantial numbers. Access to Richardson County, via the Missouri River, was comparatively easy; so was farming, thanks to excellent soil and abundant rainfall. Hence the familial immigration.

Wells County, in the north central section of North Dakota, was also agricultural, but with more bonanza farms, a shorter growing season, more extreme climate, and greater risk of drought. Most of its early settlers came not from the United States but from Wales and Scandinavia. Two-thirds of the residents were male in 1885. The young adult population was lopsidedly masculine, the children very nearly so. Over 60 percent of Wells County residents under the age of ten were boys, reflecting the tendency of immigrant farmers to bring more male children with them.

Dodge City, Kansas, represented an extreme case of gender imbalance. The absence of farm families and a surfeit of buffalo hunters, gamblers, saloon keepers, and traders explain the odd

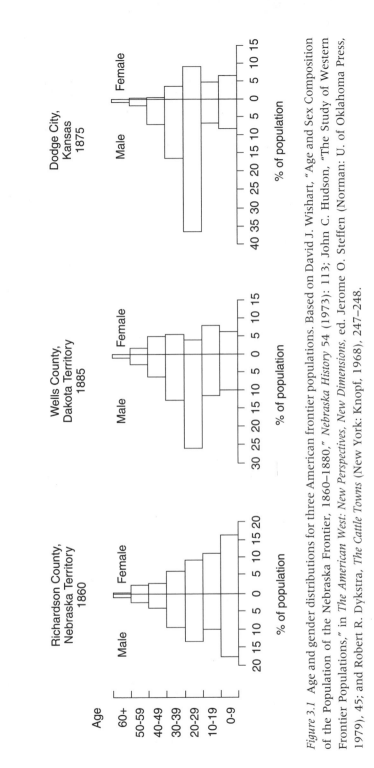

Figure 3.1 Age and gender distributions for three American frontier populations. Based on David J. Wishart, "Age and Sex Composition of the Population of the Nebraska Frontier, 1860–1880," *Nebraska History* 54 (1973): 113; John C. Hudson, "The Study of Western Frontier Populations," in *The American West: New Perspectives, New Dimensions*, ed. Jerome O. Steffen (Norman: U. of Oklahoma Press, 1979), 45; and Robert R. Dykstra, *The Cattle Towns* (New York: Knopf, 1968), 247–248.

shape of its 1875 population pyramid, so skewed that it has been likened to a deck gun. During the late 1870s and early 1880s, the peak years of Dodge City's career as a cow town, the gender ratio was even more imbalanced during the summer months, when cowboys arrived with their herds of longhorns. By 1885 the native population had begun to normalize, although the town still had a noticeable surplus of men in their twenties and thirties. The larger region in which Dodge City is located, semi-arid western Kansas, had a similar population history. Its gender ratio was 768 in 1870, fell to 124 in 1880, but remained above 110 for nearly forty more years.[22]

These three cases illustrate an important rule of frontier demographic and social history. The harsher the environment, the sparser the population, the longer and more difficult the immigrants' journey, and the lesser the importance of small-scale agriculture, the higher the gender ratio in a given frontier location. This was most apparent in the cordillera, the vast elevated region running from the eastern Rockies to the western foothills of the Sierra Nevada and Cascade ranges. Most of the remote cordilleran towns were established by miners and had wildly skewed populations, with as many as thirty-four men for every woman. The extreme gender disparities of the mining frontier passed within a decade or two, although as late as 1870 California's gender ratio was still 166, Nevada's 320, and Idaho's a lopsided 433. These ratios actually understated the true male surplus, as nonagricultural frontier regions had more than their share of homeless drifters who were missed by, or fugitive men who avoided, the federal census takers.[23]

Figure 3.2 maps the known distribution of men and women in the United States in 1870, during the climactic stage of continental frontier expansion. Except for the fertile Willamette Valley, Mormon Utah, and New Mexico with its established population, the dry plains and mountain west had high gender ratios, as did the cold and thinly populated lumbering regions on the western fringes of the Great Lakes. The well-watered lands settled by farmers during the mid-nineteenth century had normal or slightly elevated gender ratios. Eastern urban areas had female surpluses, as did large parts of the southeastern states, which had suffered the largest share of Civil War casualties.

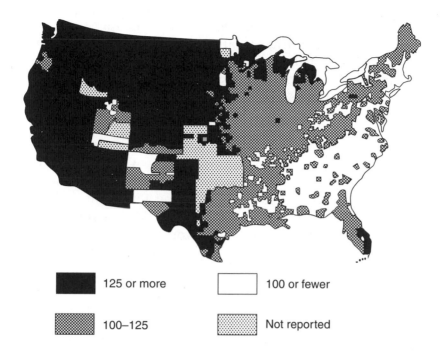

Figure 3.2 Gender ratios (number of males per 100 females) by county, 1870. Adapted from *Historical Atlas of the United States* (Washington: National Geographic Society, 1988), 49.

Seedbed of Violence

The shortage of men in the Southeast was also a consequence of migration. Poverty, soil exhaustion, and political turmoil encouraged white men to leave, just as they discouraged European immigrants from taking their places.[24] Florida was the only southeastern state that consistently gained from immigration during the period 1870–1950. Otherwise outmigration was the rule until the rise of prosperous cities like Atlanta began attracting and retaining people in the decades after World War II. Prior to the Sunbelt revival the Southeast was the nation's economic backwater, a place with a very high birth rate but little industry and few well-paying jobs. Consequently the region produced a steady stream of emigrants of whom the most common type was a man in his twenties.

White men went west, at first mainly to Arkansas, Louisiana, Oklahoma, and Texas. After 1900 they began leaving these states as well, moving farther west or to the north central industrial belt. The Depression turned southern emigration along Route 66 into a flood. California was the primary destination, as 1.2 million white southerners moved there and to other western states during the 1930s and 1940s. These "Okies" and "Arkies" and "Texies" were looked down upon as poor white trash, prone to violence, alcoholism, and incest. One California theater seated them in the balcony with blacks, the irony evidently lost on its management.[25]

The onset of World War I, which cut off European immigration and increased the demand for American manufactured goods, gave large numbers of black workers an opportunity to move to northeastern and midwestern industrial cities, where they hoped to earn better wages and escape poverty, legal segregation, and racial terrorism. "Dear Sir," wrote one, responding to a 1917 advertisement for laborers in the *Chicago Defender,* "this would be a grand opportunity for me to better my present conditions . . . I am a single man and would be willing to do any kind of work . . . There is but little down here to be gotten." There was even less in the 1930s and 1940s when a combination of declining prices, federally sponsored crop-reduction programs, and agricultural mechanization destroyed the sharecropping system and severed the main economic link between blacks and their native South. Well over a million left the region in the 1940s, a quarter of them to the West, drawn by the magnet of defense jobs. In Los Angeles alone the black population jumped from 3,000 in 1940 to 131,000 at the end of 1942. Los Angeles, Chicago, New York—the great twentieth-century migrations transformed black Americans from a predominantly rural to a predominantly urban people, from a regional racial minority to a national one.[26]

All of this made the South a seedbed of national violence. When millions of white and black southerners moved elsewhere, they took their obsessions about reputation and vengeance and deadly weapons with them. The places to which they moved, such as Central Texas and Harlem, soon became known for frequent shooting and stabbing affrays over trivial disputes. Trivial, that is, to outsiders, though not to the southern-born combatants and their sons and grandsons who faced shame and demasculinization if they failed to respond to insult or challenge.[27]

The consequences of the outmigration of violence-prone southern men were apparent in criminal justice statistics. During 1906–1935 Pennsylvania-born blacks were eleven times more likely to be committed to the Western State Penitentiary for crimes of violence than Pennsylvania-born whites, but blacks born out of state (overwhelmingly immigrants from the South) were *forty-eight* times more likely than native whites to be committed for violent crimes. More recent and sophisticated studies of murder rates have shown similar differences among white southerners, whose propensity for violence not only has kept their native state homicide rates high but has inflated the rates of other counties and states into which they have moved.[28]

Southern outmigration thus had a social, cultural, and demographic bearing on American violence. It transplanted, to use the seedbed metaphor, impoverished young men who were unusually quick to resort to violence to settle personal disputes. Insofar as postbellum southern emigration, especially that of whites, was in the direction of the frontier, it also contributed to the east-west gender polarization of the American population.

Age Structure on the Frontier

The gender ratio was not the only unusual feature of frontier demography. The age structure was also skewed. In nonagricultural regions children were few and the aged a curiosity. A scant 6.5 percent of California's 1850 population consisted of children under fourteen, compared to 40.5 percent for the country as a whole.[29] The frontier areas which had substantial numbers of dependents present from the beginning were those in which family farming predominated. Children often accompanied their parents to frontier farms; more children were soon born after their arrival since the fertility of frontier women was high. This is why there were comparatively large numbers of children under the age of ten in Richardson County, Nebraska, when the 1860 census was recorded (Figure 3.1).

Old persons were scarce in newly settled regions, at least until the pioneers themselves aged and the frontier had moved elsewhere. In 1850 only 3.0 percent of California's people were fifty or older, compared to 9.1 percent nationwide. Western miners were considered old at forty; an over-thirty cowboy was a rarity. Cowboys, to paraphrase Owen Wister, did not live long enough to become old.[30]

The youthfulness of frontier legends is often startling. John Wesley Hardin claimed to have killed five men by his sixteenth birthday. Billy the Kid (Henry McCarty) may have killed nine before being shot to death at twenty-one. (There were actually two gunfighters named Billy the Kid. The other, William Claiborne, was shot dead at twenty-two.) George Armstrong Custer, perhaps the most legendary figure of them all, was twenty-seven when his Seventh Cavalry fought Indians on the Kansas plains.[31]

Lesser mortals were also young, most often in their twenties, when they journeyed west. Few came over forty, whether married or single. The places they left had a high median age for the adult population, the places to which they moved a low median age. Letters and advice aimed at prospective emigrants emphasized the physically taxing nature of the work and suggested, at times bluntly, that the weak and aged should stay at home. There was, after all, no point in toiling beyond one's capacities in a new and unforgiving land.[32]

Nor was there any point in dying en route. Before the advent of ocean-going steamships and railroads, the prospect of a long and dangerous voyage served to discourage, or to kill off, the elderly. "Above all I warn old people who have no one but themselves to rely on against coming here," wrote a San Francisco immigrant in 1852. "Only young, healthy people are fit to travel to California— I have seen many instances of that." At that time all three of the routes to California—overland, across the Isthmus of Panama, and around Cape Horn—were risky and arduous. One San Francisco–bound army officer likened his ship to a charnel house. The danger and difficulty of the journey, together with the physical demands of mining, explain why there were few older persons (as well as few women and children) residing in California during and immediately after the Gold Rush.[33]

Here again we encounter the paradox that long-distance migration was simultaneously good and bad for American society. Insofar as it screened out the infirm and encouraged the relocation and concentration of young, healthy men, it was a boon to economic and civic life. Immigrants with strong backs built industrial America. They dug its canals and mines, laid its tracks and sewers, erected its bridges and factories. But the same process of labor concentration simultaneously increased the prospect of local violence and disorder, particularly in places like mining camps or railroad towns where the young workers resided. If the continuous influx of prime-age male workers profited the railroad magnates and cattle barons, it was equally lucrative for the liquor dealers and prostitutes. Commercialized vice targeted at bachelor laborers was as much a growth sector of the American industrial revolution as coal or steel.

Intermarriage: The Path Not Taken

Marriage, like migration, was a life adventure most often undertaken in young adulthood. The young men who went to the frontier discovered that they could not immediately embark upon both, owing to the lack of eligible brides. Adult women were generally married before moving west and hence unavailable as spouses for bachelor frontiersmen. The problem was particularly acute in places like California's Grass Valley, a mining town where a scant 3 percent of the men had wives in 1850, and only 6 percent a decade later.[34]

One alternative to bachelorhood was intermarriage with Indians. This was, in a sense, a natural solution, for intertribal warfare had often left surpluses of women. George Catlin, the celebrated painter and student of Indian life, reported that many tribes along the Upper Missouri in the 1830s had "two and sometimes three women to a man."[35]

Trappers and traders whose livelihoods brought them into contact with Indians, and who stood to gain useful alliances as well as sex, companionship, labor, and children, were the quickest to take advantage of this availability of native women. Some intermarriage took place in the seventeenth-century southern colonies, which were chronically short of white women, and along the midland backwoods frontier in the eighteenth and nineteenth centuries. Free blacks and runaway slaves also married Indian women. Casual or exploitative sexual contact, including Indian prostitution, occurred among all frontier groups. Women were sometimes "lent" to white men for the winter in exchange for food. "The girl, when sold to a white man, is generally skeary for a while and will take the first chance to run away," casually explained one Rocky Mountain hunter. "Should you take her again, and whip her well, and perhaps clip a little slice out of her ear, then she will stay."[36]

White-Indian marriage of a more civilized and permanent sort also occurred. John Rolfe, who chose an Indian princess for his bride, protested that it was not for "the unbridled desire of carnall affection," but for Jamestown, England, God, and salvation that he was marrying "an unbelieving creature," namely Pocahontas. Sir William Johnson, an imperial official and great landowner in the eighteenth-century New York upcountry, dispensed with pious rationalization and simply lived with a common-law Mohawk wife. A century later Granville Stuart, a prominent early Montana settler, took a Shoshoni wife. Unlike other early Montanans who married Indians, he did not abandon her when white women became available.[37]

Such tolerance and respect were unusual in the general run of Indian-American sexual relations, which tended toward the impermanent or the meretricious when they occurred at all. Remarkably little intermarriage took place in British and American territory, especially in comparison to French lands. Partly this was due to the very high gender ratio among French immigrants, for whom it was Indians or bachelorhood. Partly it was due to the liberality of French religious and imperial policy, which recognized and often encouraged intermarriage. But it was also due to the racial pride and Indian hating of American frontiersmen, who mostly preferred dead natives to connubial ones. Prejudice against Indian spouses, evident from Jamestown on, was formalized in colonial anti-miscegenation laws and persisted into the nineteenth century. In 1859 the journalist Horace Greeley, then touring the Far West, counted only seven Indian women living with white men among the nearly four thousand residents of Gregory's Diggings, a mining camp about twenty-five miles beyond Denver. By contrast he noted that French trappers and voyageurs in the Rocky Mountains might have two or three Indian wives apiece.[38]

Spanish men also frequently married women of native or mixed ancestry. Nacogdoches, Texas, like most frontier towns, had a disproportionately male population, roughly six men for every five women. European-Indian and European-Mestizo couples were common in Spanish Nacogdoches: between 1792 and 1804 more than half of all marriages crossed ethnic lines. After the town passed from Mexican to American control such marriages became increasingly rare. In 1860 only 6 of 1,055 married couples were Anglo-Mexican. American contempt for Mexicans, repaid in the coin of ethnic standoffishness, was common throughout the Southwest. Like Indian hating, it blocked an alternative marital path for American frontiersmen.[39]

Anglo racism is another example, like southern touchiness about honor, of how a cultural trait exacerbated the biological potential for violence and disorder inherent in concentrations of young men. If intermarriage among Europeans, mixed bloods, natives, and Africans had been as common on the American frontier as it was on the French and Spanish, the average frontiersman would have been more domesticated, better nourished, and less inclined to kill people of a different color. The "Wild West" of fact and legend was the bachelor West, the domain of the miner and cowboy and gambler. It was not the West of the banker and merchant and family farmer, men with wives and children and something to lose.

Throughout American history migration has been the chief cause of an uneven distribution of its people by gender and age, with more males and young adults in newly colonized and developing regions, more females and old persons in settled areas and cities. The imbalances have varied in magnitude and duration, but at times they have been extreme, as in the southern colonies during the seventeenth century or in the Far West during the nineteenth. Young men who found themselves on or near the frontier could not all marry white women, and they generally would not marry Indian or Hispanic women. The price of prejudice for supernumerary men was widespread bachelorhood. The price of widespread bachelorhood for society was more violence and disorder.

FOUR

The Altar of
the Golden Calf

From the standpoint of social order nearly everything that could have gone wrong on the American frontier did go wrong. Outside of family farming areas the frontier attracted armed bachelors filled with dangerous substances and deadly ideas: whiskey, racial contempt, and homicidal sensitivity about honor. Institutional restraints like efficient police, predictable justice, permanent churches, and public schools were lacking, as were the ordinary restraints of married life. Though most frontiersmen had been raised in intact families, they often had trouble forming their own families because of the shortage of unmarried white women.

Traditional accounts of frontier violence and disorder also emphasize the push effect of eastern legal troubles. Men who ran afoul of the law, accumulated debts, or killed someone headed for the Carolina backcountry or the Indian Territory or Arizona or whatever distant place happened to be the current rogue's haven. Texas became so notorious as a refuge that a "gone to Texas" sign hung on an abandoned farmhouse or cabin door was universally understood as a kiss-off to creditors and sheriffs.[1]

But those who were in trouble with the law did not go to just any frontier region. They were concerned with future income as well as escape, and there was no point in robbers, gamblers, prostitutes, and whiskey peddlers preying upon farming families, who lacked cash and an appetite for vice. So they flocked instead to the mining camps and railroad towns and cow towns where they could fatten off the wages of workers targeted as victims, suckers, johns, and drunks. The concentration of young male wage earners created a pull effect, a magnet for criminals and vice purveyors. The presence of commercialized vice in turn inflated the level of violence by inspiring drunken fights and shootings over gambling disputes and dance-hall girls. It also helped to bring about the sickness and early death of many young men and kept those who survived broke. "Like most young men we only wanted money to spend," confessed an Idaho gold miner, who spoke for many of his kind. "If I had taken my money and invested it I would have been a millionaire."[2]

The general pattern, then, was that frontier labor opportunities caused population abnormalities which in turn caused social disorder and vice parasitism. The relative absence of women, children, and old people and the oversupply of young bachelors created a pathological tangle of drunkenness, violence, gambling, prostitution, disease, neglect, and early death in male frontier groups. The rough, insalubrious, and generally short lives of railroad construction workers, buffalo hunters, teamsters, and enlisted soldiers all exemplify the process. I have chosen, however, to focus on two groups as case studies of the dangers inherent in frontier bachelor societies: the miners who took part in the great gold and silver rushes, and the cowboys who spread cattle ranching from Texas to Montana in the decades after the Civil War.

The California Gold Rush

The Gold Rush was triggered by James Marshall's celebrated discovery at Sutter's Mill in January 1848, the same year that Mexico ceded California to the United States. Eighty-nine thousand eager gold seekers from all over the world arrived in 1849; the ratio of men to women among them was twenty to one. The world they entered was almost totally anomic, a mass of unkempt men clad in flannel shirts and heavy boots who were inspired by the one desire to hurry on to the mines. Within six months one in every five of the forty-niners was dead—an astonishing statistic given that they had almost all started the journey in good health and in their prime years. So many died that life insurance companies refused to write new polices for Californians or charged substantial additional premiums for immigrants already covered.[3]

Some of the mortality was unavoidable. The Gold Rush coincided with the 1849 cholera pandemic. Cholera and other diarrheal diseases were frequent visitors along the fly-infested overland trail, which was littered with rotting food, fomites, and human excrement, and in the mining towns and camps, where sanitation was primitive. The immigrants brought malarial parasites with them; when they settled near rivers and streams, the local mosquitoes were infected and the disease became endemic. Some immigrants were also exposed to illnesses, such as Rocky Mountain spotted fever, which they had never encountered before.[4]

The lack of women ensured that illness claimed more lives than it would have in a balanced, family-centered population. Women were the everyday healers in the nineteenth century, the practical ones who, by virtue of their upbringing, were adept at nursing, sanitation, and nutrition. Men who were lucky enough to accompany them on the journey west benefited from their presence and skill. Catherine Margaret Haun, who traveled on the Oregon Trail, noted in her diary that women and their children "exerted a good influence, as the men did not take such risks with Indians and thereby avoided conflict; were more alert about the care of the teams and seldom had accidents; more attention was paid to cleanliness and sanitation and, lastly but not of less importance, the meals were more regular and better cooked thus preventing much sickness and there was less waste of food."[5]

Trail's end separated the bachelor immigrants from the women and families, who were bound for the fertile valleys rather than the gold fields. Culinary life in the latter left something to be desired. Unsoaked beans were baked in dutch ovens; puzzled men wondered why they were harder than ever when they came out. Rice was cooked without water, pans went unwashed, diets were unbalanced, scurvy was everywhere. The disease was caused by the vitamin C–deficient diet (salted meat, lard, coffee, sugar, and white flour) on which the miners subsisted during the long trip to California and in the camps. Men became weak, then listless and incapacitated, then died in cold, rain-soaked tents, victims of what has been called bachelor's scurvy.[6]

Dr. James Tyson, an eyewitness, found it strange that the men did not sooner avail themselves of such items as pickles or fresh meat or acidulous drinks. He attributed their fatal neglect to ignorance and inattention and to the fact that men were apt to neglect their health in the frantic pursuit of gold. Had women been present in larger numbers and able to collect, cultivate, and preserve more fruits and vegetables, there would have been less scurvy, to say nothing of more effective care for those who fell ill. As it was some California women profited handsomely from their dietary knowledge by retailing antiscorbutic remedies or by selling fruit from the orchards they planted for as much as a dollar a pear.[7]

What the miners had instead of women was doctors, or men who called themselves such. "The doctor can do well at practice," wrote Lt. William Tecumseh Sherman in October 1848, "as very many are sick or recovering from sickness, and all can afford to pay." Physicians poured in by land and by sea. One camp, Rich Bar, had twenty-nine doctors for its 1,000 miners. "In the short space of twenty-four days," wrote a physician's wife at nearby Indian Bar, "we have had murders, fearful accidents, bloody deaths, a mob, whippings, a hanging, an attempt at suicide and a fatal duel." Yet even this sort of sporadic mayhem was insufficient to keep the approximately 1,500 Gold Rush doctors fully employed. Many soon turned to other occupations, including barbering, prospecting, assaying, and innkeeping. The California medical market was saturated by 1850. "Most persons who come here to practice medicine are compelled to resort to some other means of obtaining a livelihood," wrote one observer. "Hydropathy is the popular treatment, and a good bath is thought to be far more conducive to health than bleeding or calomel."[8]

Those who survived their illnesses faced another problem, the ubiquity of bachelor vices. It became apparent early on in California that the only sure way to make money was to mine the miners. That meant providing goods and services of an unexceptionable sort, like groceries and laundering, or providing those of a more questionable variety, like tobacco, liquor, gambling, and prostitution. In the early days of the Gold Rush tobacco was sufficiently scarce as to nearly command its weight in gold dust. So many speculators rushed to fill the demand that the San Francisco warehouses were soon crammed with boxes of tobacco. San Francisco liquor importers were no less ambitious. In 1853 they received more bulk or wholesale containers of alcoholic beverages than there were people in the state. The imported spirits did not want for distributors, for as many as six of every one hundred Californians were involved in some aspect of the liquor trade.[9]

Eyewitnesses wrote of being astounded by the amount of liquor consumed; of seeing bottles strewn every few yards along roads and trails; of crippled and delirious men dying in shanty bunks while drunkards caroused below. They warned that alcoholic excess weakened men and made them vulnerable to infectious diseases. "The number of deaths is beyond all calculation," wrote San Franciscan Jerusha Merrill in October 1849. "Many have no friends to put them under the turf, yet those who take care of themselves and are regular in their habits enjoy good health. I warn all against the gaming house and grog shop." In a subsequent letter, written in January 1851, she noted that most of the cholera cases were drunkards. Alcohol was an insidious drug, a killer in the guise of a familiar friend. It gave the impression of warmth and well-being when in fact it lowered body temperature and depressed the nervous system. It delivered a caloric burst but was devoid of vitamins or minerals. Miners who drank their meals were starving their bodies and undermining their immune systems, setting themselves up for pneumonia or other common camp infections.[10]

Alcohol made men vulnerable to another type of parasitism, that of prostitutes and gamblers. Like all women, prostitutes were scarce, and they commanded high prices for their services. Miners paid an ounce of gold ($16) just to have one sit beside them at a bar or gaming table. San Francisco bar and café owners went further, paying women to serve as topless (and bottomless) waitresses or to pose nude in suggestive positions on elevated platforms. Those who wished to go beyond gawking paid anywhere from $200 to $400 for a night of sex. Such prices naturally attracted more prostitutes to San Francisco, which had an estimated 2,000 by 1853.[11]

Though San Francisco was the principal center of vice, prostitution quickly spread to the outlying towns. One enterprising woman, who dressed in men's clothes and rode horseback from camp to camp, claimed to have earned $50,000 in 1849. Another, more ambitious, stocked a Placerville brothel with a dozen Hawaiian girls. She charged $100 a night for her own services, $50 for those of the girls, and was said to have accumulated $100,000 in less than a year, a fortune even by California's inflated standards.[12]

Professional gamblers were more common than prostitutes, and just as skilled at siphoning off miners' earnings. "I have seen men come tottering from the mines with broken constitutions," wrote the forty-niner Alfred Doten, "but with plenty of the 'dust,' and sitting down at the gaming table, in ten minutes not be worth a cent." Saloons and gambling rooms were everywhere. "They were on the first floor, with doors wide open," Ulysses S. Grant recalled of San Francisco. "At all hours of the day and night . . . the eye was regaled . . . by the sight of players at faro." Or at monte, roulette, or poker. In California men bet on anything, even the prognosis of a shooting victim as he underwent treatment on a pool table.[13]

Indeed, there was no clear distinction between what men did for a living—sinking their labor and capital into claims that might repay their investments with nothing or a fortune—and their recreational gambling. "In the spring of 50 I had about a thousand dollars," wrote a disappointed miner named William McFarlin, "but I left the place [I was working] and went to dam the river (and by the way I have damd it often) where everybody thought we would make a pile that summer and go home in the fall but we spent all we had & five months hard labour & never got one dollar & when we settled I owed $155.00 and had but seven dollars in my pocket—one of the company took a razor & cut his throat the same night."[14]

This was a story with many variations. Men bet their lives just to come to California and their health and fortunes to pursue its golden wealth. Most lost the bet. "There are thousands of persons here who hardly ever saw a sick day in the States and are completely broken-down," wrote the California physician J. D. B. Stillman, "and many of them, if they live, will never fully recover their health."[15] In such a risk-all atmosphere, with death and illness daily prospects, gambling was a natural pastime, no more or less rational than the mining enterprise itself.

Much of the gaming and drinking took place in the winter, when men were unable to work, and on Sundays, when they flocked to towns like Coloma to gather news and gossip, lay in supplies, and patronize the saloons and gambling booths. "Sunday was the day when all the games were liveliest," wrote the forty-niner William Bennett; "the miners came in from all the gulches with big buckskin bags filled with gold dust, ounces of which they staked on a single card." Barkeeps dispensed whiskey for fifty cents or a pinch of gold dust, padding their profits by carefully sweeping up the dust that fell onto their counters.[16]

Sunday was also the day for masculine display. Miners tossed gold on the bar and bade their companions to name their drinks; reckless horsemen pulled knives from the ground at full gallop. Itinerant preachers bold enough to mount a stump and declaim against the desecration of the Sabbath were rewarded at collection time—a manifestation, perhaps, of latent guilt—but were ignored on the practical point of reformed behavior. Devout men who happened to find themselves in this milieu were appalled. One prophesied to an eastern minister that California "instead of being a blessing will prove a curse to the Union, morally and politically . . . You can form no adequate idea of the depths of sin and moral degradation to which most of the people are sunk or rather sink themselves and those too of whom we should not dream such things when they leave the States."[17]

These sentiments were shared by Hinton Helper. Later to achieve fame as a critic of southern slave society, Helper spent three weary and unprofitable years (1851–1854) in California and wrote a scathing account of the state's social and economic prospects. Helper was an unusual man, simultaneously a racist, abolitionist, Puritan, and amateur sociologist. He argued that

California's social disorder stemmed from the mammonism of its polyglot population and from the lack of women, in whose absence "vice only is esteemed and lauded." Like many other observers he noticed that the moral tone of the mining communities immediately began to change when women were present. Though he worried about the possibility that wives would be seduced away from their husbands by the many determined bachelor suitors, he nevertheless looked forward to the day when California would experience "an influx of the chaste wives and tender mothers that bless our other seaboard."[18]

This sounds like Victorianism, and it was. But it was also something deeper and more modern. Helper had grasped the fundamental principle of what is now called the interactionist school of sociology, that the self emerges and evolves as people internalize the attitudes that significant others hold toward them. When the mix of significant others changes, so does the sense of self. The typical California immigrant was neither poor nor vicious. He had been raised in a respectable family in "the States," but his home was far away and the hurly-burly of camp life was close at hand. His sense of what was permissible and appropriate was shaped by his immediate social environment, which consisted of uprooted young men thrown together with opportunists and vice figures. His masculine companions were quick to ridicule conventional virtue as weakness and self-restraint as effeminate. If he avoided the saloons and faro tables, he stayed alone in his tent or room on Saturday night, bored and lonely. If he refused to smoke or drink, he risked insult and retaliation. A person who would not partake of whiskey or tobacco was "little short of an outlaw," complained the California miner George McCowen, who took up smoking simply to avoid trouble. Louise Clappe, the wife of a mining-camp physician, observed that men who had once considered swearing vulgar and had never uttered an oath now "clothe themselves with curses as with a garment," swearing being "absolutely the fashion" in masculine California. People who had never gambled became high-stakes players. In Stockton the proprietor of the leading gambling saloon was a Methodist minister. "'Everybody gambled,'" recalled one San Franciscan; "that was the excuse for everybody else."[19]

Or almost everybody. William Swain, a devout emigrant who kept a detailed journal and wrote numerous letters home, remained mindful of the Bible and of his wife and family in New York. But communication was irregular and difficult, and other sources hint of reversion to bachelor behavior among men separated from their wives and families. "We are thousands of miles from home and comfort ourselves by thinking that a knowledge of our indulgence in vice will never reach them," confessed one heartsick miner. "Here, there is no parents eye to guide, no wife to warn, no sister to entreat, no church, no sabbath . . . in short, all the animal and vicious passions are let loose . . . without any legal or social restraint."[20]

The one sure way to change this situation was family reunification, accomplished when disappointed gold seekers sailed home or, more rarely, when their spouses journeyed to the camps. "The wives of some of the wildest boys on the creek have come down to join their husbands," observed the forty-niner Alfred Jackson, "and it has sobered them down considerably."[21] It was just this "sobering down" that Helper valued and anticipated would come about when gender balance was restored.

Helper saw something else clearly, that the violence in California was aggravated by the influx of criminals and the habit of carrying deadly weapons, the former being a justification for the latter. Ninety-nine out of a hundred miners went about armed with revolvers or Bowie knives, which were sold at local groggeries together with cigars, tobacco, and more than a hundred varieties of alcoholic beverages. This combination of young men, liquor, and deadly weapons produced a steady stream of unpremeditated homicides, most of which arose from personal disputes and occurred in or near drinking establishments. Helper estimated that California had experienced 4,200 murders in the course of six years, along with 1,400 suicides and 1,700 deaths due to insanity caused by disappointment and misfortune.[22]

Helper's estimate of murder seems too high (unless he was including murders of Indians, in which case it was almost certainly too low), but there is an abundance of other evidence that Gold Rush California was a brutal and unforgiving place. Camp names were mimetic: Gouge Eye, Murderers Bar, Cut-throat Gulch, Graveyard Flat. There was a Hangtown, a Helltown, a

Whiskeytown, and a Gomorrah, though, interestingly, no Sodom. Even innocuously named places could explode into violence. The city of Marysville reportedly experienced seventeen murders in a single week, prompting the formation of a vigilance committee. Suicide and violent death occurred in all mining regions. Witnesses wrote of men suddenly pulling out pistols and shooting themselves, of bodies floating down the river, of miners stoned to death in gambling disputes. They described men who had become beasts, biting and pulling hair, flogging one another without mercy, cropping boys' ears, laughing at executions.[23]

Corporal punishment fell most heavily on nonwhites. A white thief might receive up to a hundred lashes, but a runaway slave got two hundred for stealing himself. Another black man, found guilty of larceny simply because he had a large sum of money, was ineptly hanged by a mob and then buried alive. During 1849–1853 more than a third of the lynch-court episodes involved nonwhites, who were occasionally convicted without firm evidence and sometimes without cause. In California as in other parts of the frontier, violence had a racial edge.[24]

Little Californias

In 1849 California was the most unfettered and individualistic place in the world, the exemplar of Jacksonian America and its egalitarian values. But the situation changed in the early 1850s. The most accessible placer gold was gone, continued immigration pushed the population past a quarter million, wages declined, and the industry passed under the control of companies with the machinery necessary for vein mining. By the middle of the decade California was becoming a much more capitalistic and class-bound society, proof of the Spanish proverb that it takes a mine to work a mine. Even so, the California immigration pattern—an influx of uprooted, youthful men, a kind of accidental and imperfectly disciplined army of miners and hangers-on—was to repeat itself in the subsequent gold and silver rushes from the late 1850s through the Klondike stampede of the late 1890s. Mining camps and towns in Nevada's Comstock Lode, in Colorado, Montana, Idaho, Arizona, and throughout the cordillera were initially plagued by high mortality, heavy drinking, gambling, prostitution, ethnic conflict, and violence.[25]

This was the impression the newspaper editor Horace Greeley formed in his 1859 travels through Colorado, then experiencing a gold rush as hopeful men poured into the territory from the Mississippi Valley and points east. Greeley stressed that very few Colorado miners achieved a golden fortune. They either returned home poorer than before, fell victim to cheating gamblers, or died of insanity, suicide, or accident, their bodies found charred by forest fires or chewed by wolves. The mining-camp mix included a small but influential class of fugitives, "prone to deep drinking, soured in temper, always armed, bristling at a word, ready with the rifle, revolver or bowie knife." These toughs set the tone in mining towns like Denver, where the regular administration of justice was nonexistent and where brawls, fights, and pistol shootings were more common, Greeley believed, than any place of comparable size on earth.[26]

The Comstock Lode's most celebrated journalistic visitor, Samuel Clemens, was scarcely more charitable. Clemens, who took up silver prospecting and speculation in 1861, was sleeping at a remote Nevada inn when the Carson River suddenly overflowed its banks and surrounded the building, stranding him for eight days with an assortment of teamsters, stage drivers, and silver-rush vagabonds. Life in the inn, a diluvial microcosm of the mining frontier, was anything but pleasant. The men passed the time by swearing, drinking, gambling, and brawling. A particularly obnoxious bully named Arkansas managed to pick a fight with the landlord and was at the point of shooting him when the landlord's wife, the only woman among them, intervened. Brandishing a pair of scissors, she forced the astonished ruffian to back away from her husband. Though Arkansas was chagrined into silence, his companions went right on carousing and fighting until Clemens became so annoyed and disgusted that he tried to escape across the swollen river with two other men. He failed and in the attempt very nearly lost his life.[27]

Had Clemens perished the world would have been denied the writings of Mark Twain. One cannot but wonder, as Clemens did, how many extraordinary lives were cut short by the misadventures and violence of camp life. "Where are they now?" he inquired of California's miners, as fine a collection of young men as might be found anywhere. "Scattered to the ends of the earth," he answered, "or prematurely aged and decrepit—or shot or stabbed in street affrays—or dead of disappointed hopes and broken hearts—all gone or nearly all—victims on the altar of the golden calf."[28]

Or the silver one. Miners in the silver towns swooned into boiling slagpots, fell down mine shafts, froze in shanties, or caught their deaths from sleeping on drafty saloon floors, for which privilege they paid ten to fifty cents a night. So many died in Leadville, Colorado, in the late 1870s that the authorities took to burying them at midnight lest the death rate come to the public's attention and discourage the mining boom. In this they were successful, for the town's largely male population continued to grow, and with it the number of criminals, whiskey peddlers, prostitutes, and gamblers. By 1880 Leadville had a saloon for every 80 persons, a gambling establishment for every 170, and a bordello for every 200. There were 5,000 persons for each of its four churches, religion being less popular than sin.[29]

This was the pattern everywhere on the mining frontier. The ubiquitous vice industry reinforced a system of exploitation that, for all practical purposes, placed miners at the bottom of a hard-money feeding chain. They extracted precious metal from the ground; businessmen, professionals, saloon keepers, and vice operators extracted it from the them; and bankers, politicians, thieves, and robbers extracted it from anyone. This last sort of direct, armed parasitism was extremely dangerous, however. A Mexican outlaw named Joe Pizanthia, dispatched by Montana vigilantes in 1864, was shot, hanged, shot some more, and then burned on a pyre made from the ruins of his cabin. The next morning prostitutes panned out the ashes to see whether he had had any gold in his purse. They were not rewarded for their labors.[30]

Vigilantism, often found in newly established mining areas, was both selective and emotionally charged. In a world without insurance, where men risked their lives and exhausted their bodies to accumulate wealth, the hatred of thieves and robbers was a visceral thing. When caught they were swiftly and ruthlessly punished, as were the murderers of innocent, uninvolved citizens. But when bullies and shootists and saloon brawlers attacked one another—when, in a word, violence was confined to "players"—usually nothing was done, save to summon the doctor and mop the floor. Don Maguire, a Rocky Mountain trader who made his money selling guns, knives, dice, cards, and sundry other items at a thousand percent profit, captured one such episode in his journal. The entry, composed in a hurried, stream-of-consciousness style, was written in the course of an 1877 trip to the mining town of Atlanta, Idaho:

> The two noted characters of the town Coyote Smith and Poker Smith. My attention was first drawn to Coyote Smith. While he was engaged in a quarrel with two carpenters who were working lumber in front of a saloon, he being drunk made much disturbance and at the same time vowing to whip the two carpenters whereupon one of them gave him a kick in the hip. This set him wild. He snarled for a revolver swearing to kill the two. A revolver he could not procure. Midway up the street entered into a second altercation with Poker Smith and seizing a carving knife from the counter of a restaurant he made a stroke [passage obliterated] to sever the jugular vein for Poker Smith but missing his aim the knife struck the collar bone broke and his hand running down the blade he received a horrible wound cutting his hand from the hollow between the thumb and forefinger nearly to the wrist blood flowed freely from both parties but neither was fatally injured. There were no arrests made.[31]

"No arrests made" was the outcome of many a similar confrontation. This sort of affray kept the local surgeon busy, but not necessarily the sheriff or vigilance committee. One of the busiest surgeons was George Kenny, a physician in Salmon City, Idaho. Before he was through he managed to fill half a coffee mug with bullets dug from miners.[32]

Mining-Camp Virtues

Mining camps had their attractions. Their inhabitants were open, generous men who valued deeds above words, deplored hypocrisy, and were friendly to strangers, at least when sober and unprovoked. Their language was direct and colorful. Samuel Clemens, who knew the vernacular better than anyone, judged

Nevada slang "the richest and most infinitely varied and copious that had ever existed anywhere in the world, perhaps, except in the mines of California in the 'early days.'" Miners' swearing was also wildly inventive, though abruptly curtailed in the presence of respectable women, who were treated with courtesy and deference. "I do not recall ever hearing of a respectable woman or girl in any manner insulted or even accosted by the hundreds of dissolute characters that were everywhere," a resident of Bodie, California, recalled. "In part, this was due to the respect that depravity pays to decency; in part, to the knowledge that sudden death would follow any other course."[33]

If women were honored, erstwhile aristocrats ("biled shirts") were not. The miners' political spirit was thoroughly democratic. Practically everyone could vote. In a camp's early days even miners in their mid-teens were permitted to cast ballots. This spirit of inclusive (white) democracy, manifest in California in the late 1840s and early 1850s, was evident in all subsequent gold and silver rushes. Frederick Jackson Turner ascribed the egalitarian ethos to the frontier environment, boldly declaring: "American democracy is fundamentally the outcome of the experiences of the American people in dealing with the West."[34] This famous assertion is not so much wrong as in need of rearrangement. Democracy was a fundamental outcome of the mix of people who *went* to the West, or at any rate to the western mining regions. In a country where adult white men were the only voters, mining camps, which consisted mainly of adult white men, were necessarily democratic. The same east-west gender polarization that exacerbated frontier disorder enhanced frontier democracy. Or temporarily enhanced it, for as the male surplus inevitably disappeared, frontier regions became less egalitarian even as they were becoming more stratified.

Put formally, the assortment of traits found in frontier mining regions—violence, cruelty, recklessness, irreligion, dissipation, neglect of hygiene, bad cooking, and widespread bachelorhood on the one hand; friendliness, camaraderie, sharing, and democratic decision-making on the other—was a biologically, culturally, and socially determined byproduct of an economically driven migratory process that initially screened out the very young, the very old, and women. The demographic circum-

stance of many peers and few wives and children made for a
world of arrested male adolescence. One of the striking things
about male frontier language was the tendency of men, particularly single men, to refer to themselves and their compatriots as
"boys," as in the riposte of a faro dealer to a preacher: "Now,
boys, the old man has been showin' you how to save your souls;
come this way and I'll show you how to win some money!" The
familiar "boys," of which there are thousands of examples in
miners' memoirs and letters, was a peculiar and subtly revealing
usage in a republic where the customary plural form of adult
male address was "gentlemen"; where men were properly addressed singly as "mister" or "sir"; and where the word "boy"
often was insulting or implied servility, as in "Fetch me some
water, boy." Miners looked anything but boyish. They were
muscular men with weather-beaten and heavily bearded faces.
Yet they called themselves boys.[35]

Equally striking was the tendency of men in remote frontier
regions to go by nicknames and to dispense with their surnames
altogether. One California miner labored for a year beside another, "Doc," before learning his companion's last name. This
was a reflection of frontier informality, but also an indication
that these men had entered a new world where family background counted for little. One's standing in the male peer group,
which assigned the nicknames, counted for much. The elimina-
tion of surnames eliminated social and historical ties, perfectly
illustrating Tocqueville's dictum that democracy breaks the
chain of community. But it was also liberating, freeing a man to
realize his ability and talents. "In the east the Yankee was walled
about by forms, creeds, and conventions," observed the California miner Richard Hale. "But here there were no questions
asked about pedigree. 'Can he fill the position? If he can, well
and good, if not—let us have one who can fill it.'" The habit of
dropping surnames, using nicknames, and judging by deeds was
common throughout the Far West. In Montana a man might
simply be called Soap or Frenchy or Whiskey Bill. The last-
named, born William Graves, was hanged by vigilantes in January 1864. The frontier world of arrested adolescence was not
without its norms, the violation of which could have abruptly
fatal consequences.[36]

Counting the Bodies

Western miners, and frontiersmen generally, loved to tell and retell stories of violence, often embellishing them with new details and additional victims. The gambler Doc Holliday may have wounded or killed one black adolescent in a youthful shooting spree; in later years he was said to have deliberately massacred several.[37] Because this sort of exaggeration was common, historians interested in an accurate tally of homicides have turned from literary and anecdotal sources to the drier prose of newspapers and court files. Combing the public record is not a fool-proof method for establishing relative levels of violence, as some murders were ignored or undetected. It is nevertheless the most objective procedure available. For ease of comparison the results are expressed in the modern *Uniform Crime Reports* format of so many homicides per 100,000 persons per year.

Those who have systematically cataloged reported murders in frontier mining areas have found extremely high rates of homicide relative to both contemporaneous non-frontier regions and metropolitan areas in the late twentieth century. Figure 4.1 displays the rates in comparative fashion. Nevada County, California, location of Gomorrah, Gun Town, and other boisterous mining camps, had an average homicide rate of 83 during 1851–1856. The mining town of Aurora, Nevada, had at least 64 during its boom years of 1861–1865. However, because its records are incomplete and because a grand jury report enumerated other killings, it is quite possible that the actual Aurora rate was as high as 117. That would have been almost identical to the rate of Bodie, California, a nearby mining town that averaged 116 homicides per 100,000 during its boom period of 1878–1882. Leadville, a Colorado mining town that boomed at the same time as Bodie, had a rate of 105 in 1880.

Non-frontier or post-frontier regions with more normal gender ratios experienced far less homicidal violence. Henderson County, a rural backwater in western Illinois, had an average rate of 4.3 during 1859–1900, or just nineteen murders in over forty years. Two eastern cities, Boston and Philadelphia, had criminal homicide rates of 5.8 and 3.2 in the two decades after

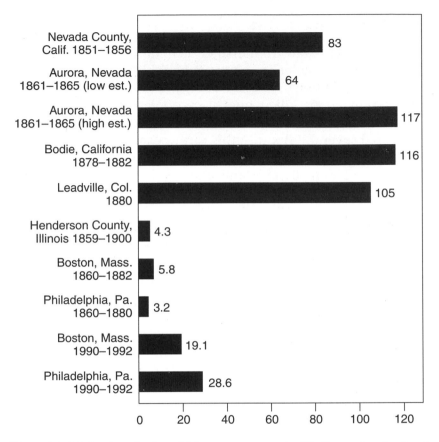

Figure 4.1 Mining frontier homicide rates compared with those of agricultural and urban areas. Based on Ben Nickoll, "Violence on the American Frontier: Nevada County, California, 1851–1856" (history honors thesis, UCLA, 1986), 4; Roger D. McGrath, *Gunfighters, Highwaymen, and Vigilantes* (Berkeley: U. of California Press, 1984), 55, 76n21, 253–254; Elliott West, *The Saloon on the Rocky Mountain Mining Frontier* (Lincoln: U. of Nebraska Press, 1979), 20; John Lee Allaman, "Nineteenth Century Homicide in Henderson County, Illinois" (D.A. diss., Illinois State U., 1989), 184–185; Theodore N. Ferdinand, "The Criminal Patterns of Boston since 1846," *AJS* 73 (1967): 89, 90, combining murder and manslaughter arrests; Roger Lane, *Violent Death in the City: Suicide, Accident, and Murder in Nineteenth-Century Philadelphia* (Cambridge, Mass.: Harvard U. Press, 1979), 60; U.S. Dept. of Justice, *Uniform Crime Reports* for 1990, 1991, and 1992.

1860. By comparison the average rates for Boston and Philadelphia in the early 1990s were 19.1 and 28.6, respectively.[38]

The inescapable conclusion is that the western mining frontier was an exceptionally violent place. This is also a conservative conclusion, for the mining-frontier rates almost certainly do not include all homicidal killings of Indians. These were particularly common in California, where the distinction between killing Indians in battle and simply shooting them down meant little in practice, and where Indian deaths of any sort were of little concern to law enforcement officials.[39]

The historian Roger McGrath, who compiled the statistics for Aurora and Bodie, has pointed out that the dark cloud of mining-town violence had a silver lining. He found that rates of robbery were comparable to, and rates of burglary lower than, those of eastern cities at the same time. McGrath believes that gun-toting citizens deterred property crime. Would-be robbers and burglars knew they stood a good chance of getting shot and that nothing would happen to anyone who killed them save highly favorable newspaper publicity. But the same guns that deterred theft made homicide all the more likely. What happened in Aurora and Bodie was a trade-off, more fatal gunplay for less larcenous crime.[40] Whether (or when) this was true of other frontier mining areas remains an open, intriguing question.

Another open question is whether the mining towns were in fact the most violent places on the frontier. The Union Pacific railroad towns—the end-of-the-line construction depots where graders and bullwhackers flocked to saloons and gambling tents at the end of their day's toil—were apparently even deadlier places. Among the most notorious was Julesburg, which served in 1867 as the temporary dwelling place for four thousand people in the northeastern Colorado Territory. An army colonel stationed there, Richard Irving Dodge, counted 127 graves, only 6 of whose inhabitants had died natural deaths. There had been, he reckoned, at least one slain man buried every day of Julesburg's brief, tumultuous existence. Many of the dead were victims of vigilante justice, hanged from the Union Pacific's telegraph poles.[41]

The end-of-track towns that succeeded Julesburg as the railroad pushed into Wyoming were as bad or worse. The journalist

James Chisholm described early Cheyenne as a human cesspool containing the roughest elements from all parts of the country, outlaws who would not scruple to kill for $10. Laramie boasted a Dickensian saloon, the Bucket of Blood, in which men were robbed and murdered and their bodies tossed into a back room, loaded onto wagons, and hauled onto the plains to be devoured by coyotes. In Benton, farther down the tracks, the 100 bodies that accumulated in the course of the town's two-month existence in the summer of 1868 were disposed of more formally, buried in graves shoveled out of the choking alkali dust. Like Julesburg, Benton averaged a murder a day. The equivalent homicide rate, in excess of 24,000, would have sufficed to wipe out the town's entire population of 1,500 in a little more than four years.[42]

Benton, of course, was exceptional, a short-lived and murderous singularity in the expanding universe of American frontier violence. What is important is the reason for, not the typicality of, its extraordinary mayhem. Like Julesburg, Cheyenne, and Laramie, Benton was an agglomeration (the word "community" is not appropriate) of young, transient, expendable, bachelor laborers whose self-image was one of toughness and whose unregulated vices attracted criminals, gamblers, prostitutes, and other armed opportunists eager to siphon off their wages. This was essentially the same set of demographic and social circumstances that made the mining camps and towns so violent relative to agricultural and eastern urban areas.

The Debate over Frontier Violence

It may seem strange that there has been a long-running debate among historians as to whether the frontier was violent. The debate pits those who believe that frontier violence, especially as portrayed in motion pictures, pulp fiction, and anecdotal histories, has been grossly exaggerated, against those who believe that the frontier's reputation for fighting and killing, even if embroidered by popularizers, is nevertheless grounded in historical reality.[43]

The debate has been complicated by the usual skirmishing about the completeness and trustworthiness of records and the uses to which they have been put, but the real reason for its persistence is that the question it poses—how violent was the frontier?—is miscast. There was no such thing as "the" frontier. Different frontier communities had different social and population characteristics. The Mormon religious colony of Orderville, Utah, and the mining town of Bodie, California, were contemporaneous American frontier settlements, but in terms of gender balance, family life, religious restraint, and the presence of liquor and vice they might as well have been on different planets.[44] In explaining the historical pattern of western violence and disorder, the key is the structure and composition of the local population, not some intangible quality of "frontierness." Mining towns like Bodie, with nine men for every woman, were places where normal marriage and family patterns were disrupted and where vice flourished, with all the increased illness and violence that such vice activities entailed.

A nice illustration of this principle is the contrast between two American gold rushes of the 1840s and early 1850s, the famous one in California and a largely forgotten one in the Gold Hill region of North Carolina. The latter attracted Cornish miners, many of whom brought their families or married local women, who were much more plentiful than on the distant Pacific coast. Aside from the inevitable mining accidents and sporadic fights, the Cornish immigrant miners experienced little in the way of premature death and violence, at least nothing to compare to what happened to the young men who flocked to California. One was an overwhelmingly single and masculine environment, the other was not, and the difference in gender balance translated into a difference in the local social order.[45]

The mining camps of California and the interior cordilleran frontier, like the end-of-tracks railroad construction depots and other boom towns with abnormally male and youthful populations, had exceptionally high levels of violence and disorder. This was true both for the straightforward statistical reason already mentioned—more young men equals more violent and disorderly behavior—and because of the pull effect that concentrated male wage-earners had on vice purveyors and criminals. Their presence made a bad situation worse, as did the weakness of social institutions and the interpersonal dynamics of male groups, which licensed and reinforced aggressive and reckless behavior.

The western miners were not alone in this predicament. The cowboys of the Great Plains also inhabited a social milieu with few women and much vice and they suffered the same consequences of more violence and disorder. The chief difference was that the cowboy got to ride to his places of dissolution while the humble miner usually walked.

FIVE

The Cowboy Subculture

The twentieth-century image of the cowboy, the most evocative of America's mythic figures, is that of a hero, a knight-errant with a horse and a gun. The gun, and his skill with it, make the cowboy a deadly antagonist, but only against rustlers, bandits, and renegades. In formulaic narratives the cowboy hero may shoot more people than all the outlaws combined, but his killings are justified and self-confidently right.

The men behind the heroic myth were less appealing figures. Journalists in western towns described cowboys as dependable and hard-working when sober but vicious menaces when drunk. Cowboys on sprees shot up towns, terrorized tenderfeet, squandered their wages on gambling and whores. "Nobody then thought of them as romantic," recalled a Montana rancher's wife. "They were regarded as a wild and undesirable lot of citizens." President Chester A. Arthur, in his annual message to Congress in 1881, complained that "a band of armed desperadoes known as 'Cowboys'" was making trouble in the Arizona Territory, "committing acts of lawlessness and brutality which the local authorities have been unable to repress." "Morally, as a class," the *Cheyenne Daily Leader* commented the following year, "they are foulmouthed, blasphemous, drunken, lecherous, utterly corrupt."[1]

The more candid memoirs are equally unflattering. The rancher Bruce Siberts remembered that most of the itinerant cowhands he saw in South Dakota in 1894 "were burned out with bad whiskey and disease." During the winter about half "were pimps, living off some cheap prostitute in Pierre . . . Most of them had a dose of clap or pox and some had a double dose. All in all, most of the old-time cowhands were a scrubby bunch." Even the cowboys' celebrated freedom has been dismissed. "The cowboy in practice," observes the western writer Wallace Stegner, "was and is an overworked, underpaid hireling, almost as homeless and dispossessed as a modern crop worker, and his fabled independence was and is chiefly the privilege of quitting his job in order to go looking for another just as bad. That, or go outside the law, as some did."[2]

The realistic image of the cowboy as a hired hand with a borrowed horse, a mean streak, and syphilis may be at odds with the heroic myth. But it is not at odds with the argument that the age and gender characteristics of a place or group in conjunction with its social institutions and norms determine the amount of violence and disorder. The cowboys of the Great Plains were young, male, single, itinerant, irreligious, often southern-born, and lived, worked, and played in male company. In the most expansive and violent years of the range cattle industry, the late 1860s and 1870s, many cowboys were combat veterans and almost all carried firearms. The nature of their work precluded drinking on the job, but they made up for it in payday binges. Those who survived the bad liquor and shooting scrapes found themselves back in the saddle, penniless, doing a job that was almost as dangerous as the whiskey mills themselves and in which few lasted for long.

Cowboys, in short, were lower-class bachelor laborers in a risky and unhealthful line of work. They were members of a disreputable and violent subculture with its own rules for appropriate behavior. The word "subculture" is, I realize, a loaded one, connoting to some a radical rejection of all values and virtues of the dominant culture. That was not true of cowboys. Their politics were usually conventional, as were the courtesy and deference they showed to respectable women. And they certainly worked hard. But much else in the cowboy code was unconventional, and therein lies the point of the term. The unwritten rules which governed their lives and which they passed on to new hands were often at odds with the norms of the Protestant core culture. For the cowboy to become a symbol of the American experience required an act of moral surgery. The cowboy as mounted protector and risk-taker was remembered. The cowboy as dismounted drunk sleeping it off on the manure pile behind the saloon was forgotten or transmogrified into a rough-edged, heart-of-gold fellow who liked an occasional bit of fun.

Origins and Character

The American cowboy subculture, like most frontier cultures, blended elements from different ethnic groups. Its deepest roots, however, were Spanish. It was the Spanish who introduced horses and cattle into the Americas and who perfected the techniques of mounted ranching, such as lassoing cattle from horseback. And it was the Spanish who first brought cattle to Texas and Alta California, two remote provinces on their northern frontier. Americans who settled in Texas in the nineteenth century combined Carolina cattle traditions with Spanish ranching techniques, equipment, and stock and added a few innovations like the chuck wagon. After the Civil War they spread themselves and their cattle into the vast grasslands formerly occupied by the bison, whose great herds were being systematically destroyed by professional buffalo hunters. The expansion of the range cattle industry reached its peak in 1885, with perhaps 7.5 million head feeding on the Great Plains north of Texas and New Mexico. The industry thereafter rapidly declined, owing to a combination of overgrazing, harsh winters, westward expansion of farming, and barbed-wire fences. By the early twentieth century the cowboys were fast diminishing, surviving more in the realm of legend than in occupational fact.

The tasks associated with the range cattle industry—rounding up cows, branding calves, castrating bulls, breaking horses, and trail drives to railheads or northern pastures—required youth, strength, endurance, and cool courage. Texas cattle were easily spooked creatures whose impressive horns and heft could kill a man in seconds. Cowboys on the trail had to be constantly alert not only for stampedes but for human and animal predators. They made do with little sleep and indifferent food, were continually exposed to foul weather, and, like soldiers in the field, had to learn to live with discomfort and minor injuries. That, or quit. Of the roughly 35,000 men who accompanied herds up the trails from 1867 through the 1880s, only a third participated in more than one drive.[3] As in gold mining, disillusionment and accidents quickly thinned their ranks. The constant attrition kept cattle herding a young man's game. The average age of cowboys in 1880 was twenty-three or twenty-four years.[4]

Many of the early cowboys were Texans or Texas immigrants, typically Confederate veterans ("TNT dressed in buckskin") or their sons who migrated to the state after the Civil War. The majority of cowboys were Anglos, though by some accounts a seventh were black men, mainly ex-slaves from Texas ranches. Perhaps another seventh were Mexicans. White southern, African-American, and Mexican-American cowboys had at least one thing in common, apart from mutual dislike. All came from cultures that stressed the desirability of decisive action to redress insult or injury. Texas-born cowboys were particularly notorious for their willingness to resort to guns to settle personal disputes, a trait which contributed to the high level of homicidal violence (32 per 100,000 in 1878) in the state in the decades after the Civil War.[5]

If cowboys were concerned with their standing in the eyes of their peers, they cared little for conventional social institutions. Few had wives or lived with their parents, unless they happened to be working on the family ranch. Their outlook was this-worldly, not so much antireligious as irreligious. "After you come in contact with nature you get all that stuff knocked out of you," explained "Teddy Blue" Abbott. "You could pray all you damn pleased, but it wouldn't get you to water where there wasn't water."[6]

A preacher who could "get to water," who could rope a calf or face down a bully, commanded the cowboys' respect. After Daniel Tuttle, the Protestant Episcopal Bishop of the Diocese of Utah, thrashed a stage driver for swearing in the presence of a woman, ranchers, miners, and even an occasional sporting man traveled from miles around to have a look at the fighting clergyman. Pugilistic Christianity was fine with cowboys. They were indifferent to the more peaceable sort and regarded regular churchgoing as unequivocally in the feminine realm. Though a few professed to worship in the "outdoor church of nature" and others claimed to have "got religion," orthodox Christianity was fundamentally at odds with the cowboys' masculine self-image.[7]

What was in keeping with their self-image was a gun. With the exception of professional hunters, cowboys were the most heavily armed civilians anywhere in post–Civil War America. They carried repeating rifles and revolvers, typically large-bore, military-issue weapons whose .44- or .45-caliber bullets did considerable and often fatal damage. Prior to 1880 these weapons were a necessary evil, given the possibility of encountering hostile Indians, robbers, rustlers, rattlesnakes, bears, and the like. But whatever the cowboys' guns bought in the way of deterrence and emergency use was paid for by an increase in accidental death and injury. Cowboy and noncowboy alike died when guns tipped over, dropped from pockets, or fell from blankets. The *Caldwell Post,* a Kansas cattle-town newspaper, estimated that five cowboys were killed by accidental gun discharges for every one slain by a murderer. Those who survived accidents were often horribly injured, living out their lives with shattered knees or shot-away faces.[8]

The other evil associated with gun toting was the increased incidence of unpremeditated homicide. "I always carried a gun because it was the only way I knew how to fight," Abbott admitted. "That was the feeling among the cowpunchers. They didn't know how to fight with their fists. The way they looked at it, fist fighting was nigger stuff anyhow and a white man wouldn't stoop to it." Abbott, whose memoirs are unusually self-revealing, explained how his trigger-happiness led to a shooting:

> I was really dangerous. A kid is more dangerous than a man because he's so sensitive about his personal courage. He's just itching to shoot somebody in order to prove himself. I did shoot a man once. I was only sixteen, and drunk. A bunch of us left town on a dead run, shooting at the gas lamps. I was in the lead and the town marshal was right in front of me with his gun in his hand calling, "Halt! Halt! Throw 'em up!" And I throwed 'em up all

right, right in his face. I always had that idea in my head—"Shoot your way out." I did not go into town for a long time afterwards, but he never knew who shot him, because it was dark enough so he could not see. He was a saloon man's marshal anyway and they wanted our trade, so did not do much about it. That was how us cowboys got away with a lot of such stunts. Besides, the bullet went through his shoulder and he was only sick a few days and then back on the job. But they say he never tried to get in front of running horses again.

Here youthful irresponsibility and intoxication combined with the need to demonstrate courage to produce a violent confrontation, the standard formula for a male group disaster. Had the bullet entered a few centimeters in and down, the hapless marshal would have been killed, dead because a drunken boy was acting out a subcultural fantasy of shooting his way out of trouble.[9]

Cowboys used their guns to act out any number of roles, the deadliest of which was *nemo me impugnit*, "no one impugns me." Harry French, a Kansas railroad brakeman, witnessed a fight between cowboys riding in the caboose of his cattle train. It began during a card game when one man remarked, "I don't like to play cards with a dirty deck." A cowboy from a rival outfit misunderstood him to say "dirty neck," and when the shooting was over one man lay dead and three were badly wounded.[10]

This was a classic scenario for homicide. Then as now most killings arose spontaneously in a group situation involving alcohol, gambling, or some other vice in which socially marginal men suddenly turned on one another with deadly weapons in response to an insult, curse, jostle, or dispute over a small sum of money. From our vantage the disputes seem trivial, though the cowboys undoubtedly viewed them differently, as crucial if dangerous tests of their mettle. "That was one thing that got many a man," Abbott conceded, "that foolish sensitiveness about personal courage."[11]

Cattle-Town Sprees

This sort of hot-tempered gunplay seldom erupted when cowboys were on the trail. Drinking and rambunctious behavior were not tolerated in a situation where an impulsive act could kill or maim innocent men and destroy thousands of dollars worth of cattle. Cowboys in the saddle were sober employees who assumed large responsibilities and discharged them well.[12] Journalists and writers who knew this side of their life often defended the cowboys from their detractors, publishing favorable accounts of their colorful and sometimes heroic activities— breaking broncos, turning a stampeding herd, thwarting rustlers. These stories of cowboy competence and courage, suitably embellished, formed the basis for the heroic myth.

Journalists and writers who only saw the cowboys when they came to town formed a very different impression. Like sailors in port, a simile that often occurred to them, they saw young men mad to spend their accumulated wages. This was especially true at the end of long cattle drives, around which rituals of pent-up consumption, pleasure, and status developed. First a visit to the barber to remove several months' growth of hair and beard, then a trip to the dry goods store for a new hat, clothes, and fancy boots. Then a meal featuring delicacies unavailable on the trail: oysters, celery, eggs. Then on to the saloon, gambling room, theater, dance hall, and brothel, perhaps ending the night by shooting out the street lights or "taking the town." The latter was a sure way to impress peers and earn a reputation, a large consideration for the greenest cowboys, who seem to have been more prone than the experienced hands to go wild.[13]

Cowboy sprees had three important consequences, all undesirable from the standpoint of individual well-being and social order. They made the cowboy's life even more dangerous and unhealthful. They kept many cowboys impoverished, dependent, and unable to marry. And they attracted vice predators, who, as on the mining frontier, heightened the level of violence and disorder.

In the heroic myth cowboys are the very picture of sinewy health. The geologist David Love, who grew up in Wyoming in the early twentieth century, recalled that they were "lean, very strong, hard-muscled, taciturn bachelors," mostly in their twenties or early thirties, who worked without complaint from daylight to dark. But he also saw something else, something left out of the myth:

Most were homely, with prematurely lined faces but with lively eyes that missed little . . . Many were already stooped from chronic saddle-weariness, bowlegged, hip-sprung, with unrepaired hernias that required trusses, and spinal injuries that required a "hanging pole" in the bunkhouse. This was a horizontal bar from which the cowboys would hang by their hands for 5–10 minutes to relieve pressure on ruptured spinal disks that came from too much bronc-fighting. Some wore eight-inch-wide heavy leather belts to keep their kidneys in place during prolonged hard rides.

The damage done by bucking animals, accidents, frostbite, and lightning storms was compounded by a monotonous and inadequate diet. Cowboy grub was long on meat, flour, and beans. It was short on fresh fruit and, ironically, dairy products. In the early years the cowboys did not even have milk for coffee, which they called "blackjack" or "bellywash" and drank hot and strong. This imbalanced, calcium-deficient diet may have contributed as much to their celebrated bow-leggedness as did long hours in the saddle.[14]

When these rickety young men rode into town they hit the saloons, false-fronted palaces full of smoke, gamblers, tubercle bacilli, and spittoons. There they used their hard-earned wages to treat themselves and their comrades to round after round of drinks, or what they took to be drinks. Liquor dealers commonly watered whiskey to maximize profits, concealing their chicanery and restoring the kick by adding stimulants like strychnine and tobacco. Cowboys drank this stuff neat and became extravagantly intoxicated, not so much drunk as on a polypharmaceutical jag, their bodies full of several different kinds of poisons.[15]

The end-of-trail binges often ended in the red-light district. The name originated in Dodge City from the railroad brakemen's custom of leaving their red lanterns outside the door to avoid interruption. Cowboys were equally avid customers of cattle-town prostitutes, some of whom were as young as fourteen years. Commercial prostitution was tolerated because of its profitability and because of the common belief that it provided a safety valve for working-class men who might otherwise sexually assault respectable women—which assaults were, in fact, rare.[16]

The social rationalizations on behalf of prostitution did nothing to alter the fact that it was a leading cause of venereal disease. Studies undertaken in the early twentieth century showed that the majority, in some instances 90 percent or more, of prostitutes harbored gonorrhea or syphilis; that prostitution was a prolific source of venereal infection; and that unmarried men were more likely to be infected than married men. The greatest venereal risk to cowboys who visited prostitutes was undoubtedly syphilis. Known to doctors as "the great imitator," the disease often returned later in life in the form of paresis, locomotor ataxia, or aortic aneurism, fatal souvenirs of their youthful encounters with whores.[17]

Sprees destroyed savings as well as health, reinforcing what was transparently a two-class system. A cattle*man* was a capitalist and employer, generally married, who lived in a ranch house built on his own land. A cow*boy* was an employee, unmarried, who tended cattle marked with another man's brand and who lived in a bunkhouse ("doghouse," "shack," "dump," or "ram pasture") built on another man's land.[18] The bunkhouse was not destiny. Cowboys who saved their wages, a dollar or at most two a day, could eventually acquire a small ranch and herd, slender but sufficient means for starting their own families. But those who kept spending their money on liquor, gamblers, and prostitutes could not achieve the stake necessary to escape their status as hirelings. Without property of their own they were not in a financial or social position to marry, potential brides being scarce and choosy about their suitors. And the absence of a wife and family made it more likely that they would continue to spend their earnings on in-town sprees. The result was a literally vicious circle.

Among those who profited from the cowboys' recurring dissipation were the gamblers and prostitutes who flocked to the cattle towns during the shipping season, moving on during the winter or when the trade was slack. Prostitutes earned their money directly while gamblers relied on a combination of skill, house odds, and cheating to separate cowboys from their wages. One New York firm specialized in selling marked or "advantage" decks to professional gamblers for $10 a dozen or $85 a gross. Loaded ivory dice were sold in sets of nine (three high, three low, three square) for $5 apiece. Why cowboys kept coming back to the saloon gaming tables against men so equipped is puzzling, though some showed clear signs of being compulsive gamblers, easy marks for a card sharp. Other cowboys, shrewder perhaps, quit the saddle and became professional gamblers themselves.[19]

Few gamblers retired to a life of luxury. The money was sometimes good but they spent it every bit as fast as the cowboys they fleeced. The prostitutes, who often lived or associated with gamblers, spent just as recklessly. A few made money and quit the trade. Some married out, though it is hard to know how many, for they covered their tracks. But the prostitutes' more usual fate was a miserable existence copulating with sweaty strangers, earning less for their trouble as they aged. The almshouse was a common end, as was suicide by overdose or poison.[20] Many sought solace in alcohol and other drugs, typically opiates in the 1870s and 1880s and cocaine and opiates from the 1890s on.

As on the mining frontier, arguments over women and cards could quickly turn into deadly confrontations. Abbott, who witnessed several shooting scrapes in bars and sporting houses, recalled that saloon men and tinhorn gamblers were as apt to get themselves killed as cowboys. The historian Robert Dykstra, who studied newspaper reports of homicides in five booming Kansas cattle towns, confirmed Abbott's impression. He found that precisely as many cowboys were victims of homicide as men identified as gamblers.

Dykstra also found that the average incidence of homicide in the five municipalities—Abilene, Ellsworth, Wichita, Dodge City, and Caldwell—was 1.5 per town per year. This may seem a small number, but so was the average population, which did not exceed 3,000. The resulting homicide rate was quite high, 50 or more per 100,000 persons per year. Someone living in (or more likely visiting) a Kansas cattle town was ten times as likely to be murdered as a person living in an eastern city or in a midwestern farming county.

Actually, more than ten times as likely. Because Dykstra did not count all homicides outside town limits or before the towns existed as municipalities (when, at least in the case of Dodge

City, there were even more killings) and because the newspaper series he used had one significant gap, the true rate was undoubtedly higher. Roger McGrath, who has reexamined Dykstra's methods and data, thinks it likely that Dodge City's actual homicide rate was in the range of that of the California mining town of Bodie, 116 per 100,000. Fort Griffin, Texas, another frontier town frequented by cowboys, buffalo hunters, and soldiers, had an even higher rate, 229 per 100,000 during its boom years in the 1870s.[21]

Fort Griffin is the perfect illustration of what happens when the biological, demographic, cultural, and social forces conducive to violence intersect in one place and time. In the 1870s the town was in the middle of the Central Texas frontier zone, an exceptionally violent region in an unusually violent state. It had a hunting, grazing, and military economy and therefore a large surplus male population, including many southern-born men who were combat veterans, sensitive about personal honor, and deeply contemptuous of other races. Family and religious life were inchoate for the transient, lower-class men, who lived and took their recreation in male groups. That recreation involved the consumption of large amounts of liquor, often in a spree pattern, and vices that could trigger sudden conflict. The conflicts were settled with deadly weapons that the combatants routinely carried. Given these circumstances, it is hardly surprising that the homicide rate was so high.

Legal Ambivalence

When differences in lethal violence are of this magnitude, homicide in Fort Griffin in the 1870s being nearly forty times as common as homicide in Boston, one is prompted to ask why the citizens put up with it. It was obvious that the spree pattern and the local vice industry were among the primary sources of violence and disorder. It was equally obvious who the culprits were. Why was the problem allowed to fester?

On this point, at least, historians are unanimous. The answer is money. A cowboy at the end of a drive had perhaps $50–$90 in his pocket, a large sum in a cash-short region. Some of his wages were bound to go to the vice parasites, but local merchants, barbers, and restaurant and hotel operators knew they would get their share, either directly from the cowboys or from the gamblers and prostitutes, who were as free-spending as their victims. Jacob Karatofsky, an immigrant dry-goods merchant who operated the Great Western Store in the heart of Abilene, understood the situation well. He sold blankets, boots, and hats to the cowboys and "fancy dress goods" to the town's prostitutes, who had expensive tastes and the wherewithal to satisfy them. When the cattle trade left Abilene Karatofsky went with it, first to Ellsworth and then to Wichita, where business was sufficiently brisk to open two stores.[22]

The profitability of such commerce made it inexpedient to have too much law and order. The disorderly behavior of their drunken visitors was a chronic problem, but businessmen knew that if the town marshal came down too heavily the cowboys would take their cattle and their wages elsewhere. The same logic applied to the suppression of vice. Cowboys would not come to town if they could not have a good time. To deny business to the local saloons and brothels was to deny it to the dry-goods stores and banks as well.

The best that could be done was to fashion a police and court system designed to keep the lid on. Cattle-town justice, to use the term loosely, was aimed at controlling, segregating, and profiting from cowboy vice sprees, not at discouraging them. It was intended to minimize both taxpayer expense and ancillary violence, though its inconsistencies—one is tempted to call them the cultural contradictions of capitalism—made control of violence difficult.

The task fell to some of the most legendary figures in frontier history, Wild Bill Hickok, Wyatt Earp, and Bat Masterson, as well as a host of less well known peace officers. The theory was to hire someone with the pluck to stand up to criminals and drunken cowboys and the lethal skill to stop them if lesser means of coercion failed. The fight-fire-with-fire approach was reasonable enough, though it sometimes failed in application, as when Wild Bill mistakenly shot and killed another Abilene policeman. And it was of no particular use during the slack season, when the saloons were empty and the gamblers and prostitutes had gone elsewhere. Marshals were then expected to serve the taxpayers in less dramatic ways, inspecting chimneys, rounding up stray swine, and, in the improbable case of Wyatt Earp, repairing the town's sidewalks.[23]

The marshals and local judges were also expected to raise money by taxing vice. Cattle-town judicial records are full of prosecutions for operating disorderly houses, but these were merely the means of securing revenue in the form of fines. In the town of Canada, Texas, creditable prostitutes were permitted to pay deposits on their fines and then were returned to the streets to earn the balance. In Fort Worth madams simply paid up and returned to their parlor houses, regardless of the number of previous convictions. Dodge City judges afforded equally lenient treatment to prostitutes for reasons of both municipal revenue and political expediency. We know, through the voyeuristic device of manuscript census records, that several of the prostitutes were living with prominent Dodge citizens, including the mayor, two policemen, and the vice president of the local bank.[24]

Gambling arrests, another source of revenue, produced their share of politically delicate moments. A sweep of gamblers in Coffeyville, Kansas, turned up a majority of the town council. Kansas saloon owners were not subject to the indignity of fines but had to pay a substantial licensing fee, which amounted to the same thing. In Wichita the saloon license fees and other vice fines produced so much revenue that in August 1873 the city treasurer announced that no further taxation would be required to support the local government.[25]

Cattle-town courts may not have been expected to stamp out vice, but they were expected to do something about serious personal and property crime. Yet even here commercial considerations intruded upon the exercise of justice. No cowboy or cattleman was ever executed for murder in the five towns Dykstra studied. Acquittals were common, as was a form of plea bargaining in which the offender pled guilty to a lesser offense, such as assault and battery instead of attempted murder. "Under the influence of liquor" was often offered, and sometimes accepted, as an extenuating circumstance. Business calculations were paramount. When in 1874 a group of Texas cowboys deliberately killed a black laborer in Wichita, no attempt was made to apprehend them. A newspaper editor criticized the inactivity of city and county officials only to have the wrath of the town's businessmen descend upon his head. They feared that the editor would stir up the citizens against the cowboys, provoking a retaliatory boycott. Or, as Abbott put it, "They wanted our trade. That was how us cowboys got away with a lot of such stunts."[26]

Vigilantism

Lax enforcement against drunken cowboys was one thing; lax enforcement against real outlaws was quite another. Cowboy sprees were dangerous but primed the local economy. Horse thieves, cattle rustlers, and highwaymen took property and lives without conferring any offsetting benefit. The official frontier justice system, inadequate and underfunded when not actually duplicitous, failed to deter such hardened criminals. They often escaped arrest or, if apprehended, the makeshift jails in which they were detained. In 1877 some five thousand men were on the wanted list in Texas alone, not a very encouraging sign of efficiency in law enforcement.[27]

The result was extralegal movements against outlaws. Most vigilante actions were limited in scope and controlled by elites, targeted thieves who would otherwise have escaped punishment, and symbolically affirmed the values of order and property. They were, in a word, socially constructive. But vigilante actions could and did miscarry, as when they were used to arbitrarily punish racial minorities or settle personal grudges. The latter form of abuse sometimes triggered private warfare, with friends and relatives of lynch victims seeking revenge against the vigilante faction.[28]

The Central Texas range country was the epicenter of vigilantism in the two decades after the Civil War. Most of these vigilante actions (known in Texas as "mob" actions) were summary executions of accused horse and cattle thieves who were hanged or simply shot down in their jail cells. Cowboys and ranchers generally played the role of executioner, but if they were caught or accused of rustling they might be executed in turn.

Vigilantism was easily abused. The "Old Law Mob," a group active in the Fort Griffin area in the early 1870s, included a rancher who was having problems with his wife. She hired an attorney to secure a divorce. The rancher warned the attorney to leave town within twenty-four hours. The attorney demurred and was found several days later with an "O.L.M." note pinned to his dangling body. No one troubled, or perhaps dared, to bury his remains, which were still visible a year later.[29]

Vigilantism, in short, was a dangerous substitute for professional police and regular courts. It is interesting that Canada's western provinces, which had both, experienced far less violence and lynching than the American frontier states. Canadian criminals were left to the North-West Mounted Police, an efficient and highly regarded force. The Mounties were aided in the their task by the prevailing Canadian attitude toward violence, which was condemned as an American aberration having no place in the realm of peace, order, and good government.[30]

Cowboy Gun Control

The Canadian frontier had something else that was initially lacking in American cattle towns: effective gun control. It was obvious to everyone that a drunken cowboy with a pistol was a good deal more dangerous than one without. Western newspaper editors and civic leaders supported laws forbidding the carrying of pistols and other deadly weapons, mainly dirks and Bowie knives. By the early 1870s most American cattle towns had nominally outlawed the practice. Cowboys were expected to "check" their guns when they entered town, typically by exchanging them for a metal token at one of the major entry points or leaving them at the livery stable before they hit the saloons.[31]

The gun laws were a good idea but poorly enforced, especially during the 1870s, the worst decade of killing on the cattle frontier. Cowboys persisted in wearing their pistols or took to concealing them, which was even more dangerous. Their defiance of the law was both a cause and an effect of the prevailing violence: as long as there were other armed men and outlaws about, it was hard to persuade them to surrender their weapons. Their resistance was as much emotional as rational. Guns were central to the subculture, objects of ritual significance to which the cowboys had been introduced in early youth. The idea that tin-star marshals (Yankees, no less) could take them away did not sit well.[32]

The situation changed in the 1880s and 1890s. As the threat of Indians and outlaws receded and the regular police system gradually became more professional and efficient, it was harder to justify carrying personal weapons for self-defense. Responsible cattlemen like Colonel R. G. Head, the superintendent of the Prairie Land and Cattle Company, began urging their hands to forgo gun toting, which he denounced as "a pernicious and useless habit," both illegal and foolish. "If you cannot freely and finally give up your pistol," he added, "then take it off, leave it at camp or rolled up in your bedding; by doing this I am inclined to the belief that you will soon learn to appreciate the absence of such an appendage." Head's successor, Murdo McKenzie, was equally adamant against firearms, and made it a point never to carry a gun himself.[33]

Gun control, enforced by determined employers, was probably the single most potent check on homicidal violence among cowboys, more effective than the specter of the lynch mob or even Wild Bill Hickok and Wyatt Earp. Getting hanged for shooting someone was a remote prospect, but getting the sack from an angry foreman was not. Head, McKenzie, and other cattlemen who insisted that cowboys lay aside their pistols understood that their men were not usually thinking straight when they pulled the trigger and that most shootings were either accidental or due to drunkenness, gambling, or hot-headed impulse. Better, then, that they should have no gun to reach for. It was a simple and obvious means of prevention and one that seems to have worked. By 1900 most cowboys had never seen a killing, much less participated in one. Many still owned guns— they were, after all, cowboys—but kept them out of sight, stowed in a bedroll or under the bunk.[34]

The emphasis on gun control, part of the larger rationalization of the range cattle industry, was complemented by a gradual change in the composition of its employees. By the 1880s the Texans, who of all the cowboys and cattlemen were the most predisposed to use firearms and to take the law into their own hands, were gradually being replaced by easterners, midwesterners, and European immigrants. The trend was especially marked on the northern ranges, where a new class of cowboys was helping to bring greater organization and discipline to the business. The newcomers were not as inclined to use their guns promiscuously or to insist on wearing them in town.[35]

If the South exported violence as its inhabitants moved to the frontier, what happened on the northern plains during and after the 1880s was the reverse, a northern order transplant. Once again, the level of violence was not simply a function of age and gender but was influenced by the immigrants' attitudes. Any population with a surplus of young men had a built-in tendency toward trouble. But the tendency was lessened if the surplus consisted, as in this case, of an increasing number of Europeans, easterners, and farm boys trying their hand at ranching and a decreasing number of heavily armed southern men.

Cowboy Myth

The gun-toting cowboy may have been declining in numbers and influence by the 1880s, but his career as a mythic hero was only beginning. It commenced in earnest with Buffalo Bill's Wild West, a popular rodeo and historical reenactment featuring cowboys racing horses, riding steers, and lassoing broncos. When not occupied with wild animals, Buffalo Bill's cowboys repulsed Indian attacks on wagon trains and mail coaches. Allied with scouts and soldiers, the cowboys were presented as the advance troops of white civilization, heroic "rough riders" who shot it out with the exotic but menacing Indians.

William F. Cody, the show's creator and manager, was a frontier jack-of-all-trades who had achieved fame as an actor and a pulp fiction protagonist. Alert to the commercial possibilities of the public's fascination with frontier adventures, Cody launched his Wild West as a touring show in 1883. By the time of his death in 1917 the Wild West had been seen by an estimated 50 million people in a dozen countries in North America and Europe. That is, 50 million people saw the cowboy por-

trayed as a trick roper and Indian-fighting hero rather than a
spree-prone hireling in a shrinking industry.

Buffalo Bill's Wild West was only the most spectacular vehicle
of cowboy myth-making, a flourishing business that ran the
gamut from hack writers like Prentiss Ingraham and Ned Bunt-
line to real talents like the novelist Owen Wister and the painters
Frederic Remington and Charles Russell. Cody's success inspired
no fewer than 116 competing shows. Most were short-lived but
at least one, the Miller Brothers' 101 Ranch Wild West Show,
managed to last until the Great Depression. By that time the
myth-making enterprise had shifted to a new and more cost-
efficient medium, the motion picture.[36]

Western themes figured in movies as far back as 1903, when
Edwin S. Porter released his innovative *The Great Train Robbery*.
By the early 1920s Hollywood had a stable of western stars,
among them William S. Hart and Tom Mix, a veteran of the
Miller Brothers' show. The popularity of the western declined
somewhat during the 1930s when star actors like Gene Autry
were confined to "B" movies, but in 1939, Hollywood's *annus
mirabilis,* the western film began a renaissance with big-budget
features like *Dodge City* and *Union Pacific.* The epic westerns of the
1940s were not simply cowboy movies. They portrayed an array
of frontier characters, although cattlemen and cowboys, whose
colorful clothing, horses, and guns and penchant for deeds over
words made them ideally suited to the action-oriented medium,
remained stock figures. In films such as *American Empire* (1942)
and *Red River* (1948) they were accorded central roles.[37]

The western film continued its dominance through the 1950s.
Between 1950 and 1961 Hollywood studios churned out more
than 1,200 films about the past, over half set in the years
between 1866 and 1890. This chronological imbalance—audiences must have thought American history synonymous with
the late nineteenth century—was due to the mass production of
westerns. Competing media were also saturated. Publishers sold
an average of 35 million paperback westerns a year. The new
television networks reprised countless western movies and were
soon producing their own western programs. By 1959 there
were thirty running in prime time, including eight of the top ten
shows. The most enduringly popular of these, "Gunsmoke," had

begun as a successful radio drama, making its television premiere in 1955. When it went off the air in 1975 it was the longest-running series in television history.[38]

"Gunsmoke" was the genre's last hurrah. Westerns declined in the 1960s and 1970s, becoming progressively fewer in number, more self-referential, and darker in tone. But they continued to have at least one thing in common with their predecessors: they apotheosized male violence and marginalized women and children. The mise-en-scène was a town, outpost, or ranch on the high-gender-ratio frontier, not a family farm in a demographically normal region. The basic plot, even if morally ambiguous and sympathetic to Indians, was still that of masculine corporate adventure. Individual men came together, fought for a common cause against a group of opposing men, and then went their separate ways, unless killed or snared by a woman in a romantic interlude. Gunfire and wedding bells were functionally equivalent in westerns. They both signaled that a man was about to be taken out of action, honorably in the one instance, prosaically in the other.[39]

Did the mass exposure of three generations of audiences to violent male adventurers in the guise of cowboys and other gun-toting western characters influence the level of actual violence in American society? This is an important yet frustrating question. Important because there are psychological reasons to suppose that such exposure made a difference. Frustrating because effects of mass media are difficult to isolate and measure.

Experimental studies of varying scope and ingenuity have shown the viewing of violent characters to be positively correlated with aggressive behavior, although the effect is not necessarily strong, permanent, or universal. The most pronounced effect (though weak in comparison to those of variables like alcohol abuse and family disruption) has been observed in less academically talented boys who are already relatively aggressive but who become more so after viewing rough-and-tumble episodes. Media violence, in other words, appears to serve as a trigger or an exacerbating influence rather than a primary cause of violent behavior.[40]

It may also reach deeper into our psyches. Our personalities emerge from the interaction of our genes, which are fixed and predispose us in some ways, and our social situations, which are fluid and present many possibilities for development and change. We become ourselves in no small part by emulating positive or negative figures in our social environment, something that has already been noted in connection with the behavior of men in barracks, saloons, mining camps, and other male preserves.

In the electronic age the social environment has come to mean more than flesh-and-blood people. It includes a thousand or so media personalities, the Elvis Presleys and Arnold Schwarzeneggers and Madonnas whom most of us have never met but whose images we nevertheless carry in our heads. Communication researchers have discovered that, for many people, these celebrities are socially real. People act like them, dress like them, talk like them, talk about them, talk *to* them, and even make love to them in their fantasies. As Wallace Stegner puts it, "We are not so far from our models, real and fictional, as we think."[41]

The dominant screen model for moviegoing and television-watching Americans in the mid-twentieth century was the frontier action hero, often though not always the mythic cowboy. He was personified by John Wayne, a cult star familiar to every American born before 1960. Wayne symbolized, and in his political statements explicitly affirmed, the belief that lethal means are necessary and appropriate to righteous ends. The cinematic personae of Wayne and other western stars not only legitimated gun carrying and violence, they fixed in the consciousness of an increasingly urbanized nation the whole mythic apparatus of the western range in the two decades after the Civil War. Though this realm was a sometimes violent and disproportionately male world, it became in its screen reincarnation ultraviolent and hypermasculine. The cattle frontier never closed. It just came back in technicolor.[42]

Or possibly in Southeast Asia. In many ways the best (though also the strangest) illustration of the pervasiveness of frontier myth in postwar America was the Vietnam War. The language of Vietnam GIs, young men who were more imbued with frontier imagery than any other group of Americans before or since, brimmed with cinematic clichés and western allusions. Nineteen-year-olds ate John Wayne cookies and John Wayne crackers out of C-rations they opened with their John Waynes (P-38 can openers). A John Wayne rifle was a .45-caliber service pistol—nobody could hit anything with it, but the Duke could mow them down at 300 meters. To "John Wayne it" was to attempt any foolish act of heroism. Stock short-timer advice to a cherry: Don't pull a John Wayne on me.

In Vietnam military operations had code names like Texas Star, Cochise Green, or Crazy Horse, the last featuring the Seventh Cavalry in helicopters. The deluxe Seabee bunker at Khe Sahn was called the Alamo Hilton. To "saddle up" was to head out on patrol against "the bad guys" in "Indian country" beyond the perimeter. "Dodge City" referred variously to the military complex at Tan Son Nhut; the contested valley between Charlie Ridge and Hill 55 in I Corps; or, for Navy pilots, Hanoi. "To get out of Dodge" was, generally, to leave any hostile or dangerous area.

"Cowboy" had a multiplicity of uses, usually ironic or pejorative. "The Cowboy" was Nguyen Cao Ky, the flamboyant South Vietnamese Air Force officer who served as prime minister and later as vice president. "Cowboys," plural, referred to draft-age male Vietnamese civilians; more specifically to the hoodlums and black marketeers who roamed Saigon on motorcycles, sometimes accompanied by prostitutes ("cowgirls"); or more specifically still to members of the ARVN Special Forces (LLDB) or to a new breed of U.S. Special Forces troopers who arrived after 1968. In Laos ("across the fence") cowboys were CIA paramilitary operatives, a secret Air Force helicopter unit the "Pony Express." FACs (forward air controllers) logged twelve hours a day "in the saddle." One FAC showed up dressed entirely in black—black cowboy hat, shirt, jeans, and boots—and announced that his reason for volunteering was that Laos seemed a good place to die. This was a man who had seen too many movies.[43]

Whatever their social consequences may have been, movie cowboys were very different from the genuine item. The historical cowboy was not a heroic gunfighter-avenger but an unmarried lower-class laborer who led a Jekyll-and-Hyde existence. He was a hard worker on the trail, loyal to his outfit and friends, and usually open, honest, and generous. But when he was on a spree, "drunk and dressed up and don't give a damn," he was a menace to himself and those around him.[44]

Cattle-town marshals did their best to keep serious trouble from erupting, though they were handicapped by the moral contradiction at the heart of the economic system. Open vice was profitable to their towns but attracted criminal elements along with thirsty young cowboys eager to shoot their pistols and blow their wages. The price of separating them from their money was a relatively high level of violence and disorder. Everyone in the real Dodge City understood this trade-off, which the location of the jail made explicit. It was on Front Street immediately opposite the cowboy saloons.[45]

SIX

The Ecology of Frontier Violence

> I don't go so far as to think that the only good Indians are the dead Indians, but I believe nine out of ten are, and I shouldn't like to inquire too closely into the case of the tenth. The most vicious cowboy has more moral principle in him than the average Indian.
>
> —Theodore Roosevelt, 1886

The westward movement of the frontier brought catastrophic losses to native human and animal populations. Among some tribes and species the losses were so heavy as to bring about extinction. Disease was the primary cause, though it was compounded by other forms of destruction, from warfare to murder to overhunting to alcoholism. Each of these was linked in some way to the abnormal demography of the white frontiersmen.

Disease, Warfare, and Frontier Demography

The historian William McNeill has provided a useful metaphor for understanding the catastrophe that befell the American Indians. All peoples, he ventures, are caught between two millstones

109

that grind away at their populations. The lower millstone is that of microparasitism, which occurs when tiny organisms like wheat rusts compete with people for food or when pathogens like malarial protozoa invade and weaken human bodies. The upper millstone is that of macroparasitism, meaning large-bodied predation (lion eats man) but also and more specifically the killing, abuse, and exploitation of one group or class of humans by another.[1]

Before Columbus Indians experienced both sorts of parasitism, enduring blights, disease, intertribal warfare, slavery, and even the ultimate form of exploitation, human sacrifice. Yet the grinding balance of the millstones was such that their overall numbers were not reduced. Indeed, they flourished. At the time of Columbus's arrival in 1492 somewhere between 40 and 113 million persons, possibly more, were living in the Americas, an estimated 4 to 12 million of them in the lands north of Mexico.[2] But after Columbus the grinding balance was decisively altered as Indians faced a deadly and ever-expanding array of new parasites from cholera bacilli to cannoneers. The 1890 Battle of Wounded Knee, at which 350 sick and hungry Sioux were surrounded by minatory troopers and raked with exploding shells from rapid-firing Hotchkiss guns, serves as a convenient symbol of four centuries of destruction.

Epidemics claimed the lives of the largest number of Indians who had little resistance to European and African diseases. Measles, influenza, bubonic plague, malaria, diphtheria, yellow fever, typhoid, and other infections reduced native populations by 95 percent or more. Smallpox was the most lethal and dreaded affliction; warriors who contracted it would rip themselves open with knives or hurl themselves into chasms rather than suffer a feverish and ignominious death. Those who sought relief in steam baths or cold streams merely hastened their ends. Entire tribes, such as the Mandan, disappeared in the wake of virulent smallpox epidemics. Their bodies rotted where they fell or were devoured by dogs and scavenging wolves.[3]

Warfare with and exploitation by whites aggravated the losses due to disease. The higher the white gender ratio the greater the aggravation. Even along the agricultural frontier the first whites Indians encountered were male interlopers, including a generous sprinkling of hard cases. Large-scale familial migration did not occur until after the Indians had been decisively defeated and removed from an area, or until a chain of fortifications had been established. Conversely, when Indians reasserted themselves, as in Ohio during the War of 1812 or in Minnesota in 1862, agricultural settlers fled until the shooting was over. A similar headlong retreat by Nebraska settlers toward Omaha in 1864 was dubbed "the stampede."[4]

This is not to say that pioneer women and children seldom saw Indians. Quite the opposite. But the Indians' contact was *initially* with white men who were unmarried or temporarily single: explorers, traders, trappers, soldiers, missionaries, prospectors, cowboys, and farmers moving ahead of their families to scout and clear the land.

Except for the missionaries the military potential of these groups was formidable. Their personnel were generally young, equipped with advanced weapons and ammunition, registered and drilled in militia companies, and, when mounted, able to move quickly. Indian braves were every bit as hardy, some so tough they struck matches from the soles of their bare feet. And they could move about even more quickly, aided by superior knowledge of the terrain.[5]

But Indian warriors were everywhere handicapped by the vulnerability of their noncombatants. Demographically, the Indian situation was just the opposite of that of the whites. Intertribal warfare (and, possibly, higher male death rates during epidemics) had produced chronically *low* gender ratios. Fewer braves had to protect more women and children, who were not as mobile and hence vulnerable to attack. In the 1620s and 1630s colonists in Virginia and New England learned that it was much easier to attack Indian villages than to go after bands of marauding warriors. This tactic was used repeatedly against Indians during the eighteenth and nineteenth centuries. The dawn assaults by militia on Cheyenne encampments at Sand Creek in 1864 and by Custer's bluecoats at Washita in 1868 are among the most infamous examples. Wounded Knee, though not planned as an all-out attack, quickly turned into one, with 120 Sioux men and 230 women and children facing impossible odds against 500 soldiers from the Seventh Cavalry.[6]

Frontier demography worked to the advantage of whites, who had more potential combatants and fewer dependents per capita. Not only did Indians have to contend with the all-male army, they faced attack from militia, vigilantes, and other groups of armed frontiersmen who were less disciplined than the regulars, though often more ruthless. I have already mentioned the fate of California Indians, more than 4,500 of whom were killed between 1848 and 1880, mainly by miners, ranchers, and militia. The situation was similar in Texas, where the Rangers, unencumbered by regular military regulations and impedimenta, simply mounted their horses, ran down hostile Indians, and unceremoniously killed any they happened to capture.[7]

Cowboys were another force to be reckoned with. Though they did not always prevail in their skirmishes with Indians, they constituted a de facto corps of mounted scouts. Armed, vigilant, and constantly on the move, the cowboys were, as one contemporary put it, "an efficient instrumentality in preventing Indian outbreaks, and in protecting the frontier settlements of the entire range and ranch cattle area against predatory incursions and massacres by Indians." One trail outfit took advantage of cowboys' reputations as Indian fighters by spreading false rumors of war parties. This assured the outfit a welcome reception by local settlers who were otherwise hostile and obstructive.[8]

Casualties in any of these military or quasi-military groups could be replaced by internal or overseas immigration. The supply of male *wasichus*, the Sioux term for unwelcome and disagreeably persistent intruders, was both endless and global. Half or more of the troopers who fought in the climactic Indian wars of the 1860s and 1870s were foreign-born, mainly Irish and German; they were joined by African-American soldiers and six thousand Confederate prisoners ("Galvanized Yankees") who volunteered for frontier garrison duty. Some Indians, isolated and without knowledge of geography, made the mistake of underestimating the population from which the *wasichus* could draw. But Little Crow, chief of the Mdewakanton division of the Santee Sioux, suffered no such illusions. "Count your fingers all day long," he warned his braves, "and white men with guns in their hands will come faster than you can count."[9]

Intertribal rivalries added to the immunological and demographic advantages of the intruders. Suspicion and a long history of warfare made Indian cooperation and concentration of force difficult, though there were exceptions, as Custer discovered at the Little Big Horn. Indian rivalries also gave whites the opportunity to play enemy against enemy, as in the army's use of Crow scouts, couriers, and warriors in its many campaigns against the Sioux. Even in the absence of recruiting, Indian competition played into white hands. When frontier expansion pushed one tribe onto another's land, the result was a chain reaction of lateral warfare, further thinning the warriors' ranks. The fur trade provided Indians with weapons that increased intertribal casualties while also providing an economic motive for aggression. Tribes that wrested control of hunting grounds from their neighbors could exchange more furs, and more enemies' scalps, for the European goods on which they were becoming dependent.[10]

Hunting Indians

Indians who survived epidemics and intertribal warfare faced a frontier immigrant population lopsided with men of military age. But if demography made whites potentially dangerous adversaries, it was white attitudes that made them actually so. Frontiersmen regarded Indians as disgusting, lazy, thieving, devious, and cruel, incorrigible obstacles to civilization's advance and, more tangibly, to whites' possession of western lands. This is, I know, a large generalization to which there were articulate exceptions, but the historical record is so freighted with white male contempt for Indians as "savages" and "gut-eaters" and worse that I feel entirely justified in making it.

Racial contempt made it socially and psychologically easier to exploit and kill Indians. Native slavery and peonage, common forms of exploitation in Spanish lands, were not widely practiced in the Anglo-American domain. Instead American Indians were driven from their coveted lands by a combination of negotiation, fraud, starvation, forced removal, and warfare. During the first half of the nineteenth century these means acquired a patina of respectability, or at least inevitability, through the doctrines of Anglo-Saxon racial superiority and America's Manifest Destiny to overspread the continent.[11]

The way in which people are killed reveals a great deal about their assailants. The weapons and tactics employed against Indians bespeak Anglo-Americans' indiscriminate hatred and contempt: poisoned meat and drink, smallpox-infected blankets, booby-trapped bodies, cannon charged with slugs, dogs unleashed on captives, and the execution of the wounded, women, and children. California Indians found "naked or wild" were gunned down without pretense or hesitation while Indian women with children were dispatched with no more compunction than stray dogs. Some white men in California, wrote a disgusted French missionary, Father Edmond Venisse, "kill Indians just to try their pistols."[12]

Equally revealing are the many episodes of Indians being attacked under the white flag of truce or surrender or during negotiations when the norms of war or diplomacy would ordinarily confer immunity. Immunity, that is, to those regarded as human beings. Indians were dishonored even in death. White men fashioned their bones into curios; they played with their mummified remains by lashing them to sticks and making them stalk about in ghost-like fashion; they pulled down bodies left in trees and scaffolds and chopped them to pieces for bait.[13]

Indians, no strangers to cruelty, repaid whites in the same fashion. They mutilated bodies and desecrated graves, flayed and burned captives, raped and impaled women, killed and even tortured children and newborns. Such deeds made for long memories. They were kept alive and embellished by campfire stories, sermons, pamphlets, newspapers, popular fiction, and captivity narratives, an ever-popular genre of which no fewer than 339 works describing the experiences of 245 individuals and families had been cataloged by 1912. Indian raids were to the frontier what slave uprisings were to the plantation South, a fear so deep and pervasive that the least rumor, however unsubstantiated, spread like prairie fire.[14]

This same fear, which compelled frontiersmen to remain vigilant against Indian attack, helps to explain the violent cast of the frontier mind. The Indian threat legitimated violence and made men practiced in its most desperate arts. It also justified the carrying of loaded weapons by those who were not well versed in their safe use. During his western travels in 1859 Horace Greeley reported hearing of a dozen accidental shootings among gold miners in the space of just two months. "Had no single emigrant across the Plains this season armed himself," he commented, "the number of them alive at this moment would have been greater than it is."[15]

The obsession with Indian attacks invited criminal mischief. Pranksters maliciously spread false rumors, scaring settlers half out of their wits. Malefactors robbed and murdered their victims in Indian disguise. Foisting the blame on Indians was a flimflam as old as the Boston Tea Party, though carried out with more success in the nineteenth century, particularly in Texas, where it was a favorite trick of marauding outlaws.[16]

Yet there was quite enough of the genuine article to inflame whites' hatred and steel their determination to exterminate Indians. "I don't know what will be done with them," wrote Sergeant Edwin Capron in 1865, describing a group of Pawnees who, pretending friendship, suddenly attacked fourteen unarmed men en route to Fort Kearney, killing two and scalping one alive:

> I think the Govt. is altogether too lenient with them and treats them too much like human beings, when the only way they *can* be governed is by fear. They never will be peaceable when they have the power to fight. Last summer [actually November 1864] Col. Chivington of Colorado attacked and destroyed a camp of Cheyennes who pretended to be friendly and were drawing rations from Fort Lyons. Now that affair has created much sympathy for the "poor Indian" and I have seen it referred to in many of the Eastern papers and in Congress as a "brutal Inhuman Massacre." In that camp of *friendly* Indians were found scalps of white men & women hardly yet dry—And property identified as having been taken from plundered [wagon] trains but a short time previous. So much for Friendly Indians. But that is enough of political economy—And the *Noble Savage?*[17]

Capron's remarks almost perfectly express the scorn prevailing among white frontiersmen. Indians were subhuman and treacherous. They were thieves and murderers who only understood force. Their depredations against noncombatants justified all-out attacks, parlor sympathizers be damned.

Almost perfectly: Capron, a New Englander of some refinement, was writing home to his sister and so may be presumed to have pulled his punches. His contemporaries employed harsher words, describing Indians as "incarnate fiends," "hellhounds," "beasts and dogs," "vermin," "cursed snakes," "guteating skunks," and "redskined Deavels," this last a bit of Irish-American malediction, phonetically spelled.[18] The beast-devil imagery is oxymoronic. A devil is a fallen angel, not an animal. Yet the traits were conjoined in white minds by the reputed cunning and diabolical cruelty of their foes. Indians may have been subhuman outsiders, but they were also extremely dangerous ones, capable of ruses and outrages beyond the ken of any dumb creature.

All of which made their scalps very attractive. Killing Indians was not simply an exercise in preemptive defense. It was a sure way to establish one's manly bona fides, something, as we have seen, of central importance in male groups and subcultures. Indians were dangerous and hence worthy game; they were a threat to the future of the white community, symbolically and actually represented in women and children; and they were unlikely to be avenged by law officers and juries who were either indifferent to the deaths or busy killing Indians themselves. Father Venisse, a cultural outsider, was wrong when he said the Californians shot Indians just to try their pistols. They shot Indians for objective reasons, to control land and preempt threats to life and property, and for subjective reasons of prestige, so that they might boast about "Indian fighting" in the saloons and winter cabins of their lopsidedly masculine land.

The historian Joe B. Frantz went to the heart of the matter when he observed that there was a premium on killing Indians, a premium whose benefits continued through life. The benefits arguably extended, in the cases of Andrew Jackson and William Henry Harrison, to the White House itself. One explanation of Custer's imprudent behavior before his annihilation at the Little Big Horn (to which he hastened without Gatling guns or mountain howitzers) was that he was determined to move quickly to secure a headline-making victory that might serve as springboard to the presidency. As it is, more people remember Custer in defeat than they do the rather undistinguished American presidents of the late nineteenth century.[19]

Achievements in Indian warfare were sufficiently important and prestigious that men took trophies to prove them. Scalping, an Indian custom adopted by whites, was common for reasons of both status and the claiming of bounties. "I regret to be obliged to admit," Colonel Richard Irving Dodge wrote in 1883, "that the majority of white men on the frontier are as prompt to take a scalp as any Indian." They also helped themselves to Indian heads, hearts, fingers, ears, bladders, breasts, and genitals. One soldier in Chivington's Sand Creek command declared his intention to fashion a tobacco pouch from a dead Cheyenne's scrotum. Here again the dead and mutilated bodies are a text in which is written the frontiersmen's sense of Indians as animals from which fleshy souvenirs might be taken.[20]

The expression "hunting Indians" appears frequently in frontier correspondence. "Genl. Mitchell is here now [at Fort Kearney] preparing to go on a grand Indian hunt . . .," Sergeant Capron observed in another 1865 letter, adding that "Mr. Indian is a difficult animal to catch, worse I think than the famous Irishman's flea." Difficult, but necessary and desirable, both from the standpoint of eliminating predators and for the prestige of bagging tricky game.[21]

The same, of course, was true from the Indian perspective. White frontiersmen were about as bad as interlopers can get. Killing them unquestionably enhanced the standing of braves, who were sensitive about matters of honor and vengeance. This was particularly true of teenage Indians who, like white boys of the same age, were anxious to prove their courage. "It is by war that they obtain wealth, position and influence within the tribe," explained one observer. "The young men especially look up to and follow the successful warrior rather than the wise and prudent chiefs." Some white veterans admitted they would rather fight Indian men than boys because the boys "had no sense, did not know what fear was and would take greater chances." By Indian accounts it was a small band of young warriors, the "suicide boys," who broke the resistance of the last knot of Custer's men at the Little Big Horn. The suicide boys were all mortally wounded, but the older warriors who followed them into the mêlée quickly finished the job.[22]

White women who killed Indians also achieved fame. Hannah Duston, who was captured during a 1697 raid on Haverhill, Massachusetts, tomahawked and scalped ten of her sleeping captors with the help of another woman and a boy. When Duston returned home she became, for a time, the most celebrated woman in New England.[23] Episodes of this sort were rare, however, and motivated by self-defense or escape. Women were not expected to join in the grand Indian hunt, nor were they inclined to do so.

White women were more sympathetic toward Indians than white men or, if not sympathetic, at least willing to concede that they had virtues as well as vices. An analysis of 100 frontier women's diaries and memoirs reveals that 16 percent held strongly positive views of Indians, 18 percent strongly negative views, and the remaining 66 percent both positive and negative views, describing some Indians as trustworthy, others as treacherous. Caroline Phelps, a young woman married to an Indian trader active in southeastern Iowa in the 1830s, typically deplored the behavior of drunken Indians but wrote with interest and concern about those who befriended or assisted her. Achieving this sort of balance was not easy, for white women had had their heads stuffed as full of massacre stories as had men, and were at first inclined to view Indians through the lens of the Savage Other. But many frontier women overcame these prejudices and developed real friendships with natives, particularly native women, with whom they felt an empathic bond.[24]

The different ways in which white men and women viewed Indians are illustrated in a story related by Benjamin Franklin Bonney, who in 1846 migrated with his family and a group of other settlers from California to Oregon. His party happened upon an eight-year-old Indian girl, naked, starving, and covered with sores:

> A council among the men was held to see what should be done with her. My father wanted to take her along; others wanted to kill her and put her out of her misery. Father said that would be

willful murder. A vote was taken and it was decided to do nothing about it, but to leave her where we found her. My mother and my aunt were unwilling to leave the little girl. They stayed behind to do all they could for her. When they finally joined us their eyes were wet with tears. Mother said she had knelt down by the little girl and had asked God to take care of her. One of the young men in charge of the horses felt so badly about leaving her, he went back and put a bullet through her head and put her out of her misery.[25]

This was no act of sadism. The young man did for the girl what he would have done for one of his horses with a broken leg. Nevertheless, it is clear that the men—and it was they who determined the Indian's fate—were inclined toward a quick and final solution while the women (and one married man) wished to nurture her. To the former she was a wounded animal, to the latter a human being, to whom the duties and injunctions of Christianity applied.

The developmental psychologist Carol Gilligan believes this sort of difference is typical. Women emphasize human relationships and nurturing, while men tend to stress impersonal individualism and achievement, in this case pressing on to Oregon.[26] Whether this generalization holds across cultures and time and whether it is rooted in biology are controversial questions, though it is safe to say that nineteenth-century frontier women, if for no other reason than their socialization into traditional gender roles, were more likely to display sympathy and empathy than men. These traits, at odds with the ethnocentric impulse, made women less inclined toward Indian hating and hunting, from which they in any case had little to gain. Their social standing rarely if ever depended on achievements in warfare.

The Failure of Government

Bonney's story of the Indian girl is revealing in another way. The decision to shoot rather than assist the child was technically a crime, though of course neither reported nor prosecuted. The killing of Indians by civilians occurred as often as it did because the federal government, nominally responsible for policing the western territories, and subsequently state and local governments, failed to stop it. Government policy toward the Indians was not, as is sometimes supposed, "genocidal." However, the desires of many individual frontiersmen clearly were. If unchecked, they produced the worst sort of depredations and retaliations. "Where the federal government . . . did not control relations between whites and Indians," sums up the historian Richard White, "conditions became a nightmare."[27]

The basic problem was that the American government was unable to stop the influx of the rapidly growing white population into Indian lands, an influx that constantly provoked the Indians and rendered futile the treaties negotiated with them. The British had originally attempted to deal with this conflict by turning the Appalachian Mountains into a racial cordon. However, the Proclamation of 1763 succeeded neither in halting white incursions nor in protecting Indians. Before the year was out a village of peaceful Conestogas had been massacred and dismembered.[28]

George Washington, who inherited the problem from the British, fared no better. In late 1795 he complained to Congress that the legislative "provisions heretofore made with a view to the protection of the Indians, from the violence of the lawless part of our frontier inhabitants are insufficient." Unless the murdering of Indians was restrained, he warned, "all the exertions of the government to prevent destructive retaliations . . . will prove fruitless." Washington's concerns were fiscal as well as diplomatic. The spiral of provocation, retaliation, and frontier warfare consumed no less than five-sixths of the government's general expenditures from 1790 to 1796.[29]

Congress responded with the 1796 Intercourse Act, which authorized punishment for white trespassers and death for those who murdered Indians on their own lands. This and subsequent nineteenth-century legislation, often of a paternalistic and well-intentioned character, nevertheless proved difficult to enforce. The army was spread too thin to control the movements of frontiersmen, while local courts and juries were invariably sympathetic toward white defendants and hostile toward the Indians.[30]

Armed and belligerent frontiersmen were more than just a problem for the natives. At times they posed a threat to their own government, particularly when they believed they were being given insufficient help against Indian attacks and outlaw depredations or otherwise felt themselves oppressed by tax, land, and monetary policies.[31] The prototypical west-to-east uprising was Bacon's Rebellion. Though it assumed class overtones before falling apart in late 1676, the rebellion began as a dispute over frontier security, pitting western settlers against Governor William Berkeley and residents of the inland counties. In the eyes of Nathaniel Bacon and his supporters, Berkeley was long on taxes but short on scalps; they therefore assumed the task of killing Susquehannahs and Occaneechees for him. Berkeley equivocated, declared Bacon a rebel—and then found the up-river men coming for him.

The historian Edmund Morgan has argued that the economic and demographic conditions of late-seventeenth-century Virginia, a high-gender-ratio colony, made it especially prone to violent episodes like Bacon's Rebellion. Indentured servants kept pouring in to cultivate other men's tobacco but, as their terms expired, they found it difficult to marry and establish their own plantations. Their mobility, marital as well as occupational, was blocked. The rapid growth of African slavery ultimately provided an unintended solution to this problem by substituting a lower class that was despised, disarmed, and black for one that was discontented, dangerous, and white.[32]

But the solution was not perfect. White losers with guns did not disappear from the colonies. They went to the frontier, where they remained a potential source of insurrection. The pattern of west-to-east defiance and rebellion persisted through the eighteenth century, as in the Paxton Boys uprising in Pennsylvania in 1763–1764 or the Regulator movements in the Carolinas from 1766 to 1771. After the Revolutionary War (itself a revolt of a young, oppressed, "frontier" people against their indifferent eastern superiors) the west-east tension persisted, notably in Shays' Rebellion of 1786–1787 and the Whiskey Rebellion of 1794. The latter featured backwoodsmen who had drunk deeply of the *casus belli* and then harassed and tortured federal excise collectors. They did not stop until Washington dispatched an army to suppress them.[33]

Disorders of this magnitude were rare during the nineteenth century despite the accelerating expansion of the frontier. This was largely due to the wisdom of the Northwest Ordinance, which established a procedure and a precedent for admitting western regions to the Union on an equal basis with existing states. Frontiersmen might have to endure a period of territorial government, but they knew that one day they would control their own political destiny.[34] There was no reason for them to contemplate sustained, armed rebellion against the distant East; hence the potential for violence inherent in their population remained a problem mainly for themselves and the native inhabitants. Put differently, the central political issue of the colonial era, whether peripheral territories would remain inferior political entities, was neatly resolved, but in a way that indirectly increased pressure on the Indians.

Unfortunately for white Americans, another and more intractable regional tension quickly arose: whether the peripheral territories would become slave states or free. Antebellum politicians were unable to finesse the North-South conflict as skillfully as their Confederation predecessors had that of West and East. This misfortune was a temporary boon to the western Indians. The Civil War, which drew troops and men from the frontier to eastern battlegrounds, gave the Indians a brief respite from regular military pressure.[35] White soldiers who killed one another were no immediate threat to them.

Hunting Animals

The soldiers came back after the Civil War, however. With them came a plague of lousy, foul-smelling men, the buffalo hunters, who symbolized the other great challenge to Indian life, the destruction of the animal life on which it depended. This destruction, which began almost from the moment of European contact, was the product of complex and often overlapping motives.

The most straightforward motive was subsistence. Frontiersmen had to eat, and the farther west they moved the more dependent they were on hunting for food. White and Indian hunters, in fact, became very similar in appearance and behavior, having borrowed and incorporated items of dress and hunting techniques from one another until they were virtually indistinguishable.[36]

But white hunters also killed for trade and profit, and so, eventually, did the Indians. The economic facts of frontier life were scarce labor, limited capital, and abundant resources, a combination that suggested to Anglo-Americans a strategy of gathering, selling, and shipping commodities for the growing Atlantic market, using as little labor as possible. An obvious resource that might be inexpensively skimmed from the environment was fur, which was taken by individual hunters employing firearms and steel traps and collected by the agents of various fur companies.

Native Americans were drawn into this enterprise by their desire to secure wampum and such trade goods as guns, gunpowder, knives, axes, kettles, blankets, sugar, molasses, tobacco, and rum, of which Indians in the northern British mainland colonies were consuming upwards of 50,000 gallons annually by the mid-1760s. Indians who became dependent on alcohol were effectively dependent on white traders, who made enormous profits by exchanging low-value liquor for the Indians' high-value furs. This was one reason why formal Indian slavery was rare along the British and subsequently the American frontier. The fur trade made it unnecessary, as Indians were induced to exchange their skilled hunting labor for liquor and other inexpensive trade goods. Some traders tried to stretch the profit margin further by diluting the liquor, though Indians caught on to the trick and began testing the spirits by spitting the first mouthful onto a fire to see if it flamed—hence the term "firewater."[37]

The notion that Indians lived in perfect harmony with the environment is a myth, though one with an important kernel of truth. Before European contact Indians were uninterested in accumulating commodities and imposed a relatively light, though appreciable, burden on their environment. After contact and the growth of the fur trade they imposed a much heavier burden, the classic instance being a band of Sioux hunters who exchanged 1,400 buffalo tongues for a few gallons of whiskey, leaving the rest of the carcasses to rot.[38] Buffalo, beaver, deer, and other animal populations were rapidly depleted by Indian hunters, who began acting more and more like their white counterparts.

This was clearly self-destructive behavior. Overhunting increased the prospect of famine which in turn increased susceptibility to infectious disease. The Mandan, wiped out by smallpox in 1837, were suffering from depleted food supplies due to excessive hunting when the epidemic struck.[39] Hunger everywhere increased the incidence of Indian begging, pilferage, and livestock raids, behaviors that reinforced white prejudices and provoked a contemptuous if not violent response.

White frontiersmen did their share of commercialized killing, especially of buffalo, whose hides brought skilled hunters thousands of dollars a year. The organized slaughter of the bison in the years after the Civil War, expedited by the railroads, finished off the great herds, whose numbers had already been substantially reduced by Indians, drought, and grazing competition. "No sight is more common on the plains," observed Theodore Roosevelt in 1886, "than that of a bleached buffalo skull."[40]

The connection between the disappearance of these herds and the disappearance of the Indians was not lost on whites, particularly ranking army officers. Instead of stopping the hunters, General Philip Sheridan admonished the Texas legislature, they ought to be commended and given bronze medals with a dead buffalo on one side and a discouraged Indian on the other. "Let them kill, skin, and sell until the buffalo are exterminated," he prophesied. "Then your prairies can be covered with speckled cattle, and the festive cowboy, who follows the hunter as a second forerunner of an advanced civilization." Readers of the previous chapter may entertain doubts about cowboys as forerunners of civilization, advanced or otherwise, but it is true enough that the destruction of bison opened millions of acres for cattle, followed by sheep and then agriculture, most often wheat farming.[41]

White Americans, who assumed that this transformation was inevitable and divinely ordained, employed two other means to bring it about, bounties and poison. To flourish, open-range livestock needed to be free of predators as well as grazing competitors like buffalo and Indian ponies. Bounties, always welcome on the cash-short frontier, encouraged the slaughter of foxes, coyotes, and wolves. These "varmints" were taken with guns and traps, though poisoned bait was the simplest and most effective means of destroying them. One technique was to lace the front quarter of a buffalo carcass with strychnine, hitch it to a horse, and drag it in a circle several miles in circumference, dropping off chunks of poisoned meat along the way. Scavengers who ate the carrion died, or perhaps vomited and drooled the strychnine over the grass, which was eaten by buffalo who in turn sickened and died. Either way the ranks of competing species were thinned.[42]

The broadcasting of poisoned bait, though devastating to the aboriginal ecosystem, was economically rational, as were all the forms of killing animals described above. But what is most striking about men's frontier memoirs, diaries, and letters is the slaughter of animals as a means of achieving masculine status and pleasure apart from commercial ends. The destruction of native animal life, which entailed the destruction of native human life, had an unmistakable element of gender.

Frontiersmen, always sensitive about their standing among male peers, could gain status through hunting. As with human enemies, the more they killed the better. Hunters often kept score, held contests, compared their prey, and, if they returned home laden with meat, had the satisfaction of being greeted as heroes. Samuel Crawford, later governor of Kansas, described a month-long hunt with fifteen companions in the autumn of 1860: "Having accomplished the purpose of the expedition and established a reputation as hunters," the men returned to Garnett, where the spoils, "four wagon-loads of choice meats and a train-load of romance . . . were distributed among the good people of Anderson County." In return, "happy girls with rosy cheeks and calico frocks" gave the hunters a rousing "buffalo dance," which Crawford reports was enjoyed by all, "especially by those who had roamed the plains for a month in search of something to kill."

There is something almost tribal in this account. At one point Crawford used the word "braves" to describe himself and his hunting companions, an interesting metaphor from the pen of a man who despised Indians. Like braves they brought home game ("choice meats") to their people and, like braves, were fêted by women in communal ceremony, something deeply satisfying to the masculine ego. The event was still vivid in Crawford's memory more than fifty years later.[43]

Other frontiersmen memorialized their skill as hunters by means of trophies. Western saloons, where men gathered to drink and brag and swap stories, often resembled natural history museums with animal heads dotting the wall. In 1902 this decor moved upscale when Theodore Roosevelt, accidental president and eastern convert to frontier recreations, festooned the White House with big game trophies. Among them was a giant moose head, incongruously hung over the fireplace of the State Dining Room.[44]

The skill by which such trophies were won, marksmanship, was honed on avian life. Wild Bill Hickok liked to shoot quail at the stable yard, the birds still being abundant in the early 1870s and practically tame. A favorite pastime around Fort Laramie in the 1870s was shooting the heads off blue grouse, a competitive sport at which the participants kept careful score. And "pigeon shooting" everywhere meant banging away at live passenger pigeons sprung from traps. Captain A. H. Bogardus, the Champion Pigeon Shot of America, introduced glass balls as a more humane substitute, but his innovation failed to halt the slaughter of passenger pigeons for sport and table. The last of the once-abundant species died in the Cincinnati Zoo in 1914.[45]

Male enthusiasm for guns, live target practice, and competitive hunting was not confined to the frontier. The pile-'em-high ethos also flourished in the South. Even so, western wildlife was subject to the same asymmetrical pressure as the Indians, an interloper population heavy with young men who were armed, restless, and anxious to prove themselves.

And bored out of their minds. "The West was not dull," observes Evan S. Connell, "it was stupendously dull, and when not dull it was murderous." Hunting was the primary male antidote for boredom, or at least a close second to drinking. In October 1865 Lieutenant Charles Herrmann Springer, a young German bachelor who had survived the fiasco of the Powder River expedition, found himself encamped near Fort Laramie in

Wyoming Territory. "The days are getting terrible monotonous," he confided to his diary:

October 10: I have the blues—
October 11: I have the blues—
October 12: I have the blues like hell—

And so on until October 20 when he and a companion went hunting. They found a large gray wolf on the Platte River bottom and began firing their Spencer carbines and revolvers at the dodging, bristling, bloodied, terrified creature:

I finally shot him down. He tumbled over got up on his haunches and made hostile demonstrations. Just as I was in the act of dismounting he recovered and struck out for the bluffs again. Another shot broke his foreleg, but he kept on. We arrived at the bluffs. I dismounted and followed him on foot, but he gave me after all the slips, and gained his hole, where there was no chance of getting him out. We returned back to camp. I felt a great deal better after the exercise.[46]

Springer was a blundering amateur compared to Henry Heth, another bachelor lieutenant. "During my sojourn on the plains," Heth recalled, ". . . I killed over one thousand buffalo. I became a buffalo fiend. I never enjoyed any sport as much as I did killing them." He did not pronounce himself fully content until he had learned to bring them down Indian-style, using only a bow and arrow.[47]

Among the higher-ranking officers Sheridan, Custer, and Ranald Mackenzie were well known as extravagant hunters. The most systematic was General George Crook, who habitually rode ahead of his column on the lookout for animals to kill, sometimes using a telescopic rifle. Before he was through Crook managed to shoot or catch practically every known species of game or type of fish and had learned taxidermy to preserve his own trophies.[48]

Bad Habits

Indian acculturation into the ways of commercialized hunting is only one example of the influence of white frontiersmen. They in turn adopted many Indian practices, such as cultivation of corn and squash. Much of this cross-fertilization was beneficial, as when woodland Indians learned new techniques of log carpentry. Some was embarrassing, as when Indians began mimetically calling white men and their vilified freighting wagons "goddams."[49] And some was deadly, especially when Indians acquired the vices of drunkenness and prostitution.

Indians who secured liquor from white traders often drank excessively, turned belligerent, and cut one another to pieces, a story so often repeated by so many different observers that it cannot be written off as prejudice. Drunken Indians exterminated themselves. Yet we know that violent conduct is not an automatic, biological response to alcohol. Aggressiveness and other forms of drunken comportment are learned behaviors. Normally these behaviors are acquired through socialization. People learn what their society "knows" about drunkenness, internalize it, and become living confirmations of their society's teachings. But the North American Indians, who had no distilled alcohol before white contact, had no store of social knowledge to draw upon. The only role models they had were whites who lived near or traveled along the frontier. Indians thus learned to drink from the worst possible tutors: *coureurs de bois*, soldiers, mule skinners, miners, cowboys, and the like. They did not see children sipping cider or the gentry nursing after-dinner brandies. They saw men who went on prolonged binges, swilling rotgut whiskey and becoming dangerously, obstreperously drunk. Small wonder that they did the same or suffered the same consequences.[50]

Indian prostitution went hand in hand with Indian drinking. While formal marriage between American frontiersmen and Indian women was comparatively rare, sexual relations were not. The situation was particularly bad in Gold Rush California, where the pent-up sexual demand of young white men was partly met by the supply of Indian women, some of whom were prostituted for a bottle of whiskey or a bit of sugar. Meretricious commerce, unknown before Spanish and especially American contact, demoralized the California Indians and further reduced their numbers. The spread of syphilis and gonorrhea, accelerated by prostitution, claimed more lives and undermined the capacity to produce new generations of healthy children, a price the rapidly disappearing tribes could ill afford.[51]

Beyond prostitution was the rape of Indian women. California newspapers published accounts of at least twenty-seven flagrant incidents during the 1850s, undoubtedly just the journalistic tip of the rape iceberg. Some of the victims were as young as ten years.[52] Little was done about these outrages, although rape was then regarded as a heinous crime and, if detected and proved against white women, swiftly punished. The difference was the perception of Indian women as subhuman others against whom the baser instincts might be given freer play, much as they were against female slaves.

Sheriffs and vigilantes did not usually concern themselves when Indians were the victims of felonious crimes but acted otherwise when Indians were the accused. One hapless California brave named Collo, accused of murdering a white boy, was hanged before a crowd of nearly two thousand onlookers. Half were Indians rounded up to witness the execution so "that they might be impressed with a wholesome fear of the white man's justice, and thus be deterred from committing any more murders."[53]

The whites who viewed the execution were presumably impressed by another message, that Indians were killers. In fact the frequency of Indian homicide *was* increased by drinking and prostitution, activities that inevitably gave rise to violent quarrels, just as they did among whites.[54] Violent crime by Indians in turn reinforced anti-Indian prejudice, even though the frontiersmen who judged the Indians were really glimpsing their own vices in the distorting mirror of the Savage Other.

Recent scholarship on Indians and frontier whites has emphasized the syncretic nature of their cultures, the mutual borrowing of customs, plants, and technologies that produced for both a genuinely new experience of the world. To this I would add an important qualifier. Because of the unbalanced character of frontier demography, Indians did most of their cultural borrowing from an atypical segment of white society, the one that was most prone to violent and disorderly behavior. It is not, I think, accidental that the high rates of alcoholism and violent death that have continued to plague Indians in the twentieth century were common problems among the frontier whites with whom they first came into contact. Frontiers, to paraphrase Turner, are like glaciers; when they are gone they leave a rocky cultural moraine.[55]

They also left a large number of dead Indians. Though Turner's account of "advancing" whites settling on "free land" along an "empty" frontier has rightly been denounced as culturally biased, there is a sense in which it is biologically apt, for the deaths of millions of native inhabitants created an ecological opening into which immigrants and their livestock could move. The primary, unthinking agent of their destruction was disease. The age and gender structure of the white frontier population was relevant to Indian infection in the specific case of venereal disease and, more generally, through the effects of overhunting, starvation, and the combination of killing, abuse, and exploitation that William McNeill dubbed macroparasitism. Natives, as the medical historian Stephen Kunitz has pointed out, did not simply drop dead whenever they found themselves downwind from a European. They were most likely to succumb to disease when they suffered catastrophic displacement from their lands, typically at the hands of miners or pastoralists.[56]

The displacers were mostly armed young men, the segment of the white population that had the greatest potential for lethal and predatory behavior. The potential was compounded by ethnocentrism and unleashed by its triumphalist racial adjunct, the West as the White Man's Land. The determination of frontiersmen to achieve and profit from this expropriating vision despite the half-hearted attempts of their government to delay them and secure justice for the Indians produced the most tragic and sustained episode of violence in American history.

SEVEN

Women and Families

Frontier regions with high gender ratios were social and ecological disaster zones plagued by premature death and wanton destruction of native and animal populations. But they were by no means permanent disaster zones, for the abnormal population structure that caused or exacerbated the problems was a self-limiting phenomenon. The reason mainly had to do with frontier women—when and whom they married, how many children they bore, and with whom they allied themselves socially and politically. Though the story of the triumph of law and order on the frontier is often told from the vantage of determined marshals and hanging judges, it is more properly and essentially a story of women, families, and the balancing of the population.

Hardship and Scarcity

Women over the age of twenty-one who journeyed toward the frontier were, as a rule, already married and reluctant to go. The decision to migrate was not theirs but was made by their husbands, who chose to gamble on the West for reasons of economic advancement, independence, and adventure. But for women the gamble meant the loss of their female relations and friends. Mothers, sisters, cousins, and neighbors lent emotional and, in crises like childbirth, crucial practical support. Migration

131

destroyed these familiar channels of intimacy and assistance,
provoking tears, resentment, homesickness, and, on occasion,
decisive action, as when pregnant women on the nineteenth-
century southern frontier packed up, left their husbands, and
went back home to have their babies.[1]

The work of frontier women was exhausting, a dawn-to-dark
regimen of baking, brewing, stewing, and sewing compounded
by the cares of raising large families in an environment where
children could wander off into disaster. The floors of their cabins
and sod houses were of packed earth, their visitors seldom of the
bipedal variety. Rats leapt into beds, spiders lurked under the
outhouse seat, and centipedes, mosquitoes, lice, bedbugs, fleas,
and poisonous snakes were everywhere. It was a country, an
army officer laconically noted in his diary, that St. Patrick did
not visit.[2]

The endless battle with dirt and vermin, the worries over
sickness, crops, children, and Indians, and the daily drudgery
taken for granted by their husbands wore emigrant women
down. The Great Plains, with its stark, featureless landscape and
constant, unnerving wind, was perhaps the most demanding
and depressing environment, though the haggard, prematurely
aged woman was a staple of all types of western memoirs and
the butt of the frontier aphorism "this country is all right for men
and dogs, but it's hell on women and horses."[3]

For all the hard work and homesickness, frontier life offered
some advantages for women, or at least for those in locales with
high gender ratios. Precisely because they were scarce and because they had mastered essential tasks at which men were
maladroit, they could command wages that far exceeded eastern
norms. Mary Ballou, a California pioneer who hated the place
and warned other women off, could at least write home in 1852
that "sometimes I am taking care of Babies and nursing at the
rate of fifty dollars a week." "I get fabulous prices for sewing," a
young Denver woman named Mollie Sanford confided to her
journal in 1860. Other western women profited from teaching,
washing, ironing, baking pies, and growing fruits and vegetables
in demand as antiscorbutics. Running a restaurant or boarding
house was another common means of earning additional income, and one appreciated in ways other than strictly monetary.

When a traveling salesman complained about the cooking of Nellie Cashman, the popular proprietress of Tucson's Russ House, a "tall miner" unholstered his pistol and instructed the man, "Stranger, eat them beans."[4]

Any insult to a respectable nineteenth-century frontier woman was considered a serious matter. One mining town, Yellowstone City, specified death by hanging for such offenses, an instance of Victorian sentimentalism hypertrophied by female scarcity. Some cowboys were afraid to even *talk* to respectable women, lest they mention "a leg or something like that that would send them up in the air." As late as the 1910s Wyoming ranch hands would call out "Church time!" when a married woman approached and then lapse into complete if awkwardly respectful silence.[5]

Hypergamy

For single frontier women—scarce people indeed—gender imbalance posed opportunities beyond silent courtesy and good pay. Prostitution was a lucrative option, though it entailed grave risks of venereal disease, abuse, alcoholism, and narcotic addiction, as well as guilt, suicide, and stigmatization. The rule of respect for women that prevailed in frontier towns stopped at the brothel door. Some unknown percentage of prostitutes escaped the trade by marrying out, occasionally to wealthy and respectable men. But the safer and more conventional marital strategy for an eligible young frontier woman was to shun prostitution and aim directly at a hypergamous marriage, or one in which she married above her social station.

This pattern was established early in American history in the Chesapeake region, the prototypical gender-imbalanced frontier. In 1621 the Virginia Company, "takinge into . . . consideration, that the Plantaĉon can never flourish till families be planted, and the respect of wives and Children fix the people on the Soyle," promised to ship fifty more single women to its struggling colony. The women were, however, to be married only to freemen or tenants of substantial means, "for we would have theire condiĉion so much bettered as multitudes may be allured thereby to come unto you." This became a standard ploy.

Colonial promoters promised prospective female emigrants "of honest stock" that they might "pick their husbands out of the better sort of people." It cannot be said that this promise was entirely false. Poor women had much better marital prospects in America, especially in the frontier regions and southern colonies, than they did in seventeenth-century Europe, where low gender ratios and dowries were the rule.[6]

Hypergamy persisted in America's remote masculine regions (though not in its longer-settled areas) from the colonial era into the early twentieth century. Irish servant girls were able to marry rising men, widows and divorcées to marry doctors, housekeepers ranch owners, governesses army officers, and teachers prominent politicians and judges. If a single story may stand for many, it is the poignant one of Julia Etta Parkerson, a devout twenty-one-year-old resident of Manhattan, Kansas. Etta, as she was known, faced practically every marital handicap imaginable. She was poor, suffered migraine headaches, and was bent over by scoliosis, a congenital curvature of the spine that left her barely four feet tall. Yet she had a suitor, an older man named Alvin Reynolds, an honorably discharged soldier who worked as a skilled stonemason.

Alvin, tired of his lonely bachelor existence, made it clear that he was ready to tie the knot. Etta held back. In a remarkable journal she kept between January 1874 and July 1875 she poured out her doubts about marrying him. She worried about her disability and the risk of pregnancy, but most of all she worried about Alvin, the adequacy of his religious beliefs and his use of tobacco, a vice with which she was obsessed. "I am afraid if he yields to tobacco he will sooner or later do the same to whiskey. O Father—*Jesus* help him." As their family photograph attests, Etta eventually overcame her misgivings and married Alvin in 1876. But what is striking, in social historical terms, was that a handicapped woman was calling the matrimonial shots to the point of making her suitor bury his tobacco. This had much to do with the demography of Manhattan, Kansas, where there were six men for every five women. It is hard to imagine a similar drama unfolding in Manhattan, New York, or any other city with a low gender ratio. What the late Tip O'Neill said of politics is equally true of matrimony: all marriage markets are local.[7]

Hypergamy meant that frontier men often married down or, in the case of poor ones, not at all. This was certainly true of propertyless cowboys, but the most easily quantified example is that of soldiers in the frontier army. A sample of manuscript census returns shows that the majority of officers, but only a fraction of the enlisted men, had wives. In 1870 just three of the ninety-four enlisted men (3 percent) at Fort Larned, Kansas, were married compared to four of the six officers (67 percent). In 1880 some 6 percent of the enlisted men at Fort Sisseton, Dakota Territory, were listed as having wives, but fully 100 percent of the officers. The lowest percentages for both groups were found at Fort D. A. Russell, Wyoming Territory, where 45 percent of the officers were married in 1880 compared to 0.3 percent of the enlisted men.[8]

The higher a bachelor officer's rank, the more eligible he became. Women who married captains and above had more household income and better quarters, could employ servants, and enjoyed higher social standing, which was specified when they were formally addressed by their husband's rank: Mrs. Lieutenant-Colonel George Armstrong Custer. Gossips wondered whether Miss Betty Taylor, who was taken with a dashing but impecunious young lieutenant named Dick Garnett, would choose him or a more educated and well-to-do suitor, Major William Bliss. In the end Betty chose the major. Prudently so, as he had the firm approval of her father, Zachary Taylor, major general and soon-to-be president of the United States.[9]

The Lieutenant Garnetts of the world were not without prospects, however. Other officers' unmarried female relations from the East came "husband hunting" at western outposts, where they were enthusiastically welcomed. Matchmaking flourished and was a fixture of officers' dances, segregated, like much else, from the common soldiers. Enlisted men, who earned between $13 and $23 a month and many of whom were foreign-born or black, had to make do with barracks, payday sprees, and prostitutes or, for the few corporals and sergeants who married, a servant girl or laundress on the fort's Soap Suds Row.[10]

The matrimonial history of the frontier army, and of high-gender-ratio western regions generally, was the plot of *The Virginian* writ large. The winners got the brides—if they moved quickly and decisively. Pretty girls were booked up for dances months in advance. Eligible women could count on determined bachelor "visitors" and were regarded as curiosities if unwed for more than a year. Engagements were short and sometimes risky. Even a frontiersman as formidable as Davy Crockett could find himself cut out. In 1805 Crockett thought he was engaged to Miss Margaret Elder of Dandridge, Tennessee, having gone so far as to obtain a marriage license. When he came calling he learned that she was to wed another man the next day. The record for marital alacrity on the frontier, however, was set by one Henderson Couch in December 1846. The foreman of the jury that granted the first divorce in Dallas, Texas, Couch married the divorcée in question, the former Mrs. Charlotte Dalton, the same afternoon.[11]

(Re)Marriage and Fertility

Widows in recently settled areas could count on quick remarriage if they were so inclined. By remarrying they might acquire not only new husbands and families but, in cases of longevity and repeated inheritance, substantial wealth. Seventeenth-century Virginia has been described only half-jokingly as a "widowarchy." The more long-lived women managed to inherit sizable amounts of property along with an impressive string of deceased husbands' surnames, such as that of the redoubtable Mrs. Sarah Offley Thorowgood Gookin Yeardley of Norfolk County.[12]

During the eighteenth century widows seem to have encountered financial hardships rather more often than suitors, at least if they lived in settled eastern areas with lower gender ratios. But along the backwoods frontier they had a much better chance of remarriage. Sometimes, as it transpired, prematurely so. The American Martin Guerre was a Kentucky militiaman named McMerter, thought to have been killed in the 1782 Blue Licks debacle, a late battle of the American Revolution. His widow, a young, intelligent, and beautiful woman with two children, married again a year later, whereupon the lost McMerter returned to general consternation. A decent man, McMerter told his wife he attached no blame and proposed to his rival that she be allowed to choose between them "and whoever she said she preferred . . . the other promised, upon the honor of a gentleman, to withdraw and never interfere." She chose McMerter, the father of her children and her first love. The second husband, true to his word, withdrew.[13]

The more frequent remarriage of western widows and the early marriage of young western women meant that the overall percentage of women with husbands would be higher as one moved toward the frontier. Two surviving colonial censuses include information about marital status. New Hampshire's in 1773 showed that, the lower a county's gender ratio, the lower the percentage of women married and the higher the percentage of widows. Connecticut's in 1774 showed that women twenty and older were more likely to be married if they resided in a recently settled county with a higher gender ratio like Litchfield, in the northwestern portion of the state. Women in Litchfield also tended to marry earlier in life than women in longer-settled counties.[14]

Census and other evidence strongly suggests that gender ratio differences continued to affect American marriage patterns throughout the nineteenth century and into the twentieth. Indeed, the positive correlation between the gender ratio and the percentage of women who are married or who marry early seems to be a nearly universal social pattern.[15]

Youthful brides were particularly common in regions with very large male surpluses, a pattern that emerged early in American history. Anne Burras, the first woman married in Jamestown, was a fourteen-year-old servant girl who wed a man twice her age. Marriages of twelve- and thirteen-year-old girls were not unheard of in the Chesapeake colonies and were noted during the California Gold Rush. In frontier Michigan the legal age of female consent to sexual intercourse was eleven years. Harriet Martineau, the indefatigable English traveler and observer, complained in 1837 of "the early marriages of silly children in the south and west, where, owing to the disproportion of numbers, every woman is married before she well knows how serious a matter human life is." Or how unpredictable and transient. A thirteen-year-old bride in Morris County, Kansas, gave birth to two children before becoming a widow at nineteen.

She then married the man into whose hands her dying husband had entrusted her care.[16]

That contemporaries remarked such cases in their journals and memoirs shows that the marriages of scarcely menarcheal girls and remarriages of teenage widows with children were regarded as unusual. The norm for a first marriage for women in high-gender-ratio regions was closer to the mid-to-late teens. The average age of marriage for women born in Somerset County, Maryland, before 1670 was 16.5 years. The age at first marriage of women in the Peters colony of north central Texas during the period 1841–1850 was 19.4 years, collectively six years younger than their bridegrooms.[17]

Women who married young produced numerous children, particularly if they lived on farms and in a era or subculture hostile to contraception. Country wives, remarked an anonymous New York colonial official, were "good breeders." They were young, he reasoned, and did not sometimes "Lye fallor" like city wives. While not the sort of person one might wish to come courting, the official expressed a demographic truth. Rural wives who wed early had more years to produce offspring and an economic incentive, their children's agricultural labor, to do so. Land was not a constraint on population growth as it was in Europe. Certainly it was not a restraint along the frontier, where the destruction of the native inhabitants created an economic and ecological opening favorable to the immigrants. Cheap land and rude plenty reinforced the tendency of high gender ratios to produce early marriages and large families. Eventually, as population density increased and the numbers of males and females evened out, the average marriage age of women increased and their fertility declined.[18]

The life of Margaret Dwight, a niece of a president of Yale and great-granddaughter of the evangelist Jonathan Edwards, was emblematic of these demographic forces. In 1810 she left New Haven to live with her cousins in then-remote Warren, Ohio. A year after her arrival she married William Bell Jr. He was thirty, she was twenty. Although the Bells ultimately moved back to Pittsburgh, Margaret's early marriage made it possible for her to bear thirteen children. Whether it was desirable was another matter, for she died at the age of forty-three.[19]

Margaret Dwight's life was an unconscious replay of seventeenth-century New England history. Her Puritan ancestors had faced much the same situation she did in Ohio, an initial surplus of men, and had responded in the same fashion, with earlier marriages and hence larger families than had been typical in England. Because infant mortality was low in New England, an unusually large number of these children survived and began their own families, triggering a population explosion in which the white population of Massachusetts more than sextupled between 1640 and 1700.

Population growth of this sort automatically eroded high gender ratios. Since the new children were roughly divided between males and females, they began to even out the gender balance of the population. So did the disappearance of unmarried adult males who either died prematurely or migrated elsewhere as the frontier moved on. As children grew and entered the labor force, there was less need to rely on immigrant workers; hence the bachelor workers who died or left were less likely to be replaced. The death or emigration of unmarried men together with the high fertility of young brides operated as a homeostatic mechanism: the deck-gun "barrel" of the abnormal population distribution eventually dropped off, even as its base was broadening. The result was an increasingly symmetrical population pyramid and, with it, a gradual increase in female age at marriage.

Two decades sufficed to balance most frontier populations, especially those in farming areas where the initial imbalance was less extreme. Washington County, Kansas, a stretch of arable prairie between the Flint Hills and the Nebraska border, had 149 men for every 100 women in 1860, but only 124 in 1870 and 114 in 1880.[20] The gender ratios of midwestern farming areas like Washington County seldom dropped below 100 because of the demand for farmhands, but these reproductively "extra" male workers were usually attached to families, which served both to maintain social order and, by their relatively high fertility, to drive the gender ratio downward.

On occasion the homeostatic process broke down. If immigrant women could not marry early because they arrived in their twenties, if they were bound as indentured servants, if they and their children died young, or if male immigrants continued to pour into the community in large numbers, then gender imbalance would persist for a longer period of time. The one region where all of these problems were in evidence was the seventeenth- and early-eighteenth-century Chesapeake, whose population consequently took much longer to grow naturally and to become balanced.[21] The population of Middlesex County, Virginia, shown in Figure 7.1, required thirty-six years to achieve the pyramidal shape characteristic of most premodern populations, and even then there were vestiges of male predominance.

Shortcuts to Population Balance

The speed with which a given population achieved balance was also affected by the rapidity, comfort, safety, and price of transportation and, to a lesser extent, the cost and availability of mass communication. In the seventeenth and eighteenth centuries women who wished to move to a region with more potential husbands had to make a tedious and dangerous overland journey or, if emigrating from Europe, a long and costly ocean voyage. By the 1870s women in a similar position could simply purchase, at considerably less risk and expense, a ticket on a steamship or a westbound train. Lou Conway Roberts, who settled with her husband, a former Texas Ranger, in New Mexico in 1882, wrote of an influx of "disconsolate widows" and "forlorn old maids." Such persons were able to marry by moving to New Mexico, she observed. They did not have to be attractive so long as they were "American women."[22]

Of course it did not hurt to be attractive, nor did it hurt to advertise the fact. Newspaper personals were the other technological means of increasing the odds of finding a suitable spouse. In July 1857 Ned Bowers, a twenty-one-year-old bachelor in Douglas County, Kansas, advertised his availability in the local *Freeman's Champion,* repeating the ad several times. He had been considered good looking when he lived in the States, he wrote, though he admitted to being "somewhat uncouth in my appearance now; am hale, hearty, strong, and full of fun and frolic; have been, and am sometimes now, a little wild, but think I should be steady as a deacon, if I had a congenial partner to love and protect." It was an old line but one with a certain sociologi-

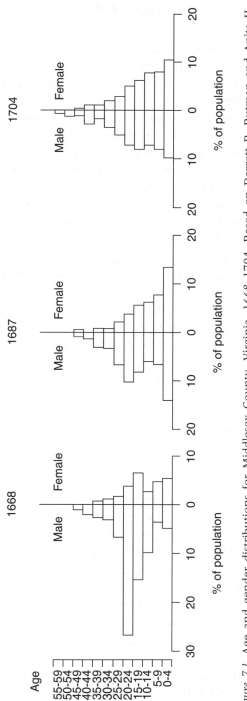

Figure 7.1 Age and gender distributions for Middlesex County, Virginia, 1668–1704. Based on Darrett B. Rutman and Anita H. Rutman, *A Place in Time: Middlesex County, Virginia, 1650–1750* (New York: Norton, 1984), 77.

cal plausibility. Sixteen to twenty-one was the age range he was looking for, Ned explained, and poverty was no bar. Respondents need not have a cent to their name as long as they were lady-like and pretty.

Ned was evidently stronger than he was smart, for he forgot to include an address. This prompted a Miss Lovina Littleton of Peoria City, Kansas, who chanced to read his ad, to write a letter to the editor of the *Freeman's Champion,* which he gleefully published. Lovina announced that she was a candidate for matrimony, the right age and very good looking ("acknowledged by a host of admirers to be the very ideal of beauty and witticism"). But, she continued, certain things needed to be understood at once: no gambling and no drinking. She was not about to forfeit her happiness to liquid poison nor would she ever unite herself to a drinking man.

A public marital negotiation between two parties is unusual enough, but then the editor himself got into the act. "A capital chance," he opined. "Her letter certainly exhibits indications of good sense . . . and there can be no doubt but what she is worth looking after. Oh! 'pitch in,' Ned!" Whether Ned did so is a mystery which a search of the county marriage records failed to resolve. But if he did not the chances are good that the determined Lovina found an abstemious suitor before long.[23]

Church Time

The growing presence of women and children changed the moral climate as well as the population structure of frontier regions. In family farming areas where there were fewer extra men the change was less noticeable, particularly in the religious colonies. They were peaceful anyway, always excepting the possibility of Indian uprisings or, in the special case of the Mormons, conflict with Gentiles. But in secular and heavily male domains the homeostatic process of population balancing produced dramatic social changes, widely remarked by contemporaries.

There is in any established community a spectrum of religious temperaments, interwoven beliefs about God, morality, and the self that transcend particular denominations. Devout, churchgoing, self-denying people form one end of this spectrum and more worldly, unchurched, self-assertive people the other, with varying degrees of religiosity and self-control in between. In the eighteenth and nineteenth centuries Americans who might be called, for the sake of brevity, the moral conservatives tended to be native-born Protestant women or married men of the middle class or aspiring lower-middle class who had had a conversion experience. Their temperamental opposites, moral libertarians, were mostly men, especially young men of society's genteel upper reaches or, in ever-increasing numbers, laborers who had not had a conversion experience and who devoted little time or serious attention to religion in any form. These two groups were locked in an emotional and political conflict that centered on public and, to the devout, scandalous male recreations such as horse races, dice and card games, whoring, and tavern and saloon drinking. The last-mentioned emerged as the key issue as the nineteenth century wore on.

There was nothing unique about the conflict between Americans of different religious temperaments, which had then as it has now cultural equivalents in every part of the world. What was unusual about the American case was the way migration and frontier expansion continuously reshuffled the moral deck, giving a temporary advantage in the new settlements to one camp or the other. In the case of the religious colonies, the advantage obviously lay with the moral conservatives. In the cordilleran mining camps and plains cattle towns and other primitive places dominated by transient bachelor laborers, the numerical and interactionist advantage lay with the moral libertarians, a fact that helps to account for their wide-open character.

Open vice was hard for devout frontier women to bear. In 1780 Sarah Peairs survived a nightmarish journey down the Mississippi, a water-borne Donner Party minus the cannibalism but complete with disease, starvation, and a death lottery in which a young girl drew the fatal lot from her own father ("O! daddy will you kill me O! daddy will you kill me"). Peairs intervened, dissuaded the stupid man, and managed to stay alive until they finally reached Natchez. Grateful for her deliverance, she was nevertheless so appalled by the "general corruption of manners" in the frontier river town that she begged passage for herself and her surviving children to return "to a gospel land," eventually sailing via New Orleans to Philadelphia.[24]

It was much the same in Gold Rush California, from which many a disillusioned moralist likewise sailed home. California women wrote of being sickened by piles of "yellow kivered" (pornographic) literature, of their revulsion against drunkenness and violence, of their unease at newly rich men throwing jewelry and coins at the feet of young actresses of doubtful virtue.[25] Even though they might personally be treated with respect and well paid for their work, there was no hiding the fact that they lived in a land of moral eyesores, another and not the least hardship borne by pioneer women in predominantly male lands.

Or temporarily borne, for the ineluctable balancing of the population brought with it progressively better chances for moral counterrevolution. The presence of women and children made men more self-conscious of and embarrassed by commercialized vice. A brothel or saloon may have been tolerable in a mining camp but not in a town or neighborhood teeming with children. Married, middle-class men with children were particularly apt to have reservations about the propriety of open vice, not to mention their own participation in it.[26]

The demographic shift likewise encouraged the formation of churches. Boom towns with overwhelmingly male populations were visited by preachers who declaimed against sin in the midst of the sinners, but theirs was an itinerant ministry. The establishment of permanent churches (in Newton, Kansas, one took over a former saloon, bullet holes and all) with full-time clergy depended on the growing presence of women. They made up the majority of regular worshipers in Protestant congregations throughout the West as in the rest of the nation.[27]

These new churches became the local bases from which masculine vice was attacked, if not necessarily driven from its economic and political lair. Clergymen, female moralists, and their respectable male allies (generally husbands, converts, and Masons) used a variety of means, from petitions to sit-in demonstrations, to protest Sabbath breaking, brothels, dance halls, gambling palaces, and saloons. Reformist newspaper editors, anxious to better their towns' reputations, assisted the moral conservatives by writing anti-vice editorials and by what one historian has called dingbat moralizing. Dingbats were the ubiquitous column-filler and separator lines like "*Whiskey Brings Men to Jail*."[28]

One of the best known of the reformist editors was James King of William, a colorful character who devised his unusual patronymic to distinguish himself from others who bore his common surname. In 1856 King, then editor of the San Francisco *Evening Bulletin*, was shot to death by James Casey, an Irish election fixer who did not care for King's brand of investigative journalism. The murder created a sensation. It catalyzed the formation of the famous 1856 Vigilance Committee, which was dominated by mercantile interests and strongly backed by respectable women. One lady reportedly said that if the men did not hang Casey, the women would. She need not have worried. He and three other malefactors were soon dispatched. A score of others, mostly Irishmen of suspect politics, were forced out of town.[29]

Women in the maturing western cities and towns did not confine their efforts to ad hoc protests but organized elaborate "home missions." These involved such projects as a house of refuge for Chinese prostitutes in San Francisco, one for unwed mothers in Denver, and another for Mormon wives fleeing plural marriages in Salt Lake City. Western women were also quick to join in statewide and national reform organizations, the best known of which was the powerful Woman's Christian Temperance Union (WCTU), which claimed 176,000 members by the turn of the century. What these groups had in common was hostility toward the worst aspects of masculine culture and, some historians believe, a tendency to encourage protofeminist consciousness in their members. Women whose reform efforts were delayed or blocked by male businessmen and politicians linked to the vice industry were not blind to the possibilities of enfranchisement. Some, like WCTU president Frances Willard, openly espoused the vote for women.[30]

Motives and means are seldom pure in history, and the women's reform movements were no exception. Though religious conviction was always a key factor, women had various reasons for joining the anti-vice organizations that mushroomed after 1870, status seeking and female companionship among them. In the interests of achieving their goals they were willing to build coalitions, beginning with their husbands. On occasion they also joined forces with men who, for purely self-interested reasons, wished to attack the foundation of the local vice industry.

The classic case of a mixed reform alliance was that of Abilene, Kansas, the original cattle town. Abilene was the brainchild of Joseph G. McCoy, a visionary cattleman who in 1868 saw the sleepy hamlet's possibility as a collecting point for Texas longhorns, which could be shipped east via the railroad that had just reached the town. McCoy's scheme was realized over the next three years as vast herds were driven up the Chisholm Trail to Abilene, bringing rapid growth and a measure of prosperity. But with the cattle and their fever ticks came the cowboys and their vice parasites, scandalizing the respectable settlers in and around the town. Though cowboys deferred to ladies, the tipsy whores who paraded about in gaudy dresses sometimes insulted them. The situation was not improved when the whores' employers erected a brothel near the schoolhouse.[31]

The most celebrated scandal was the 1869 affair of the Bull's Head Saloon, whose flare front was emblazoned with a crude painting of a "big red bull in all its grandeur." That citizens should be so offended by a painting of a bull's penis and testicles when the real thing could be seen in action everywhere around town struck some as amusing. But we live by symbols and this one managed to encompass just about everything that the townspeople hated about the Faustian pact with the cattle trade, not to say an affront, as they put it, to the modesty of women and innocence of children. The proprietor of the Bull's Head, a Texan, told the protest committee to go to hell and made a little speech of his own: "I'm not to be dictated to by the mealy-mouthed or scared off the trail by girly fellers." In the end, though, he gave in and painted out the offending organs.[32]

By 1872 the moral reformers had managed to paint out the cattle trade altogether. They made common cause with agricultural land speculators, who wanted the cattle gone so that they might sell more acreage, and with farmers who were sick of having their corn trampled and their own livestock killed by imported Texas fever. This mixed but formidable coalition issued a manifesto that the county residents would "no longer submit to the evils of the trade" and persuaded the state legislature to fix the cattle quarantine line farther west, making it impossible to ship from Abilene. The cowboys and their wages disappeared. The town reverted to its orderly and considerably less prosperous self, sunflowers sprouting in the quiet main streets.[33]

Elsewhere the course of reform was less dramatic, a matter of incremental change and political seesaw. Laws enforcing Sunday closings or suppressing prostitution would be enacted in towns like Cheyenne or Wichita only to provoke an angry reaction and repeal a short time later. The resistance to the moral counterrevolution occasionally assumed an ironic form. Three saloons were named for the hatchet-minded prohibitionist Carry Nation; she managed to wreck one of them. The general drift of anti-vice legislation and enforcement from 1870 on was clearly in favor of the reformers, however. When they failed to secure ordinances specifically outlawing commercialized vice they were usually able to achieve its spatial and temporal segregation. In 1890, for example, the town of Ballinger, Texas, made it unlawful for men to be seen in public with a prostitute between four in the morning and nine in the evening or for prostitutes to enter any public building during the daytime, so that they would not be seen by and give offense to respectable women.[34]

Other towns solved the problem of moral eyesores by confining prostitution to a single neighborhood, typically on the fringe of the central business district and overlapping with the entertainment district and the local Chinatown. The prevailing wisdom was that segregated prostitution provided a regrettable but necessary sexual outlet for lower-class men, although even this rationalization was rejected during the 1910s when reformers and clergymen finally managed to end official acquiescence to redlight districts. By that decade most of the western states were also solidly in the prohibition camp, owing to the progressive balancing of the population, the enfranchisement of women, and the reasoned appeals of a new, less strident generation of temperance advocates that won over some Catholic and labor voters.[35]

Education, Recreation, and Cultural Life

Beyond serving as a catalyst for anti-vice reforms, the presence of families, women, and children expanded the range of educational, recreational, and cultural activities. The life of the mind was not a priority on the raw frontier. "One fifth of the men out here cant right or cipher," admitted John Ferguson, an early resident of Washington County, Kansas. "I was elected last spring as Justice of the Peace in this township so you may know by that the men out here isent non the smartest or I wouldent been picked on to fill that office for I am sure I ent fit for it." Ferguson bore his own limitations cheerfully but was deeply worried about the educational prospects for his children.[36]

This was a common concern, particularly among Protestant settlers who understood literacy as the key to the Bible and salvation as well as to worldly success. Energetic women like Helen Chapman, the wife of an army officer stationed in Brownsville, Texas, worked hard to gain support from community leaders for primary education, arguing that their communities could not pretend to respectability until they had schools and churches. Western women also acted as educators in their own right, whether as home instructors or private tutors or as teachers in the Sunday and public schools that were eventually established.[37]

The progress of public education was steady though difficult. Because of the thin tax base, schools were an expensive proposition. Underfunding, primitive facilities, transient students, and recruitment of teachers were chronic problems. The citizens of one mountain town had to lure away the community's best-educated woman from her job as the piano player in the local saloon. But a rudimentary system had been established almost everywhere in the West by 1880, a development that had as important implications for social control as it did for literacy. Assignments, bells, deadlines, and the constant requirement of sitting still and paying attention helped the rising generation of students, particularly boys, to acquire self-control and master their impulsiveness. Their common texts, the graded *McGuffey's Readers*, stressed the Victorian imperatives of self-discipline, punctuality, and hard work and inveighed against disobedience, debt, and drunkenness. It is of some interest that the *Readers* were originally designed for students in the newly settled lands of the West and South, though they were so successful that they were adopted nationwide, selling 122 million copies between 1837 and 1920.[38]

Social reformers understood that moral improvement entailed more than building schools and enacting thou-shalt-nots. Bachelor laborers gravitated to saloons and gambling dens and brothels because they were lonely and bored. They wanted companionship, news, and such basic amenities as light, warmth, food, and toilets. Women's church and WCTU chapters began developing alternative resorts like dry lunch rooms and small libraries where men could gather to converse, read, relax, and hear occasional lectures on such self-improving topics as "Hygiene." Dashaway Hall, a San Francisco temperance establishment that flourished during the 1860s, featured Wednesday night dances and Thursday evening socials where sober-minded men could mix with the Ladies Dashaway Association. The ice-cream parlors and soda fountains that sprang up in western cities and towns were another respectable alternative, popular with married and courting couples, who were increasingly common as the population became more balanced.[39]

The growing presence of women transformed the higher cultural life of western communities. Nineteenth-century American men, especially frontiersmen, were notorious for their anti-intellectualism and indifference to the arts, which, like religion, they took to be the domain of women. This prejudice was so entrenched that the greatest composer of his generation, Charles Ives, felt compelled to pursue a career in business to avoid seeming abnormal. A reporter in Chicago once counted the number of men attending a lecture by Henry James. He found two, one of whom was asleep.[40] Given the prevailing masculine lack of interest, no community could regularly support sophisticated artistic and humanistic enterprises without a critical mass of women, who were indispensable as audiences, critics, performers, and instructors. Women organized lectures and debates, joined reading and discussion clubs, patronized and staffed libraries, put on amateur theatricals and attended professional performances, wrote books and articles, studied and taught music, collected and preserved artifacts, genealogies, and historical materials. To recast a cliché, women civilized western communities in the sense of reducing violence and squalor while at the same time enhancing their aesthetic and intellectual lives.

The history of the maturation of frontier towns is the history of women turning them into places actually worth living in.

The restoration of a more normal age and gender distribution entailed moral, political, and cultural changes that reduced the violence and disorder characteristic of heavily male frontier populations. Even where the reformers and cultural improvers were frustrated politically the growing presence of women and children affected, in an elementary statistical sense, the local rates of violence and disorder. The incidence per 100,000 of a problem like homicide or alcoholism or venereal disease was bound to decline as the number of women and children and older persons in a community's population increased. That is one important reason why the rates of homicide in eastern cities were so much lower than those in western mining districts and cattle towns. Late-nineteenth-century Boston and Philadelphia had plenty of young, unmarried men strutting around with guns and flasks, but they made up a much smaller proportion of the total municipal populations, ensuring, by the laws of probability and long division, much lower rates of murder.

By the same logic, and by reason of the association between men and violence, population balancing brought greater social peace to frontier regions throughout the world. The passing of the colorful but bloody gaucho era on the Argentine Pampas is a parallel case, though the best-documented example is that of New South Wales, Australia, founded by the British in 1788 as a penal colony to replace their lost American dumping grounds. Immigration gave New South Wales a heavily male population. Men initially outnumbered women by four to one; this ratio fluctuated between three and two to one over the next half-century.

The result was widespread drunkenness, prostitution, corporal punishment, and lethal violence, both among the colonists and against the Aborigines. New South Wales was an early version of the tumultuous world of the American Gold Rush. In fact, the "Sydney Ducks" who remigrated to California during 1849–1852 had bad reputations by California standards, which is saying a lot. But the same inexorable demographic forces that tamed California tamed New South Wales, turning it into a civil place by the late nineteenth century. Peter Grabosky, who compared criminal statistics from New South Wales during 1826 to 1893 to economic conditions, gender distribution, urbanization, police manpower, and police expenditures, came to the conclusion that rates for serious crimes against persons and property were almost solely a function of the oversupply of men in the population. The other variables virtually did not matter. In New South Wales as in nonfarming areas of the American frontier, social problems grew out of a skewed, largely male population. As it became more normal so did the amount of violence and disorder.[41]

EIGHT

Chinatown

The same process of population adjustment at work in frontier communities altered the composition of heavily male immigrant groups. The passage of time naturally restored the balance of men and women and young and old, reducing the rate of violent and disorderly behavior and diversifying social life. The process could, however, be disrupted and delayed by unwanted government interference. That was what happened to the Chinese immigrants during the last half of the nineteenth and the first half of the twentieth centuries. As exceptions to the rule, their case is both instructive and disturbing. It shows how racial contempt magnified American violence not only by justifying riotous attacks but also and more subtly by blocking the balancing of the population and prolonging the tendency toward disorder inherent in male populations.

The Chinese in America

Nineteenth-century Chinese immigrants came from the area in and around Canton (Guangzhou), a chaotic region suffering from overpopulation, famine, warfare, and banditry. They were chiefly men between the ages of eighteen and thirty whose concern was earning money to support their impoverished families. The available evidence (much documentary material was destroyed in the 1906 San Francisco earthquake and fire) indicates that a majority were married, though for cultural and economic reasons they left their wives at home. In any case they were planning on returning, not on staying in the United States. A few did accumulate money, repatriate, purchase property, and retire to a life of wealth and respectability. However, for reasons that will become apparent, this was not the norm.[1]

The demand for labor generated by the California Gold Rush and rapid development of the Pacific states and territories made the United States a logical destination. Steady work at the Gum Sann (Gold Mountain) was a tantalizing prospect for peasants and laborers who earned the equivalent of ten or fifteen cents a day and who were worried about finding enough rice and firewood. But they had to borrow substantial sums from merchants to pay for their passage and to procure entry papers, an outlay of well over $200. The total debt, principal plus interest, represented more than ten years' wages at home. The willingness to assume such a burden was a sign of the immigrants' desperation and their optimism about prospects in the United States.[2]

In America their wages were garnished to repay these loans. Most also remitted a portion of their earnings to sustain their relatives in China. Both traits fueled anti-Chinese sentiment. The indebtedness of Chinese workers led to charges of unfair competition from "coolie" or "pauper labor," the practices of scrimping and sending money home to charges of "carrying away our treasure." The truth was that Chinese laborers in America were not virtual slaves, like their wretched counterparts who were worked to death in the guano pits of Peru. But neither were they entirely free. No Chinese laborer could book passage out of California until he had been cleared by the Zhonghua Huigan, the Chinese Six Companies. This powerful governing organization was dominated by merchant-creditors and saw to it that all debts were repaid before laborers returned home.[3]

At first Chinese immigration to California was small-scale and occasioned little opposition. From 1848 through 1851 merchants set themselves up in the retail trade and laborers took jobs mainly as cooks and launderers, conventionally female jobs that badly needed doing but posed no threat to American miners. This abruptly changed in 1852 when approximately 20,000 Chinese landed in California, all but 50 of them men. This wave, more than five times the size of all previous Chinese immigration, had come for gold. The placer mines were regarded as a white American preserve and were in any case beginning to play out, making foreign miners doubly unwelcome. Chinese competition brought racial hostility to the surface and aroused fears that California might not be a white man's land after all.[4]

Opposition to Chinese miners assumed the legal form of a discriminatory but lucrative miners' tax, which was collected with a vengeance in California and other western states and territories. Joseph Boyd, the deputy sheriff of Shoshone County, Idaho Territory, recalled that the tax on Chinese miners was $5 a head, of which he was allowed to keep 20 percent. "Often when the Orientals saw the collector coming they would run into the woods or other hiding places and I had to round them up and force them to pay their tax," he wrote. "Sometimes they would claim they did not have the money and I marched them in pig tail file down the trail to the store where they would borrow the required sum from the store keeper."[5]

Though forced deeper into debt, these men were lucky. In California the Foreign Miners' Tax collectors were notorious for their brutal tactics. "I was sorry to have to stab the poor creature," rationalized one collector, "but the law makes it necessary to collect the tax; and that's where I get my profit." By 1862 at least eleven Chinese miners in California had been murdered in this fashion.[6]

Other whites attacked, extorted, robbed, kidnapped, and killed Chinese miners without any pretext of law, committing violent crimes that drove the immigrants from rich mining areas and netted an estimated $1 million in gold dust. The robbers and killers knew they stood little risk of successful prosecution, as Chinese testimony against whites was not allowed in court. Of eighty-eight known murders of Chinese before 1862, just two resulted in conviction and execution.[7]

As a rule Chinese were permitted to work only those sites abandoned by whites as unremunerative, a restriction that prevailed not only in California but in Oregon, Washington, Nevada, Idaho, and other western states and territories into which Chinese miners ventured. "You might fire a cannon ball down the main street without danger of hitting anyone unless some stray Chinaman should chance to get in the way," was how one correspondent described Coloma, site of the original gold strike, in 1870. "The Chinese slip into these towns as the white men leave, and in their contentment with small wages, not only exist, but appear to be exceedingly happy." They might have been a good deal happier if they had been permitted to work decent claims, but when they chanced to get one angry whites showed up and drove them away.[8]

One response to abuse and discrimination was to return home, which more than 50,000 Chinese did between 1851 and 1868. Another was to stay and seek other forms of employment. Chinese labored in vineyards and wheat fields, excavation and drainage projects, fisheries and canneries, cigar and shoe factories, in every case proving themselves steady and efficient workers. The accomplishment for which they are best remembered was their success in cutting the Central Pacific Railroad through the Sierra Nevada mountains. They froze in blizzards, perished in explosions, were buried by avalanches. One in ten died, but the survivors got the job done. "They prove nearly equal to white men, in the amount of labor they perform," their employer Charles Crocker wrote in 1865, "and are far more reliable. No danger of strikes among them."[9]

Chinese biddability seemed less of a virtue to competing laborers. The completion of the transcontinental railroad in 1869, Turner's labor safety-valve actualized in timber and steel, produced a stream of white workers in search of better jobs in the West. They did not take kindly to Chinese competition during the depression years of the 1870s. Attacks on the Chinese became increasingly politicized and systematic, culminating in a full-scale race riot in San Francisco in July 1877. Exclusion was by then a powerful political issue and the key to controlling the labor vote. It also touched a deep racial nerve, as revealed in this extraordinary exchange between two lawyers testifying before a special congressional committee in late 1876. Frank M. Pixley was representing the City of San Francisco, Benjamin Brooks the Chinese:

Mr. Pixley. . . In relation to [the Chinese] religion, it is not our religion. That is enough to say about it; because if ours is right theirs must necessarily be wrong.

Mr. Brooks. What is our religion?

Mr. Pixley. Ours is a belief in the existence of a Divine Providence that holds in its hands the destinies of nations. The Divine Wisdom has said that He would divide the country and the world as the heritage of five great families; that to the blacks He would give Africa; to the whites He would give Europe; to the red man He would give America, and Asia He would give to the yellow races. He inspires us with the determination not only to have preserved our own inheritance, but to have stolen from the red man America; and it is settled now that the Saxon, American or European group of families, the white race, is to have the inheritance of Europe and of America and that the yellow races of China are to be confined to what God Almighty originally gave them; and as they are not a favorite people they are not to be permitted to steal from us what we robbed the American savage of.[10]

Missionaries who testified before the committee had other ideas as to which of His peoples God might have favored, not to say different views on kleptotheology. They did their best to defend Chinese immigrants, as did wealthy capitalists who had profited from their industrious labor. But the business elite had not obtained its position by championing lost causes. By 1880, the year of a bloody anti-Chinese riot in Denver, it was plain that social and industrial peace could be purchased only at the price of an end to Chinese immigration. California senators introduced, Congress passed, and in 1882 President Chester Arthur signed legislation to exclude the immigration of Chinese laborers for ten years, a ban that was to be subsequently tightened and extended. It was the first time in American history that a group had been barred on the basis of race.[11]

And class. Chinese merchants, diplomats, students, clergymen, and travelers were permitted to come to the United States and bring their wives with them, but the same spousal privileges were denied to laborers, including those long resident in the United States. Two 1884 federal court decisions ruled that laborers' wives in China were ineligible to immigrate. (Not that large numbers of Chinese workers, indebted and forced into marginal jobs in which they earned two-thirds of the average white wage, could afford to bring them over anyway.) Resident Chinese laborers could return to China to visit their wives and families and then come back to the United States, although further restrictions enacted in 1888 made even this arrangement practically impossible.[12]

The campaign to bar Chinese women had in fact begun well before the Exclusion Act and its amendments. A large majority, between 70 and 90 percent, of those who came prior to 1870 were prostitutes, mostly women between the ages of sixteen and twenty-five who had been sold, tricked, or kidnapped into the trade. It was an ugly business. Women who resisted were tortured until they resumed performing sexual services. Almost all became diseased; few lasted in the brothels more than four or five years. Unlike those of dead Chinese laborers, whose bones were usually shipped back to China for burial, their remains were discarded in the streets of Chinatown.[13]

The moral and racial revulsion occasioned by Chinese prostitution led to the passage of the 1875 Page Law, a federal act that provided substantial penalties for the importation of women for purposes of prostitution. The effect of this legislation was to slow Chinese female immigration. There were, of course, Chinese prostitutes already active in the United States, but they did not survive for long. Their demise, together with the economic and legislative barriers to female entry and the sharp rise in male laborers' immigration in the early 1880s (in anticipation of exclusion), created a set of circumstances that kept the Chinese community lopsidedly male longer than any comparable group in American history.[14]

The Chinese community also became progressively smaller, at least until the 1920s. Although Chinese laborers continued to enter the United States illegally after 1882, they were too few to replace those who died or returned to China, driven out by violent intimidation. In 1885 alone there were large-scale riots against Chinese workers in Seattle, Tacoma, and Rock Springs, Wyoming Territory. The last was a massacre in which miners armed with revolvers and Winchester rifles shot down Chinese men "fleeing like a herd of hunted antelope." A total of twenty-eight Chinese died in the Rock Springs Massacre, which caused an international episode and eventually forced the United States government to pay more than $147,000 in damages. Sixteen white men were arrested for the murders, but the local grand jury returned no indictments and no one was ever convicted.[15]

As with the Indians, to whom whites often compared the Chinese, the way such killings were carried out revealed a deep, almost feral hatred. Chinese men were scalped, mutilated, burned, branded, decapitated, dismembered, and hanged from gutter spouts. One Chinese miner's penis and testicles were cut off and then toasted in a nearby saloon "as a trophy of the hunt." This was plainly racial terrorism, and it had its intended effect. Brutalized, discouraged, and relegated to low-paying jobs, many Chinese headed for the East Coast or, if they had paid off their debts, left the United States for good.[16]

Those who stayed faced the stark fact of female scarcity. In 1890 the Chinese gender ratio was 2,679, roughly 27 Chinese men for every woman. Three decades later the ratio was still a very high seven to one. Intermarriage was discouraged by white racism and, more concretely, by fifteen state anti-miscegenation laws, two of which carried penalties of up to ten years in prison. In places where the practice was not strictly forbidden some Chinese men defied custom and married or cohabited with white women—one New York City official estimated about 200 such arrangements in 1900—but they usually had to settle for the dregs of white society, alcoholic or addicted prostitutes. An alternative (and, in the larger context of American social history, highly unusual) sexual gambit for those who rejected white women was polyandry. One Chinese woman might live with as many as ten men.[17]

The extremity of the prejudice against Asian intermarriage in the United States is highlighted by the experience of the Chinese in Southeast Asia, the Pacific Islands, and former Spanish colonies. Like their American counterparts, the Chinese immigrants in these lands were almost all men, but they were not confronted with insuperable cultural or legal barriers to taking native wives. They solved the problem of gender balance by marrying Siamese and Malay women, Filipinas, Hawaiians, and Mexican mestizas. Not only were such marriages permitted, they were in many cases preferred by native women, who regarded Chinese men as hard workers and good providers. These marriage markets were free and meritocratic.[18]

Not so the American marriage market, at least as far as the
Chinese were concerned. Most sojourners remained de facto
bachelors until they left or died, often by taking their own lives
when age or injury prevented them from supporting themselves.
Those who did manage to reproduce themselves genetically and
socially were the merchant "winners" who raised their American-born sons and daughters in a closely guarded bourgeois
world. What finally and decisively changed this situation was
the partial lifting of restrictions on Chinese immigration during
and after World War II. The majority of the refugees and immigrants who legally entered the country between 1945 and 1965
were women. Their presence and childbearing rapidly balanced
the Chinese-American population, which was nearly equally
divided between males and females by 1980 and had a slight
female surplus by 1990.[19]

Chinatown Vice

What most Chinese who lived in the United States before World
War II had instead of resident families were the crowded ghettos
known as Chinatowns. These were simultaneously places of
physical and cultural refuge, bachelor dormitories, winter quarters, labor distribution centers, mercantile hubs, and vice districts. Men of every laboring status—employed, underemployed,
unemployed, and between seasonal jobs—crammed into cheap
hotels and apartments, as many as twenty to a room. They
pooled their pennies to purchase food, played mah-jongg on
packing-crate tables, slept in shifts in double or triple bunks.[20]
Chinese men who shuttled back and forth from Chinatowns
to the migrant labor camps in the countryside fared little better.
They worked all day picking apples or grapes and at night
squeezed into dreary bunkhouses, ten to a room. "Saturday
night's the only night you go out and do anything, if you do
anything at all," recalled Kam Wai, a long-time farm worker.
"Course, if you're married, it's a different thing altogether . . .
You might go to a show or something like that." But for single
men like himself Saturday night meant "time in a gambling
joint, that's one thing. Or I could go around to the prostitution

towns, making all the rounds . . . At that time, life didn't mean too much to us."[21]

But emotional and sexual release did, and that was the point of the Chinatown vice spots. Certain districts, such as the section of San Francisco bound by Stockton, Pacific, DuPont, and Washington streets, were virtual vice bazaars. Gambling parlors, brothels, and opium dens were chockablock with barber and pawn shops, restaurants, and lodging houses. Although Chinese vice practices varied in their cultural details, the economic and social consequences were the same as those in white bachelor laborer communities: more debt, more disease, more death, and more disorder.

Chinese workers and peasants believed in a world governed by fortune. Gamblers in a land of gamblers, they were drawn to games of chance that held out the prospect of economic freedom. A winning lottery ticket or a lucky night at the fan-tan table might mean debts cleared; a big bet a trip back to China— or into penury. Some laborers lost years of savings in a single night at the Chinatown gaming tables. Others became so impoverished through gambling that they could not set aside money to have their remains returned to their native villages, a cultural and religious catastrophe akin to being left in limbo.[22]

The pleasure and release purchased in a brothel set workers back from twenty-five to fifty cents, more if they visited a higher-class prostitute who maintained an exclusively Chinese clientele. (For the immigrants, in their own way as ethnocentric as their persecutors, the most disgusting thing Chinese women could do was to have sexual relations with white men, an act that declassed the women and lowered their value.) Fifty cents was half or more of a day's wages, and there was always the chance that venereal disease would ruin health and diminish earnings.[23]

Themes of regret and warning appear often in the *Jinshan ge ji* (Songs of Gold Mountain), a remarkable anthology of Cantonese vernacular poetry composed in San Francisco in the early 1910s:

> My life's half gone, but I'm still unsettled;
> I've erred, I'm an expert at whoring and gambling.
> Syphilis almost ended my life.

I turned to friends for a loan, but no one took pity on me.
Ashamed, frightened—
Now, I must wake up after this long nightmare;
Leap out of this misery and find my paradise.
But others laugh that old habits die hard and I'll never change.[24]

The hardest habit to shake was opium smoking, to which perhaps as many as one in four Chinese laborers was addicted. Though the Chinese seldom drank to excess, opium smoking was an economically equivalent vice, an unfortunate piece of cultural baggage the immigrants brought to America. The practice had been encouraged in China by the British, who illegally imported large quantities of Indian opium to China in the late eighteenth and early nineteenth centuries, ultimately forcing legalization of the trade through the Opium War of 1839–1842. Prior to 1842 the British had shipped their opium exclusively through the Canton area, the region from which most of the California-bound laborers were to come. Not all Cantonese immigrants were experienced opium smokers. But they certainly knew of the vice and had the opportunity to practice it when they came to America, away from restraining family influences. The Fook Hung Company of Hong Kong and other suppliers took advantage of the situation and shipped large quantities of the drug to the United States. Its importation was legal up to 1909, though subject to a sin tax in the form of a stiff customs duty.[25]

Weary Chinese laborers smoked opium in the evenings and on holidays to forget their troubles and lose themselves in pleasant reveries. But too many draws on the pipe could lead to addiction, and addiction cost fifty cents or more a day, fully half a laborer's earnings. An opium habit did not immediately destroy the ability and will to labor. Myths of stupefaction to the contrary, some addicts were able to keep working for years. "I'd smoke, go to work, come home, smoke again," one illegal Hong Kong immigrant told me, explaining how he juggled an opium habit and restaurant jobs in New York City in the 1920s. He smoked to work and worked to smoke, spending nearly all of his wages on the drug.[26]

Few could manage this trick indefinitely, however. Physicians and missionaries who worked with the Chinese observed that even moderate and self-disciplined smokers were on a slippery slope leading to compulsive use, anorexia, impotence, demoralization, idleness, poverty, and death. This was a common Chinese view as well:

> Face haggard, turning yellow and puffy,
> Waist, bent like a drawn bow.
> Lying on his side next to a small lit lamp,
> He holds the pipe as his family fortune goes down the hole.
> Look at him:
> Soon he will be six feet underground.
> Lazy, remiss, he won't move even if you drag him.
> He's about to meet King Yimlo at Hell's tenth palace.

King Yimlo was the mythological ruler of the eighteen palaces of the underworld and judge of mortal deeds. Chinese addicts who had the misfortune to be arrested and thrown into California jails must have thought themselves already in his domain. Their screams made the nights hideous with pleas for opium.[27]

The puking addicts, ruined gamblers, and diseased prodigals who could not return home represented more than lost lives and personal tragedies. Chinatown vice was systemic and so were its consequences. It would not be going too far to say that it was a form of organized parasitism. The professional gamblers and criminal societies that controlled the vice industry profited directly. Government officials collected fines and taxes on imported opium and took bribes. And the merchant-creditors and labor contractors prolonged their control over immigrants, who were bound to work until their debts were repaid. Chinese laborers slipped into the cycle of work and spree as easily as their white counterparts, but in their case the vicious circle was even harder to escape because of the added burden of debt.

Crime and Demography

Chinese made up a disproportionate number of those who were arrested and convicted of misdemeanors and felony crimes in the United States in the late nineteenth and early twentieth centuries. This was partly a matter of harassment, transparently so in the case of ordinances against such activities as "carrying

baskets with shoulder poles." Prejudice and selective prosecution inflated the number of Chinese arrests for gambling, prostitution, and drug-law offenses, though it should be kept in mind
that the violations were not simply fabrications and there is no
reason to doubt that Chinese were in fact heavily involved with
these vices. And prejudice alone cannot explain the disproportionate arrests of Chinese men for serious personal and property
crimes. In Portland, Oregon, for example, the Chinese made up
8 percent of the city's population from 1871 to 1885 but accounted for 31 percent of arrests for homicide, 21 for aggravated
assault, 14 for robbery, 30 for burglary, and 19 for larceny. As
might be expected from these figures, Chinese made up more
than their share of prison inmates. In 1890 the national rate of
imprisonment for "Mongolians" (Chinese plus the much less
numerous Japanese) was 3.8 times that of whites.[28]

Walter F. Willcox, the statistician who took note of these
prison figures, offered a simple explanation. "The Chinese and
Japanese in the United States are nearly all men," he wrote,
applying Ockham's Razor, "from which class prisoners mainly
come." Others have subsequently confirmed and elaborated this
judgment, arguing that the lawbreaking and widespread vice in
the early Chinese immigrant communities were rooted in their
demographic structure, which was partly (after 1882 largely) a
product of institutionalized racism. Prejudice and fear of labor
competition led to exclusionary and anti-miscegenation laws,
which prolonged gender imbalance, which increased crime and
fed the vice industry, which produced reams of lurid newspaper
publicity ("Heathen Life in Chinatown," "Slaves to Opium,"
"Her Back Was Burnt with Irons," and so on), which reinforced
prejudice and steeled the determination to maintain barriers
against entry and intermarriage, which further prolonged gender imbalance.[29]

The circularity of the problem was obvious to sympathetic
religious and reform figures. The Presbyterian women who established and presided over the Chinese Home Mission, a San
Francisco refuge for women trying to escape the brutal world
of the alley brothels, were opposed to exclusion, regarding open
immigration as a lesser evil than forced prostitution. The cru-
sading journalist Jacob Riis made a similar point about opium

smoking in New York's Chinatown. Riis, like many of his contemporaries, was disgusted by the presence of young white
women in Chinese opium dives. The practice, though exaggerated, was not wholly illusory. During the 1870s opium smoking
had spread from the Chinese to the American underworld and
had become an increasingly common vice of white prostitutes
and demimondaines. The specter of white women smoking
opium with supposedly scheming, lecherous Chinese men gave
more ammunition to the exclusionists and prompted a crack-
down on opium dens, particularly those frequented by white
patrons. But Riis drew a very different conclusion in *How the
Other Half Lives,* his 1890 exposé of life in the slums. "Rather
than banish the Chinaman I would have the door opened
wider—for his wife; make it a condition of his coming or staying that he bring his wife with him. Then, at least, he might
not be what he now is and remains, a homeless stranger
among us."[30]

The experience of the Japanese in America underscores Riis's
point and confirms, by way of contrast, the role of exclusion and
gender imbalance in explaining Chinese crime and vice. Male
Japanese laborers first entered the country in substantial numbers during the 1890s and continued to do so until the Gentlemen's Agreement of 1907–1908, an exchange of diplomatic
notes through which the Japanese government agreed to issue
no further passports to laborers bound for America. Although
the Japanese already in the United States experienced racial
discrimination, they did not initially face the same severe legal
barriers against family formation and reunification that confronted the Chinese. They were permitted to summon their
wives, to return to Japan to marry and then come back to the
United States, or, if sufficiently prosperous, to resort to *shashin
kekkon,* "photo marriage." This was a mail-order-bride system in
which photographs, letters, and intermediaries were used to
arrange long-distance marriages. Once an agreement had been
reached the "picture brides" could legally join their husbands in
the United States. Although there were occasional complaints
about retouched photographs, *shashin kekkon* worked quite
well—so well, in fact, that the overall Japanese gender ratio in
the United States fell precipitously. In California, where the

majority of Japanese lived, it dropped from 563 in 1910 to 172 just ten years later.[31]

Then the window of marital opportunity was slammed shut. In December 1919 the Japanese government decided to cease issuing passports to picture brides, largely to placate American exclusionists. In 1924 Congress effectively cut off Japanese immigration altogether. But by virtue of the influx of wives and brides in the first two decades of the century the Japanese had, relative to the Chinese, a head start on achieving a normal population distribution. The Japanese women who came to America were young and had a very high birth rate, three times that of white Americans. The Japanese population in the United States nearly doubled in twenty years, from 72,000 in 1910 to 139,000 in 1930, by which time fully half of the Japanese were native-born Americans.[32]

These demographic differences showed up in numbers of arrests. In 1928 the family-centered Japanese community of Stockton, California, which made up about 5.5 percent of the local population, accounted for only 0.4 percent of all arrests and no serious crimes. The pattern was reversed for the Chinese in San Francisco in fiscal year 1929: their share of arrests was more than three times their share of the urban population. Of course San Francisco's Chinatown was still a vice center and home to a large number of single laborers, aging yet more likely than married men or women and children to get caught in gambling and drug raids.[33]

Vice, Violence, and Organized Crime

The thriving Chinatown vice industry also gave rise to violence, although in not quite the same way it did in white mining camps and cattle towns. Opium, the Chinese intoxicant of choice, was a powerful tranquilizer. Those who were under its influence seldom exhibited the irritable aggressiveness of men drinking liquor in saloons, nor did they beat women and children. But opium smoking did lead to theft by impoverished addicts, especially after prohibitory federal legislation drove up the price of the drug. The opium traffic was also an indirect cause of criminal violence in the form of rivalry among the tongs, secret Chinese organizations that fought for control of the vice industry.[34]

The tongs' oath-bound members employed systematic bribery, intimidation, and violence to keep people in line and illicit revenues flowing. In this they closely resembled the Mafia families, their later and more famous counterparts. Tong members made money by extorting protection money from Chinese businessmen, but the key to their success was steady profit from what were essentially male vices. The tongs smuggled opium to avoid the high duty and legal restrictions against Chinese importers. They supplied the opium dens, which were outlawed in most cities. They ran gambling houses and earned income from brothels, either through direct ownership or through the collection of an extortionate tax on prostitutes. When someone tried to muscle in or refused to pay a debt, "highbinders" (a word that originally referred to Irish toughs but was extended to Chinese enforcers) were dispatched to settle accounts. The highbinders also pursued men who ran off with their prostitutes, a common though not surprising occurrence, given the shortage of women.[35]

If the culprit was a member of another tong, the result could be warfare. "You want to know how a lot of tong wars started?" asked Big Pete, a seventy-two-year-old gambler and member of the Suey Sing Tong, interviewed in the early 1970s. "Say, I own a girl and somebody tries to take her away from me and he succeeds. If he happens to belong to a different tong or a different family, that's it. He pays the damage." The damage might amount to $5,000, the cost of purchasing and smuggling the girl into the country. "He can have her," Big Pete continued, "but he gotta pay that five thousand dollars or he'll never see those lights again!" Lew Wah Get, an eighty-four-year-old officer of the same tong, remembered the last big fight in 1921. It erupted when the rival Hop Sing Tong took over a prostitute and refused to reimburse the expense of her illegal importation. "Not only that, but while they were doing business with us, they shot and killed one of our members . . . We decided to take revenge and fight back." The ensuing war lasted ten months and required an outside mediating committee to settle matters.[36]

Tong warfare had a cultural as well as an economic dimension. The Cantonese were, in the words of Chinese Imperial

Commissioner Ji Ying, a violent and obstinate people who were "fond of brawls and made light of their lives." Known for their clannishness, physical courage, and alertness, the Cantonese immigrants in some ways resembled the rugged backwoodsmen from the fringes of northern and western Europe, with the important difference that their ideas of prestige and retaliation were centered on the group instead of the individual. When challenged tongs were capable of extremely violent and seemingly irrational responses, fighting pitched battles over unpaid debts as small as $15 "with every conceivable weapon." In the early days the weapons often included small axes, hence the term "hatchet men," a synonym for highbinders and a colorful addition to the American language. But the hatchets were quickly supplanted by revolvers concealed in the billowing sleeves of the highbinders' outer garments. In the twentieth century machine guns briefly came into fashion.[37]

By then, however, organized violence was subsiding. Gauging the extent of tong membership and conflict is difficult, as these were things the Chinese concealed. At their peak in 1882–1906 the tongs employed perhaps three thousand fighting men, or roughly 3 percent of the total Chinese population. Five hundred to a thousand of these were active in San Francisco's Chinatown, the largest in the United States. The highbinders' depredations finally became so disruptive and scandalous that Chinese consular officials threatened to imprison tong members' relatives in China for crimes committed in the United States, a drastic form of legal blackmail that appears to have had some deterrent effect. The 1906 earthquake and fire also hurt the San Francisco tongs by destroying their accustomed headquarters, hideouts, and flow of income from vice dens.[38]

Even without the fire and the official threats the tongs could not have prospered indefinitely. Chinese gangsterism in America was the criminal epiphenomenon of an artificial bachelor society. When the sojourners returned to China or died and the American-born population finally began to increase rapidly, involvement in gambling, prostitution, and narcotics sharply declined and with it illicit revenue that sustained and gave purpose to the tongs. By the 1940s and 1950s, if not before, they and their sworn members had become aging anachronisms, widely ignored by the growing, family-centered, middle-class Chinese-American community to which the future belonged.[39]

Other Lower-Class Immigrant Groups

The historical experience of the Chinese laborers in America was unique in that they were the only major lower-class male immigrant group deliberately denied access to spouses and families for such a long period. In this regard paupers and slaves were treated with more consideration than the Chinese. James Oglethorpe, who in 1732 founded Georgia as a refuge for debtors and as a buffer against Spanish Florida, soon learned that it was essential to send women to join his male colonists. This was true, he wrote, for reasons of both social order ("from single men there are great Inconveniences") and population growth, natural increase being "much the cheapest way of peopling the Country."[40]

The male slaves who made up a large and growing percentage of the population in eighteenth-century southern colonies were likewise provided with women, and for reasons equally as calculated. Explaining in 1769 why he ordered young African women sent to his Mount Royal and Amelia Island plantations in British East Florida, John Perceval, Earl of Egmont, wrote that he wished to render his male slaves "happy and contented, which I know they cannot be without having each a Wife." Imported wives, he reasoned, "will greatly tend to keep them at home and to make them Regular and tho the Women will not work all together so well as ye Men, Yet Amends will be sufficiently made in a very few years by the Great Encrease of Children who may easily [be trained] and become faithfully attached to the Glebe and their Master." Slave children represented both a natural dividend and an emotional lever. Their fathers might be induced to work harder to earn extra rations for them or to prevent them from being sold. The one drawback was absenteeism occasioned by visiting "broad wives," spouses who lived away from ("abroad" of) the home plantation. A stock piece of slaveowners' advice was to minimize this problem by forbidding unions elsewhere and encouraging them, if at all possible, within their own quarters.[41]

Such was not the case with Chinese laborers. If they and their children had been enslaved in the same way that black Africans were, or if they had been objects of humanitarian sympathy and military design, like Georgia's white debtors, no objection would have been raised to the immigration of wives or marriageable Chinese women. They were instead despised and unwanted and hence subject to more than half a century of exclusionary legislation and court rulings, perhaps the greatest injustice in the history of federal immigration policy.

Chinese exclusion was also arguably the most counterproductive policy, illustrating how racial (and, secondarily, class) prejudice undermined the social order. The role of racial hatred was crudely obvious when a riot erupted or a Chinese man's genitals were hacked off, but its most powerful and long-term consequences were indirect, the result of forcing large numbers of men to live as de facto bachelors. In this regard the unwillingness of Anglo frontiersmen in the West to take Indian or Hispanic wives and their determination to block Chinese marriage or family reunification were deeply parallel. Both prejudices were grounded in a sense of contemptuous superiority and the belief that the new land and its future belonged to the white race. Both had the result of frustrating marriage and family formation. And both had the predictable and unhappy consequences of more vice, more violence, and more disorder.

NINE

The Floating Army

The geographically and ethnically uneven distribution of American violence and disorder to the end of the nineteenth century can be explained by three sets of factors, one cultural, one racial, and one demographic. Cultural beliefs and habits, like southern sensibilities about guns and honor or the Irish penchant for aggressive drinking, help explain why some regions or groups consistently had higher rates of murder and mayhem. Racism was important both because it encouraged and exacerbated conflict with minorities, such as the Indians, and because it contributed to the economic marginalization of black men and restrictions on Chinese immigration. Then there were local and regional variations in population structure, notably the age and gender imbalances on the nonagricultural frontier. Through a combination of pooled biological tendencies, widespread bachelorhood, and male group dynamics, these produced more drinking, gambling, prostitution, quarreling, carrying of weapons, and other traits associated with bad ends. The ensuing high level of violence was like a passing epidemic. It raged for a time in heavily male frontier regions and then subsided as the migrant population became more balanced.

This is, I trust, a persuasive model consistent with historical and scientific evidence, the laws of probability, and common sense. The one obvious qualification is that the last factor, regional variation in population structure, diminished in importance after about 1890, the date popularized by Frederick Jackson Turner as the closing of the frontier. Whether and precisely when the frontier actually closed has occasioned the expenditure of much scholarly ammunition, Turner's words having on America's historians roughly the same effect as population imbalance on its society.[1] This, at least, is clear: western regional gender ratios continued to decline rapidly during and after the 1880s and 1890s, as shown in Figure 9.1. The east-west gender polarization of the American population, so apparent in the two decades before and immediately after the Civil War, had become muted by the early twentieth century.

Which is not to say that single male migrants and their problems disappeared from American society. Overseas immigration remained voluminous and disproportionately male; the national gender ratio remained high, peaking at 106 in 1910; and pockets of bachelor laborers could be found all over the country.[2] Many, perhaps most, of these surplus men moved continuously in search of work. The search might take them from orchard to city to lumber camp to oil town to hobo jungle to copper mine to wheat field and back to the city again. They were not frontiersmen in the conventional sense of remote western pioneers and settlers, though many spent at least part of their working lives in the developing West. Such men were common enough in the antebellum era, working on projects like canal construction, but their real heyday was from the late 1860s to about 1920.

Migrant Labor and the Urban-Industrial Transformation

These were the years of America's transformation into an urban and industrial nation. In 1860 most Americans still lived on farms or in small towns connected by meandering dirt roads. They labored with plow and churn and hand tools to produce agricultural and artisanal products for an economy in which the value of farm output still exceeded that of factories. The Civil War that was about to engulf them was fought by farmers, field hands, and craftsmen who had grown up in a casual, small-scale world.[3]

Sixty years later that world was as dead as the men who had fallen at Antietam. By 1920 most Americans lived in large towns

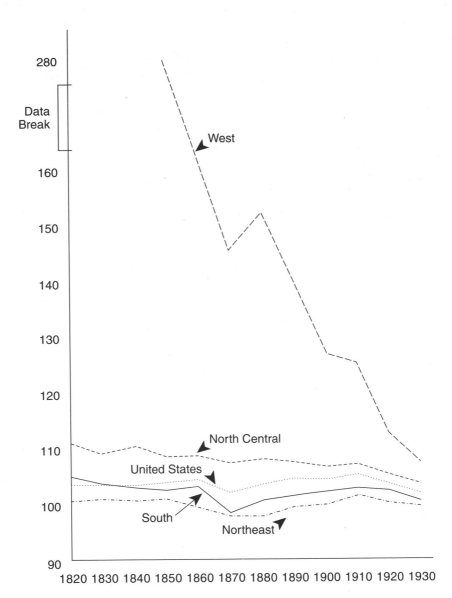

280

Data
Break

160

150

140

130

120

110

100

90

1820 1830 1840 1850 1860 1870 1880 1890 1900 1910 1920 1930

West

North Central

United States

South

Northeast

Figure 9.1 Regional gender ratios, 1820–1930. Adapted from Warren S. Thompson and P. K. Whelpton, *Population Trends in the United States* (rpt. New York: Gordon and Breach, 1969), 28n1, 182.

or rapidly growing cities connected by nearly 300,000 miles of railroads. They labored with the help of machinery powered by steam, electricity, and other inanimate forms of energy, the consumption of which had increased seven times since 1860. The Great War of their era was fought with divisions as regimented and mechanized as the new industrial order.[4]

The urban-industrial transformation could not have occurred without an infrastructure, the expanding web of tracks, bridges, roads, canals, docks, warehouses, sewers, and telegraph lines that knit the system together. Nor would it have been possible without a continuing flow of raw materials, fuel, and food for the factories and the cities. All of this was provided by a floating army, half a million or more strong, of itinerant workers who built and fed modern America. Now vanished and largely forgotten, they were overwhelmingly male and single and under forty and were commonly, if not quite accurately, called tramps.[5]

The primary means by which tramps traveled to their far-flung work was the interurban rail network. Largely completed by the mid-1880s, the main lines connected hubs like Chicago with vast grain and timber lands that required seasonal workers. When they were not laboring in the countryside or working on the railroad itself, these itinerant men often returned to what they called the main stems, the low-rent city neighborhoods near the marshaling yards where lodging houses, greasy spoons, used-clothing stores, pawnshops, missions, soup kitchens, employment agencies, saloons, burlesque houses, and brothels could be found in abundance. The main stem of any city was in effect a non-Chinese Chinatown, a place where homeless, single men spent the winter months, collected information about job prospects, and blew off steam and wages.[6]

The main stems were located chiefly in northern, midwestern, and western cities. Few were in the South, a region that floaters tended to avoid because it had fewer cities, railroads, jobs, lodging houses, and other prerequisites of tramp life. The South also had a reputation for penal abuses. A tramp who caught the eye of the local sheriff could find himself in the county jail on a vagrancy charge and then leased out as a convict laborer. The work camps, where the annual death rates ranged from under 5 to as high as 40 percent, were hell on convicts though cruelly useful for developing the South's lumber and mineral resources and building its roads. The one offsetting attraction of the South was its milder winter, which emboldened some tramps to make a seasonal pilgrimage to such coastal cities as New Orleans, St. Augustine, and Jacksonville. The snow-birds had to be extremely cautious, however, "for the jails in the South are man-killing holes in many and many an instance."[7]

Black men who traveled about the South in search of work had to tread even more carefully. Few prospects awaited them in southern towns and cities, where the demand for black labor was for female domestics. But there were jobs to be had on large plantations, in lumber and turpentine camps, sawmills, mines, mills, and railroad and levee construction sites. This rural-versus-urban pattern of opportunities for black men and women created local gender imbalances and separated family members. It also put migrant workers at grave risk, for white anxieties about race were focused on peripatetic black men. A local black resident who had a little property and for whom whites would vouch was relatively safe, but a black stranger accused of vagrancy or petty theft was likely to be condemned to hard labor, or worse. Although lynchings of black men are usually understood as a universal southern phenomenon, they were, like other forms of violence, unevenly distributed. The counties with the highest numbers of lynchings were those with high levels of black transiency and a thin and scattered white population fearful of those whom they called "strange niggers."[8]

Outside the South most tramps were white and native-born. Those born abroad came mainly from the English-speaking lands of northwestern Europe. Their familiarity with the language contributed to the widespread impression that tramping was an essentially American phenomenon, although in fact the Irish, long identified with itinerant construction work, were consistently overrepresented in tramp surveys. So were unskilled or semiskilled workers. Teamsters, hostlers, graders, field hands, and other manual laborers were the ones most likely to ride the rails in search of work. Skilled and white-collar workers drifted in search of jobs only during serious depressions, when the number of homeless itinerants sharply, if temporarily, increased. Conversely, when wars broke out and the demand for soldiers and war workers grew, the number of tramps noticeably declined.[9]

A Dangerous Subculture

The floating army was a subculture in several senses of the term. Its members were socially marginal, shared traits like maleness and bachelorhood, spoke a common argot, and gravitated toward the ghettoized and gender-segregated main stems. But it was a special and highly unstable kind of subculture, one that was constantly expanding and contracting and one in which its members participated with markedly different degrees of persistence and enthusiasm.

Veteran men, the "repeaters," "revolvers," and "blowed-in-the-glass tramps," formed the core of the subculture. They were the homeless, long-term migrants who called themselves "profesh," short for professionals, and claimed to be proud of their calling. "It's habit forming," one hobo explained; "it's a disease . . . you piss out a boxcar once, you're hooked." When most people think of hobos or tramps, it is this sort of sentimentalized figure who comes to mind.[10]

But for most men tramping was a temporary expedient, a means of acquiring a first job, replacing a lost one, or earning a small stake. For others it was a way of escaping routinized work. The novelist Sinclair Lewis called them a cheerful pariahdom, restless young men with bundles and black sateen shirts who would suddenly light out and drift from state to state. "They are not permanently tramps," he observed. "They have home towns to which they return, to work quietly in the factory or the section gang for a year—for a week—and as quietly to disappear again."[11]

All of which sounds fine, opportunistic, adventuresome—in a word, American. To believe this, however, is to believe a fiction. Life in the floating army was cruel and precarious, especially if it became extended. The longer a worker stayed on the tramp the more likely he was to be maimed, imprisoned, diseased, or killed.

The worst danger was the railroad itself. Tramps got around by "flippin'"—stealing rides on trains. They clambered into, between, on top of, and even under the cars, a risky technique called riding the rods. They usually made their moves in darkness, lowering the chance of detection but increasing the risk of a misstep and fall onto a rolling guillotine. In one five-year period, 1901–1905, nearly 24,000 railroad trespassers were killed in accidents and another 25,000 were injured. Many of the injured became single or double amputees, known among tramps as "halfies," and were reduced to a life of begging and penury.[12]

Those who left the rail yards with their bodies intact were by no means safe. The lumbering, mining, and construction industries to which they flocked were dangerous and unhealthful. John Fitzmaurice, a journalist who wrote a classic account of life in the lumber camps, estimated that in Michigan alone in the logging season of 1884–1885 about 3,000 of the 40,000 loggers became ill. Another 3,000 were injured and 60 were killed outright, dispatched by blows so crushing that pocket watches were flattened and their works reduced to small fragments. Conditions were equally bad in the northwestern lumber camps and mills, where men lost arms to unshielded saws and counted lost fingers beneath notice.[13]

Worse yet were the mines, smoke- and urine-filled pits where men were cheaper than timber and every bit as replaceable. They perished in cave-ins, were electrocuted when their tools touched uninsulated high-voltage wires, and were blown to bits by dynamite. At times supervisors had to puzzle out who and how many were dead by checking the living against the payroll.[14]

Lung diseases plagued miners and tunnelers. The best known of these, silicosis, afflicted men who blasted and drilled through granite, sandstone, or anthracite coal. Just how devastating silicosis was and with what indifference its victims were treated is illustrated by the Hawk's Nest incident. This involved a hydroelectric tunnel drilled beneath Gauley Mountain, West Virginia, between March 1930 and September 1931. Within five years at least 764 of the 5,000 workers had died of silicosis. Their deaths could have been prevented by wet drilling, a simple technique in which streams of water were used to suppress airborne dust. But wet drilling was as much as 50 percent slower, and Union

Carbide and its contractors stood to save money if the work was completed quickly. Though the power drills had hose attachments, the tunnel workers, mostly black migrants, had to drill and excavate without water, surrounded by clouds of silica dust so thick that they could not see more than a few feet. Respirators were issued to the engineering staff when they went into the tunnel but not to the migrant crews. It was as if the workers were used and discarded.[15]

Even in industries like agriculture, where the risks of trauma and occupational disease were not particularly high, migrant workers perished at rates much higher than would be expected of men in the prime of life. From 1906 through 1913 Japanese consular officials kept track of deaths among the Issei, the Japanese immigrants in California. The influx of wives and picture brides was only beginning to transform the Japanese population, which in those years still consisted mostly of unmarried men in their twenties and thirties who lived in primitive agricultural work camps. The average death rate of Issei aged fifteen and older was at least 11.3 per thousand per year, a rate roughly 50 percent higher than men of comparable age in the general population.[16]

Four percent of the Issei deaths were suicides. I know of no comparable estimate for non-Japanese migrant workers, although there is eyewitness medical testimony that suicide by opium overdose was widespread among Chinese laborers too sick or injured to work and much anecdotal or newspaper evidence of suicides among white floaters. Tramps pitched themselves off buildings, swallowed cyanide, hanged themselves from trestles, or blew their brains out by railway embankments. The drink-anything alcoholism of skid-row tramps can be understood as a kind of slow-motion suicide of those past caring about early death. These sad ends were, in one sense, to be expected, given the mass of empirical research showing that suicide is most common among unmarried and socially isolated men.[17]

The risk of homicide was also high, judging from the fragmentary statistics for the end-of-tracks towns in which railroad work crews squandered their wages. Julesburg, Benton, and the other railroad construction sites were the most murderous places in the United States, worse even than the mining camps and cattle towns. It seems that many of the supposedly accidental deaths of railroad trespassers were really acts of negligent manslaughter or homicide committed by railroad police who threw tramps off trains. Other undetected murders were perpetrated by "yeggs," roving criminals who slugged train-jumping workers returning from the harvest, stole their wages, and tossed their bodies onto the tracks.[18]

Exploitation and Counter-Exploitation

Theft and robbery were facts of life in the floating army. Though most men were interested in honest employment and took to the rails for the purpose of finding it, there were among them those who did not hesitate to steal if the opportunity arose, including hard-core tramps who disdained all work and specialized in panhandling and theft. Snoring drunks, henhouses, and melon patches were favorite targets and so, for obvious reasons, were the contents of railroad boxcars. Train jumpers rifled crates and boxes looking for portable or edible objects, often damaging the rest or burning them for warmth. Sometimes the fires got out of control, sending whole boxcars up in smoke.[19]

This posed a dilemma for the railroads. On the one hand tramps were a useful pool of itinerant labor. They worked in railroad construction and maintenance crews and provided the means of picking, harvesting, and extracting the commodities the railroads profitably hauled from place to place. In this sense the fares lost to trespassers were really a means of subsidizing the transportation costs of the labor that made railroads possible in the first place.

On the other hand pilferage and damaged equipment were serious problems. By the 1890s railroad officials had concluded that the nuisance cost of tramps outweighed their labor value, which was declining as more and more of the infrastructure was completed and as seasonal work in the West and Midwest was taken over by local laborers. They beefed up their private security forces and dispatched burly men with guns and truncheons to deal with the tramps, who hated the railroad bulls and did everything in their power to avoid them.[20]

Municipal police likewise changed their policies toward tramps during the 1890s. Prior to that decade it was common for police stations to lodge tramps at night, admitting them to sleep on the floor or in unused cells, providing a little soup or bread and, on occasion, mandatory vaccinations, though the indignant tramps swore they had recently been "scraped." Nineteenth-century police were in the business, as the historian Eric Monkkonen puts it, of managing the "dangerous class" of which tramps were a part. Sensibly enough this management entailed rudimentary welfare services as well as selective repression in the form of arrests. However, reformers like Josephine Lowell and Theodore Roosevelt objected to police lodging because it crowded the station houses with verminous and supposedly idle men without requiring any work from them. During the 1890s they were able to shut down or substantially reduce police lodging operations. From the early twentieth century on police officers, apart from mercifully arresting the odd gutter drunk to keep him from freezing, abandoned their welfare functions and concentrated on crime suppression and traffic control.[21]

This reorientation meant that the police were increasingly in an adversarial position vis-à-vis the tramps. When citizens became anxious about the presence of homeless, unemployed men, as happened in San Luis Obispo County, California, after 1895, the police responded by stepping up arrests for vagrancy and petty theft. Concern for economy led to chain gangs both to offset the cost of the prisoners' board and to discourage the presence of other tramps, who were imagined to be incorrigibly lazy.[22]

Tramps saw the matter differently. Vagrancy laws and chain gangs were to them a form of legalized slavery, an unjust punishment for the crime of being temporarily out of work. Their unemployment itself was often of an illegal nature. Private employment agents, "labor sharks," were known to sign up men for attractive jobs, pocket their finders' fees, and ship the men off to remote destinations where the jobs either did not exist or were inferior to the ones advertised. A common variation on this racket was the three-gang system. Collusive contractors kept one crew coming, one working, and one going by quickly firing the newly hired workers, splitting the fees with the employment agents who kept sending a fresh supply of victims. The extreme of exploitation was achieved by a South Dakota sheepman named Kunnecke, who made a habit of hiring floating herders. He worked them for six months or a year and then, to avoid paying their wages, murdered them and buried their bodies.[23]

The frustration of irregular employment and rage against employer abuses had political consequences. In 1894, in the depths of a severe depression, the Populist businessman Jacob Coxey led a contingent of several hundred unemployed men in a march on Washington. The aim was to petition the government to finance road building and other relief measures. Coxey's was only one of seventeen different "armies" of unemployed men to begin marching on Washington that year, but his was the best known and came to symbolize the movement. The last major west-to-east men's protest march in American history, Coxey's Army was but a shadow of the wild seventeenth- and eighteenth-century frontier insurrections. It was easily suppressed—Coxey was arrested by police and charged with damaging the Capitol's grass—though not before his ragtag marchers had managed to arouse a good deal of fear and had secured for themselves a place in the hard times of American history.[24]

A similar feat was achieved by the Industrial Workers of the World. Founded in 1905, the IWW was a revolutionary anticapitalist union that drew most of its members from the ranks of unskilled and itinerant workers, principally the loggers and miners and bindle stiffs who endured the hard life of western labor camps. The chief organizer of the IWW, the one-eyed William D. "Big Bill" Haywood, understood their world only too well. Before he became active in the union he had been a bunkhouse miner, cowboy, prospector, surveyor, thresher, farmer, and saloon poker dealer. Haywood and other IWW organizers played upon the grievances of the floating army, including the fact that few men could afford to marry. At first they enjoyed considerable recruiting success, despite police harassment. By 1917 the union had 100,000 members and hobo train jumpers carrying red IWW cards were a common sight. But the IWW's strong opposition to American involvement in the European war made the organization unpopular and vulnerable. Concerted action by vigilantes and government officials disrupted its leadership and put more than 2,000 members behind bars. The IWW survived the persecution but never recovered anything like its prewar influence and strength.[25]

Part of the IWW's problem was its reputation for industrial violence and sabotage, a reputation based on its class-war rhetoric. Whether or how the IWW delivered on its threats is another matter. "No Wobbly," points out the historian Joseph Conlin, "was ever proved to have committed an act of violence." Sabotage, when it occurred, most often took the passive-aggressive form of slowdowns, a tactic implicit in the IWW motto "Good pay or bum work." When IWW members were actually involved in violence it was more often as victims of mob action than as perpetrators of radical terror.[26]

It would be a mistake, however, to conclude that tramp terrorism was a myth. It did exist, though as a result of spontaneous, uncoordinated actions and not as a revolutionary conspiracy. One victim was John Ovenbeck, a farmer in Friendship, Wisconsin, who in unfriendly fashion refused food to hungry tramps. They returned to his barn later that night and slashed the throats of three of his cows. Ovenbeck found a note jabbed on one of their horns: "Remember us when we call for something to eat again." Other tramps in a mood for vengeance set fire to straw, hurled rocks at "horstile" train crews, and shot it out with interloping brakemen.[27]

The most dreaded form of tramp crime was the robbery and murder of isolated rural dwellers. Waldo Cook, who published the first systematic study of homicide in Massachusetts, summarized one such case:

> Allan J. Adams killed Moses B. Dickinson November 25, 1875. Dickinson was a farmer who lived alone outside Amherst town. Adams came along tramp fashion and was hired by Dickinson to do farm work. The murder was done with an axe, and the motive was robbery. Adams was of native stock, lazy, and of very low type of character. He was a cider drinker.

There was not then and is not now any consensus as to how common serious criminal behavior was among tramps, cider drinkers or otherwise. One study of three Montana counties for 1895–1915 is at least suggestive, however. Beaverhead, the county that consistently had the highest rate of arrests for major

crimes, was the one most heavily dependent on large numbers
of seasonal workers for cutting hay. It was common for floating
laborers to use aliases, changing their names as often as once a
month when the paymaster opened a new time book. "This was
the custom," remarked one who had changed his own name
three times, "as so many who went out there were just one jump
ahead of the sheriff."[28]

Though hinting at a tramp-crime connection, this evidence in
no way proves that a majority of itinerant workers engaged in
serious crimes of robbery and vengeance. It is quite possible that
some drifters were accused and convicted unfairly, singled out for
convenient and ritualistic prosecution, so many virgins tossed
into the volcano to appease the criminal-justice gods. Several
towns in Ohio and Indiana dispensed with judicial trappings altogether and subjected unlucky tramps to "timber lessons," vigilante gauntlets organized by local boys and men. "I came out of
the scrape with a rather sore back," wrote Josiah Flynt Willard,
who was forced to run through Oxford, Indiana, under a barrage
of blows and stones. "One of my fellow-sufferers, I heard, was in
a hospital for some time. My other companion had his eye gouged
terribly, and I fancy that he will never visit that town again."[29]

Tramps, in short, were suspect men picking their way through
a social minefield. Their talk in the rail-yard jungles, as they ate
their mulligan and drank coffee made from reused beans, constantly turned to the question of "horstiles"—those train crews,
sheriffs, railroads, towns, and states that were to be avoided.
Stay out of "Lousy Anna," they warned one another, but the
"Milk and Honey route" in Utah was all right. The Mormons
were generous and would usually give a hobo a break.

Tramps had their own signs, cryptic symbols chalked on gates
and barns and water tanks, which gave detailed directions
through the local minefield to those able to read them. An X or
a rotund female figure followed by three stick children meant a
kind woman, good for a handout—hence the expression that
someone is a mark. But a C warned of a cheap town, linked
circles the handcuffs of hostile police, and a 6 a possible six-
month term in jail. A comb, its teeth signifying a dog, warned
tramps of lurking canines, while a slanted stick figure scrawled
in haste meant "run like hell."[30]

"Just a Common Drunk": Fourth Precinct Station House, Oak Street, New York City, 22 February 1895, 11:15 P.M. The sergeant on duty explained to John James McCook that police patrols would be augmented after midnight "because saloons close and send their contents out to commit disorder."

Bound for Potter's Field: the morgue, New York City, 23 February 1895. Homelessness, alcoholism, and violent death have been disproportionately male problems throughout American history.

THE NEW LIBERTY 22-CALIBER
REVOLVER.
$1.29

We have a large demand for a revolver at a lower price than the double action revolver costs, and in order to fill the demand we have gotten out the New Liberty Revolver in 22-caliber. The Liberty Revolver is fitted with a 2½-inch smooth bored barrel, 7-shot, fancy rubber handle, nickel plated throughout, and shoots the 22-caliber short rim fire cartridge. Weighs about 7 ounces and is 5¼ inches long. It is as well made as any single action revolver selling generally for $1.50 to $2.00.

Catalogue Number	Caliber	Length of Barrel	Finish	No. of Shots	Weight	Price
6K1489	22 rim	2½ in.	Nickeled	7	7 ozs.	$1.29

If by mail, postage extra, 10 cents. Insured mail, 15 cents.

Mail-order gun, 1908: from the Sears, Roebuck and Company catalog. Men in groups make for competition; men drinking in groups make for trouble; men drinking in groups with cheap handguns in their pockets make for homicide, usually of an unpremeditated sort.

Sat. Oct. 30, 1943

Hi sis —

Well here I am in Port Hueneme, Calif. livin' in a tent and learnin' to be a commando!

The bos'n keeps us pretty much on the jump but in spite of all his efforts to break me both physically + morally I'm feeling better than I have for a long time. Never the less there is lots to do so I'll

The bos'n is trying to break me both physically and morally: illustrated letter from boot camp, 1943. The armed forces have historically inculcated masculine vices and hardened attitudes in recruits.

"Two Pike County Arrivals": a Frederic Remington illustration for an article on early California in *Century Magazine*, 1890. "Pike is a county in the state of Missouri noted for its huge stature and rough disposition of its inhabitants," wrote Colonel Richard Irving Dodge. Thousands of such men—but few women—flocked to California after the discovery of gold.

"The Used-Up Man": from Alonzo Delano's *Pen Knife Sketches*, 1853. The last line of the accompanying poem is "I'm living dead in Califor-nee."

"Judge Lynch," California, 1848, as imagined by Stanley Berkeley in 1905. Improbable in several details—melodramatic poses, sturdy fence, tidy cabin, glazed widows with mullions and transoms— the subject matter was nevertheless real enough. Note the pistol by the murderer's boot and the two black faces in the crowd, one peering over the brush pile behind the cabin.

Miners and recently arrived immigrants sleeping in the sawdust of a saloon in Leadville, Colorado, circa 1880. Saloon proprietors charged anywhere from a dime to fifty cents for the privilege.

"Here lies poor Jack; his race is run," by C. M. Russell, 1901. Cowboy life was dangerous on and off the trail. Men were killed by everything from lightning strikes, rabid skunk bites, and stampedes to gun accidents, drunken misadventures, and saloon brawls.

A trader offers a Plains Indian a bottle of whiskey. From *Leslie's Illustrated Weekly*, 23 September 1871. The introduction of liquor was a disaster for North American Indians and indirectly for the environment, as Indians increased their hunting and trapping to barter for alcohol and other commodities.

Rabbit hunters on the Kansas prairie. The photograph, half of an Underwood and Underwood stereograph, is probably from around 1900. Note the posing of the most successful hunters in the foreground and the range of ages. Hunting was a male initiation ritual that transmitted enthusiasm for killing game across generations; by the time this photograph was taken the Kansas prairie contained only a fraction of the wild animals it had supported half a century before.

"The Danites": an undated cartoon satirizing the instant and assiduous court-ship of eligible young women in western mining districts.

Julia Etta Parkerson Reynolds, Alvin Reynolds, and their son, William, in 1883.

An anti-Chinese cartoon, better drawn than spelled, from the *Wasp*, a satirical San Francisco newspaper, 1876. The Reverends Otis Gibson and Augustus Ward Loomis, whose views are being attacked, were Protestant missionaries and outspoken defenders of the West Coast Chinese.

Lumberjacks' bunk house, Minnesota. Unmarried men in their twenties and thirties, lumberjacks worked so hard that they consumed more than 5,000 calories a day. Apart from indulgences like tobacco, they had few opportunities to spend their wages in the woods and so accumulated a "stake" worth between $200 and $400 by the end of the season.

"Riding the Rods" as demonstrated by Providence Bob and Philadelphia Shorty, two experienced train flippers, on 5 December 1894. The grooved board that straddles the rod was known as a "ticket." A slip meant death or serious injury.

"A Timber Lesson": from Josiah Flynt Willard's *Tramping with Tramps* (1899). "I must say that it is one of the best remedies for vagabondage that exist," he wrote of the gauntlet. "But it is very crude and often cruel."

John James McCook presiding over his Trinity College classroom. Deeply religious yet socially cost-conscious, he worried about saving men's souls and taxpayers' dollars. An indignant concern over large municipal expenditures for alms in Hartford led to his pioneering study of tramps.

William "Roving Bill" Aspinwall, 8 June 1893. McCook paid to have this studio shot made by a photographer in Bennington, Vermont, so that he might have some idea of what Aspinwall looked like. Aspinwall's moniker was a sure sign that he was a confirmed member of the tramp subculture, though his tool kit and neat clothes showed that he was among the elite, not a vulgar "shovel bum."

The Billy Goat saloon, 153 Park Row, East Side, New York City, 22 February 1895. The owner, Bernard Kommel, is in the left foreground, facing the camera. McCook estimated that there were forty-five to fifty men in the long room, only one of whom was black and most of whom were bums. Kommel insisted they were longshoremen and that he "wouldn't let a bum stay."

SPEAKING OF VICE—

Anti-saloon cartoon, 1911. Dry propaganda to the contrary, saloons were not completely exploitative. Their keepers passed on job information and sometimes served as informal bankers, holding a man's stake for the winter. But the long-term financial consequences of saloon patronage—symbolized here by the falling coins, patched knee, and emasculating crush of the saloon vice—were undoubtedly bad.

Wedding photograph, taken 18 March 1944 for Yeoman Second Class Paul W. Heinz of the USS Ranger. The great marriage boom began during the war and continued through the late 1940s and 1950s.

California gunfighters, circa 1970. Children, boys especially, mimicked frontier action heros. The unanswered question: How much actual impact did violence in the media have on postwar homicide and other violent crime rates?

Despair of an old head, Red Hook, Brooklyn.

Street portrait, North Philadelphia. The crack epidemic was accompanied by a big increase in the number of emergency-room patients with multiple gunshot wounds.

Inmates watching television at the Detention Center of St. Johns County, Florida, 1994. As part of a popular "get-tough" policy toward crime, county prisoners are only permitted to watch the Public Broadcasting Service affiliate between 7:00 and 11:00 P.M. Viewing habits on the outside are more latitudinarian.

Michael Bell, new frontiersman, on trial for first-degree murder. He was convicted in 1995 of killing two young men outside a Jacksonville, Florida, liquor
store by firing thirty AK-47 rounds into their car. "Finally got his ass," said Bill
Bolena, the homicide detective who had been pursuing him since the late
1980s. "He's the most vicious guy I've ever arrested."

Clambering Out of the Social Pit

In retrospect the floating army had "run like hell" chalked all over it. Although itinerant work may have been a reasonable choice for a young man just starting out or for an unemployed man trying to ride out hard times, it was a guaranteed dead end for anyone who tried to make a career of it and a trip to potter's field for those who stayed too long. Social historians have long noted the paradox that, despite nineteenth-century Americans' habit of moving restlessly from place to place, the surest route to wealth and power was staying put. To set down roots in a community, or at any rate in one that was not in irreversible decline, was to acquire access to valuable information about jobs and investment opportunities, to make friends and gain trust, to meet potential spouses, and to have a chance to accumulate the credit and property that made family life possible.[31]

The one notable exception was the foreman who had charge of the bachelor work crews. Though often on the move, he generally earned enough to support a family and, as was common practice on ranches and in lumber camps, could live with his wife in separate quarters. This situation invited jealousy, or at least unfulfilled longing. "She was a young, smiling, good-natured woman who treated everybody nice," Teddy Blue Abbott recalled of one foreman's wife; "the whole outfit was in love with her."[32]

And doubtless focused on her in their sexual fantasies. Relegated to life in a succession of bunkhouses, the transient workers had to make do with masturbation, pornography, occasional trips to the brothel, or even a pimp-supplied "dingfob," an inflated, life-sized rubber woman of Japanese manufacture. Nor were homosexual liaisons unknown. They occurred in bunkhouses and main stems and boxcars and were most frequently observed between veteran tramps, called jockers or wolves, and their companion adolescent boys, often runaways, known as punks or prushins.[33]

The primary heterosexual outlets were prostitution and harvest unions. Harvesting of hops and berries was among the few activities that attracted substantial numbers of female workers, including mill hands and prostitutes from nearby cities. The men and women loaded boxes during daylight and frolicked after dark. "Hop dances are all the go every night," wrote a tramp named Bill Aspinwall, "sometimes Sunday included. Some dances are Respectable; others free and easy." The revels spilled over into nearby saloons, from which the harvesters reeled, penniless, to sleep it off in fields and ditches. Others took advantage of the temporary availability of women to shack up. "A great many [hobos] gets a wife very suddenly about these times and build a shantie in the woods," Aspinwall continued. They kept house for a while but inevitably parted with "black eyes, sore Heads and may be an arest of both, three months in jail or work house." More marital burlesque than marriage, these harvest unions were clandestine, alcoholic, abusive, and mercifully brief.[34]

It is possible to think of these misadventures in Darwinian terms. Aside from temporary cohabitation and heterosexual prostitution, with its remote possibility of an unaborted pregnancy, the tramps' sexual outlets were all biologically sterile. Hands, mouths, anuses, and dingfob vaginas provided release but no offspring. From an evolutionary perspective this sterility, together with the hazardous character of work and life on the road, made a tramping career genetically and personally suicidal, something against which both sexual and natural selection operated.

The shrewder and better educated saw the futility of the floating army and got out quickly, suffering no detriment in later life. The Supreme Court Justice William O. Douglas and the actor Clark Gable were hobos. So was the writer Jack London, who quit tramping and went back to school, glad to have escaped what he called the Social Pit. Another survivor was Francis McCredy Hutchinson, an educated young Philadelphian who traveled to Minnesota in May 1871 to work as a chainman and rodman on the Northern Pacific Railroad. Homesick and troubled by financial worries, Hutchinson did not much like the world in which he found himself. In his journal he described his room in St. Paul as

a regular hole in the wall. The dimensions would have barely sufficed for a bachelor mosquito, let alone one of the genus homo . . . On the floor was a filthy apology for a carpet, a war scarred wash stand which from appearances might have been run over with a curry comb, a superannuated chair, a miserable bed upon which was linen of very questionable purity, while the walls were frescoed with the blood of man's particular enemy the fiendish "Bed Bug."

What Hutchinson did not say, and what reveals a great deal about his background and outlook, is that by tramping standards these were *good* accommodations—better than the usual lousy barracks or communal flop on damp newspapers on a lodging-house floor.[35]

Hutchinson did not mind life in the open summer air, especially when his crew supplemented its diet with black bass and pike and wild strawberries. But there was always the danger of sudden storms, stinging hail, and the ever-present annoyance of mosquitoes and fleas. Biting insects bothered him almost as much as the drunken antics of the railroad crews, whom he judged the most depraved men in existence. He stuck it out until February 1872, returned to Philadelphia, did one last stint in the West as a surveyor and railroad tie inspector, then quit the transient life for good in 1873, settling down to become a journalist for the *Philadelphia Record*.[36]

Bruce Siberts was a twenty-two-year-old farm boy who, on the evening of 8 July 1890, climbed into a baggage car in Mount Pleasant, Iowa, and embarked for the "land of adventure." He found it in the form of three drunken tramps who chased him and another young traveler on top of the boxcar, yelling that they would throw them under the wheels. One of the three pursuers smashed into an overhead viaduct and was hurled screaming from the train. The other two tramps got off at the next stop, but Siberts and his companion went on, afraid they might be arrested and charged with murder.

Siberts learned any number of lessons over the coming months, among them how to delouse clothes by setting them on an anthill and why it was a good idea to stay out of saloons. After a year of sleeping in hay and oat shocks and drifting in a world of chiselers, drunks, whores, and tin-horn gamblers, he was ready to settle down to cattle and horse ranching in the Plum Creek region of South Dakota. He worked at that calling for fifteen years, married in late 1905, sold his ranch and stock, and moved with his wife to Oklahoma, where he accumulated 8,000 acres.[37]

Hutchinson and Siberts were young men who never closely identified with the subculture of transient workers and who got out while the getting was good. Sometimes whole groups of men were able to escape. Bridgeport, a Chicago neighborhood originally called Hardscrabble, was first settled in the 1830s by Irish navvies digging the Illinois and Michigan canal. Irish canal workers were then known, and deservedly so, as the wildest laborers in the United States. But the men who stayed in Bridgeport were able to create the foundation of something different and much better. They built a stable ethnic community that by the late nineteenth century was socially and demographically normal, peopled with workers, priests and policemen, ward heelers and widows, wives and servant girls, as well as the inevitable criminals and toughs. Into that community was born Richard J. Daley, the son of a sheet-metal worker and a native Bridgeport woman, who would in his time rise to become mayor of Chicago, Democratic Party kingmaker, and arguably the most powerful politician in the United States.[38]

What was good for the Bridgeport Irish was good for society, or at any rate reductive of crime. Riotous behavior and urban felony rates declined in the late nineteenth century, a trend usually ascribed to the deterrent effect of better and more numerous police or the psychological consequences of the urban-industrial transformation with its character-shaping apparatus of factories, time clocks, whistles, and bureaucratic rules. But such a change required residential stability. For men to be subject to systematic police scrutiny and industrial discipline as well as the restraints of married life, they had to be settled in one place, not on the road sleeping in barns, working irregularly, and changing their names as they shuttled in and out of the main stems. The new factory order may well have molded the character of the persisters, as the historian Roger Lane has argued, but it is hard to see how it affected the floaters. Charlie Chaplin understood this. He called the protagonist of his film *Modern Times* (1936), the one who passes unscathed through the gears of the huge machine, the Tramp.[39]

Sober Professor, Drinking Rover

Not everyone who did a stint in the floating army managed to get out and stay out. We know from police lodging data, vagrancy arrests, and other institutional records that thousands of men, and a much smaller number of women, continued to tramp about even when times were good. We also have memoirs and letters from a handful of articulate tramps who tried to explain why they stayed in the floating world even after they had become acquainted with its dangers.

The most detailed of these is a twenty-five-year correspondence between John James McCook and William "Roving Bill" Aspinwall. McCook was an Episcopal priest and a professor of modern languages. Deeply religious yet cosmopolitan in outlook, he knew a dozen languages, married and fathered eight children, taught at Trinity College, served as the pastor of a parish in East Hartford, Connecticut, and in 1890, as if he had nothing else to do, began the most systematic study of tramp life ever undertaken in the United States.

McCook left no stone unturned. He investigated itinerants who wintered in the Hartford almshouse, followed homeless men and mapped their begging routes, and visited tramp jungles, saloons, and lodgings with a photographer in tow. In November 1891 he sent questionnaires to the mayors of forty cities, asking that they be passed on to those in charge of the charitable or police institutions where tramps were housed. He received 1,349 replies from fourteen cities, data he mined for a series of magazine articles on the tramp problem. He also drew on interviews and correspondence with numerous tramps, of whom Aspinwall was the most thoughtful.

Aspinwall, like McCook, had served in the Union Army in his youth, but there the similarities ended. Aspinwall was a wanderer who made his money by mushfaking, or mending umbrellas, and by repairing clocks and sewing machines, doing seasonal farm work, and occasionally working in woolen mills. A proud man, he did not beg unless he was desperate or received an unsolicited offer of money or food. Something of a loner, he usually walked alone to his work—in the photograph his leather shoes are so warn and dusty as to be almost white—although he sometimes rode the rails, slept in boxcars, and associated with other tramps. Certainly he knew enough about the subculture to send McCook long and at times Rabelaisian accounts replete with descriptions of down-and-outers, vote sellers, and sodomites. One wonders what went through Reverend McCook's mind as he read all this.[40]

Aspinwall professed to enjoy the road and the free and leisurely life it offered. On beautiful spring days, he wrote, he liked to find a secluded spot in the woods, lie in the shade of a friendly tree, listen to the birdsongs, and then sleep for hours—"such sweet sleep, such nice dreams . . . I often think God intended man to live as the Indians used to—all the land common property. What happy times if we was all in the woods together!"

McCook analyzed these sentiments in near-Freudian terms. We are all, he wrote, yoked with the habits of civilized life. We are taught to believe that goodness and happiness consist of doing our daily tasks, eating regular meals, going to bed in the same place, rising at the same time, wearing certain kinds of clothes, behaving respectably. "Religion gives its awful sanction to this theory," McCook observed; "habit fortifies it; successive generations of what we call civilization even creates an instinct which makes us think, or at least say, we like it." But when someone like Aspinwall made the discovery—McCook characteristically called it a fatal discovery—that it was possible to turn away from all this, hit the road, go anywhere, get along, associate with anyone, and drop all responsibilities, then it was hard to go back to the settled routine.[41]

There was more to Aspinwall's story, however, than atavism, the tripping of some hunter-gatherer switch deep in the recesses of his brain. Bill Aspinwall was an alcoholic. Despite his professed love of the roving life, he did occasionally try to settle down and work at steady jobs but dissipated his earnings in drinking bouts. He admitted to McCook that he would be well-to-do if it were not for his drinking, which had begun in the army. In his later years, when he lived in a series of veterans' homes (a safety net not available to most tramps), he was still fighting his battle with the bottle.[42]

Aspinwall was also a victim of industrial downturns. One of his more ambitious attempts to settle down and open a repair shop in Pittsburgh in 1893 was doomed by bad timing. The severe depression that hit that year forced him to close the shop for want of business and sent him back on the road where he observed a huge increase in wandering, unemployed men. McCook came to the same realization, noting a large increase in the number of lodgers during depression years. Although McCook originally believed that drink was the primary cause of tramping, he had second thoughts and concluded that it was chiefly due to the intertwined effects of drinking and the business cycle.

McCook's mature views were subtle and command our attention. He understood, of course, that drinking dissipated savings. Men blew their stakes on drunken sprees, sometimes pawning the coats on their backs, and then either had to stagger back to work or, if too sick and exhausted, apply for a ticket to the almshouse. He was not alone in this judgment. Other observers, including young Harry Truman, a $30-a-month timekeeper for the Santa Fe Railroad, saw exactly the same thing. Truman noted sadly that the hobos were paid off every two weeks on Saturday night in a saloon so that they would drink up their wages and return to work on Monday morning. East and West, inside and outside the subculture, there are dozens of accounts of the spree pattern and its ill effects on itinerant men. They corroborate McCook's own survey findings, which indicated that 63 percent of his large sample of tramps and casual lodgers was intemperate.[43]

But McCook discovered something else, that liquor put men at a much higher risk of unemployment when hard times hit. He interviewed the personnel managers of twelve large firms in Hartford, eight of which had drinking men and tramps in their employ. He was told that when business fell off and the payroll had to be cut, the first to go were the drinkers, then the single men, then married men last of all. This industrial triage meant that tramps, most of whom drank and almost all of whom were single, faced double jeopardy. First laid off and last rehired, they had to move on in search of work again.[44]

Tramps, in brief, were in a predicament similar to that of gold miners, Plains cowboys, Chinese laborers, and deep-water sailors, yet another group of expendable laborers floating on a male

frontier. Itinerant workers could and often did spend long periods working in isolation and sobriety, accumulating wages that,
if saved and spent judiciously, promised a way out. A stake could
mean tuition, tools, a down payment on a shop, or even a small
farm—the dream that animates George and Lennie, the doomed
hobo protagonists of John Steinbeck's *Of Mice and Men* (1937).
But too often the stake was lost in the steamy confines of a
main-stem bar or in the arms of a prostitute. "A man can't get
along without that—it's God's arrangement," explained one
Irish drifter, still patronizing whores at the age of fifty-eight.[45]

The physical and psychological effects of sprees were cumula-
tive. Alcohol-related malnutrition, tremors, liver and venereal
diseases, and related health problems diminished a man's ability
to work and the likelihood he would be hired or, if hired, kept
on the job. The string of drunken binges also encouraged a
defeatist attitude that became more pronounced as—if—he grew
older. "Booze put me on the bum," explained one derelict alcoholic, an ex-carpenter and union member who ended up on
Chicago's West Madison Street in the early 1920s. "Now, I'm
here and I'm too old to be good for anything, so why not keep
it up?"[46]

Victorians viewed this sort of fate as a matter of defective
character and moral weakness. They had a point, or rather half
of one. A lack of discipline and future-orientation might explain
why some individuals and not others succumbed to vice and
languished in the floating army, but they ought not blind us, as
indeed they did not blind thoughtful contemporaries, to the
systematic, profit-driven, and corrupt character of the vice industry. The political economy of the lumber towns, for example,
was simply that of the cattle towns writ larger. Saloons and
brothels relieved the timber workers of their accumulated seasonal wages and circulated the money, politicians turned a blind
eye, and the marshals (when not busy running their own
whorehouses, as in Bay City, Michigan) simply tried to quell the
worst violence and keep the boys quiet on Sunday and out of
respectable neighborhoods. Where they really kept them, intentionally or otherwise, was in the cycle of work and spree.[47]

The exploitative process was transparent when employers cut
out the middlemen and went into the drink business for them-

selves. The precedent was set by antebellum canal companies that sold whiskey to their Irish crews, subtracting the cost from their wages and effectively keeping alcoholic workers tied to the job. This practice had terrible consequences; one observer put the life expectancy of the hard-drinking navvies at eighteen months. For sheer ruthlessness, however, it is hard to match the record of the western railroad contractor who set up a saloon at the end of the tunnel his men were drilling. When they ran out of money, he accepted their bank checks at a discount of ten cents on the dollar.[48]

The nineteenth-century revolution in alkaloidal chemistry presented new possibilities for exploiting workers. "At every company store," complained Big Bill Haywood, referring to the southern turpentine and lumber camps, "cocaine, morphine, and heroin are sold. The workers, once addicted, cannot think of going away from their source of supply." Social conservatives had their own reasons for deploring such practices, especially the sale of cocaine to black laborers. In 1909 Harris Dickson, a municipal court judge in Vicksburg, Mississippi, went so far as to state that anyone who deliberately put cocaine into a Negro was more dangerous than a person who would inoculate a dog with hydrophobia. Setting aside the racist trope, there is no reason to doubt the point of Dickson's investigations, that some railroad and levee construction companies knowingly sold dangerous and addictive drugs to their work crews, acting out another variation on the theme of the expendability of migrant labor.[49]

Prohibition

Evangelical women and men regarded entrepreneurial vice, above all the liquor industry, as a hydra-headed evil. The drink business was, in the powerful if mixed metaphor of the Reverend Mark Matthews, moderator of the Presbyterian General Assembly, "the most fiendish, corrupt and hell-soaked institution that ever crawled out of the slime of the eternal pit."[50]

In the years from 1890 through 1917 Evangelical leaders like Matthews found new allies in the rising generation of Progressive reformers. Though the Progressives resembled the Evangelicals in several important respects and were often motivated by moral and religious convictions, they cast their criticism of the liquor industry in cooler scientific terms. They pointed to the growing body of evidence that drink ruined health and lowered life expectancy, reduced industrial safety and efficiency, contributed to unemployment, poverty, and crime, triggered domestic beatings, and disrupted family life.

The ill effects of drink may have been concentrated in the lower classes, but the Progressives argued that the costs were ultimately borne by everyone. An inebriated fur trapper in the Rocky Mountains was one thing, a drunken switchman or hung-over section gang on a busy railroad quite another. Urban-industrial America paid for drink in the form of more and costlier accidents, more police, and higher outlays for prisons, almshouses, hospitals, asylums, and other institutions filled with the human debris of alcoholic excess. Drink produced profit and labor-control advantages for the few, misery and disorder for the many, imposing social losses that efficiency-minded Progressives and a growing number of business leaders calculated and emphasized as grounds for coercive change.[51]

Progressives were equally sensitive to irresponsible corporate behavior, of which the big distillers and brewers were guilty on several accounts. Notorious for corrupting legislatures and buying votes, they had also created a distribution system that practically guaranteed abuse. By the late nineteenth century brewers owned 70 percent or more of the saloons in the United States, a move calculated to provide a steady outlet for their products, much the way oil companies would later franchise gas stations. The brewers' expectations put pressure on the saloonkeepers to keep the product moving. Given the intense competition, they could accomplish this only by selling liquor to the underage and the already soused or by harboring vice activities to attract more customers. In New York City saloons took advantage of an 1896 revision of the state licensing code to add bedrooms and become, technically, hotels. What these new bedrooms were used for soon became apparent and aroused a storm of indignation, as did the notorious drink-sex-flop "barrelhouses" of the Chicago main stem. Saloons had always been centers of male vice, but sharp competition made the problem conspicuously worse in the two decades before World War I.[52]

These well-publicized abuses did much to bring the liquor question to a head. Not all Progressives embraced prohibition. McCook, for one, favored a system of fixed-profit municipal liquor monopolies and reformatories for drunkards. But a combination of social and political pressures—the saloon scandals, the lobbying of the Anti-Saloon League and other grass-roots organizations, the enfranchisement of women, and the war itself, with its patriotic fervor, pressure for grain conservation, and backlash against all things German, including beer—created an irresistible momentum for the root-and-branch solution of national prohibition. The Eighteenth Amendment and its enabling legislation, the Volstead Act, took effect in January 1920, although many parts of the country were by then already dry through state and local legislation. National prohibition lasted almost fourteen years, until December 1933, when a combination of skillful and well-financed wet propaganda, concern over gangsterism and bootlegging, the Depression and Democratic ascendancy, and an urgent need for tax dollars brought about repeal of the amendment.

The once popular and politically useful myth that Prohibition turned America into a nation of speakeasy-going drunkards has been exploded by historians and alcohol researchers. There is widespread agreement that per capita alcohol consumption dropped by half or more as a result of Prohibition, that alcohol-related diseases sharply declined, and that urban wage earners spent billions of dollars less on drink, using the savings to purchase such durable consumer goods as automobiles. "Prohibition," sums up John Burnham, a historian who led the revisionist charge, "was substantially successful."[53]

But was it substantially successful in liberating itinerant workers from the work-spree cycle? Here the answer must be a tentative no. Resistance to prohibition laws, as Burnham himself has observed, was most widespread among tramps and other irreligious, lower-class, and mostly single men who resented the Protestant do-gooders and their crusades against liquor, gambling, prostitution, pornography, and other bachelor vices. These men often came from cultures that approved of drinking and had acquired a taste for alcohol themselves. "Blind pigs," or low-rent speakeasies, flourished in and around main-stem neighborhoods, giving tramping men easy access to alcohol while they wintered in cities. When Nels Anderson, a second-generation hobo turned sociologist, studied Chicago's main stem in the early 1920s, he promptly discovered that tramp teetotalers were few and that alcoholism and spree drinking were still widespread problems, Prohibition or no.[54]

When bootleg liquor was unavailable there were other ways to get high. Floaters drank rubbing alcohol, bay rum, vanilla extract, and the ever-popular Sterno, a dangerous vestige of Prohibition that persisted into the 1930s and beyond. "Drinking this fluid results in a physiological and neurotic degeneracy which is as disastrous as narcotic addiction," wrote one observer. "Individuals habituated to 'smoke' ordinarily do not return to the comparatively mild effects of whiskey or beer. There is nothing, moreover, which the 'derailer' will not attempt to consume, lacking his favorite, canned heat." The most extreme alternative was a mixture of two parts milk to one part kerosene. When boiled, skimmed, cooled, and drunk the result was "an efficient loss of all control of rational processes and behavior."[55] Whatever good Prohibition did for the nation as a whole it was of no help to tramps who persisted in this sort of intoxication. They were not merely dissipating their wages. They were headed over a cliff.

The End of the Floating Army

Yet the hard-drinking, train-jumping, jungling workers were disappearing by the early 1920s. "The hobo," summed up Anderson, looking back over this period, "was on his way out."[56] Why, if not for reforms like prohibition, did this decline occur?

One answer is that the jobs created by the building of the urban-industrial infrastructure were self-liquidating. When the main rail lines were completed, the tunnels dug, and the dams built, all that was required was maintenance crews, not massed gangs of laborers. There was still a demand for harvest and other seasonal help, but as the western populations began to grow naturally more of these jobs were taken by nonmigrating work-ers such as teenagers, students, or local men and women looking to earn additional income. The automobile, which became increasingly common during the late 1910s and especially during the 1920s, made it much easier for these laborers to travel to their jobs. Commuting, not freight hopping, was becoming central to American workers' lives.

Technological change altered labor demand in other important ways. Combines reduced the need for field hands during the harvest rush by two-thirds or more. Steam shovels replaced ditch diggers, chainsaws replaced axmen, and refrigerators replaced tramps who had once eked out a living cutting blocks of ice. In 1879 a man with a strong back and a willingness to travel could count on finding temporary work somewhere, but by 1929 the demand for unskilled migrant labor had greatly diminished or was being met by local workers.[57]

Then came the Great Depression and with it a huge jump in the number of transients. By August 1932 as many as two million homeless persons were roaming America, including 200,000 children. The volume of those riding the rails was a fever chart of hard times. On the Missouri Pacific the number of trespassers observed on or ejected from trains rose from under 40,000 in 1929 to nearly 280,000 in the crisis year of 1933 before tapering to 100,000 in 1937.[58]

The men who hopped freights and the families who took to the road in battered flivvers during the 1930s were quite distinct from the old-style tramps. The new wanderers were desperate economic refugees with little realistic hope of finding industrial jobs, while the hobos of thirty years before could at least count on a variety of work, some of it, as in the lumber camps, comparatively well paying. Nor were the itinerant job-seekers of the 1930s attuned to the tramp subculture. The most famous Depression-era refugees, the Okies who streamed into California, were anything but bindle stiffs. They came in families, planned to relocate permanently, and had no intention of becoming lifelong migratory workers. They settled near rural towns and cities, tried to send their children to school, and, when the family breadwinners followed the harvest, did so from a residential base.[59]

The Federal Emergency Relief Administration and other government agencies were able to provide some help to homeless

Americans during the 1930s, but what really ended the crisis was the reabsorption of the unemployed into the war economy or the armed forces in the early 1940s. It then became clear how completely the male tramp's world, or at least the economic underpinnings of it, had vanished. There were still migratory agricultural workers, but these were increasingly families with cars and sometimes trailers who followed the harvest and were in no way dependent on the railroads or wintering in the main stems. The main-stem neighborhoods had themselves changed. They were not so much urban dormitories for working men as they were skid-row slums, home to aging pensioners squeezed by inflation, disabled men on relief, and an assortment of alcoholics, blood sellers, panhandlers, and other derelicts kept on the move more by their arrest records than by the seasonal rhythms of labor.[60]

Before 1900 it was possible for homeless American men to lead lives that were socially marginal but economically useful. They harvested crops and cut down forests, herded cattle, built railroads, opened new mines. "Such labor granted them a place in the economy while allowing them to remain on society's edges," Peter Marin writes, "an option rarely available to women save through prostitution."[61] This mixed status—necessary workers, troublesome pariahs—explains the peculiar, almost schizoid, response to itinerant unskilled workers: why railroad officials alternately let them ride and threw them off trains, why towns tolerated them at harvest time but later administered timber lessons, why police stations functioned as both tramp hotels and prisons. Even the Chinese bachelors, one of the most despised groups in Victorian America, were regarded as an important labor asset by western landowners and magnates.

A hundred years later the situation had changed dramatically. Most jobs required skills, regular hours, and a sedentary, disciplined style of living. The demand for casual day laborers either had disappeared or was being met by immigrants. In these circumstances men who lacked homes, families, education, sobriety, and alarm clocks were economically *and* socially marginal. In the eyes of the public they were not only superfluous but dangerous as well. For all his problems the late nineteenth-century tramp could at least lay claim to having built industrial America. Fairly or unfairly his late twentieth-century counter-part, the homeless urban man, is widely viewed as just another threat to tear it apart.

TEN

Marriage Boom, Urban Bust

The near disappearance of tramps in the first half of the twentieth century was part of a larger decline in the relative numbers and influence of single men. The gradual achievement of gender balance and rising affluence encouraged family formation, especially during the marriage boom of the 1940s and 1950s. The shift is illustrated in Figure 10.1, which shows the marital status of American men over fourteen. In 1890 nearly five American men in ten were single, widowed, or divorced. By 1955 it was three in ten. Most of these were simply men in their teens or twenties who had not yet married but would do so in the coming flush years.

The End of the Male Surplus

In a monogamous society marriage is a gigantic game of musical chairs. Because one woman can legally wed one man and vice versa, any marked adult gender imbalance will necessarily leave some unmarried persons, who may or may not be content with their single state. Conversely, the chances of marriage and family formation are most favorable when the numbers of women and men of appropriate ages are most nearly equal.

A rough numerical balance of just this sort was temporarily achieved in the mid-twentieth century when the overall male

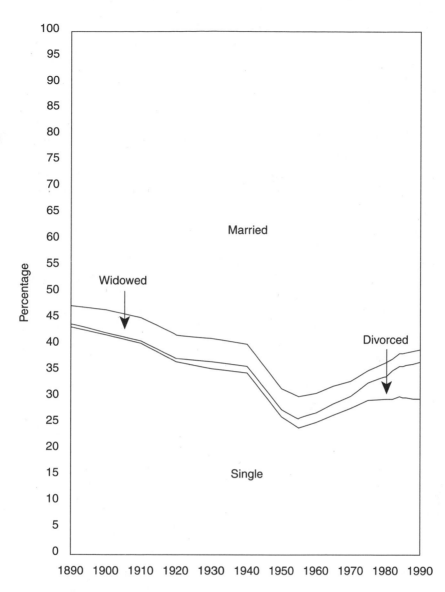

Figure 10.1 Marital status of American men aged fourteen and older, 1890–
1990. Based on Donald J. Bogue et al., *The Population of the United States:
Historical Trends and Future Prospects,* rev. ed. (New York: Free Press, 1985), 147,
supplemented by U.S. Bureau of the Census, *Marital Status and Living Arrangements,* series P-20, Current Population Reports for 1984 through 1990. (Because of a change in census categories the data for 1980–1990 are for men over
fifteen.)

surplus finally disappeared. The disappearance was caused by two important changes. One was in immigration patterns, the other in the growing difference between male and female life expectancies.

From 1900 to 1914 overseas migration to the United States swelled to unprecedented levels. Over thirteen million immigrants entered the country, mostly young workers from southern or eastern Europe. At its peak in 1906–1907 the immigrant gender ratio was 262 men for every 100 women, the largest such disparity recorded since the early 1820s. More men immigrated in the early twentieth century for the same reason that there were more male tramps: industrialization and the need for manual laborers to build America's infrastructure. Slavs and Italians and Greeks toiled in mines and quarries, dug ditches and laid track, and undertook countless other jobs spawned by the urban-industrial transformation. Not all of them stayed, but enough did so that the U.S. gender ratio hit its high-water mark in 1910.[1]

A chain of events then diminished and reversed the male immigration surplus. When Europe went to war in August 1914 it suddenly became much harder for young men, who were wanted for military service, to leave for America. As many as 600,000 of those already in the United States repatriated. Some were conscripted, some rejoined their families for the duration, some left to take advantage of the demand for war workers in their native lands. In 1918 Josiah Rowe Jr., a young American pilot training in Foggia, Italy, estimated that a third of the Italian men he met had formerly worked in America. It was funny, he wrote, to walk along the street and hear someone call out, "Hello Keed." As soon as the war was over, he judged, these men and others would head back to the States on the first available ship. But for the duration the war caused net immigration (arrivals minus departures) to fall in magnitude and change in composition, becoming predominantly female for the first time in 1915–1919.[2]

Male immigration did make a comeback in the 1920s, though not to anything like prewar levels. It might have but for nativist sentiment, which had been gaining in intensity for two decades as immigration shifted away from northwestern Europe, and which crystallized in a campaign for restriction after the war. The campaign's legislative fruits, the 1921 and 1924 quotas, discriminated against immigrants from southern and eastern Europe, whence most of the male industrial workers came.[3]

The new immigration regime of the 1920s had one loophole, but it was a big one. The laws gave preferential status to the wives and children of male immigrants who were already U.S. citizens or permanent residents. Except in the case of Asian groups like the Chinese, who were singled out for virtually total exclusion, the laws cut the flow of male immigrants but not the follow-on migration of families and spouses. The latter included wives acquired through trips back home or arranged marriages, another option denied resident Chinese and, for that matter, the Japanese after exclusionists torpedoed the picture-bride system. In brief, European immigrants who elected to stay in the United States could legally form or reunite families in the 1920s and 1930s while Asian immigrants could not.

The preferential treatment of spouses continued to be an important factor during World War II and the Cold War, when millions of young American servicemen were stationed overseas. The foreign women they married were permitted to come to the United States and did so in large numbers. In 1946 through 1948 nearly 113,000 war brides entered America, or one quarter of all legal immigrants during that period. It is interesting (and, given the history of Asian exclusion, somewhat strange) that by 1983 fully 200,000 Asian wives of American servicemen were residing in the United States.[4]

The upshot was that mid-century immigration to the United States became and stayed mostly female. From 1929 to 1979 female immigrants made up a majority of the new arrivals, two-thirds of whom were women or children.[5] Thus the force that had for so long contributed to the nation's male surplus had finally begun to work the other way. By the 1930s the net effect of immigration was to create or reunite families, rather than to supply more and more bachelor laborers.

The other important population change was the widening mortality gap between women and men. In 1920 the life expectancy at birth of white women was one year longer than that of men. By 1950 it had grown to nearly six years and by 1975, when white women could expect 77.2 years of life and men 69.4 years, it was nearly eight years. Among blacks the gap was even more pronounced, 72.3 years for women in 1975 compared to 63.6 for men.[6]

This widening gap was caused by safer births (over 100 times less risky for American women in 1980 than in 1915–1919), heavier male consumption of cigarettes and alcohol, greater male exposure to stress and likelihood of violent death, and the natural superiority of the female immune system. Its consequence was to accelerate the decline of the national gender ratio, which fell from 106.2 in 1910 to 100.8 in 1940 to 94.8 in 1970, a more than eleven-point swing in just sixty years. Although the ratio increased slightly in the 1980s and 1990s, it has remained low by historical standards, hovering in the 95–96 range.[7]

Most of the female surplus was among the elderly. If men survived the dangerous years of their late teens and early twenties, they typically married, aged, developed a fatal illness like heart disease or cancer, and then died. Their widows kept on aging, developed a string of chronic illnesses, lost their health and independence, and then died. This is, of course, a simplification, but as anyone who has ever visited a nursing home can attest, it is not far from the truth. By 1980 widowhood was more than four times as common among seventy-year-old women than among seventy-year-old men.[8]

While lingering widowhood has emerged as a serious domestic and fiscal problem, posing challenges to caretaker families, the solvency of the Social Security system, and health-care financing, it never has been a problem of social order. From the standpoint of violence and disorder, the marital status of aged women does not much matter, as they are unlikely to make trouble in any case. It is when young men cannot or do not marry that socially disruptive behavior is intensified.

The surfeit of elderly widows was of no marital help to young men, who in the United States as elsewhere preferred younger women to much older ones. But the feminization of immigration was clearly a boon, particularly to foreign-born men prevented by religious, ethnic, and class differences from marrying native-born women. And all American bachelors, immigrant or native, had their marital prospects enhanced by the gradual equalization of regional gender ratios, as shown in Figure 9.1. By the 1940s and 1950s gender imbalance had ceased to be a significant impediment to marriage in all but the remotest parts of the nation.

The Great Marriage Boom

Spousal availability is a necessary rather than sufficient condition for monogamous marriage and family formation. Political, cultural, and especially economic circumstances play critical roles in the extent and timing of marriage. Hard times make for fewer marriages and reduced fertility. In 1932, during the depths of the Great Depression, the crude marriage rate hit a historic low of 7.9 per thousand. But it climbed back up in the later 1930s and then leapt to 12.7 in mid-1941.

The Selective Service Act, passed in September 1940, had much to do with this increase. J. R. Woods and Sons, a wedding-ring manufacturer, reported a 250 percent increase in sales after the draft law was passed. Young men and women adopted a now-or-never attitude toward the marital bed. "I've told him I don't love him," admitted one woman. "But he's an aviator and he says I should marry him anyhow and give him a little happiness. He says . . . he hasn't any chance of living through the war." This last-chance mentality was especially pronounced after the attack on Pearl Harbor, when marriages jumped 60 percent over the previous December. An estimated 1,000 women a day married servicemen over the next five months.[9]

A quickie wartime marriage was not necessarily a lasting marriage, a problem dramatized by the breakup of the Derrys (Dana Andrews and Virginia Mayo) in the 1946 film *The Best Years of Our Lives.* The crude divorce rate, which stood at 2.0 per thousand in 1940, shot up to 4.3 in 1946. But the crude marriage rate for 1946 was far higher, a record 16.4 per thousand. Moreover, the divorce rate dropped to a low plateau during the late 1940s and 1950s while the marriage rate remained very high. In round numbers there were 33 million marriages in those years compared to 8 million divorces, hence the pronounced increase in the percentage of men who were married.[10]

The great marriage boom was abetted by unprecedented national prosperity. The war and military spending ballooned the gross national product from $90 billion in 1939 to $212 billion in 1945, with the sharpest income and employment gains occurring among the poor. Pent-up consumer demand for housing, automobiles, and appliances kept the economy and family incomes growing after the war. In 1946 a worker with three dependents earned, after federal taxes, an average of about $43 a week. In 1959 the same worker's disposable wages were over $80 (both sums in 1960 dollars). Many of the jobs available in the late 1940s and 1950s were in the manufacturing and construction sectors, did not require much education, and were unionized and relatively well-paying. It was economically possible for couples to marry shortly after high school or even before. The median age of first marriage for men, 25.1 in 1910, dropped to 22.6 in 1955. Two-and-a-half years may seem a small change, but it had dramatic consequences. At the turn of the century only about one of every five men under twenty-five was married; at mid-century it was one of every two.[11]

For women the median age of first marriage dipped even lower. In 1955 it was just 20.2 years, or about what it had been in Plymouth Colony in the early seventeenth century. Formal engagements at seventeen were common. A *New York Times* feature writer went so far as to warn that a "girl who hasn't a man in sight by the time she is 20 is not altogether wrong in fearing that she may never get married."[12]

Veterans who wished to pursue their education beyond high school could do so with the help of the 1944 Servicemen's Readjustment Act, better known as the GI Bill. University of Chicago president Robert Hutchins pitched a public fit over the legislation, warning that the nation's "colleges and universities will find themselves converted into educational hobo jungles." It was a risible prophecy. By 1947 nearly half of all college enrollees were veterans, and they had proved themselves hard-working students intent on professional careers. Some 450,000 became engineers, 360,000 schoolteachers, 240,000 accountants, 180,000 doctors or nurses, and 150,000 scientists. Their skills helped sustain the national economic expansion and their incomes provided a solid financial foundation for marriage and middle-class family life.[13]

Student-veterans did not have to postpone marriage until graduation. The GI Bill provided allowances for spouses and children along with college expenses. Half of the veterans who attended college were married and half of these already had one or more children. As in so many other aspects of social life, marriage proved an advantage. Despite cramped quarters, housing shortages, and squawking babies, the married vets, mostly mature and highly motivated men, consistently got higher grades than their bachelor peers.[14]

If demography, prosperity, and educational opportunity all favored marriage, so did the postwar *Zeitgeist*. The mass media bombarded Americans with images of romantic love and marital fulfillment in popular magazines and movies like William Wyler's *The Best Years of Our Lives*. The film's central figure, Captain Fred Derry, is haunted by the memory of combat, has trouble finding a good job, and is dumped by his two-timing wife. But in the moving final sequence it becomes clear that he will wed the banker's daughter Peggy Stephenson, even as the handless Navy veteran Homer Parrish prosthetically slips a wedding ring on the finger of Wilma, his loyal childhood sweetheart. Love conquers all, even traumatic stress and double amputation.

The nation agreed with Hollywood. Fewer than one postwar American in ten believed an unmarried person could be happy. Marriage was supposed to be a benign destiny, especially for women, who were regarded as mannish freaks if they chose a career over matrimony. In 1959 two out of three women who entered college dropped out, usually to go to the altar. "Education, work, whatever you did before marriage," recalled one young woman of the era, Bonnie Carr, "was only a prelude to your real life, which was marriage." "I just wanted to get married," commented another, Cathy Lee Shipley, "and start my life."[15]

The marital efflorescence of the late 1940s and 1950s was in many respects historically unique. The social historian Stephanie Coontz has gone so far as to call it a qualitatively new phenomenon discontinuous with the marital trends of the previous hundred years. That which had been declining for a century, fertility and the disparity between married men's and women's education, suddenly began increasing. That which had been increasing, the divorce rate and female ages for marriage and motherhood, suddenly began decreasing. On top of everything else, the postwar family had a new locus, the suburb.[16]

Postwar Suburbs

Suburbs were not new but the scale of postwar suburban expansion was. Newlyweds were desperate for private housing, construction having been curtailed during the war. Families doubled up with relatives or squatted in Quonset huts, trolley cars, trailers, and grain bins. Wanted-to-rent ads in late 1945 newspapers are short essays in desperation, so many cents per word. Apartment seekers swore respectability of character, permanence of residence, Christian faith. They said they had no bad habits and no pets, or none that was not well trained. A few said they would live anywhere and that price was no object. Would-be landlords did not have much to offer in return. "Big Ice Box, 7×17 feet," ran an Omaha newspaper ad, "could be fixed up to live in."[17]

Bill Levitt had a better idea: affordable, mass-produced housing erected on inexpensive farmland within commuting distance of the central city. Levittown, his first and most famous development, went up on 4,000 acres of Long Island potato fields twenty-five miles east of New York City. Before they were through Levitt and his associates built 140,000 houses and helped to inspire the single most important postwar urban trend, suburban sprawl. By 1960 almost 60 million people, a third of the American population, resided in the ever-expanding suburbs. Most were families with young children living in Levitt-style Cape Cods, colonials, and ranch houses. The Levitt house, the historian Kenneth Jackson has written, was to postwar suburban development what the Model T was to the automobile.[18]

As important as Levitt and other private builders were, the suburban explosion would not have occurred on the scale it did without government assistance. The policy of allowing income tax deductions for mortgage interest payments and local property taxes amounted to a massive subsidy for new home ownership. So did loan guarantees by the Federal Housing Administration and the Veterans Administration, both of which made low-cost mortgages available to millions of postwar Americans. "The majority of guys . . . did not use the GI Bill for school," the journalist Mike Royko recalled of his working-class Chicago neighborhood. "They used it for a loan for a home. That's when the younger couples started moving out. Guys got married and went lookin' to live somewhere else. The neighborhood got older and never really recovered. The guys went out to Park Forest, Rolling Meadows. They were the new suburban pioneers."[19]

The pioneers, if that is the right word, depended on government-subsidized roads for transportation. In the 1940s and early 1950s most jobs and major stores were still in the central cities, and commuting, via narrow and crowded roads, was a necessity. The solution to the growing traffic problem, foreshadowed by the Futurama exhibit at the 1939 New York World's Fair, was a system of superhighways that could carry thousands of cars at high speeds between built-up areas. The superhighways and ancillary roads were built through the efforts of the most broadly based and powerful lobby in American history, a combination of oil, car, and truck companies, banks, labor unions, road contractors, realtors, and land developers, all of whom stood to gain from the rapid growth of suburbs knit together with new roads and geared to automobiles. In 1951 even the atomic scientists got into the act, arguing that larger, decentralized cities with depopulated urban cores would be less susceptible to nuclear attack. When the legislation authorizing the interstate highway system was enacted in 1956, with 90 percent of the cost paid by the federal government, one of the official rationales was the quick evacuation of urban targets in the event of atomic bombardment.[20]

What the new roads and highways actually permitted was quick white evacuation from increasingly black parts of town. Levitt's own family had promptly left Brooklyn's Bedford-Stuyvesant neighborhood when the first black family moved in. For two decades blacks were legally barred from buying into his proliferating Levittowns and similar developments. "Everybody wanted to have a house away from the niggers," admitted Paul Pisicano, a New York Italian who used the GI Bill to become an architect after the war. "Now guys were talking about niggers: I gotta move out or my kids . . . I think American suburbs are bound by their antiblack sentiments. That's the common denominator."[21]

Not everyone agrees. Kenneth Jackson, for one, thinks that economic factors, the pent-up demand for and relative cheapness of subsidized suburban housing, were more decisive than race. Be that as it may, there was unquestionably a racial impetus to suburbanization, an anti-black push as well as an economic pull. The larger the postwar migration of southern blacks to inner cities—at one point in the 1950s 2,200 black men and women were moving to Chicago's South and West Sides every week—the stronger the impetus and the more pronounced racial polarization became. By 1970 blacks made up 22.5 percent of central-city dwellers but only 5.7 percent of suburbanites. Suburban blacks, including those of the middle class, were usually confined to older, closer-in, less desirable neighborhoods, while affluent white families kept moving farther out to newer, more expensive suburban (ultimately, exurban) housing and better schools protected from black incursion by municipal and district lines.[22]

Pax Domestica

The 1940s and 1950s marriage, baby, and suburban booms had important consequences for the amount and pattern of American violence and disorder. Two stand out. The first was that the decline in the number of single men and the efflorescence of family life contributed to the substantially lower overall rates of violence and disorder in American society after World War II until about 1960. The second was that the pattern of urban violence and disorder became increasingly centripetal, with crime and delinquency occurring much more often in the inner cities than the new, family-oriented suburban neighborhoods.

The statistical basis of the first proposition begins with Figure 10.2, which displays three common measures of violent death, the rates of mortality from homicide, suicide, and motor vehicle accidents, plus an aggregate of these three statistics, for the years 1933–1973.[23] Figure 10.3 displays four demographic and social statistics correlated with the rise and fall of the violent death rates: the percentage of American men fourteen and older who were single, divorced, or widowed; the percentage of Americans who told pollsters they did not attend a church or synagogue on

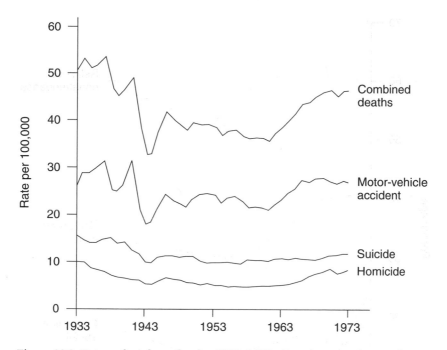

Figure 10.2 Rates of violent death, 1933–1973. Based on Paul C. Holinger, *Violent Deaths in the United States: An Epidemiologic Study of Suicide, Homicide, and Accidents* (New York: Guilford Press, 1987), 207–213.

a weekly basis; the unemployment rate; and the percentage of the total population aged fifteen through twenty-four.

The years 1933-1973 were chosen for reasons of comparability. Suicide and especially homicide data recorded before 1933 are less consistent and reliable, in part because deaths from motor-vehicle accidents were often recorded as murders. In 1906 Woodrow Wilson, president of Princeton, declared reckless drivers the worst menace facing the nation. "I am a Southerner and know how to shoot," he reminded his New York City audience, adding that he sympathized with those who blazed away at hit-and-run drivers. The animus against Mr. Toad–like motorists and careless teamsters, once quite common, likely contributed to the overcharging which contaminates early-twentieth-century homicide data.

After 1973 auto death rates fell because of the oil crisis and highway speed-limit reductions ("55 Saves Lives"). Moreover,

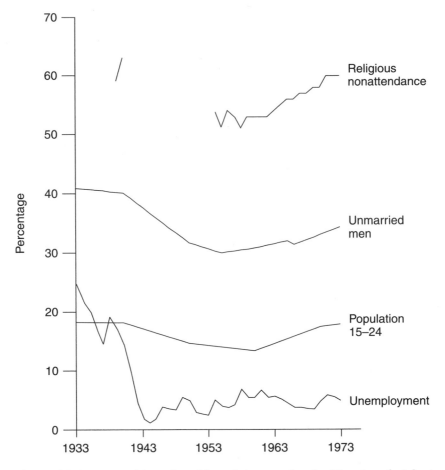

Figure 10.3 Demographic and social statistics correlated with rates of violent death, 1933–1973. Data from Donald J. Bogue et al., *The Population of the United States: Historical Trends and Future Prospects,* rev. ed. (New York: Free Press, 1985), 45, 147; "Religion in America," *Gallup Report* nos. 201–202 (June–July 1982): 44; Albert W. Niemi, *U.S. Economic History,* 2nd ed. (Chicago: Rand McNally, 1980), 275.

the rapid, Vietnam-inspired improvement in emergency medical services in big cities after the early 1970s prevented the deaths of many trauma, stabbing, and gunshot victims, "bleeders" in police parlance. Better odds for the bleeders, not to mention mandatory seat-belt laws, air bags, and other auto-safety measures make it anachronistic to compare late-twentieth-century rates of violent death to those of the mid-twentieth century. As strange as it may seem, the violent death rates of the late 1980s and early 1990s, popularly and with some justice believed to be appallingly high, were, in historical and medical terms, artificially low.[24]

A number of researchers believe that homicide, suicide, and motor-vehicle death rates move in unison and that the three categories are socially and psychologically related. A person who is reckless, self-destructive, or intoxicated or has little to lose may easily end up with any one of the three on his death certificate. Conversely those who avoid undue risk, act soberly and responsibly, and have something to lose are far less likely to meet a violent end, unless they simply happen to be in the wrong place at the wrong time.[25]

Figure 10.2 supports the idea that violent death rates moved together in roughly U-shaped curves that were high in the 1930s, lower in the 1940s and 1950s, and then rose again in the early 1960s. There were a few anomalies, but these are easily explained. The dip in motor-vehicle death rates during World War II was due to gas and tire rationing and hence fewer miles driven. It was probably also due to the fact that so many young men were in boot camp rather than behind the wheel. Likewise the homicide downturn during the war, followed by an upturn in 1946, was the usual sponge effect of the armed forces absorbing, isolating, and then releasing men back into civilian society.[26]

In the years 1942–1945 American men did most of their killing overseas. In the racial cockpit of the Pacific theater violence took on a ferocious, mutilatory quality reminiscent of the Indian wars. Dead Japanese soldiers were field-stripped of teeth, ears, noses, hands, skulls, and other souvenirs; returning soldiers clearing customs in Hawaii were routinely asked if they had any bones. One cocky, bearded young minesweeper skipper hanged the mangled body of a kamikaze pilot from the top yardarm of his mast. But none of this latter-day barbarity showed up in domestic violence statistics.[27]

What did show up are post-1946 declines in all four death curves, declines that corresponded to the diminishing percentage of single, divorced, or widowed men. (Figure 10.4 lists the correlations for this and other variables.) The postwar marriage, economic, educational, and suburban booms combined to give a

	Homicides	Suicides	M-V accidents	Combined deaths	Unmarried men	Religious nonattendance	Unemployment	Population 15-24
Homicides	1.00	.752	.695	.884	.650	.752	.647	.828
Suicides	.752	1.00	.575	.827	.875	.764	.925	.777
M-V accidents	.695	.575	1.00	.918	.382	.705	.489	.573
Combined deaths	.884	.827	.918	1.00	.654	.838	.728	.778
Unmarried men	.650	.875	.382	.654	1.00	.741	.766	.867
Religious nonattendance	.752	.764	.705	.838	.741	1.00	.375	.860
Unemployment	.647	.925	.489	.728	.766	.375	1.00	.588
Population 15-24	.828	.777	.573	.778	.867	.860	.588	1.00

Figure 10.4 Correlation matrix for rates of violent death and four independent variables, 1933–1973. Sources: see Figures 10.2 and 10.3. All correlations are based on 41 cases, except for those with religious nonattendance, which are based on 23 cases—the years for which the Gallup Poll data were available. All relationships are statistically significant at $p < .01$ except for that between motor vehicle deaths and unmarried men, which is significant at $p < .02$.

record number of American men a huge emotional and financial stake in the system: wives, kids, jobs, respectability, homes, and mortgages. It was the middle-class experience mass-produced, and it exerted the same restraining influence that it had in the nineteenth century except that the number of affected men was proportionately larger.

Marriage, fatherhood, and homeownership were not the only causes of the decline of violent death rates after 1946, nor can they be disentangled from several other important factors. One is religion. George Gallup's pollsters estimated weekly church or synagogue attendance in 1939, 1940, 1950, and yearly from 1954 on (Figure 10.3). Their findings point to a substantial religious revival in the late 1940s and 1950s. The fraction of Americans who did not attend weekly religious services, 63 percent in 1940, dropped to a twentieth-century low of 51 percent in 1958. In 1950 just under 87 million Americans belonged to churches; in 1960 over 114 million were members. Church buildings sprouted in pastures; seminaries and college religion courses were full. The Revised Standard Version of the Bible and other religious books were runaway bestsellers. Young revivalists like Billy Graham and Oral Roberts launched spectacular careers. Evangelical denominations gained in confidence and numbers. The Catholic Church's increasingly prosperous and still-loyal congregants packed Masses and sent their children to crowded parish schools. The Church's postwar success was so manifest that anti-Catholic writers like Paul Blanshard resurrected the hoary nativist plaint that "superior Catholic fertility" and the institutional clout of the hierarchy threatened the American nation.[28]

Nothing could have been further from the truth. The busy bishops and parish priests, the no-nonsense nuns—and the Pentecostal revivalists, the refugee rabbis, the Nation of Islam's ministers, clergy of every type and color—were a force for order in postwar American society. From a social perspective it is not denomination that matters as much as depth of conviction and active involvement in religious life. Regular churchgoers do not have rap sheets, or at least not long ones.

True, the postwar revival faltered in the 1960s and 1970s, undermined by the triumph of consumer culture. The mainline congregations in particular went into a spiritual and numerical decline that has not yet been reversed. But the revival was real enough in the 1950s and likely had a restraining effect on violent and reckless behavior, judging by the correlations in Figure 10.4. Notice that nonattendance at religious services in those years was also correlated with the percentage of unmarried men and the portion of the population aged fifteen to twenty-four. In the 1950s as in earlier periods of American history young, single, lower-class men were the most religiously indifferent element of the population. Married, middle-aged, middle-class men with children more readily joined churches. That is, the postwar religious revival was itself partly caused by the marriage boom and the upward mobility of a large segment of the population. Both of these were in turn made possible by the rapid expansion of the economy and the creation of millions of jobs. When unemployment went down, so did all measures of violent death.[29]

Unemployment was a particularly good predictor of suicide, the rate of which was very high during the Depression and much lower subsequently. This was an old story. Serious industrial downturns and widespread layoffs have always increased suicides among workers despairing of employment.[30] Joblessness, however, was less strongly correlated to homicidal and motor-vehicle deaths. An odd thing happened during the 1960s. Unemployment was low—during the Vietnam build-up extremely low, around 3 or 4 percent—but the accident and homicide rates were shooting up anyway.

One explanation for this anomaly is demographic. The marriage boom gave rise to the baby boom, and by the 1960s and early 1970s the 49 million babies born between 1941 and 1954 were becoming adolescents and young adults. The portion of the population aged fifteen to twenty-four jumped from 13 percent in 1960 to nearly 18 percent in 1973. For men and women alike fifteen to twenty-four are years during which the chances of drunken driving accidents, violent quarrels, drug experimentation, and suicide are much higher than in childhood or mature adulthood. Hence the higher violent death rates, full employment or no.[31]

The violent tendency inherent in the youthful bulge was magnified by interrelated economic, technological, legal, and moral changes of the 1960s and 1970s. Women's increasing entry into the workforce delayed or, in some cases, indefinitely postponed marriages. Medical innovations—birth control pills and IUDs, plus continued antibiotic progress against venereal diseases—made sex without marriage easier and safer, though in doing so they removed traditional reasons to get and stay married.[32] As a result of the new marital disincentives and of the growing affluence and emphasis on expressive individualism and erotic gratification, more young men began delaying or forgoing formal marriage. More middle-aged ones took advantage of liberalized divorce laws and "traded in" their aging wives for younger ones by way of remarriage.

The net effect of these portentous changes, collectively known as the sexual revolution, was to increase the numbers of single adults and fatherless children. In 1960 Americans spent an average of 62 percent of their adult lives with spouses and children, an all-time high; in 1980 they spent 43 percent, an all-time low. "This trend alone," comments the sociologist David Popenoe, "may help to account for the high and rising crime rates." Violent crimes were largely committed by unattached males, he reasons, and when their number rose, so did the crime rate.[33]

The 1960s and 1970s were also characterized by growing tolerance and use of psychoactive drugs, of which the most publicized were marijuana, LSD, and heroin. Their increased use caused more overdoses and accidents and generated turf and robbery homicides in illicit drug markets. At the same time alcohol consumption, which had been low and stable from 1947 to 1959, shot up from around 2.02 gallons of absolute alcohol per person in 1960 to 2.69 in 1973, an increase of 33 percent in just fourteen years. This increase undoubtedly contributed to the higher violent death rates, as did the beginning of the cocaine revival. Practically nonexistent at midcentury, cocaine began a comeback in 1969–1973 and continued to grow in popularity for the next fifteen years.[34]

It was as if, in the late 1940s and 1950s, all the irenic planets in the American solar system had finally come into alignment. Gender balance, predominantly female immigration, widespread and stable marriages, educational and employment opportunities, religious revivals, and low levels of alcohol and drug abuse all worked to diminish the number or constrain the behavior of America's young men. From the standpoint of preventing violence and disorder, just about everything that could have gone right did go right, as in the mining camps and cattle towns nearly everything that could have gone wrong did go wrong.

It is true that in the postwar era homicide remained high in the United States in comparison to European nations like Britain. Guns were still widely available, notions of honor and justifiable killing lingered in the South and West, and motion pictures and television glorified the violent frontier action hero. Moreover, the homicide death rate of nonwhite men, though declining from 51.5 in 1947 to a low of 33.6 in 1961, remained very high relative to the rate for white men and inflated the national total.[35] In relation to other developed countries postwar America was still a violent land, though by its own historical standards (if not those of peacetime Europe) it had become relatively tranquil. It would remain so until its irenic planets drifted out of alignment during the 1960s and 1970s.

The Collapse of the Inner Cities

The other major and, as it turned out, more lasting effect of the postwar marriage and suburban boom was to reinforce the tendency for urban violence and disorder to be concentrated in or near city centers. From their inception in the railroad boom of the nineteenth century, American suburbs had been essentially middle- or upper-class enclaves populated by propertied families with stable incomes. As such they had much lower rates of crime and delinquency than crowded inner-city tenement districts, where people were poorer, life was more precarious, vice operators were more abundant, and the children of immigrants often ran in gangs and afoul of the law.

Pre–World War II American cities were nevertheless fairly compact. Even in the biggest cities the distance between the lowest and highest crime zones—in Chicago, say, between suburban Oak Park and the downtown Loop—might be as little as five miles. But by the 1970s the distance between the safest, most affluent suburbs and the most crime-ridden inner-city neighborhoods could easily be five or ten times that distance. The reasons were cars, highway construction, and the suburban explosion.[36]

Let me illustrate, if I may, with a story. In the summer of 1974 a friend and I were visited by a young German Marxist we had met while studying in Europe. Our German acquaintance arrived at Kansas City International Airport and was driven by interstate beltway to my friend's commodious suburban home.

On the principle of when in Rome, he agreed to go with us to a football exhibition game. We drove along the interstate to Arrowhead Stadium, watched the game, and returned home. "I enjoyed very much the match," the German said politely, "and you have a fine *Autobahn*. But I have a question. Where are your factories? Where are your ghettos?"

I looked him straight in the eye and said, "It's all communist propaganda. They don't exist."

His expression was one of complete bafflement. His mind told him I was pulling his leg but his experience told him something quite different. In two days he had not seen a shred of industry or poverty, so well were these things concealed by the city's sprawl.

Who could not tell a similar tale? The isolation and segregation of the poor have not only confused foreign visitors and eased the consciences of the affluent, they have disastrously increased the economic, familial, and social problems of inner cities in a way that has made the affluent more determined than ever to keep their distance. The automobile has become middle America's instrument of applied sociology. Postwar suburbanites, including those who were not openly or consciously racist, took advantage of cars and the existence of distant, often municipally separate communities to practice geographical and statistical discrimination. They knew where the bad neighborhoods were and used their automobility to avoid them, thereby reducing their chances of being mugged or burglarized or having their children educated in inferior schools.

The neighborhoods they abandoned or shunned were increasingly occupied by poor immigrants, often though not always black, for whom moving to the city was a step up. As the journalist Nicholas Lemann has pointed out, an extraordinary thing occurred in the rural South after the war. Hundreds of thousands of poor blacks, sharecroppers and small farmers displaced by agricultural mechanization, could quadruple their incomes by merely relocating to a city a long day's train journey away. They streamed to the North, as did thousands of poor southern whites. They were joined by a wave of Puerto Rican immigrants, the so-called Marine Tigers, named for a Liberty ship that shuttled back and forth between New York and San Juan after the war.[37]

They might as well have booked passage on the *Titanic*. Rural-to-urban migration worked well enough in the 1940s and early 1950s when unskilled and industrial jobs were abundant in the center cities. But as more and more people and employers left for the suburbs and as the industrial base of the economy began shrinking, the legitimate economic prospects of inner-city dwellers diminished. Many of the entrepreneurs who did stay were in some way connected to vice: loan sharks and pawn brokers, liquor-store and tavern owners, drug dealers, pimps, prostitutes, and numbers runners. This not only increased the amount of violence—vice institutions and transactions, as always, were flash points—it drained away money and sharply increased alcoholism and addiction among the newcomers and their children.[38]

Drug and alcohol abuse were among the most tragic consequences of the great black migration. Southern racial mythology to the contrary, blacks did not have serious problems with alcohol or narcotics at the turn of the century. Most of them were poor and lived in remote and often legally dry rural areas. Despite occasional Saturday night and holiday sprees, chronic alcoholism among country blacks was practically unknown. It is not going too far to suggest that in 1900 rural blacks were the soberest people in the nation, apart from totally abstemious groups like the Mormons.

But when blacks began moving to the cities and settled in or near vice districts the situation changed. Unemployed black men were particularly prone to get into trouble with liquor or drugs, both commonplace in the ghetto environment. Narcotics arrests and hospital commitments among blacks went up sharply in the 1940s, 1950s, and early 1960s as the tempo of the southern black exodus increased. In 1974 Washington, D.C., by then a largely black city, had far and away the highest rate of alcohol abuse in the country, with nearly one in four adult residents an alcoholic. By contrast Mississippi and Alabama, two states with large rural black populations, then had the lowest alcoholism rates in the nation.[39]

Heavy drinking and drug abuse aggravated inner-city violence, not least among young, turf-conscious black and Latino gang members. A notorious instance was the 30 July 1957 killing of Michael Farmer, a fifteen-year-old polio victim who lived with his parents in New York City. He was jumped by members of the Egyptian Kings and Dragons gang, who had been drinking cheap wine and whiskey and were out looking for their enemies when Farmer and a companion happened along. "You know, I was drunk," admitted one assailant, "so I just stabbed him. [Laughs] He was screamin' like a dog." When Farmer's mother identified his body in the hospital morgue she said his expression looked as if he were calling for help.[40]

The trial, then the longest in New York City's history, created a sensation and focused attention on the growing problem of gang violence. (So did the musical *West Side Story*, which opened with a cast of more sympathetic characters two months after the Farmer slaying.) One of the New Yorkers who decided to get involved in the problem was a young priest named William O'Brien. Following the Farmer murder, he recalled, "hundreds of kids were referred to me, and ninety percent of them were using drugs." The solution O'Brien ultimately hit upon was a therapeutic community called Daytop Village in which addicted, alcoholic, and violent youth were resocialized in an artificial authoritarian family.[41]

Daytop was a noble effort. It was also a drop in the proverbial bucket. By the late 1960s and 1970s widespread alcoholism and drug abuse were established facts of ghetto life. They led to violence directly through intoxication, bad judgment, drug rip-offs, and other disputes; indirectly by compounding problems of marital and family stability, which were also being worsened by job loss and the steady growth of a self-contained, increasingly isolated, and deeply troubled urban "underclass."

I shall have more to say about the problems of ghetto families in the next two chapters. The point I want to emphasize here is simply that migration patterns in the postwar decades exaggerated the centripetal character of urban violence and disorder as suburbs filled up with people who were affluent, family-oriented, sober, and well educated, leaving behind people who were less and less likely to share these traits. In the end the exodus turned out to be a matter of class as well as race. The black middle class, greatly expanded by the Civil Rights movement and growing access to public-sector jobs, got out or made plans to do so. "I still live in the black community," a black parole officer complained to a black sociologist. "I want to get away from all riff-raff, but I'm just not able to afford one of those big mortgages yet, ha-ha." He was, he admitted, "afraid of some of these younger guys, what they'll do to people like me and you. They don't care, don't worry about jail. They'll take you out of here." Looked at honestly, such fears of violence and predatory crime and their proposed remedy, flight from the inner city, were identical to those of middle-class whites. Identical too were the consequences: concentration in the ghetto of those with the poorest economic prospects and the fewest pro-social role models.[42]

A black man interviewed in 1981 under the alias "Teddy" had an unusual perspective on the ghetto implosion. In 1965 he was sent to prison on charges of attempted robbery and attempted murder, his fourth felony conviction. He did not get out until 1977. When he returned to Harlem late one evening he experienced a time-machine effect, so drastically had the area changed. "Harlem wasn't Harlem no more," he remembered:

> I saw the trains were all marked up with graffiti, and that the platforms were dirty. I said to myself, "What the fuck has happened?" I got off the subway at 135th Street. I looked at the neighborhood and there weren't any more houses, just bricks and garbage and shit piled up. I said, "Goddam!" I walked down another block, and I saw that all the stores that weren't closed up were barred up. You couldn't see anything in the windows no more. There weren't any people in the street, and this was summertime. When I left there were people all over the streets. You could hear music, and kids laughing. Now it was almost like a ghost town.

When Teddy reached his mother's house, a once-grand edifice on Seventh Avenue that had been chopped up into apartments, he saw that it had fallen into complete disrepair. "The lights were hanging down, the walls were marked, the halls smelled like piss . . . I went into the apartment and said, 'Mom, what's going on?' That apartment used to be spotless, but now the plaster and shit were falling down." When he woke up the next morning he looked out the window: "It was just completely turned around. Across the street the houses were boarded up, nailed up. And the first thing I see is a guy out there selling dope."[43]

What happened in Harlem happened all over the country in the 1960s and 1970s with the same bloody results. In Cleveland the homicide rate jumped 320 percent between 1958 and 1974; most of the slayings were black-on-black ghetto shootings. In Michigan so many black men were deliberately or accidentally killed during the 1960s that the life expectancy of that group fell by three years. In the nation as a whole, more blacks were killed by other blacks in a single year, 1977, than were killed in combat in Vietnam from 1963 to 1972.[44]

By 1980, when the American homicide rate hit a new high, the urban environment had become so polarized and the situation in the slum neighborhoods so bad that the life expectancy of male ghetto dwellers was approaching that of people living in the world's least developed countries. In Central Harlem, where 40 percent of the excess mortality in 1979–1981 was due to cirrhosis, homicide, or drug addiction, the chances of a man reaching his sixty-fifth birthday were worse than they were in Bangladesh.[45]

Night as Frontier

Twentieth-century urban violence and disorder have been unevenly distributed in ways other than geographical. The criminologist Marvin Wolfgang, in a well-known study of homicides in Philadelphia in 1948–1952, found not only that the killings were concentrated in the inner city but that nearly half took place on just two days, Friday and Saturday, and nearly half occurred within the span of just six evening hours, 8:00 P.M. to 1:59 A.M. Studies of homicide patterns in other cities have confirmed that a disproportionate number of murders and assaults take place after dark. "Our day begins when your day ends," homicide detectives are fond of saying. The same is true of emergency room personnel, who become very busy with bleeders in the early morning hours.[46]

The best way to understand this phenomenon is to think of the night as a frontier. If one considers a frontier to be partly a collection of human characteristics ("a form of society," as Turner put it), then it is reasonable to ask whether those characteristics exhibit a temporal as well as spatial pattern. They do. Electric lighting, automobiles, and other technological innovations have made it possible for twentieth-century Americans to carry on more and more of their activities after dark. It was, in the words of the sociologist Murray Melbin, "as if the flow across the continent swerved into the nighttime rather than spilling into the sea."[47]

But the colonization of the night, like that of the western frontier, has been a selective demographic process. Melbin analyzed a large sample of passersby at various sites in central Boston in 1974. He found that men were more numerous than women at any given time but that their majority was only 52–61 percent during daylight hours versus 67–89 percent at night. The ages of the passersby were just as skewed. No one over the age of fifty-nine was observed on the streets after midnight and no one over forty from 2:00 to 5:00 A.M. Not coincidentally there was more violence after dark. The largest number of fights, for example, was reported around midnight despite the fact that most Bostonians were asleep.[48]

This has been and remains the pattern in all American cities. In Boston and elsewhere the urban motor-vehicle death rate quadruples after dark. Nor is this simply a matter of poor visibility. Nighttime drivers are more likely to be under twenty-five, intoxicated, or both. Murder and rape are everywhere crimes of the night. In Jacksonville, Florida, a woman is four times as likely to be raped at midnight as she is at noon, although the Jacksonvilleans active at midday far outnumber those up and about late at night. Nighttime provides cover and, in a statistical and moral sense, an abnormal population. Avoiding that population by avoiding the late-night hours is a form of precautionary temporal segregation, just as moving to a suburb is a form of precautionary residential segregation.[49]

What people shun in reality they often seek out in fiction. The nighttime has provided writers and filmmakers with many of their most successful settings, plots, and characters. Beginning in the 1920s the hard-boiled school of American detective fiction became temporally fixated on the floating night world of speakeasies, roadhouses, gambling joints, and cheap hotels. The dark urban settings of Dashiell Hammett, Erle Stanley Gardner, and Raymond Chandler in turn influenced and lent themselves to the dominant visual style of Hollywood in the 1940s and 1950s, the stark, black-and-white cinematography of *film noir*. Just as pulp fiction and western films had mythologized the ranching frontier, preserving the humble cowboy in the magnifying amber of popular culture, *noir* movies glamorized the tough-guy gumshoes, the Sam Spades and Philip Marlowes whose personal sense of honor and willingness to resort to violence to uphold it resembled the frontier code.[50] Thus the fictionalized version of the colonization of the night injected into the collective American consciousness something it did not especially need, another set of larger-than-life and homicidally violent male action figures.

The colonization of the night by youthful crime- or accident-prone men has had legal and political consequences. Municipal curfews on teenagers, spot checks for drunken drivers, feminist "Take Back the Night" campaigns, and paramilitary vigilante operations like the Guardian Angels, who patrolled New York City's subways, are all instances of organized responses to the dangers posed by the abnormal demography of the nighttime frontier. In a way they are updated versions of the anti-vice and law-and-order campaigns of the maturing mining and cattle towns. History, sociology, epidemiology, literature, myth, and politics all point to the same basic lesson. Whenever and wherever young males congregate, violent trouble is likely to follow.

At mid-century, however, most middle-class men were not active in the dangerous late-night hours. They were instead daylight creatures of regular habits who worked in small businesses or, increasingly, in large organizations from which they commuted home in the evening. Whatever experience they had of frontier violence was vicarious. They watched their share of shoot-'em-ups but also Milton Berle, Lucille Ball, and Ed Sullivan, America's strait-laced impresario. They took their kids to picnics and ball games and Scout meetings. They cut the grass and played golf on Saturday, went to church on Sunday morning, watched football, tucked their kids in bed, retired to their rooms, made love to their wives, rolled over, drifted into snoring sleep, got up, shaved and showered, climbed into the car, and drove back to work on Monday morning.

This lifestyle has been subjected to endless intellectual and artistic ridicule. It has been mocked as bland, conformist, soulless, sexist, speechless. "My generation, coming into its own," complained John Updike, "was called Silent, as if, after all the vain and murderous noise of recent history, this was a bad thing."[51]

The jibe hits home. All social history consists of trade-offs, and all politics is about which trade-offs should be made. While the postwar marriage and suburban booms undoubtedly narrowed the options of married women and bled center cities, it seems equally undeniable that they were, at least in the short run, a potent force for social order, welcome in a country that had been through a lot. The marriage boom gave purpose to, restrained the behavior of, and added years to the lives of a generation of young men. To fairly evaluate the 1950s or any other decade it is important to remember what did not happen as well as what did. Judging from the violent death curves, what did not happen during the marriage-boom era was the premature, senseless, and traumatic deaths of tens of thousands of American men.

ELEVEN

Ghetto Violence

By the mid-1980s it had become fashionable to announce that the upsurge of criminal violence in American society that had begun in the 1960s was finally over or at least slowing down. Reported violent crime was declining and the homicide death rate had fallen from over 10 to about 8 per 100,000 population. Increasingly sophisticated trauma units were saving more victims, but the root cause was supposed to be that the baby boomers were outgrowing their wild days. Fewer young men relative to total population meant lower rates of crime. The authors of one article went so far as to plot predicted rates of homicide, robbery, burglary, and auto theft to the year 2000. All the projected curves showed steady declines through the 1990s. "As the baby boom ages," they commented, "better days lie ahead for the nation's police departments and for its citizens."[1]

A funny thing happened on the way to the better days. In the late 1980s rates of violent crime and drug abuse began shooting upward, particularly in big cities. In Chicago, for example, the number of cases of aggravated assault, rape, robbery, and murder jumped 16 per cent between 1985 and 1988 despite no increase in the city's population.[2]

This was no local anomaly. Problems of social order, particularly homicidal violence, worsened throughout the United States in the late 1980s and early 1990s with the homicide rate hitting a new peak in 1991. Though rates of burglary and theft were comparable to those of European nations, the American rape rate was by then eight times, the murder rate four times, and the heroin addiction rate twice the European average. With just 4–5 percent of the world's population, Americans were managing to consume half the world's supply of cocaine. Americans had also achieved the highest rate of incarceration in the world, 455 per 100,000. South Africans, a distant second, had 311. The Japanese had 45. America had plainly become one of the world's most violent and self-destructive nations at the very moment demographers had forecast things would be getting much better.[3] What went wrong?

There was nothing faulty about the demographers' logic, at least as it applied to homicide, the single most closely watched index of violence. The rate of homicide among the aging baby boomers did go down during the late 1980s and early 1990s. But these gains were more than canceled out by an unanticipated explosion of murderous violence among males aged fourteen to twenty-four, who were committing more than half of all homicides by 1992.[4]

It was also clear that the problem of homicide, and the problem of violent crime generally, was centered on young minority men, especially black men, who lived and died in urban ghettos. In New York City in 1990–1991 the homicide rate for black males aged fifteen to twenty-four was 247 per 100,000, higher than that of the Texas frontier town of Fort Griffin in the 1870s. As on the historical frontier, most ghetto slayings involved handguns. Nationally the firearm murder rate for black males fifteen to nineteen, the group that experienced the biggest percentage increase in homicide deaths, was 105 per 100,000, or eleven times that of white males in the same age group.[5]

Blacks were on both ends of the gun. In the early 1990s there were more black murderers than white murderers, although blacks made up only an eighth of the population. Most of the killing was of the intraracial player variety, black men killing other black men who were involved in drugs and street life or who had committed violent crimes themselves.[6] What made the 1994 indictment of O. J. Simpson for murder extraordinary, apart from the defendant's celebrity, was its deviation from this rule. If Simpson had been accused of killing another black man in his youthful San Francisco gang days, the media would have taken no notice.

The police would have taken notice, though their investigation would have been routine, perhaps desultory. The work of big-city homicide squads has long been politically and morally stratified. Certain cases, such as the murder of a child, generate tremendous pressure for a quick solution. Homicide detectives call them red balls or holy-shit cases, and they are taken very seriously. But even in cases without a high media profile detectives distinguish between those in which there is a "real victim" and everyday player violence, such as one gang member or crack dealer shooting another. Gender counts as well as race. Murders of women are investigated more rigorously than the more common murders of men.[7]

Player violence and drug trafficking are often difficult crimes to prosecute. Witnesses tend to be scarce, uncooperative, or afraid to talk. But enough cases eventually result in convictions to have dramatic penal consequences, particularly for black men. By the mid-1990s nearly one-third of black American men in their twenties were under some form of correctional supervision. In Washington 42 percent and in Baltimore an astonishing 57 percent of black men between eighteen and thirty-five were in prison, on probation or parole, out on bail, or being sought on an arrest warrant. Even allowing for prejudicial arrests and biased sentencing, it was simply not possible that all these convictions and sentences were a manifestation of oppression. Something was amiss in black America, above all in the inner cities.[8]

Fatherless Bachelors

That something had to do with the universal problem of youthful males and social disorder. Boys experience parental discipline and modeling in the families in which they are raised and self-discipline and adult responsibilities when they form their own families. Men subject to first the one and then the other type of family control are unlikely to behave destructively. Men who are raised in intact families but do not marry are more prone than their married peers to violent and disorderly behavior as well as to higher mortality. The worst case, however, occurs when young men who are inadequately disciplined and socialized in single-parent families of origin also do not marry and establish their own families of procreation. They are doubly prone to irresponsible and sociopathic behavior because their moral horizons, habits of self-control, and economic opportunities have been truncated at both ends of the reproductive cycle.

Illegitimacy is a recipe for anomie. Illegitimate children often lack not only fathers and decent family incomes but the whole array of socially obligated kin (paternal grandparents, uncles, aunts, cousins) who come with an official or publicly acknowledged marriage. A male child who is illegitimate is, by definition, missing half his kin and the social and economic capital they represent. He may have many relatives in the sense of shared genes, but any claims he may make upon their time or resources are socially contingent and legally avoidable.

A man who does not marry or acknowledge paternity likewise lacks another set of relatives, his wife, children, and in-laws, for whom he is responsible and from whom he might also benefit through family alliances. Brothers-in-law are useful fellows. They can help find jobs, loan money, serve as children's role models. The myth of individualism notwithstanding, people get up and on in the world through families and family alliances.

Illegitimacy and singleness frustrate this process and, when they reach a certain point, begin to perpetuate themselves. Illegitimate children raised in a social milieu where fatherless families are the norm often grow up poor and conceive children who become, at an early age, unmarried parents, and so on across generations. Within the limits imposed by heredity we mold our sexual behavior—in fact, we become ourselves in every sense—by emulating the behavior of others in our social environment.[9]

The fatherless bachelor phenomenon has been most widespread among black Americans, who have long had higher rates of family disruption than whites. Black couples have been more often separated or divorced, and bachelorhood has been more common among black men than among white. In 1992 40.4 percent of black men over age eighteen had never been married compared to just 24.2 percent of white men.[10] This statistic alone would translate into higher black rates of crime and violent death.

The biggest and most ominous difference, however, has been in illegitimate births. In 1960 only about one in fifty whites and one in five blacks were born out of wedlock. By 1990 the numbers were one in five whites and well over three in five blacks. These ratios would have meant little socially if they had represented technically illegitimate births in stable cohabitations or common-law marriages, but in fact most illegitimate children in America grow up without a father to provide discipline, moral instruction, a positive role model, and regular financial support. By 1991 the combination of widespread illegitimacy, divorce, separation, and abandonment had made the single-parent or "blended" stepparent family the rule in black America, where only one child in four lived in a traditional nuclear family with both biological parents.[11]

Enter Moynihan

The modern debate over the causes and consequences of black family disruption and illegitimacy took off in 1965 with the publication of Daniel Patrick Moynihan's Labor Department study, *The Negro Family: The Case for National Action.* The Moynihan report, as it became known, was an argument that black social problems, including crime, delinquency, and poor school performance, were rooted in the deterioration of black urban families, evidenced in high rates of marital dissolution, illegitimate births, and female-headed, welfare-dependent households.

Moynihan supposed that black family life in America had been difficult from the beginning, owing to the disruptions and separations imposed by a harsh system of chattel slavery. Things had been made worse by the unsettling effects of rural-to-urban migration and catastrophically high levels of black unemployment since the onset of the Depression, relieved only by periods of full employment during wartime.

Yet joblessness was not the whole story. One of Moynihan's discoveries was that from 1948 to 1962 the nonwhite male unemployment rate and the number of Aid to Families with Dependent Children (AFDC) cases opened during the year moved in lockstep, the correlation being +.91. Black men apparently abandoned families they could not support, increasing the need for welfare services. But then something snapped. In 1963 and 1964 the number of AFDC cases kept growing even as the nonwhite unemployment rate was plummeting. The correlation, having been strongly positive for years, was suddenly negative. Moynihan, who feared that the situation had begun feeding on itself, was at a loss to explain this disturbing new phenomenon.[12]

He was not at a loss for critics. He was variously accused of racism, of being hung up on middle-class family norms, of misunderstanding the strength and resiliency of black kin networks, of putting too much causal weight on slavery, and, in a famous phrase, of "blaming the victim." The last charge ignored the report's sociological bent and Moynihan's insistence that fatherless families caused chaos in all human communities, none excepted. But the critics had their way. Within a year Moynihan had become a kind of political nonperson and his report had been all but officially suppressed.[13]

During the 1980s the report was politically rehabilitated, thanks in no small measure to the fact that so many of its troubling prophecies had come true. Indices of black family disruption continued to rise in good times and bad, black illegitimacy became the norm rather than the exception, and the evidence that violent and disorderly behavior, substance abuse, poor academic performance, and mortality rates were all exacerbated by family disruption and illegitimacy continued to accumulate. One Ohio study of death certificates found that children born out of wedlock were five times more likely to die by homicide than children in the general population. Illegitimacy was a better predictor of childhood homicide risk than the mother's race, education, residence, or any other factor.[14]

But there was no agreement on what was causing illegitimacy and single-parent families in the first place. During the 1980s the two most publicly discussed views were the welfare thesis and the job-loss thesis. The former, articulated by a host of conservative commentators, stressed that generous welfare benefits ("transfers") had created perverse incentives. "Any social transfer," declared Charles Murray, "increases the net value of being in the condition that prompted the transfer."[15] Lyndon Johnson's Great Society and its subsequent legislative additions had made it possible for healthy adults to withdraw from the labor market, for alcoholics and drug addicts to stay high and live off food stamps and SSI (Supplemental Security Income), and most critically for sexually active women to marry the state rather than husbands, secure in the knowledge that their children would be supported by AFDC. Men could abandon or refuse to marry the women they impregnated, certain that others, however grudgingly, would pay to raise and educate their offspring. Government transfer payments thus removed an ancient check on male sexuality and behavior, the necessity of family involvement to insure the survival of children. In the new ghetto-cum-welfare environment the optimal male strategy for having a good time, enhancing reputation, and passing on genes was simply, and atavistically, frequent intercourse with as many fertile women as possible.

This line of thinking was rebutted by liberals who denied the notion that welfare support was in any sense generous. AFDC payments, for example, steadily declined in real dollars after 1972. If illegitimacy were tied to such benefits, the number of out-of-wedlock births should have gone down, not up. A likelier explanation was structural changes in the labor market. Family formation and family stability required decent jobs. But decent working-class jobs were increasingly hard to find. Deindustrialization, government cutbacks, union decline, automation, retrenchment, global competition, and other economic changes had reduced the availability of secure employment for people with high school educations or less. When in 1990 the City of New York announced an examination for prospective sanitation workers (starting salary $23,000, no high school diploma required), more than 100,000 people signed up to compete for 2,000 positions. Many of the applicants were from the city's large minority population and lived in race- and class-segregated neighborhoods where legitimate economic opportunities were scarce.[16]

The liberal prescription for this problem was to provide the means—public transportation, affirmative action, daycare, education, adult retraining—to make it easier for inner-city residents to get, and get to, jobs. Over the long run more and better jobs would presumably translate into more marriages, fewer illegiti-

mate births, greater family stability, and less violent and disorderly behavior, as had been the case in the 1940s and 1950s.

But this approach also came in for its share of criticism.
Teaching poor people to be welders or meat cutters was fine, but
unless the number of such blue-collar jobs kept growing the
training and placement programs would simply substitute one
group of employees for another, having no effect on the overall
unemployment rate. The alternative, to train people for skilled
careers in growth sectors of the economy, ran into the fact that
children from poor, single-parent families spent less time on
homework, did less well in school, and consequently ended up
less literate and numerate than the general population.[17] A child
in this predicament was necessarily much harder to train later in
life for good jobs in the postindustrial economy. The same dilemma confronted rehabilitation efforts of every stripe. It was,
after all, much harder to rehabilitate someone who had never
been habilitated in the first place.

The Culture of Poverty

Though debate between conservative critics of welfare and liberal advocates of employment during the 1980s was acerbic and
politicized, there was at least one piece of common ground. Both
sides agreed that the behavior of ghetto residents was in some
sense economically rational. That is, marrying the state and
using transfer payments to raise children was reasonable: why
earn and spend your own money when you can have access to
other people's? For market conservatives the basic problem was
misguided policy, not individuals' opportunistic response to it.

Liberals accounted for the socially destructive behavior of
unwed or irresponsible parents by posing a question of their
own: Why even think of getting or staying married if it was
financially impossible to support a family? In their analysis the
basic problem was the lack of decent incomes and job opportunities, not the individuals' rational if unfortunate adaptation of
sexual behavior to chronic unemployment.

But cultures as well as individuals adapt, and cultures are
harder to change by altering the details of public policy. In fact
cultures can become so distorted by intractable poverty that they

become the means by which impoverishment is transmitted across generations. Countervalue norms—why bother, squares work, hustling is hip, high is cool, get it now—are psychologically adaptive, providing a kind of defiant design for living for those who would otherwise succumb to hopelessness and despair. Yet these same norms encourage behaviors that guarantee economic and familial failure over the long run.

This thesis, popularized in the 1960s by the anthropologist Oscar Lewis as the "culture of poverty," has been the main counterpoint to left-right market discourse about ghetto disarray. The concept has had an important influence on conservative thinkers who have stressed the moral dimension of poverty and disorder and, at least initially, on liberal thinkers who believed they had the power and responsibility to break the cycle of deprivation and demoralization that made the lives of the poor so enduringly miserable.

Or some of the poor. Lewis made an important distinction between being poor, which was often temporary, and being trapped in the culture of poverty, which was not. Most Eastern European Jews, for example, were impecunious when they arrived in America. But because they had what was an essentially middle-class outlook, emphasizing learning, religion, thrift, and community organization, they soon prospered.[18]

There was another possible explanation as to why some groups escaped poverty and others did not. In the early 1970s a handful of social thinkers, notably the psychologist Richard Herrnstein, began offering a dysgenic version of the culture of poverty thesis. Intelligence and temperament, Herrnstein argued, were to some degree inherited. Because of social isolation and homogamy (like mating with like), members of the lower class were apt to have intercourse with other members of the lower class, conceiving children who were on average less intelligent, more impulsive, and harder to discipline than children of middle- or upper-class parents. Insofar as these traits contributed to educational, economic, and familial failure, they guaranteed that the lower class, black as well as white, would remain poor, troublesome, and self-perpetuating, particularly in an economy that rewarded people with college degrees and high cognitive abilities.[19]

The idea that low intelligence and other heritable defects were responsible for problems of social order was not new. It had been an article of faith among early twentieth-century social engineers, whose initiatives had ranged from screening programs to identify and treat feebleminded offenders to laws for sterilizing certain criminals and mental defectives. Genetic explanations and programs fell out of favor after World War II, when the culture-learning model reigned supreme in the social sciences, until Herrnstein and other neo-Darwinians began to revive them.[20]

The dysgenic argument, as it applies to differences in IQ and social class, comes down to a chicken-or-egg question. Moynihan pointed out that black children whose fathers were present had normal IQ scores while black children whose fathers were absent scored an average of only 91.[21] Was that difference due to growing up in a poor environment? Or was there something defective about the intelligence of the parents of illegitimate children? Or was it both, nurture and nature working together to form the interlocking jaws of a terrible trap?

There is, to put it mildly, no consensus on the relative weight of environment and genetic endowment in the formation of the urban underclass and its problems. This may well prove to be one of the outstandingly controversial questions in the social sciences for the next generation. What seems incontrovertible, however, is the role of racial and class prejudice (and hence economic marginalization and social isolation) in creating and exacerbating those problems. A good example is the original American urban underclass, the Chinese. They had very serious problems of violence and disorder, and yet their descendants have consistently scored *high* on IQ tests.

What also seems incontrovertible is that something like Lewis's culture of poverty, non-genetic version, is indeed operating in the contemporary ghetto. That is, an oppositional lower-class subculture has taken root and has divided the black community along lines of value and class. The sociologist Elijah Anderson, employing the terms of the subjects he interviewed, refers to this division as the conflict between "the culture of decency" and "the culture of the street."

The black culture of decency values the same things as most

middle- and working-class Americans: close if not invariably traditional nuclear families, financial stability, religion, the work ethic, and getting ahead. It disapproves of that which middle America disapproves: crime, drug abuse, and teenage pregnancy. Mature black men ("old heads") steeped in these values were once role models for men coming of age, but with the disappearance of well-paying blue-collar jobs and the rise of the hyperghetto they have lost prestige and credibility among the young, who have become increasingly attuned to the culture of the street.

For young men the key value in the street culture is hipness, or status based on one's person and personal reputation rather than on one's conventional achievements. Indeed conventional achievement and comportment—doing well in school, being civil to whites, speaking standard English—detract from street reputation rather than enhancing it.

So does sexual restraint. Within the peer group, often a neighborhood gang, sexual conquest provides impoverished young black men with a libidinous outlet, reinforces masculine identity, and enhances their standing. Marriage and being good providers do not. Remote prospects in any case, they are more likely to be a prelude to leaving the group than a means of ascent within it. The object, writes Anderson, is to smoothly "play" the girls but never to "play house." They hit on vulnerable, naive, and often fatherless teenage women and then run, maintaining personal freedom and independence from matrimonial ties. When such ties exist, they are to be on the young man's terms.[22]

Street culture encourages men in the view that women are sexual objects to be cajoled and exploited rather than treated with consideration and dignity, much less regarded as lifelong partners. "For a lot of poor young black males," Patrick Welsh writes in a candid memoir of his career as a high-school teacher,

> the tradition of fatherhood seems absent. Many of them have no real fathers themselves. It's a kind of joke with them. When my wife was pregnant with our first baby, a couple of guys I taught quipped that their then thirty-nine-year-old English teacher was

"way behind." "I've already got two," said one seventeen-year-old boy . . . Black girls I've known from English class tell me most boys deny parenthood. "Get out of my face, bitch! That ain't my kid," one girl quoted her boyfriend as saying when she confronted him with his paternity.[23]

The unmarried fathers who do acknowledge paternity are usually part-time husbands and fathers. They may visit and provide a few dollars for Pampers, Similac, shoes, and other necessities, but their spending priorities are elsewhere, often with dating other women and purchasing hip accoutrements. "I don't know if the statement 'the clothes make the man' truly exists anywhere else," says Sharron Corley, a member of a Brownsville shoplifting gang called the LoLifes, "but in Brooklyn it is considered a motto. With this in mind I have no problem admitting my being materialistic."[24]

This behavior is encouraged by young women who expect their boyfriends to be sharply dressed and to provide them with expensive presents, never mind where the money comes from. "Got no cash, got not time," summed up one Detroit girl. "I want nice things," said another. "I likes BMWs, Volvos and Benzos. Some niggah tried rapping to me, talking about going out on a date, taking the *bus* . . . I said, 'Niggah, please!'" The no-money no-sex equation poses a Darwinian dilemma for young men without legitimate jobs. "I risked my life for pussy," complained a former drug dealer. "All this scrambling [dealing] and shit is how we can get with [the girls], because if you don't have that money you ain't nobody to them . . . So unless you ready to give up the sex or give up the drugs, give up the gun, you take the risk."[25]

Girls are also extremely conscious of their own appearance and compete among themselves over who is the cutest, or who has the cutest boyfriend. The competition extends to their babies. Far from being viewed as unwanted nuisances, babies are objects of status. Anderson reports that some young mothers spend as much as 75 percent of their welfare checks on fancy baby clothing, to the point of neglecting their own and their infants' nutrition. Street culture, remarks another observer, is a feminist nightmare.[26]

Make You Tall

Street culture is also extremely violent. Aggression among women most often assumes a verbal form, "he say, she say" gossip designed to tear down another's appearance and reputation. But among men matters of reputation are settled in more direct fashion, often with deadly weapons. As in the South, in which almost all urban black men have personal or ancestral roots, to permit oneself to be insulted is to lose one's self-respect. "Where I lived, stepping on someone's shoe was a capital offense punishable by death," remembers Sanyika Shakur, a Crip gangster in South Central Los Angeles. "Regardless of the condition of the shoes, the underlying factor that usually got you killed was the principle [of] respect, a linchpin critical to relations between all people, but magnified by thirty in the ghettos and slums across America."[27]

Willingness to retaliate has a practical as well as an emotional logic. Any young man who backs out of a ghetto dispute sets himself up as an easy mark, a target for future attacks: "You got to dog everybody or they gonna dog you." A violent response guarantees status and discourages challengers. So does "going for bad," maintaining a social posture that practically radiates violence by threatening demeanor, gangster clothing, or even signs like the one left in English and Spanish in the window of a brand-new BMW parked on a New York City street: "Yes, I have a motherfucking radio and I dare you to fuck with it."[28]

A violent response to an affront can produce a wild, almost primitive pleasure. "I just stood there thinking," the reporter Nathan McCall writes of a youthful encounter with a rival at a carnival, "*This niggah is gonna make me do something I didn't come here to do.* Not only had he disrespected me again, but he'd done it in *front* of my lady. I *had* to do something. That's when I decided to shoot him." McCall's antagonist, a loudmouth named Plaz, kept right on bullyragging him: "Niggah, you better get outta my face 'fore I stomp your ass! I'm tired a' you and that bitch . . ."

Unwise words. McCall pulled a .22 out of his shoulder pouch and fired point-blank into Plaz's chest. A red speck appeared and Plaz flopped backward, while his startled companions scattered at the report of the gun. Shock and terror showed in his defeated eyes. "In that moment," McCall remembers, "I felt like God. I felt so good and powerful that I wanted to do it again. I felt like I could pull that trigger, and keep on pulling it until I emptied the gun. Years later, I read an article in a psychology magazine that likened the feeling of shooting a gun to ejaculation. That's what it was like for me. Shooting off."

One of McCall's friends, a cooler head, grabbed the gun before he could fire again. Cupping his hand to his bleeding chest, Plaz struggled to his feet, started to run, then collapsed between two parked cars. The carnival grounds turned chaotic with onlookers screaming and running about, to McCall's great satisfaction: "I didn't know whether to beat my chest and yell at the top of my voice or shout some pithy, John Wayne-esque remark to be quoted when the shooting was recounted on the streets." He settled for yelling, to no one in particular, "I hope the motherfucka dies."

As it happened Plaz did not die, but in street terms McCall had proved himself. "I was a bona fide crazy nigger. Everywhere I went after that, guys on the street said, reverently, 'Yeah, man, I heard you bust a cap in Plaz's ass.' My street rep shot up three full notches."[29]

What is most revealing about this story—and it is unusual only for its vivid detail and the emotional candor with which McCall, a professional journalist, recalls it—is the role of third parties. Left to their own devices the two young men might not have exchanged words, let alone fought. But they had an audience, several men and a woman, McCall's girl, whom Plaz dissed as a bitch. For either to have backed down would have been socially catastrophic and emotionally devastating. In lower-class honor cultures a man may lack property but still have worth, though only and exactly as much worth as others confer upon him. If they confer nothing he is nothing. Hence he has little to lose and much to gain, socially and sexually, through the violent, public defense of his reputation.[30]

The audience factor helps to explain why gangs are so important in ghetto violence. In the public mind black gangs like the Crips and the Bloods are embroiled in violence because of internecine drug wars. That is only partly true. Street gangs are not simply or even usually organized criminal groups. They are instead surrogate families, well adapted to the psychological needs of outcast teenage males who find in them the companionship, protection, opportunities, and respect often missing in their own households. "A gang gave me a sense of love," explained nineteen-year-old Jamal Hall of Albany, Georgia. "They would do anything to help me, and I would do anything to help them." Anything includes backup, or armed assistance for fellow members. "There'll always be someone to set you up with a gun or whatever you need," said one fifteen-year-old. "You feel safe." Sharron Corley agreed that there was safety in numbers. "If you got props, you got respect and you got a crew. People think twice about cappin' you, 'cause then there are people who are coming back."[31]

A member or wannabe who fails to live up to the gang's stand-up values is out. If he shows nerve or pluck in a dangerous situation he is in and his status enhanced. Young men in groups egg one another on; young, undersocialized, armed, and intoxicated men in gangs egg one another on to crimes. These range in seriousness from vandalism to robbery to murder. "Ain't no fun just sittin' here," explained a fourteen-year-old Crip who claimed to have been jumped into his set at eight. "Anybody can just sit around, just drink, smoke a little Thai. But that ain't fun like shootin' guns and stabbin' people. *That's* fun. Like, see . . . people you kill . . ." He paused, then held up his hand to indicate his height. "Okay, look, I'm so high and killin' somebody, that make me higher. 'Cause you got enough heart to kill somebody, then, like you got the heart to destroy. Make you tall."[32]

It can also make you dead, particularly if your victim happens to be a member of another gang. Insults or trespass, let alone a killing, will trigger retaliation. In Los Angeles one conflict between two Crips factions, the Rollin' Sixties and the Eight-Tray Gangsters, claimed twenty-five lives over twelve years. That was more than died in the St. Valentine's Day Massacre, more than were killed by the outlaw legends Bonnie Parker and Clyde Barrow, more than perished in the notorious Hatfield-McCoy feud. Honor cultures have an almost unbelievable capacity to elevate the trivial to the tragic. The Hatfield-McCoy feud originated in a dispute over two hogs; the Rollin' Sixties war in an obscene insult hurled by a jilted suitor.[33] Yet few Americans outside of Los Angeles have ever heard of the latter, an indication perhaps of the extent to which the larger society is inured, or simply indifferent, to the slaughter in the ghetto.

The most thorough statistical study to date of urban gangs, crime, and violence was undertaken by the Los Angeles District Attorney's Office and published in 1992. Even bearing in mind that Los Angeles has an unusually serious gang problem, the results were startling. Los Angeles County was home to an estimated 1,000 gangs, some 800 of which were involved in criminal activity. At least 70 percent of the 150,000 gang members used illicit drugs and 50 percent engaged in violence, rates respectively seven and four times those of youths not in gangs. While non-gang murders in Los Angeles had been declining for several years, gang killings were up sharply, hitting a record 771 in 1991. In fact all of the growth in homicide since 1984 was attributable to gang slayings. At least three-quarters of these killings were intentional, but anywhere from 10 to 25 percent of the dead were innocent bystanders, known in gang parlance as mushrooms. (They popped up in the wrong place and got mowed down.) In Los Angeles as in the rest of the nation the unexpected increase in the homicide rate in the late 1980s and early 1990s was driven by the surge in youthful inner-city murder and manslaughter.[34]

The Los Angeles gangs were overwhelmingly concentrated in ethnic neighborhoods and composed of teenagers and young men from poor or single-parent families. Only 0.5 percent of Anglo men in their early twenties were involved in gangs, compared to 6–7 percent of Asian, 9–10 percent of Latino, and 47 percent of black men of similar age. Doubtless more young black men end up in police data bases because police associate young black men with gang activities. But allowing a discount for prejudice, there is no question that gangs have become a deadly problem in ghetto neighborhoods in Los Angeles, or in Chicago, East St. Louis, Detroit, Philadelphia, New York, and other cities with substantial black populations.

Nor can there be much doubt that gangs flourish where conventional families do not. To join a neighborhood gang in South Central Los Angeles, one former member observed, "is the equivalent of growing up in Grosse Pointe, Michigan, and going to college: everyone does it." "Most people in gangs come from families where parents don't care about you and don't want to know what you're doing," admitted Hector Guzman, a sixteen-year-old gang associate. "You wake up steppin' over people on the floor of your house," a veteran Blood explained. "Mom's smoked out, she don't care 'bout nothin', for sure not you. You roll up out on the street, same ol' homies. And no father around at all."[35]

Black Population Structure

For someone who is purportedly missing, the absent father is everywhere in the literature of ghetto social problems. Conservatives trace his absence to welfare, liberals to unemployment, culture-of-poverty sociologists to the baneful effects of macho street culture. But there is yet another explanation, one that is both surprising and surprisingly powerful. It is the idea that illegitimacy and female-headed households are common in the ghetto because of a chronically *low* gender ratio.

The notion that sexual behavior is connected to the balance of men and women dates back to the pioneering work of the sociologist Willard Waller, who studied American courtship during the 1930s. Waller, an unflinching realist, thought sexual relationships were governed by the "principle of least interest." The person who had less to lose—who was less in love, less dependent—exercised power over the other person, who was more willing to sacrifice to keep the relationship alive. The gender ratio figured in the least-interest equation because men would have more alternative partners available if it was low, women if it was high. That is, the minority party in a relationship had less to lose if the relationship broke up and hence could make more demands. On college campuses where women were scarce, Waller observed, they had the upper hand in courtship. But during the summer term, when men were briefly in the minority, women were more willing to pay for dates or grant sexual favors. The most stable, least stressful situation occurred when the gender ratio was even and couples settled into a routine of going steady.[36]

The principle of least interest, rechristened "dyadic power," was central to a wide-ranging 1983 book entitled *Too Many Women?* The social psychologists Marcia Guttentag and Paul Secord argued that in high-gender-ratio situations most women would prize their virginity and expect to marry up, marry young, stay home, and bear large numbers of legitimate children, at least in cultures where contraception was not yet common. Low-gender-ratio situations produced the opposite pattern: more premarital sex and illegitimacy; more female-headed households and female labor-force participation; later marriages for women and more divorce.[37]

These hypotheses have been corroborated by comparative historical and cross-cultural studies. For example, Italian women in nineteenth-century Rochester, New York, married younger than their counterparts in Southern Italy and were more successful in resisting premarital sexual advances. A firm "no" did not hurt their chances of marrying well because they were greatly outnumbered by Italian immigrant males who were denied the alternative of WASP brides by nativist prejudice. The reverse was true in impoverished Southern Italy, where men were scarce because of the overseas exodus and hence exercised greater dyadic power.[38]

The sociologists Scott South and Katherine Trent, in a systematic study of late-twentieth-century data from 117 countries, found much the same thing. Controlling for differences in socio-economic development, women in low-gender-ratio nations consistently had lower rates of marriage and fertility and higher rates of divorce and illegitimacy.[39] Given favorable sexual odds it seems that men everywhere act like, and produce, bastards.

Black America, which has had the lowest gender ratio of any of the country's major ethnic groups for the last century and a half, is no exception. The difference begins at birth. The gender ratio for black newborns typically ranges from 102 to 103, compared to 105 to 106 for whites. The higher mortality of black male children and young men causes the gap to widen with age. At ages twenty to twenty-four the black gender ratio is 97, the white 105. By ages forty to forty-four the black ratio is 86, the white 100.[40]

The gender ratio alone understates the extent of the problem. Young black urban men are far more likely than whites of comparable age to be unemployed, imprisoned, institutional-ized, crippled, addicted, or otherwise bad bets as potential hus-bands. The increase in interracial marriages following the Civil Rights movement has further contributed to the unavailability of black men, who take white wives more than twice as often as black women take white husbands.[41]

The situation has given rise to frustration, anger, and deepen-ing poverty among black women, whose marital prospects have declined steadily since 1960. In that year only 17 percent of black females aged twenty-four to twenty-nine had never mar-ried; by 1987 it was over 53 percent. The problem has been particularly acute among educated and successful black women, for whom the pickings have become increasingly slim. They have either had to do without husbands or marry down, the opposite of the pattern on the female-scarce frontier. "I don't care what kind of problems you have," McCall reports one anxious female suitor as saying, "drugs, alcohol, whatever—I'm willing to work with you."[42]

Dyadic power equals sexual leverage. Black women unwilling to engage in premarital sex are at a huge disadvantage in an already tight market. Black men know this and can easily exploit the situation. But such sexual opportunism increases the pros-pect of illegitimacy, and illegitimacy feeds the problems of pov-erty, unemployment, and violence that gave rise to the shortage of marriageable men in the first place. Low gender ratios turn out to be as circular as every other black urban social problem.[43]

Let me anticipate an objection. Having offered so many exam-ples of problems stemming from *high* gender ratios it may seem contradictory to claim that low gender ratios are likewise fraught with social peril. Should not fewer men translate into less crime? Yes, but as the sociologists Steven Messner and Robert Sampson have shown, the effect of fewer men is, over time, more than canceled out by the effects of increased illegitimacy and family disruption. There may be proportionately fewer men in the ghetto, but because they are less often socialized in intact fami-lies or likely to marry and stay married they more often get into trouble.[44]

So the relationship between the gender ratio and violence turns out to be paradoxical. Both too many and too few women can lead to problems. The best case, as Waller discerned, is a marriage market in equilibrium. When a population's structure is conducive to marriage it is conducive to social order. But migrations, economic upheavals, and changes in mortality patterns are constantly shifting the male-female balance, guaranteeing that America—or any other nation—will never rest permanently in the optimal situation.

The other unusual demographic feature of black America is lower median age. Sexual activity begins comparatively early among blacks. Unmarried mothers conceive and give birth while still in their teens. Their children have children at a similarly early age. Women in the projects are sometimes great grandmothers by their mid-forties. Because of earlier conception and higher mortality, the median age of blacks in the United States is fully six years less than that of whites. More than half of the U.S. black population is composed of children, teenagers, and youth in their twenties, who are much more likely than older people to run afoul of the law. Urban black society not only has proportionately more undersocialized males than nonblack society, it has more *young* undersocialized males, a combination guaranteed to increase violence and disorder.[45]

The root cause of the wave of black inner-city male violence that began building during the 1960s and 1970s and rose again in the late 1980s and early 1990s was the decline of stable two-parent families and the institution of marriage in the context of an entrenched culture of poverty in an isolated, youthful subsociety with diminishing employment opportunities and a chronically low gender ratio. This combination of factors will increase problems of social order in any society. A young man of any ethnic background who is undersocialized and unrestrained by domesticity is potentially dangerous because of his physical capacity for and biological tendency toward copulation and aggression. Libido, a transracial universal, requires the check of the superego, and it is through stable family life that the superego, as well as a sense of social responsibility and connection to ancestry and posterity, is best and ordinarily formed.

Imagine a kind of negative of American history, in which the country had been explored and colonized by black adventurers and settlers who exploited their immunological advantages over the Indians. Imagine further that they had enslaved, then freed, then ghettoized white laborers in isolated, vice-ridden inner cities characterized by widespread poverty and single-parent family life. Under those circumstances the young white men, or at any rate the most disadvantaged among them, would have been overrepresented among criminal offenders.

But it happened the other way around. It is young black men who are overrepresented not only in the statistics of violence but in drug dealing, rape, robbery, and other serious criminal offenses. It is the not-so-secret will of affluent Americans to deal with this problem by avoiding it through residential segregation, an ancient crime-control tactic given new impetus by the automotive revolution. Ever-more-distant suburbs and gated, privately policed communities are the real "solutions" that underlie a veneer of public discourse and policy tinkering. The tinkering divides along ideological lines: more urban enterprise zones, workfare, prisons, and stiffer sentences for the right, versus Head Start, job training, condom distribution, and Medicaid-funded abortions for the left. Whether any of these measures begins to address let alone resolve the familial crisis that is at the heart of ghetto violence and disorder is another matter.[46]

Critics on the left are correct about one point: family life has a material as well as a cultural and religious basis. The percentage of unmarried men was strongly correlated with the unemployment rate throughout the mid-twentieth century. There is no reason to think this is any less true near the end of the century. Nor is there reason to doubt that structural shifts in the economy hurt the job prospects of inner-city residents. "Moynihan was right to point to the deterioration of the black family as a crucial factor in the growth of the underclass," sums up the writer Michael Massing. "Yet . . . black family life is itself highly susceptible to broader forces in American society. Among the most important of these is the nature and availability of work."[47]

The rub is that job prospects, though they may be a necessary condition for stable urban family life, are not always sufficient to change behavior. Labor-market improvements do not guarantee immediate improvements in black family stability, as Moynihan himself discovered when he looked at the AFDC numbers for the 1960s. The street attitudes that have become common among some men in poor black neighborhoods—the casual sexual exploitation of women, the contempt for adult authority and legitimate work, the murderous sensitivity about reputation—have assumed a life of their own and have been passed across generations by everyday acts of role modeling. A boy is much more likely to join a gang, for example, if older relatives (brothers, cousins, uncles) are already involved. Street banter has its own effect. A child growing up in the ghetto hears work referred to as "slaving," women as "bitches," men as "motherfuckers," and good as "bad." A boy calls his gang associates "my people," his closest friend "my gun." Places where sex is performed are "slaughter houses." The values conveyed by this sort of language are not simply the byproducts of this month's unemployment rate and they will not disappear at a wave of the wand of transfer payments.[48]

The same is true of black urban demography. Bigger checks or new jobs in the inner city will not abruptly balance the gender ratio or increase the median age of the black population. (They might even lower the age by triggering a baby boom.) Jobs and better family prospects would eventually help equalize the gender ratio by giving more black men an incentive to stay alive. The more at stake the smaller the number of "zeros," ghetto slang for men who have nothing to lose. But the socially beneficial effects of gender balance would emerge over many years and then only if the job opportunities persisted.[49] Although on the frontier the elementary facts of human reproduction ensured that the gender imbalance would abate, there is no comparable homeostatic mechanism built into black inner-city populations. This is yet another reason why ghetto violence and disorder have assumed such an intractable character.

TWELVE _____

The Crack Era

Most contemporary analyses of problems in the urban ghettos have emphasized structural or subcultural factors. Chronic unemployment, a long history of racial segregation, systemic welfare dependency, an entrenched culture of poverty, low median age, and a persistently low gender ratio have all been evoked to explain family decline, increased illegitimacy, high rates of violence, and kindred social maladies. These factors are like the minute hand on the historical clock described in the introduction: relatively slow moving and extending back over generations. Though they are certainly important causes, they are not necessarily the only ones. Other developments, which might be described as recent or sweep-hand factors, have contributed to rising ghetto violence and disorder in the late twentieth century. Among them are the overlapping sexual and media revolutions, the cocaine epidemic, and the declining efficiency of the criminal justice system. None of these is a deep historical cause of ghetto disarray, but they have collectively made a bad situation much worse.

Outside Agitators

During the 1960s and 1970s elite and to a lesser extent middle-class opinion about sexual mores—the propriety of premarital and extramarital sex, the stigma attached to illegitimacy and divorce, the morality of abortion and pornography—underwent a sea change. American culture, once officially prudish, became visibly and commercially eroticized. Cities sprouted singles and topless bars, nudity on stage and screen became commonplace, divorce and abortion became easier and more frequent, high schools stopped expelling pregnant students, and college dormitories did away with visiting hours. The old rules of sexual conduct and responsibility were clearly being relaxed.[1]

This was not necessarily the best collective message to send to black Americans, then finally achieving the status of full citizens after a century of disfranchisement and legal oppression. If civil rights had come when they should have, after emancipation, blacks would have had a chance to make their way in an industrializing Victorian society that would have provided both economic opportunity and social approval of strict sexual morality at a time when, despite the disruptions of slavery and civil war, the black family was still in reasonably good shape. As it was their historical opportunity came at the worst possible moment, when American society was both deindustrializing and deemphasizing traditional middle-class sexual mores. Blacks may have won their freedom in the 1960s, but the fashionable new ideas about what to do with that freedom (to "get it on") were not conducive to escaping the culture of poverty and the cycle of family disruption and illegitimacy that had become established in the ghettos. The sexual revolution was a cultural variation on the old economic saw that when white America catches a cold, black America gets pneumonia.[2]

The primary means through which the sexual revolution was publicized—some say propagandized—was the mass media, in particular television. Poverty in America is, in one sense, historically unique. Unlike the impoverished in most parts of the world, the poor in urban America have seldom been unable to afford a television set or to receive broadcast signals. Since the early 1960s television viewing has become as firmly entrenched in the ghetto as in the larger society. Thus, a paradox: although the ghetto has become more and more physically removed from white society, it has been wired into the white-dominated electronic fantasy world of sex, violent action, and consumption, "a toxic soup of mixed moral messages" that have as their ultimate effect the arousal of desire.[3]

Among the first to recognize this was the militant black nationalist H. Rap Brown. "America is a country that makes you want things, but doesn't give you the means to get those things," he explained in 1969:

> Little Black children sit in front of the t.v. set and all they see are fine cars, perfumes, clothes and everything else they ain't got. They sit there and watch it, telling the rats to sit down and stop blocking their view. Ain't nobody told them, though, they don't have any way of getting any of that stuff . . . And white folks wonder why niggers steal and gamble. I only wish we would stop this petty stealing and take care of Chase Manhattan Bank, Fort Knox or some armories.

Nobody, black or white, was about to do Fort Knox. But looting of the sort that occurred on a large scale during the 1960s race riots and sporadically in cities like Miami and Los Angeles during the 1980s and 1990s, was an attainable goal. Mostly young, mostly male, and mostly poor, the "commodity rioters," frustrated and tantalized by the seductive images of consumption, helped themselves when the opportunity arose. Television showed them how to do it. (It also showed them—a nice irony—how to steal televisions.) Riots spread by contagion, and video footage was the single most important means of communicating the details, tactics, and rewards of commodity riot behavior.[4]

Television has been a template of individual as well as collective violence. In an era in which parents are increasingly absent, preoccupied, working, or watching television themselves, children have been tutored by the third media parent that violence is a quick and decisive way to solve problems and that killing is ubiquitous. By the age of eighteen the average American reportedly has, in the course of twenty-five viewing hours a week, witnessed 200,000 acts of televised violence and 40,000 murders. Exposure is even higher among blacks, who collectively spend as much as 47 percent more time watching television than whites.[5]

Perhaps the one saving grace of television gore is that it is consumed at home. A young person experiencing violence vi-

cariously on the couch is at least not out on the street learning
the real thing from peers. This is less true of violent movies,
however. They are often attended by groups of young men and
have become in recent years increasingly violent. The body
count in the gangster film *Public Enemy* (1931) and the urban
vigilante fantasy *Death Wish* (1974), both highly controversial
films when they were released, was eight apiece. The average
body count in more recent action pictures like *Rambo II* (1985),
Robocop (1987), *Die Hard* (1988), *Rambo III* (1988), and *Total
Recall* (1990) was just under sixty per movie. The primary audience for such movies was sixteen- to twenty-year-olds, who in
1990 constituted 20 percent of the cinema admissions but only
9 percent of the population. The most violent movies, in short,
are most often watched by the most violence-prone age group.[6]

The same is true of the most violent music, rap and its white
counterpart, heavy metal. Hard-core rappers defiantly celebrate
the violence and sexism entrenched in street culture. "They
rapped often about selling dope," recalled Jerrold Ladd, a young
black man from Dallas:

> the glory of its success, how they had robbed, murdered, kicked,
> AK 47 sprayed down, Uzi'ed down, beat down, pimped girls,
> fucked up niggers, and slapped bitches. A lot of us, especially the
> upcoming dope dealers and the younger generation, were absorb-
> ing these messages, having them reinforced over and over again
> through the music we people loved so dearly, the rhythms and
> beats we enjoyed so much.[7]

The actual effects of this sort of posturing entertainment are
hard to quantify, though there is broad if not quite unanimous
consensus that the effects of violence in music, movies, television, and other electronic media are real and socially destructive.[8] To the extent that they are real, however, they would
logically be most deleterious in subcultures in which young
people consume large amounts of violent fare unmediated by
parental supervision, which pretty much describes listening and
viewing habits in poor black neighborhoods.

The critic and philosopher Cornel West has gone so far as to
charge that the mass media are a leading cause of social and
psychological pathology among black Americans. His theory is

one of relative vulnerability. The media's saturation violence, macho sex, and mindless consumerism are bad for everyone, but they do greatest harm to those with the fewest constructive, pro-social alternatives, especially black people who are young and poor. Isolated and undereducated, they are, in effect, set up to be sucker-punched by profit-driven models of immorality and self-indulgence.[9]

Poor children who while away their time with television and other electronic diversions are also less likely to do well in school. Black students report spending an average of about four hours a week on math, science, social studies, and English homework; non-Hispanic white students six hours; Asian-American students seven. The parents of this last group take a dim view of television, dating, and other distractions. Not surprisingly, their children, who in comparison with black students have put in more than a thousand extra hours of homework by high school graduation, make better grades and score higher on standardized tests. Just as someone who runs every day will do better in a race than someone who occasionally jogs, children who study daily will do better academically than television-distracted peers who sporadically crack the books. One wonders how much of the black-Asian differential in IQ is simply a reflection of differences in parental willingness to turn off the television and seat their children at a desk or table. But a difference is no less real for being nongenetic. Any cultural or familial trait that hinders educational achievement in an information economy is bound, over time, to make family formation more difficult and thus indirectly increase the amount of violence and disorder.[10]

Television viewing has magnified the fear of violence as well as violence itself. Police-blotter programs such as *Cops* and *Real Stories of the Highway Patrol* have become common fare. Television news has become strobe-lit with blue lights. From 1989 through 1991 the three network evening newscasts collectively spent 67 minutes per month on crime stories; by late 1993 the amount of "crime time" had more than doubled to 157 minutes per month. Local news was even more police-oriented. A study of late-night news in Denver, for example, found that 54.5 percent of the news coverage was devoted to crime stories, including eleven of fifteen lead stories and two-thirds of all stories longer than two minutes. Related issues like poverty were given no coverage at all.[11]

The Cocaine Revival

A big part of the expanded crime coverage on television has been the war on drugs, above all the war on cocaine. The coverage, however, has often been simplistic and ritualized: buy and bust, shove and cuff, cut to the powder on the table. Little attempt has been made to explain the origins of this modern plague.

Like most psychoactive drugs, cocaine entered American society under medical auspices. During the 1890s, however, it became popular in the white and black underworlds, and by the early twentieth century a full-blown cocaine epidemic was under way. Prostitutes coked themselves up, street urchins snorted "blow," tabloids ran exposés, politicians fulminated, legislatures passed laws. The epidemic ran its course, as epidemics will, and by mid-century cocaine had lapsed into obscurity. The drug was of little concern to the police, invisible to the general public, and regarded as a rare and expensive treat by street addicts who were geared toward mainlining heroin. Even in New York City, the nation's drug entrepôt, cocaine was a scarce commodity.[12]

Then, at the end of the 1960s, the drug began to come back. One source of the revival was, curiously, the growing availability of methadone maintenance programs for heroin addicts. At a sufficiently high dose methadone blocked the euphoric effects of heroin while satisfying addicts' physical need for the drug. Methadone patients soon discovered, however, that non-opiate drugs, including cocaine, could still produce pleasure. To acquire the cocaine they sometimes sold or traded part of their supply of methadone. By 1970 one Philadelphia methadone patient in five was showing traces of cocaine in his urine.[13]

Restrictions on amphetamines played an unexpected role in the cocaine revival. Introduced in the 1930s, the amphetamines were relatively inexpensive and legal stimulants. Some 200 million tablets were given to American troops during World War II. By the 1950s amphetamine use had spread to college students, athletes, truck drivers, and housewives in the United States. In fact the growing popularity of the amphetamines may well have contributed to cocaine's mid-century eclipse. By the early 1970s, however, amphetamines were becoming subject to tighter restrictions and adverse publicity. These changes made cocaine seem an attractive alternative, at least until 1986, the year the college basketball star Len Bias collapsed and died after using the drug.[14]

Most of the new cocaine users were young adults entering their prime drug-experimenting years. They had cut their teeth on marijuana, a cheap, double-duty drug smoked for the high and for symbolic protest against the forces of war and segregation. Those who tried marijuana and who suffered no ill effects grew skeptical (if they were not already) of drug abuse warnings, which they dismissed as so much propaganda.[15]

Snorting cocaine was, for many, the next step. The drug was subtly pleasurable, sexually stimulating, easy to use, considered to be safe, and, though expensive, affordable for those with substantial allowances or good jobs. At some universities the percentage of undergraduates who experimented with cocaine increased tenfold between 1970 and 1980. The American mass media, slavering for trends among the young and affluent, played up the cocaine renaissance. Cover stories on the drug and its revised history appeared in conventional and countercultural magazines. *Easy Rider,* one of the most popular and profitable films of 1969, opened with a cocaine deal on the Mexican border. It was followed by a string of 1970s hits like *Superfly* and *Annie Hall* in which cocaine played at least a cameo role. Retailers capitalized on the trend by stocking cocaine handbooks and gilded paraphernalia, symbols of sexual prowess and conspicuous consumption. As the 1980s began, the dominant impression of cocaine sniffing was that it was an expensive vice, not exactly harmless but not especially addictive or déclassé or associated with violence.[16]

Then everything changed. By 1986 cocaine had acquired a reputation as America's most dangerous and addictive drug. It was linked, as it had been at the turn of the century, with poverty, crime, depravity, and death.

What happened was a shift in the pattern of cocaine use triggered by an increase in supply, a lowering of wholesale and retail prices, and the introduction of new ways of administering the drug, freebasing and smoking crack. Colombian drug traffickers, who in the late 1970s realized that they could earn far more by smuggling cocaine than marijuana, developed an elaborate network for acquiring, processing, and transporting the drug. By 1982 these smugglers had become so sophisticated that they were air-dropping cocaine in watertight containers to waiting speedboats which raced off to Miami. They secured protection for their operations by means of systematic bribery and violence. In Colombia, where assassinations and car bombings became commonplace, uncooperative government officials were subjected to a reign of terror.[17]

Producers in Peru and Bolivia, whence most of the coca leaves came, expanded their acreage to take advantage of the rising demand. More cocaine entered the smuggling pipeline, driving down prices. Between 1980 and 1988 the wholesale price of the drug in the United States dropped from $60,000 to as low as $10,000 a kilo. Some of these savings were passed on to lower-level dealers and consumers. The standardized price, defined as the price paid per pure gram of cocaine in a one-ounce transaction, declined from over $120 at the beginning of 1981 to just $50 in late 1988.[18]

As cocaine became cheaper in bulk it also began to be sold in smaller and less expensive units. The key was the development and popularization of crack. Beginning in California in 1974 avant-garde users took to converting black-market powder cocaine, which was adulterated and noncombustible, into cocaine freebase. The method, which involved heating cocaine hydrochloride in a water solution with ammonia and ether, was complicated and time-consuming, but it produced pure crystalline flakes of cocaine that were suitable for smoking (actually, vaporization) in a pipe. The vapor went from lung to arterial blood to heart to brain, jolting the user with a powerful rush. Just as smoking cigarettes was a more intensely pleasurable way of using tobacco than dipping snuff, freebasing was a more intensely pleasurable way of using cocaine than sniffing. By the late 1970s freebasing was in vogue in Hollywood and environs, though cost and complexity limited its appeal. The near-death in 1980 of the comedian Richard Pryor, who reportedly set himself on fire while preparing freebase cocaine, served to warn that the process could be dangerous. What was needed from a marketing standpoint was a form of freebase that was cheap and ready to use.

The answer was crack. Heating cocaine hydrochloride in a simple solution of baking soda and water produced a residue of cocaine that was not as pure as freebase but that was nonetheless suitable for the pipe and easy to sell in small chunks. Because the chunks made a crackling sound when smoked, they came to be called "crack."

Crack's big advantage was low unit cost. Cocaine powder generally retailed for $75 or more a gram, but crack could be sold in small vials for $5 or less, bringing it within reach of the poor. By 1984 the crack trade, fueled by ever larger and purer shipments of smuggled cocaine, was flourishing in such impoverished districts as South Central Los Angeles and Miami's Overtown and Liberty City. By 1985 the crack revolution was transforming the cocaine business in Washington Heights, Harlem, and other New York City neighborhoods populated by blacks and Latinos. Heroin, the inner-city drug of choice a decade earlier, was partially eclipsed by cocaine—in Miami, almost totally so. Addicts using only heroin became increasingly rare. In San Francisco and Oakland heroin addicts began smoking crack after injecting heroin-cocaine solutions into their veins.[19]

Crack abuse was by no means confined to the ghetto. Suburbanites, white kids in Camaros, cruised the mean streets to purchase crack for home consumption. But the heaviest users were concentrated in poor black and Latino neighborhoods. This was particularly true from the late 1980s on, as more and more middle-class users were frightened off. In the ghetto, crack sales, use, and dependency became part and parcel of the daily drug scene. Crack joined heroin, powder cocaine, marijuana, and forty-ounce bottles of malt liquor as a permanent fixture in the inner-city landscape.[20]

With this difference: crack sales involved teenage runners and dealers to an unprecedented degree. Selling crack was a ghetto youth industry. In Washington, D.C., black teenagers who sold crack could expect to earn an average of $30 an hour, more than four times the hourly wage of the legitimate jobs open to them.

Like the young white men who went west in the nineteenth century, they were trading greater risk for higher earnings. "Fuck that factory rap," said one young Detroit gang member, "we going to sell some dope and get paid." "The only business in our hood that bloods run is 'caine for the dope fiends," said another. "Selling 'caine makes more doughski than little bullshit shops in the hood." The crack business was truly their own: no white or "A-rab" bosses to placate, no strictures on language, dress, or demeanor, no forms to fill out, no taxes to pay. Chances for advancement were better than in the legitimate service sector. For those whose future prospects were otherwise bleak, hustling crack was an appealing job.[21]

Crack and Violence

If they survived. Whatever the monetary advantages of peddling crack, the personal and social costs were steep. Like alcohol, crack distorted judgment. It also led to aggressive, often paranoid behavior in heavy users. It produced violent disputes over rip-offs and territories and financed the acquisition of automatic weapons. It encouraged crime and prostitution and undercut the life chances of drug-exposed infants. And it disrupted, impoverished, and destroyed the lives of individuals, families, and neighborhoods.

Small amounts of cocaine taken at irregular intervals do not usually produce violent behavior. Large amounts taken at frequent intervals by inhalation or intravenous injection—the most direct routes to the brain, and the most toxic—are another matter. Cocaine acts at the brain's synapses to stimulate the release and block the reuptake of norepinephrine, epinephrine, and dopamine, substances associated with aggressiveness, impulsivity, and hyperactivity. Long-term cocaine use also increases dopamine sensitivity at the postsynaptic receptors, a neurological change associated with paranoia. Just as a male group will have a greater statistical tendency toward violent behavior because (among other things) it has a higher testosterone level than a female group, a cocaine-using group will have a greater tendency toward violent behavior than a nonusing group because its altered neurochemistry favors aggressive, impulsive, and paranoid behavior.[22]

Two studies conducted in New York City are particularly suggestive. The first involved fatalities from Russian roulette during the years 1984–1987. Russian roulette, a deadly game popularized by the 1978 movie *The Deer Hunter,* involves putting a bullet in a revolver chamber, spinning the cylinder, putting the barrel to the temple, and pulling the trigger to find out what happens, click or bang. The losers who came under the autopsist's knife were mostly black and Latino men, unmarried and unemployed, who challenged one another in the presence of others to "prove they were men." Nearly two-thirds of the victims tested positive for cocaine, a rate almost twice as high as the control sample.[23]

The second New York study involved all known homicide deaths among city residents in 1990 and 1991. Nearly a third of the victims had cocaine metabolites in their blood, with the highest rates for Latinos and blacks. The authors believe that the victims may have provoked their own deaths through irritability, paranoia, or verbally or physically aggressive behavior, all known pharmacologic effects of cocaine. Most of the deaths, particularly among young minority men, involved guns.[24] With cocaine as with alcohol, set and setting matter. Cocaine use is especially dangerous among the young and the armed, just as drinking stimulant-laced whiskey was so dangerous among pistol-toting frontiersmen.

The expanded cocaine trade itself gave rise to violence. Drug trafficking is a big business, but because it is illegal and unregulated it operates in Darwinian fashion. It is structured as a parasitic chain, with drugs coming down from the cartel bosses to kilo connections to street dealers to users, and cash moving back up the chain until it is collected, laundered, and deposited in offshore banks. Anything that interrupts the flow of drugs or cash—a rip-off, a customer who refuses to pay, too much cocaine or heroin into a dealer's own nose or arm—is apt to provoke an extremely violent response, no excuses accepted. "You know—fuck that—that's just yo' ass," shrugged a middle-level distributor. One New York City dealer who "messed up the money" was beaten with iron pipes, then dragged to a curb and placed with his feet extending into the street. His connection then drove a car over his legs, crippling him for life. Another young dealer who ran afoul of his suppliers was stripped naked, had a tube inserted in his rectum, and was pumped full of raw alcohol. Knowing that the game is played in this fashion, and knowing that their profits make them inviting targets for theft, drug dealers take pains to arm themselves, thereby increasing the chance that their disputes will end lethally. Guns and ruthlessness are prerequisites for surviving in the world of drug dealing. The more ruthless a dealer is, the more apt he is to move up the chain.[25]

The drug trade is highly territorial. Dealers do not like competition. They have been known to "drop a dime" on their rivals, using the police to eliminate them, or to attack them directly. By 1986 and 1987 the big-city crack trade was beginning to attract heavily armed gangs like the Shower Posse, so named for showering automatic fire on their opponents. A 1990 study of drug dealing in the nation's capital concluded that, between turf disputes and robberies, a ten-year career selling drugs in the District entailed a one-in-seven chance of violent death and a seven-in-ten chance of serious injury.[26]

The time-honored solution to such bad odds was to get out of Dodge. As the bodies and drugs stacked up in the metropolises, driving profits down, enterprising gang members began taking their product elsewhere, branching out into second-tier cities like Seattle or Kansas City and even Mississippi Delta towns like Clarksdale. "Too many dope dealers in Los Angeles," explained one gang member. "So they take it out of town. The profits are better. Here you can sell an ounce for $600, over there you can sell it for $1,500."[27]

A fair share of the crack proceeds went for guns, especially for expensive automatic or semiautomatic weapons that had previously been out of most gang members' reach. In the old days, one veteran Blood explained, gangs got their guns by stealing whatever was lying around other people's houses. "But then, when the cocaine thing came around—shit, just go *buy* a gun. And then, as the cocaine came around more and more, most of those people whose houses you used to break into, they started in smokin', so they bringin' the guns to you now, to trade."[28]

Before the crack revolution a typical street gang had perhaps one good gun stashed away somewhere out of sight and not easily accessible. After crack more and more members, whether they were dealing or not, went about armed with their own high-powered, rapid-fire weapons. They were compact, easily concealed, affordable, available on the black market, status symbols within the group, and objects of juvenile fantasies. "To me a gun changes a person," observed a youthful Boston gang member. "It makes 'em brave. Sometimes, I would go on the roof and shoot in the air. I felt like, 'let 'em come up on me, I'd be like Hercules.'" Others believed that guns offered protection. "You get it because you fear what is happening out there," explained a New York City teenager. "Once you have it you feel like a god. You feel invincible."[29]

This is exactly wrong. No one is safe in the midst of a teenage arms race, which is bound to increase the frequency and lethality of hot-headed, spur-of-the-moment shootings. In 1984 only 5 percent of the shooting victims treated at Chicago's Cook County Hospital trauma unit had been hit by more than one bullet. In 1994 it was 30 percent. The effect of the automatic barrage was to offset the advances in emergency medical care that had kept the homicide rate down in the early 1980s. The best emergency room in the world could not do much for someone with three rounds in the torso.[30]

Automatic weapons greatly increased bystanders' deaths and injuries. Gang members, who lack the discipline and opportunity to practice regularly, are notoriously bad shots. But when they are armed with assault weapons that spray a dozen bullets with one squeeze of the trigger, marksmanship becomes secondary: someone is going to get hit. Insofar as these casualties required payback from rival gangs, the shootings fed on themselves. Feuding is bad enough. Incompetent feuding with automatic weapons firing high-velocity, wall-penetrating rounds in neighborhoods fought over by revenge- and turf-conscious teenage gangs has proved to be a complete disaster.[31]

The cocaine epidemic and the related spread of automatic weapons help to explain the big increase in the number of teen homicide offenders and victims in the late 1980s and 1990s. Historically the twenties have been the prime age for male homicide, but this has changed as more teenagers have become involved in selling drugs. They work more cheaply than adults, do less time if caught, and will take chances that adults would shun. They have also been emboldened by powerful, rapid-firing guns. When killing was close-in work done with knife or bludgeon or cheap, small-caliber handgun, someone who was, say, twenty-five had a physical advantage over someone who was fifteen, so the latter was less inclined to take on the big boys or for that matter his own peers. But automatic weapons certainly lessen, possibly eliminate, and may even reverse the teenage disadvantage, given the immaturity and fearlessness of the very young. "Guns and kids are probably the most dangerous combination there is," comments Peter Reinharz, a New York City prosecutor. "A 13- or 14-year-old holding an Uzi submachine gun has no understanding of his own mortality, let alone your mortality."[32]

One index of just how bad shootouts with cocaine-financed weaponry had become by the early 1990s was the nostalgia people expressed for the "good old days" of heroin trafficking. Claude Brown, a writer and former narcotics user, pointed out that at the height of the heroin epidemic only one four-block area in New York City (114th Street to 118th Street on Eighth Avenue, the "DMZ") was controlled by armed dealers. "But with the advent of the crack epidemic, people came out of nowhere and took over entire communities, and people were afraid to come out of their houses." Crack dealers even came into buildings, ordering tenants not to come and go during certain hours when their presence would interfere with business. "And, of course, you didn't want to give them an argument because they had some pretty heavy firepower to persuade you."[33]

A few people, mostly working-class men, fought back. "They were laughing at the whole neighborhood," said Perry Kent, a twenty-nine-year-old Detroit man who got fed up and helped burn down the local crack house. "The kids couldn't play outside. The police said to wait till something bad happened. Well, we couldn't do that." Indicted and tried for arson, Kent was promptly acquitted by a sympathetic jury. "I would have been more violent," one juror explained. In Philadelphia a group called Mantua Against Drugs attempted to close crack houses by harassing their patrons. "We're not Gandhi and King here," explained Herman Wrice, the group's six-foot, four-inch leader. "Cops need hard evidence to fuck with you. Neighbors don't." Nor do voters. Elected judges who dared to set dealers' bail too low were stared down in their own courtrooms and their names circulated in a newsletter.[34]

The emergence of urban vigilantism, though it has been criticized in some quarters, is hardly surprising. It is a time-honored response to the absence or breakdown of regular law enforcement. What is surprising is how anemic and uncoordinated contemporary vigilantism is compared to that of the frontier. One reason is undoubtedly fear. Inner-city residents understand only too well the dangers they face. Teenage gangsters and crack dealers will shoot if crossed, keep on shooting, and if they should miss or run out of ammunition their running partners will not. "Kids with automatic weapons and no sense," was how one man described the situation. "These young boys were like crazed animals," said another, referring to a local gang. "The boy that was the leader, he wasn't really 15, he wasn't like no teenager, he was a cold-blooded man, a ruthless killer . . . Old people, young people, everybody is scared of these gang boys."[35]

The crack trade made for addiction as well as terror, and addiction also contributed to a rise in neighborhood crime. Much of it was petty and nonviolent: drug-hungry addicts shoplifting, stripping metal from buildings, selling food stamps at a discount. But it could also be predatory, as the eighty-one-year-old Civil Rights heroine Rosa Parks found out the night of August 30, 1994. Joseph Skipper, a young black crack user, entered her Detroit home, beat her, and robbed her of $53. After she identified him in a police line-up she moved into an apartment building protected by white security guards, an act that said as much about the strange career of race relations in late twentieth-century America as any that might be imagined.[36]

By the late 1980s it was clear that many inner-city crack smokers, in some places a slight majority, were women. This was highly unusual in that nonmedical drug addiction had previously been concentrated among lower-class men. (The change was partly due to the fact that crack was cheap and did not have to be administered with a needle, the usual, unappealing way of administering adulterated street heroin.) Many of the newly addicted female crack smokers resorted to free-lance prostitution or its equivalent, trading sex for drugs. The exchange often took place in "freak houses," a freak being a woman who would perform any type of intercourse, oral, anal, and unprotected vaginal. "It was an aphrodisiac nightmare," wrote a Dallas observer, who witnessed acts of public sexual degradation. "I do things for crack that I would never do for heroin," one woman admitted. Thus crack contributed to the other great epidemic of American life in the 1980s and 1990s, the spread of HIV infection.[37]

It also gave rise to a new pathology, crack babies. *In utero* cocaine exposure increased sharply after 1985. In that year 5.3 of every 1,000 New York City birth certificates reported exposure to cocaine or crack; in 1990 the rate was 17.6. About 66 percent of the cocaine-exposed babies born in New York City in 1990 were black, 20 percent Puerto Rican. Similar statistics from other cities emphasized that the problem of crack babies, like crack smoking itself, was concentrated among the nonwhite and the poor.[38]

Researchers have disputed the magnitude and source of crack babies' medical problems, but it is a safe assumption that cocaine dependency is not the most propitious way to begin life. If there is anything to the theory that the underclass is composed of people of low intelligence, this may be it. Children who are exposed to cocaine—or alcohol, or tobacco, or any other toxic drug that is more common in the ghetto than in the general population—and who consequently suffer low birth weight and neurological problems are in jeopardy. They are likely to do less well in school than peers who are not exposed to drugs, be less employable in the information economy, and hence have diminished prospects of saving money, forming stable families, and escaping the ghetto, in which their own, often illegitimate and drug-exposed, children will be born.

Children also suffer if their biological fathers are mixed up with drugs. "Stepping off," refusing to acknowledge and support offspring, is more common among young men who become involved with drugs and related street crime. This holds for all urban ethnic groups, white and Latino as well as black. Conversely, acquiring a spouse and children can lead young men previously involved with drug use or trafficking to reassess their situation and quit for the sake of their families, another instance of the protective effect of marriage.[39]

Children without parents are themselves more likely to get into trouble with drugs or to have more trouble getting off of them. "The family is there," recalled one young man who kicked after being addicted for two years:

> No matter how bad it is or how shameful, you can always go back to them. And that's what I did . . . I knew I could always go back. I knew a lot of my friends that wanted to kick didn't have no place to go but jail. I remember cats, man, that would be glad to go to jail because at least they are eating a square meal and they could de-tox. So, "Hey, take me, man." That was their family—jail, man. I discovered a lot of people didn't have no place to go. Nowhere. They didn't want to go to jail so they stayed out there in the street life. They stayed out there. But I had a family to go back to, which probably saved my ass.[40]

This young man happened to be a heroin abuser, but the same principle applies to those dependent on cocaine, alcohol, and other drugs. Recovery is more likely with strong family support. And recovery is personally and socially imperative, for without it the compulsive user's trajectory is toward degradation, crime, illness, and early death.

The drug trade ruined neighborhoods as surely as it ruined individuals. Armed crack dealers and larcenous addicts made normal life impossible. Mothers who would otherwise have sought employment were unwilling to risk traveling to and from work or leaving their children alone. In a survey of Atlanta residents published in 1989, 74.7 percent listed drugs as the most serious local problem, followed by crime and violence. Only 2.3 percent cited housing conditions as their top concern and a bare 0.4 percent a lack of jobs. More than four-fifths of the sample said they stayed indoors at night as a matter of course. In Chicago several public housing residents who were, by court order, relocated to the suburbs reported taking jobs for the first time: "They previously had seen no point in working because it only made them more conspicuous targets for robbery or theft."[41]

From a purely economic point of view the crack trade and its attendant crime and prostitution would not have been so devastating if the proceeds had stayed in the neighborhood. They did not. The money ultimately ended up in Colombian or Mexican traffickers' counting rooms, Bahamian banks, or the tills of mall jewelry stores, boutiques, and gun dealers. The ethnographer Ansley Hamid has likened crack to a giant vacuum cleaner sucking money from the inner-city economy, with teenage dealers merely the free-spending labor force through which it passes on its way out of the neighborhood.[42] Like alcohol in the main stems or opium in the Chinatowns, crack cocaine is a leech drug.

Crack, in brief, made life increasingly dangerous and miserable for the black urban poor and accelerated the rate at which their neighborhoods tipped into hyperghettos. Once tipped they stayed that way, assuring that the young grew up in an atmosphere of fear and violence with street-culture role models and fewer and fewer decent educational or employment opportunities. The usual cliché about America in the 1980s, that the rich got richer and the poor got poorer, is correct but incomplete. What happened, at least in the big cities, was that the rich got richer and the poorer got crack cocaine.

The Drug War and Its Aftermath

The disturbing consequences of crack smoking and dealing became known to the American public in 1986 when the media seized upon the story and gave full play to its most sordid elements. Although mass-circulation newspapers and articles had not been alarmist about cocaine in the 1970s or early 1980s, crack was portrayed as extremely addictive and a prolific source of urban crime. Similar fears were voiced in congressional hearings where crack was compared to the Black Death. Crack catalyzed what came to be known as the drug war, formally declared by President Ronald Reagan in August 1986. By 1993 the drug war had produced three nationally televised presidential addresses, two omnibus federal antidrug laws, a national "drug czar," and a fivefold increase in the federal drug control budget.

It was the most dramatic, sustained, and controversial governmental response to drug abuse in American history, and a marked contrast to the nineteenth-century tactic of simply fining or ostracizing vice purveyors. Under the new laws drug dealers were risking their assets, their freedom, and even their lives.

The drug war succeeded in making a dent in casual cocaine use. By 1988 cocaine was declining in popularity among more affluent users made wary by the negative publicity and new emphasis on its addictive potential. Crack was also becoming less popular among potential initiates. The drug war had less impact on those who were already regular consumers, however. An aging cohort of heavy users who had begun their careers in the 1970s or 1980s persisted in abusing cocaine and began developing serious health problems as a consequence. The number of such users has been disputed, but it is widely agreed that during the late 1980s cocaine abuse became increasingly confined to a residual group of hard-core users who were concentrated in urban minority groups.[43]

The transformation of cocaine from golden drug to ghetto drug was reinforced by the way the drug war was conducted. Nationally blacks were four times as likely—in some cities more than twenty times as likely—as whites to be arrested on drug charges. The high rate for blacks has been variously attributed to racism, search tactics based on minority profiles, and the fact that minority drug dealers and couriers are highly visible, easy targets for police. Whatever the motivation for the large number of black arrests, their ritualized presentation in newspapers and television news programs intensified the impression that cocaine use and dealing were the near-monopoly of the poor black community, reinforcing the determination of the middle class, white and nonwhite, to stay as far away as possible.[44]

Another consequence of the drug war was to further overburden the nation's courts and prisons. In 1986, year one of the Reagan drug war, the number of days of imprisonment a felon could expect per serious crime was already only about a fifth of what it had been in 1959. The stepped-up campaign against crack and other drugs jammed court dockets and made prison crowding worse, particularly in the federal system. By 1992 six in ten federal inmates had been convicted of drug charges, compared to fewer than three in ten in 1980.[45]

States with widespread illicit drug use and trafficking also experienced serious prison crowding. "Earlier in [1993], almost all our early releases were violent offenders, and a lot of those taking up their bed space were just first-time drug offenders or couriers," complained Kevin Roberts, a controlled-release officer of the Florida State Parole Commission. The drug war, agreed the law professor William Stuntz, was one of the main reasons for the paradoxical state of the American criminal justice system: shockingly low levels of expected punishment for offenses like robbery or assault combined with a shockingly high prison population.[46]

All of this was made worse by mass-arrest tactics like street sweeps of lower-level dealers, which compounded the overload and increased the number of cheap plea bargains. Short sentences and prison overcrowding in turn fed public skepticism about whether criminals would be punished for any length of time. The skepticism contributed to a national decline in the willingness to report offenses. By 1990 only an estimated 38 percent of all crimes and 48 percent of violent crimes were being reported to police.[47]

Daniel Patrick Moynihan has called this trend "defining deviancy down." Because the amount of deviant behavior in American society has expanded much faster than the institutional capacity to deal with it, deviancy has been redefined to exempt conduct that previously was stigmatized. We have, Moynihan believes, quietly raised the normal level in categories where the behavior is in fact abnormal by any previous standard. Ignoring incivility, dumbing down schools, and failing to investigate (or simply not reporting) crimes are all symptoms of a social malaise rooted in the growing inability of families and other institutions to shape and restrain behavior. With so many holes suddenly appearing in the dike of social control, authorities have been reduced to plugging the most serious leaks.

The historian Roger McGrath has explored the defining-down phenomenon in his own city. "I grew up in a Los Angeles that had very little crime," he writes. "We locked the door to our house with a skeleton key, when we remembered." The plots of the

Dragnet radio series that first aired in the early 1950s accurately reflected what the police did: Sergeant Joe Friday might occasionally collar a robber or killer, but he spent much of his time doggedly pursuing shoplifters, hot rodders, and bicycle thieves.

Try calling the LAPD today, McGrath sardonically suggests, to report that your bicycle has been stolen. Though the city's population has risen about 75 percent from the *Dragnet* days, rape has gone up 350 percent, auto theft 1,100 percent, murder 1,350 percent, and robbery 1,540 percent. The norm was seventy murders a year in the early 1950s compared to ninety or more a month by the early 1990s. In these circumstances offenses like petty or auto theft were either ignored or processed in a routine, statistics-gathering fashion. Korean merchants complained that thieves were brazenly pocketing merchandise and walking out of their stores, confident in the knowledge that the police were too busy to respond to such crimes.[48]

The drug war itself has been affected by the defining-down phenomenon. A good way to convict traffickers is to make cases for tax evasion or money laundering rather than drug smuggling per se. Big-time dealers seldom handle drugs themselves, though they do take in large amounts of money. Attempts to conceal or launder the profits can leave a trail. But money-laundering investigations, which are complicated and time-consuming, are hampered by a shortage of personnel and prosecutorial resources. In Los Angeles, a major money-laundering center, by 1991 the U.S. Attorney's office had simply given up prosecuting drug money cases involving less than a certain amount, reportedly $500,000. Mere "smurfs," professional criminals who specialized in laundering drug money by making multiple deposits in amounts less than $10,000, had little to fear in L.A.[49]

The criminal justice systems in Los Angeles and other big cities are like huge and not very efficient engines that have begun to break down under an ever-growing load. The national murder clearance rate (the proportion of cases resulting in arrest) fell from 91 percent in 1965 to about 65 percent in 1995, largely because drug- and robbery-related slayings had become so numerous and so difficult to solve. Homicide detectives are not pleased when strangers kill strangers. There are no obvious suspects of the jealous-spouse variety and witnesses, if any, are reluctant to talk.

Or, if they do, they are not always believed by a jury. One Kansas City murder case featured a ten-year-old girl who had the side of her head blown off by a drive-by bullet. The jurors decided not to accept the plea-bargained testimony of one of the assailants. The other three defendants were acquitted. "I don't believe in justice anymore," said the girl's embittered father.[50]

In New York City murder victims' families sometimes avoid the police altogether, preferring to take care of the matter themselves. "They don't have any faith in the criminal justice system and I can't really blame them," said Lieutenant Mike Sneed of New York's Ninth Precinct. "If a loved one of yours gets killed and we catch the guy that did it and we manage to convict him, what's he going to get? Three or four years max. Most of the homicides don't even make the newspapers."[51]

The journalist David Simon made a careful study of the disposition of 200 murder arrests in Baltimore for 1988. Ninety percent of these involved blacks accused of killing other blacks, and only 60 percent resulted in convictions. Factoring in unsolved homicides, the chance of being caught and convicted after killing someone was only a little more than 40 percent despite the fact that most of the murderers were sloppy, leaving behind material evidence of their crimes. Half of the killings, Simon estimated, were tied to drugs.[52]

The problem of drug-related violence and the overcrowding of the courts and prisons with drug offenders has contributed to a growing movement for the controlled legalization of substances like cocaine. Legalization is an old idea, but by 1990 it had a cast of new and reputable supporters, ranging from the Nobel Prize–winning economist Milton Friedman to Baltimore's mayor Kurt Schmoke. If the spirit of their argument was libertarian, the logic was utilitarian. Drug prohibition was simply causing more trouble than it was worth. While drug abuse was admittedly a bad thing, abuse in a milieu of armed suppliers selling adulterated drugs at black-market prices was a fiasco—the same argument that had been advanced against prohibition of alcohol in the 1920s and 1930s.

The catch was that no one knew what would happen under legalization. There might be millions more addicts, each perhaps a little less harmful than the illegal users but in the aggregate imposing a much heavier burden on society. Whatever one thinks of the merits and risks of drug legalization it is a revealing bit of policy history, a perfect example of Moynihan's point that a society swamped by rising disorder will find reasons to define deviancy down.

When Moynihan addressed himself to ghetto disarray in 1965 he attributed the problem to instability of the black family. The matriarchal arrangement, as he called it, was a legacy of slavery, the chronic lack of good employment opportunities, and the emergence of a self-sustaining culture of poverty. Though historians subsequently cast doubt on the slavery thesis, social-scientific and ethnographic inquiry has sustained Moynihan's claims about the importance of intact families, the destructiveness of long-term unemployment, and the reality of a ghetto street culture in which generations of young men have made virtues of unpleasant necessities.

What Moynihan could not have realized in 1965 was how seriously the structural and subcultural problems of the black ghetto would be worsened by outside forces. Among these were the sexual revolution and heavy consumption of television shows, movies, videos, and music that depicted or celebrated acts of violence; a Vietnam-era epidemic of heroin addiction followed by an even more widespread and destructive wave of cocaine abuse; and the concurrent decline in the effectiveness and credibility of the criminal justice system. By the time of the crack wars the justice system had taken on the aspect of a nuisance or rite of passage for many ghetto youth or even, perversely, a refuge from their gun-toting enemies.[53] Any sane ghetto youth contemplating shooting someone is far more worried that a payback bullet worth thirty cents will dispatch him than that the man downtown will catch him and spend several million dollars of taxpayers' money over the course of fifteen years to strap him into an electric chair or tie him to a gurney and infuse poison into his veins.

Not that the man downtown is inclined to do any such thing. The chances are he will settle for a plea bargain, content to send another black man to prison, call it a day, get in his car, and drive home to his family in the suburbs.

CONCLUSION

Life in the New Frontier Society

The study of violence and disorder, like the study of religion, has two basic plot lines, decline and persistence. Analysts of violence tend, as Bill Buford put it, to see violence either as a deviation from the past or as continuous with it. That is, commentators stress that the violence of their own times is somehow worse or different from that of preceding generations or they argue that it is fundamentally the same thing, the unvarying sordid product of poverty or oppression or crowd psychology or whatever human characteristics they take to be causally relevant and to transcend time and place.[1]

I have endeavored to combine these two points of view. There is something both fundamentally old *and* fundamentally new about late-twentieth-century American violence. What is continuous—in fact, as old as the species—is that a disproportionate share of violent and disorderly acts involve young men. The tendency is in their bodies, in their chemistry, in their genes. In the words of the psychologist Thomas Bouchard Jr., "The genes sing a prehistoric song that should today sometimes be resisted but which it would be foolish to ignore."[2] This idea is not yet generally accepted by historians, who are suspicious of its political implications and content to labor within the familiar paradigms of cultural or economic determinism. But it does have strong support from biological and social scientific research. Anyone who wants to understand the history of violence and disorder in American society—in any society—should watch the young men closely, for it is with them that evolution has centered the problem.

Yet gender and age are only two aspects of violence and disorder. Cultural norms and social arrangements are equally critical. Young men who are sensitive about honor and race, intoxicated, irreligious, gathered in armed and undisciplined groups, and without family ties are more prone to mayhem than other young men. This also is historically continuous. The social dynamics of a group of touchy, drunken bachelors in a backwoods tavern in seventeenth-century Virginia would not have been much different from those of a group of touchy, drunken bachelors in a bar in twentieth-century Harlem, and the color of the blood on the floor was surely the same.

But when we ask *why* these two groups of bibulous men were unsupervised and single, we discover an important difference. The historical change, the something new, involves the reasons for the weakness or failure of the family as an instrument of moderation and control.

Familial social control in America (or, more precisely, in remote parts of America) was for a long time frustrated by demographic and social forces. The economically driven migration of peripatetic bachelor laborers, both into the society as a whole and more particularly into masculine domains like gold fields and range country and bonanza farms, distorted local marriage markets. The distortion was aggravated by women's preference for and migration to cities, by racist and nativist assumptions that ruled out potential spouses from different ethnic groups, and by the work-spree cycle, the privately profitable but socially disastrous siphoning off of itinerant bachelor laborers' wages, which might otherwise have gone into savings and family formation.

The migratory problem, as it happened, was self-resolving. Over time the demand for itinerant male labor declined and the gender ratios evened out, both nationally and regionally. Imbalanced marriage markets ceased to be a major problem except in distant places like Alaska. The favorable demography and prosperous, mature industrial economy of the 1940s and 1950s made it possible for record numbers of Americans in all social classes and ethnic groups to marry, many of them at an early age. The marriage and baby booms generated their share of problems, from crowded schools to suburban sprawl, but they also had a domesticating effect. Rates of crime and violent death fell.

Then came the 1960s, a decade that looks more and more like the hinge of modern American history. The baby boomers entered their teens and twenties; rates of drug and alcohol consumption began to go up, as did divorce, illegitimacy, sex and violence in the media, and the propensity to avoid or delay marriage and to live alone. For reasons of racism, segregation, and structural economic change, as well as the persistence of a subculture of poverty, these changes were most apparent in the inner city. It was the ghetto residents who suffered most from the upsurge of youthful male violence and disorder, especially after the crack trade upgraded weapons and destroyed families and whole neighborhoods.

It is as if what had been a transient demographic anomaly in nonagricultural frontier regions, the temporary breakdown in the familial mechanisms for controlling young men, has become a permanent feature of ghetto life despite (or, as some have suggested, because of) the low gender ratio. Indeed, it is possible to think of the urban ghettos as artificial and unusually violent frontier societies—vice-ridden combat zones in which groups of armed, unparented, and reputation-conscious young bachelors, high on alcohol, cocaine, and other drugs, menace one another and the local citizenry, undeterred if not altogether untouched by an entropic justice system.

Calling ghettos in the decaying hearts of big cities "frontiers" may seem an odd metaphor, but it is not an anachronistic one. It has often occurred to contemporaries. Sanyika Shakur, a former Eight-Tray Gangster Crip who took to studying history in prison, decided that the incursions of his set into enemy territory were like those of American settlers into Indian lands. Scouts would be sent in, the "natives" probed for weaknesses, raiding parties would "mount up," a military presence would be established, then "in come the citizens—in this case, gang members."

When Secretary of Housing and Urban Development Henry Cisneros toured Chicago's Ida B. Wells public housing project in 1993 (accompanied by a security patrol) he decided that what he saw was "almost like a western frontier." Local residents began calling North Kenwood, another Chicago war zone, "the Wild West." The founders of the Jamaican drug gangs took their generic name, "posses," from western films. One young New York City drug dealer who went to Buffalo in search of sweeter profits and softer markets even evoked the frontier analogy in Turnerian fashion. "There's more opportunity in Buffalo," he explained. "You know back in the days when you went West to claim gold? Buffalo's like that."[3]

The language of gangs resembles that of the masculine frontier. It is vivid, profane, and unconsciously self-denigrating. Just as men in western mining camps and bunkhouses dubbed themselves "boys," black gang members call themselves "homeboys" and "niggers." Nicknames like G-Roc and Tiny Vamp replace formal names, which are often unknown to other gang members, as they were unknown to other miners in the gold fields.[4] In both cases the conventional virtues and connections implied by polite social discourse—Mister, given name, surname—are jettisoned in favor of *noms de guerre* and defiant, juvenile language that reflect the disposability and puerility of its speakers.

Outsiders have understood the situation in much the same way. The nonagricultural frontier was, in deed and reputation, the most tumultuous region of the expanding nation; the inner city has earned the same distinction in the twentieth century. The parallel even turned up in the language of the Vietnam War. When Navy pilots flew off to bomb Hanoi, they said they were going to "Dodge City." Air Force pilots, more up-to-date in their choice of metaphors, said they were going "downtown." The two images, a century apart in their origins, connoted exactly the same thing: the zone of maximum danger.

A good analogy, like a good argument, should not be pushed too hard. There are also important differences between violence and disorder in the nonagricultural West and in the late-twentieth-century ghetto. Far more ghetto youth are illegitimate, hence undersocialized, and unemployed, hence unproductive in the legitimate economy, than was the case along the frontier. If the dominant pattern of frontier vice was work and spree, that of ghetto vice is hustle and spree, adding another dimension of crime and degradation to the violence surrounding the vice industry. Young frontiersmen, whatever their marital prospects may have been, did not want for work. The dollars they spent on liquor and whores were usually come by honestly, not by robbery or shoplifting or drug dealing. Street gangs of the sort common today in the inner city were practically nonexistent.

The historical sources (as opposed to western novels and movies) also indicate that there was less sociopathic violence on the frontier. The reasons for the killing—nobody calls me that, goddam skulking savages, coolies take our wages—may seem lamentable to modern eyes, but at least they were reasons. Settlers were not much worried that a kid with a gun and no regard for human life would mow them down while gunning for someone else. People were not, in fact, much worried about kids at all.[5]

They are now. One of the most disturbing and politically explosive aspects of inner-city violence, terrifying to black and white communities alike, has been the rapid increase of felonious crime and gunplay among unsupervised inner-city youths, not excluding children. Miami police chief Donald Warshaw has encountered ten-, eleven-, and twelve-year-olds "running around with guns and drugs, and when we track down their parents, we find they are on drugs, too. It's out of control."[6]

And it keeps getting worse. Michael Bell, a resident of Jacksonville, Florida, who began selling drugs at thirteen, managed to accumulate a record of sixteen arrests on narcotics, gun, theft, and battery charges before finally being convicted of two murders at the age of twenty-four. He used an AK-47 and ambushed his victims. He was the prime suspect in at least four other killings. "He doesn't seem to have a conscience at all," said the homicide detective who doggedly pursued him. "This guy has absolutely no remorse about any of the killings we questioned him about." On trial for his life, Bell spent his time amusing himself by sticking out his tongue and making obscene gestures.[7]

The Jacksonville sheriff's office has created a composite portrait of future Michael Bells. Called SHOs, for serious habitual offenders, they are juveniles who have a minimum of five arrests, including three felonies within a twelve-month period, and have a record of violence or drug charges. Four of five SHOs are black males. One in twenty lives with both parents. Their average age is 16.7 years.[8]

No trend continues forever. After 1991, rates of homicide and other serious crimes began declining again following their spectacular run-up in the late 1980s. The decline has been attributed to a leveling off of crack consumption and the stabilization of urban drug markets; the mass incarceration, often on drug charges, of young black men; and the creation of larger, more aggressive police departments, of which the "unchained" NYPD is taken to be the model. Having been defined down for so many years, deviancy has begun to be defined back up, at least in New York City.[9]

What is often missing from the discussion of the recent past is the idea that the crime statistics *should* have been falling, given the movement of the baby boomers into sedate middle age. Viewed in perspective, the decline in the five years after 1991 is more a restoration of normal demographic trends than a law-enforcement miracle. And it may well prove short-lived. Crime and violence among juveniles remain at unprecedented levels and several experts have predicted that they will actually worsen, both because of a projected increase in the number of teenagers and because more of these teenagers will be illegitimate.[10]

This is the other key difference between the old and the new patterns, the outer and the inner frontier. Western violence and disorder were passing migratory anomalies in a society dominated by Victorianism and the work ethic. The vice-linked troubles of a Dodge City or an early San Francisco were intense and deadly, but of brief duration. The same cannot be said of the ghetto, where violence and disorder have become endemic in the context of very different social and demographic circumstances. There is no built-in mechanism to balance inner-city populations as there was along the frontier, where the population inevitably moved toward balance and any large male surplus usually disappeared within a decade or two. Nothing in contemporary ghetto life assures that the numbers of marriage-

able men and women will come into balance, or that prospects
for family formation will thus be enhanced.

The entangled problems of social order described in this book
are not going away any time soon, either in the ghetto or in the
larger society. What has happened in the inner city may well be
a harbinger of worsening problems for the entire nation. Changing labor-market realities and the new dispensation of sexual
individualism in an eroticized, youth-oriented, media-based
consumer culture have undermined family stability and self-discipline throughout the United States, not just in urban ghettos.
Levels of family disruption and illegitimacy among whites three
decades into the sexual revolution are almost exactly where
they were for black families when Moynihan sounded the alarm
in 1965.[11]

Seen in perspective these events are a continuation, possibly
the culmination, of a momentous historical trend, the decline of
the family as the basic social unit and the appropriation of its
functions by the state, professions, and corporations. Two centuries ago American families were society, or at any rate its
centers of desire, conception, labor, production, consumption,
authority, discipline, training, credit, and care for the sick, aged,
and dying. But in the course of the nineteenth century families
began losing power and authority. The usual suspects are the
commercial and industrial revolutions, the decline of agriculture
and rise of cities, the spread of public schools, factories, asylums,
prisons, hospitals, and the creeping intrusions of bureaucracies
and professions into the lifeworld of the home. In the course of
the twentieth century (aside from the temporary and perhaps
anomalous marriage boom of the 1940s and 1950s) the nuclear
family itself began to break up. More and more of its socializing
and punishing functions devolved upon the professions, private
enterprise, and the state, the parent of last resort.[12]

State parenting is neither a cheap nor a satisfactory solution
to the problem of maintaining social order. The voice of family-
instilled conscience is always more cost-effective than that of a
police officer, especially if the officer is part of a criminal justice
system that has become irrelevant to all but serious offenses and
then not guaranteed to produce results. Voters have obviously
become frustrated over this failure, which has been a conserva-

tive warhorse since the 1968 election and has contributed heavily to the Republican ascendancy in state and national politics.

Some of this anger might be better directed into a mirror. While it is true that politicians have often affected the amount of violence and disorder—think of the failure to protect Indians or the success of the educational provisions of the GI Bill—they have usually done so at the margins. Those who think that the right array of policies will quickly and painlessly reverse the post-1960 trends are deceiving themselves. No one who considers the history of American violence and disorder should be a policy nihilist. Lives gained or lost at the margin are still lives gained or lost. Statutory details matter, and so does the effectiveness of law enforcement. Yet it is equally hard to escape the conclusion that the key to controlling young men's violence and disorder lies not in the legislative process or in simply adding police and prisons but in society's basic familial arrangements, which means with all of us.

This insight is at the heart of the "new familism," a movement that has attracted a diverse group of social scientists and journalists. The basic point of the movement, that families nurture, control, and integrate, is the same one Durkheim made more than a century ago. When families do not perform these functions the larger society always suffers. Too many boys with guns, sums up the writer David Blankenhorn, is the result of too few boys with fathers.

The policy corollary is that the prison-building spree of the last two decades, whatever its partisan dividends, has been socially misguided. Prisons, Blankenhorn continues, are just a costly quarantining strategy for dealing with the consequences of illegitimacy and fatherless families. Michael R. Gottfredson and Travis Hirschi reach a similar conclusion in their widely discussed book *A General Theory of Crime*. In their view law-breaking originates in poor self-control, which is in turn caused by negligent parenting in the first six to eight years of life. Unconcerned or absent parents who fail to supervise young children and to recognize or punish their deviant behavior breed impulsive delinquents who will persist in breaking the law until they are incapacitated, killed, or burned out. Observing that governments are neither the cause of nor the solution to the crime problem,

they advocate policies to enhance the ability of families to social-
ize children as the only realistic hope for substantial reduction
in crime.[13]

The psychologist David Lykken has gone a step further. He
argues that skillful parenting is crucial, especially for boys whose
genetic makeup inclines them toward fearlessness, aggressiveness, impulsivity, and sensation-seeking. Tough kids need tough
love from vigilant parents. But widespread illegitimacy (to
which Lykken attributes the high black crime rate) has undermined parenting and produced a bumper crop of mostly male
sociopaths, "stowaways on our communal voyage who have
never signed the social contract." Because each sociopath gener-
ates large social costs, drastic preventive measures are in order:
more foster homes, boarding schools, and even parental licensing. People who are not competent to be parents should not
reproduce, Lykken asserts, and if they do they should be subject
to forced contraception.[14]

Few of the new familists share Lykken's enthusiasm for state
eugenics. They do, however, share his basic idea, that life's script
is written early. Much in this book supports this view, though
much also qualifies it. To look at the American situation over
four centuries is to realize that there is more to antisocial conduct than parental non-, mis-, or malfeasance acting upon a
child's innate temperament. Other factors such as population
structure, cultural and subcultural norms, racial prejudice, economic opportunity, the interactive effects of male groups, the
availability of guns, drugs, and alcohol, and the restraining effect
of marriage are necessary to make sense of the historical pattern
of violence and disorder.

Stated logically, defective socialization is a sufficient but not a
necessary condition for increased violence and disorder. Consider California during the Gold Rush. With the possible and
partial exception of the Sydney Ducks and some French paupers,
the California immigrants were self-disciplined men raised in
intact families.[15] The vice, violence, and disorder of their lives
were products of demographic, situational, and cultural factors,
such as the racially motivated exclusion of Chinese women. It
was not a matter of broken families or inattentive parenting. The
same might be said of the cowboys, hard workers whose payday

blowouts had little to do with early childhood and much to do with the temptations of the cattle towns. That said, those who emphasize early upbringing still make an important point. Families rather than governments are the first and best line of defense against violent and disorderly behavior.

The family advocates are also right about cost effectiveness. Societies that attempt to control behavior by relying on police and prisons rather than families will have more crime and heavier taxes, plus ever-larger outlays for private security. This is the other great virtue of attentive parenting in stable families: it is by far the least expensive way to maintain social order. Men who are raised by two parents and who then marry and become parents themselves will not require costly legal deterrence or medical treatment as often as those who are not.

There are, to be sure, exceptions. Family life is not for everyone, and there are certainly married men (and women) who drink too much, attack their spouses, brutalize their children, and run afoul of the law, just as there are children of conscientious parents who turn out willfully, inexplicably bad. But in an aggregate statistical sense society will always be more orderly and less costly if more of its male members are domesticated.

Domestication does not mean a patriarchal family, or one in which the father is the sole breadwinner. The one belongs to the past, the other is no longer feasible for millions of Americans. Nor am I suggesting that women have an obligation to marry, or that they should marry poorly behaved men in an effort to "rescue" them. Let the louts fend for themselves. However, other things being equal, the total *amount* of violence and disorder in society is negatively related to the percentage of males in intact families of origin or procreation, and therefore it is desirable for governments and other institutions to encourage marriage.

Some might reply that marriage, far from dampening male violence, merely transfers it within the family: the wives and kids get hit instead of the boys in the bar. This is, in a tautological sense, true. There would be no spouse abuse if there were no spouses, no child abuse if no children. But it is unrealistic to suppose that men would pose no danger to women and children if marriage did not exist or that society would somehow be safer and more orderly without the institution. Monogamy and married fatherhood reduce the likelihood of sexual jealousy and the uncertainty of paternity, two potent causes of violence against women. In one study using data from 1990–1991, unmarried pregnant women were found to be more than three times as likely to report physical attacks by their boyfriends than married pregnant women were to report similar abuse by their husbands. Not being married was a better predictor of abuse than education, race, age, or any other factor.[16]

In the broadest terms, marriage and family life restrain men because they change the mix of significant others, roles, expectations, resources, and consequences, and so change behavior. If this principle is false, it would be well to jettison the whole interactionist school of sociology as well as the conclusions of this book. The regionally, racially, and temporally skewed pattern of violence and disorder in America's past and present is simply not comprehensible without taking into account marriage markets and other structural or cultural determinants of family life. Where married men have been scarce or parental supervision wanting, violence and disorder have flourished, as in the mining camps, cattle towns, Chinatowns, black ghettos, and the small hours of the morning. But when stable family life has been the norm for men and boys, violence and disorder have diminished. That was one important reason why, during the mid-twentieth-century marriage boom, violent death rates showed a sustained decline.

Whether politicians can legislatively rescue the comparatively tranquil days of the 1950s from the riptide of modern history is something we may reasonably doubt. What we should not doubt is the social utility of the family, the institution best suited to shape, control, and sublimate the energies of young men.

Bibliographic Note

Abbreviations

Notes

Index

Bibliographic Note _____

Francis Loewenheim, the diplomatic historian, once remarked to me that it was unlikely historians would discover something significant about the past unless it had also been noticed by contemporaries. That proved to be my experience in writing this book. I read widely in letters, journals, and memoirs, concentrating on those that described frontier conditions. Many if not most of the themes of this book were suggested, confirmed, elaborated, or qualified by eyewitness accounts.

These accounts were sometimes found in archives and special collections—I owe the staff of Chicago's Newberry Library a special debt—but I was pleasantly surprised by the richness of the published primary sources. The writings of major frontier figures, and a good many minor ones, are easily available in book form. Works like *The World Rushed In: The California Gold Rush Experience*, J. S. Holliday's superbly edited version of the forty-niner William Swain's diary and correspondence, provided much of the foundation for the historical chapters of this book.

I have also benefited from the recent outpouring of accounts of life on the inner-urban frontier, ranging from memoirs like Sanyika Shakur's *Monster: The Autobiography of an L.A. Gang Member* to ethnographic studies like Terry Williams's *Crackhouse: Notes from the End of the Line*. Works of closely observed journalism such as David Simon's *Homicide: A Year on the Killing Streets* were another source of insight and detail, as were my own interviews of inner-city residents.

As indispensable as eyewitness accounts are, it is necessary to fit the raw matter of human experience into an intelligible pattern. To do this I have drawn on the literatures of anthropology, biology, criminology, demography, epidemiology, psychology, sociobiology, sociology, and social history. I have found the work of researchers who employ evolutionary insights, such as Martin Daly and Margo Wilson, to be particularly suggestive. Robert Wright's "The Biology of Violence," *New Yorker* 71 (13 March 1995): 68-77, offers a thoughtful précis of the evolutionary account of male violence. Readers interested in scientific and social scientific accounts of a more detailed or technical nature will find several listed in the notes for the first two chapters.

Abbreviations

AAAPSS	*Annals of the American Academy of Political and Social Sciences*
ADPP: China	*American Diplomatic and Public Papers: The United States and China.* Series II: *The United States, China, and Imperial Rivalries, 1861–1893*
AHR	*American Historical Review*
AJPH	*American Journal of Public Health*
AJS	*American Journal of Sociology*
ASR	*American Sociological Review*
IJA	*International Journal of the Addictions*
JAH	*Journal of American History*
JAMA	*Journal of the American Medical Association*
JFH	*Journal of Family History*
JMF	*Journal of Marriage and the Family*
JSC	U.S. Senate, *Report of the Joint Special Committee to Investigate Chinese Immigration,* Senate Report no. 689, 44th Cong., 2nd sess. (1877)
JSH	*Journal of Southern History*
NEJM	*New England Journal of Medicine*
LC	Library of Congress Manuscripts Division, Washington
Newberry	Newberry Library, Chicago
NYRB	*New York Review of Books*
NYT	*New York Times*
PHR	*Public Health Reports*
PacHR	*Pacific Historical Review*

SRP   Social Reform Papers of John James McCook (microfilm), Antiquarian and Landmarks Society, Inc., Hartford, Connecticut

SHQ   *Southwestern Historical Quarterly*

UPV   *Understanding and Preventing Violence*, 2 vols., ed. Albert J. Reiss Jr. and Jeffrey A. Roth (New York: National Academy Press, 1993)

WAC, Beinecke   Western Americana Collection, Beinecke Rare Book and Manuscript Library, Yale University

WMQ   *William and Mary Quarterly,* 3rd series

Notes

Introduction: The Historical Pattern

1. I am keenly aware that the word "frontier" is controversial and freighted with triumphalist connotations, and that nowadays many historians prefer to avoid using it. Jettisoning the word, however, seems to me both cumbersome and anachronistic. Rather, following the example of the historian William McNeill, I retain and employ the term in a neutral, ecological sense to describe a shifting zone of interaction between indigenous and nonindigenous populations. For reasons of simplicity and historical consistency, I also refer to the indigenous peoples of the Americas as Indians.

1. Biological and Demographic Roots

1. Roger Lane, *Violent Death in the City: Suicide, Accident, and Murder in Nineteenth-Century Philadelphia* (Cambridge, Mass.: Harvard U. Press, 1979), 29, 37, 100–101.
2. Lawrence R. Friedman and Robert V. Percival, *The Roots of Justice: Crime and Punishment in Alameda County, California, 1870–1910* (Chapel Hill: U. of North Carolina Press, 1981), 108.
3. U.S. Census Office, *Report on Crime, Pauperism, and Benevolence in the United States . . . 1890*, part 2 (1895), 173, 207. James Q. Wilson and Richard J. Herrnstein, *Crime and Human Nature* (New York: Simon and Schuster, 1985), 110, updated by U.S. Dept. of Justice, *Uniform Crime Reports, 1990* (1991), 191; U.S. Dept. of Justice, *Historical Corrections Statistics . . . 1850–1984* (Rockville, Md.: Westat, 1986), 19; Jack Levin and James Alan Fox, *Mass Murder: America's Growing Menace* (New York: Berkley, 1991), 46–47.
4. Paul C. Holinger, "Violent Deaths as a Leading Cause of Mortality," *American J. of Psychiatry* 137 (1980): 474; Austin L. Porterfield, "Traffic Fatalities, Suicide, and Homicide," *ASR* 25 (1960): 897–901.

5. Wilson and Herrnstein, *Crime and Human Nature,* 110, and U.S. Dept. of Justice, *Uniform Crime Reports, 1994* (1995), 224; U.S. Dept. of Justice, *Historical Corrections Statistics,* 66.

6. James Patterson and Peter Kim, *The Day America Told the Truth: What People Really Believe about Everything That Really Matters* (New York: Prentice Hall, 1991), 108–109.

7. E.g., Morton Hunt, *Sexual Behavior in the 1970s* (Chicago: Playboy Press, 1974), 150, 258, 261; Donald Symons, *The Evolution of Human Sexuality* (New York: Oxford U. Press, 1979), chs. 6–7; Patterson and Kim, *The Day America Told the Truth,* 77, 81.

8. Quetelet, *A Treatise on Man and the Development of His Faculties,* intro. Solomon Diamond (Gainesville, Fl.: Scholars' Facsimiles and Reprints, 1969), 90–95; Neison, *Contributions to Vital Statistics . . . ,* 3rd ed. (London, 1857), 391, 392 (combining divisions 1 and 2); Durkheim, *Suicide, A Study in Sociology,* trans. John A. Spaulding and George Simpson (New York: Free Press, 1951), 71; James Buchanan Given, *Society and Homicide in Thirteenth-Century England* (Stanford: Stanford U. Press, 1977), 134; Martin Daly and Margo Wilson, *Homicide* (New York: Aldine de Gruyter, 1988), 146–149, 202–203.

9. Roy G. D'Andrade, "Sex Differences and Cultural Institutions," in *The Development of Sex Differences,* ed. Eleanor E. Maccoby (Stanford: Stanford U. Press, 1966), 198, 201; Daly and Wilson, *Homicide,* 144; Erik Trinkaus and M. R. Zimmerman, "Trauma among the Shanidar Neandertals," *American J. of Physical Anthropology* 57 (1987): 72; Leonard Krishtalka, Richard K. Stucky, and K. Christopher Beard, "The Earliest Fossil Evidence for Sexual Dimorphism in Primates," *Proceedings of the National Academy of Sciences* 87 (1990): 5223–5226.

10. E.g., A. Joan Klebba, "Homicide Trends in the United States, 1900–74," *PHR* 90 (1975): 198–199; F. Landis MacKellar and Machiko Yanagishita, "Homicide in the United States," *Population Trends and Public Policy,* no. 21 (Feb. 1995): 4–5.

11. Allen D. Sapp et al., *A Report of Essential Findings from a Study of Serial Arsonists,* National Center for the Analysis of Violent Crime (1994), 4–5; Robert E. May, "Young American Males and Filibustering in the Age of Manifest Destiny," *JAH* 78 (1991): 861, 863; Otto Kerner et al., *Report of the National Advisory Commission on Civil Disorders* (New York: Bantam, 1968), 7; William M. Tuttle Jr., *Race Riot: Chicago in the Red Summer of 1919* (New York: Atheneum, 1970), 215, 264; U.S. Dept. of Justice, *Uniform Crime Reports, 1990,* 186–189.

12. Erich Goode, *Drugs in American Society,* 3rd ed. (New York: Knopf, 1989), 86, 89, 140–142; Mark A. R. Kleiman, *Against Excess: Drug Policy for Results* (New York: Basic Books, 1992), 95–96.

13. Stanley H. Schuman et al., "Young Male Drivers: Impulse Expression, Accidents, and Violations," *JAMA* 200 (1967): 1026–1030; H. M. Simpson, D. R. Mayhew, and R. A. Warren, "Epidemiology of Road Accidents Involving Young Adults," *Drug and Alcohol Dependence* 10 (1982): 45.

14. David T. Lykken, *The Antisocial Personalties* (Hillsdale, N.J.: Erlbaum, 1995), 93; Derral Cheatwood and Kathleen J. Block, "Youth and Homicide," *Justice Quarterly* 7 (1990): 268; Herrnstein and Wilson, "Are Criminals Made or Born?" *New York Times Magazine*, 4 Aug. 1985, 32.

15. Edward O. Wilson, *Sociobiology* (Cambridge, Mass.: Harvard U. Press, 1975), 242–243; Wilson and Herrnstein, *Crime and Human Nature*, ch. 7; Eleanor Emmons Maccoby and Carol Nagy Jacklin, *The Psychology of Sex Differences* (Stanford: Stanford U. Press, 1974).

16. Harry Holbert Turney-High, *Primitive War: Its Practice and Concepts*, 2nd ed. (Columbia: U. of South Carolina Press, 1971), 158–159; David P. Barash, *Sociobiology and Behavior* (New York: Oxford, 1977), chs. 6–9; Martin Daly and Margo Wilson, *Sex, Evolution, and Behavior: Adaptations for Reproduction* (North Scituate, Mass.: Duxbury Press, 1978), ch. 4; idem, *Homicide*, chs. 6–8; Edward O. Wilson, *On Human Nature* (New York: Bantam, 1982), 114–119; Lionel Tiger, *Men in Groups*, 2nd ed. (London: Marion Boyars, 1984), 43–44; Robert Wright, *The Moral Animal: Evolutionary Psychology and Everyday Life* (New York: Pantheon, 1994), pt. 1.

17. Symons, *Evolution of Human Sexuality*, 180–181, 203–205; idem, "Darwinism and Contemporary Marriage," in *Contemporary Marriage: Comparative Perspectives on a Changing Institution*, ed. Kingsley Davis (New York: Russell Sage, 1985), 133–155.

18. James Q. Wilson, *The Moral Sense* (New York: Free Press, 1993), 168–170; David M. Buss, *The Evolution of Desire: Strategies of Human Mating* (New York: Basic Books, 1994), chs. 1–3.

19. Auke Tellegen et al., "Personality Similarity in Twins Reared Apart and Together," *J. of Personality and Social Psychology* 54 (1988): 1031–1039; Thomas J. Bouchard Jr. et al., "Sources of Human Psychological Differences: The Minnesota Study of Twins Reared Apart," *Science* 250 (1990): 223–228.

20. Frederick Naftolin, "Understanding the Bases of Sex Differences," *Science* 211 (1981): 1263–1264; Simon LeVay, *The Sexual Brain* (Cambridge, Mass.: MIT Press, 1993), chs. 2, 10.

21. John Gunn, *Violence* (New York: Praeger, 1973), 28–29, 52; Kenneth E. Moyer, "Sex Differences in Aggression," in *Sex Differences in Behavior*, ed. Richard C. Friedman et al. (New York: Wiley, 1974), 344–346, 363–366; Daly and Wilson, *Sex, Evolution, and Behavior*, 193–202.

22. Michael Elias, "Serum Cortisol, Testosterone, and Testosterone-Binding Globulin Responses to Competitive Fighting in Human Males," *Aggressive Behavior* 7 (1981): 215–224; Robert Pool, *Eve's Rib: The Biological Roots of Sex Differences* (New York: Crown, 1994), 179; Theodore D. Kemper, *Social Structure and Testosterone: Explorations of the Socio-Bio-Social Chain* (New Brunswick: Rutgers U. Press, 1990), chs. 1–2.

23. Alan Booth and D. Wayne, "The Influence of Testosterone on Deviance in Adulthood," *Criminology* 31 (1993): 93–117.

24. C. Barker Jørgensen, *John Hunter, A. A. Berthold, and the Origins of Endocrinology* (Odense, Denmark: Odense University Press, 1971), 16; June Machover Reinisch, "Prenatal Exposure to Synthetic Progestins Increases Potential for Aggression in Humans," *Science* 211 (1981): 1171–1173; Stephanie Van Goozen, Nico Frijda, and Nanne Van de Poll, "Anger and Aggression in Women: Influence of Sports Choice and Testosterone Administration," *Aggressive Behavior* 20 (1994): 213–222 (James Dabbs called this and other sources to my attention).

25. Richard Strauss, "Anabolic Steroids," in *Drugs and Performance in Sports,* ed. Richard Strauss (Philadelphia: W. B. Saunders, 1987, 64; Dorothy E. Dusek and Daniel A. Girdano, *Drugs: A Factual Account,* 5th ed. (New York: McGraw-Hill, 1993), 171; William N. Taylor, *Hormonal Manipulation: A New Era of Monstrous Athletes* (Jefferson, N.C.: McFarland, 1985), 16–24; Gary I. Wadler and Brian Hainline, *Drugs and the Athlete* (Philadelphia: F. A. Davis, 1989), 56, 61, 65.

26. Paul Fredric Brain, "Hormonal Aspects of Aggression and Violence," *UPV,* vol. 2, 226, 228; Kelly L. Burrowes, Robert E. Hales, and Edward Arrington, "Research on the Biologic Aspects of Violence," *Psychiatric Clinics of North America* 11 (1988): 499–508; Kemper, *Social Structure and Testosterone,* 30–35.

27. Robert V. Wells, *Revolutions in Americans' Lives: A Demographic Perspective on the History of Americans, Their Families, and Their Societies* (Westport, Conn.: Greenwood Press, 1982), 30–31, 50–51, 80–83; Donald J. Bogue et al., *The Population of the United States: Historical Trends and Future Projections,* rev. ed. (New York: Free Press, 1985), 15–16, 40–44.

28. Virginia Bernhard, "'Men, Women and Children' at Jamestown," *JSH* 58 (1992): 603, 616; Herbert Moller, "Sex Composition and Correlated Culture Patterns of Colonial America," *WMQ* 2 (1945): 113–153.

29. Marcia Guttentag and Paul F. Secord, *Too Many Women? The Sex Ratio Question* (Beverly Hills: Sage, 1983), 15; U.S. Bureau of the Census, *Historical Statistics of the United States: Colonial Times to 1970,* pt. 1 (1975), 9.

30. See Moller, "Sex Composition"; Darrett B. Rutman and Anita H. Rutman, *A Place in Time: Explicatus* (New York: Norton, 1984), 180–

182; A. Roger Ekirch, "Bound for America: A Profile of British Convicts Transported to the Colonies, 1718–1775," *WMQ* 42 (1985): 194–195; David Galenson, *White Servitude in Colonial America* (Cambridge: Cambridge U. Press, 1981), 3–4, 25.

31. Betty Lee Sung, *Mountain of Gold: The Story of the Chinese in America* (New York: Macmillan, 1967), 115–121, 320; Shih-Shan Henry Tsai, *The Chinese Experience in America* (Bloomington: Indiana University Press, 1986), 40 (quotation); Judy Yung, *Chinese Women of America: A Pictorial History* (Seattle: U. of Washington Press, 1986), 14.

32. Hasia R. Diner, *Erin's Daughters in America: Irish Immigrant Women in the Nineteenth Century* (Baltimore: Johns Hopkins U. Press, 1983), 28–35; Wells, *Revolutions*, 105, 184.

33. Charles Issawi, "The Costs of the French Revolution," *American Scholar* 58 (1989): 372; Jean-Jacques Becker, *The Great War and the French People*, trans. Arnold Pomerans (New York: St. Martin's, 1986), 330; Maris A. Vinovskis, "Have Social Historians Lost the Civil War?" *JAH* 76 (1989): 37–38; *History of World War II*, ed. A. J. P. Taylor and S. L. Mayer (London: Octopus, 1974), 278–279; William Petersen, *Population*, 2nd ed. (New York: Macmillan, 1969), 660–665; Bureau of the Census, *Historical Statistics*, pt. 1, 9.

34. Vinovskis, "Social Historians," 43n21 (World War I estimate based on comparison of 1911–1914 with 1915–1918 U.S. immigration figures); William M. Fowler Jr., *Jack Tars and Commodores: The American Navy, 1783–1815* (Boston: Houghton Mifflin, 1984), 148–149.

35. Wells, *Revolutions*, 82, 182–183; Galenson, *White Servitude*, 100; Kenneth Morgan, "The Organization of the Convict Trade to Maryland: Stevenson, Randolph and Cheston, 1768–1775," *WMQ* 42 (1985): 221; Robert William Fogel and Stanley L. Engerman, *Time on the Cross: The Econometrics of American Negro Slavery* (Boston: Little, Brown, 1974), 75–77.

2. Cultural and Social Roots

1. Beatrix A. Hamburg, "The Psychobiology of Sex Differences: An Evolutionary Perspective," in *Sex Differences in Behavior*, ed. Richard C. Friedman et al. (New York: Wiley, 1974), 375–376.

2. Mead, *Male and Female: A Study of the Sexes in a Changing World* (New York: William Morrow, 1949), 160.

3. Lois A. Fingerhut and Joel C. Kleinman, "International and Interstate Comparisons of Homicide among Young Males," *JAMA* 263 (1990): 3294; Martin Daly and Margo Wilson, *Homicide* (New York: Aldine de Gruyter, 1988), 284–286.

4. Bertram Wyatt-Brown, *Southern Honor: Ethics and Behavior in the Old South* (New York: Oxford U. Press, 1982), chs. 2, 13, 14; Edward L. Ayers, "Honor," *Encyclopedia of Southern Culture*, ed. Charles Reagan Wilson and William Ferris (Chapel Hill: U. of North Carolina Press, 1989), 1483; Ted Ownby, *Subduing Satan: Religion, Recreation, and Manhood in the Rural South, 1865–1920* (Chapel Hill: U. of North Carolina Press, 1990), 12–14; Elliott J. Gorn, "'Gouge and Bite, Pull Hair and Scratch': The Social Significance of Fighting in the Southern Backcountry," *AHR* 90 (1985): 36, 42.

5. David Hackett Fischer, *Albion's Seed: Four British Folkways in America* (New York: Oxford U. Press, 1989), 765; Richard Erdoes, *Saloons of the Old West* (New York: Knopf, 1979), 130; Richard Maxwell Brown, *No Duty to Retreat: Violence and Values in American History and Society* (New York: Oxford U. Press, 1991).

6. Bernard Bailyn with Barbara DeWolfe, *Voyagers to the West: A Passage in the Peopling of America on the Eve of the Revolution* (New York: Knopf, 1986), 506 (quotation); Terry G. Jordan and Matti Kaups, *The American Backwoods Frontier* (Baltimore: Johns Hopkins U. Press, 1989), chs. 1–4; Grady McWhiney, *Cracker Culture: Celtic Ways in the Old South* (Tuscaloosa: U. of Alabama Press, 1988), ch. 6; Fischer, *Albion's Seed,* 618–639, 759–771.

7. Myra C. Glenn, *Campaigns against Corporal Punishment: Prisoners, Sailors, Women and Children in Antebellum America* (Albany: SUNY Press, 1984), 48–49; Ownby, *Subduing Satan,* 16; William D. Valentine Diaries, vol. 2, 20 April 1838, Southern History Collection, U. of North Carolina at Chapel Hill.

8. Roland Oliver, *The African Experience* (New York: Icon, 1992), ch. 10; Ayers, "Honor," 1484 (fallout metaphor); Richard E. Nisbett, "Violence and U.S. Regional Culture," *American Psychologist* 48 (1993): 441–449; Michael Nyenhuis, "Southern Violence," *Florida Times-Union,* 18 April 1993, C1; *Gangs, Crime and Violence in Los Angeles* (Los Angeles: District Attorney's Office, 1992), 34, 54–56, 63–64.

9. Wilson, *On Human Nature* (New York: Bantam, 1982), 122–123; Johan M. G. van der Dennen, "Ethnocentrism and In-Group/Out-Group Differentiation," and Robin I. M. Dunbar, "Sociobiological Explanations and the Evolution of Ethnocentrism," in *The Sociobiology of Ethnocentrism,* ed. Vernon Reynolds et al. (Athens: U. of Georgia Press, 1987), 18–20; 56.

10. Ian Vine, "Inclusive Fitness and the Self-System," in *Sociobiology of Ethnocentrism,* ed. Reynolds et al., 74.

11. Hylan Lewis, *Blackways of Kent* (Chapel Hill: U. of North Carolina Press, 1955), 67–72, 203–221; Joel Williamson, *The Crucible of Race: Black-*

White Relations in the American South Since Emancipation (New York: Oxford U. Press, 1984), 57–59, 212.

12. Enrico Ferri, *Criminal Sociology* (New York, 1898), 117; Laurence Jolidon, "Sands Dry, Troops Dry, Crime Blotter Dry," *USA Today,* 11 Dec. 1990, 5A.

13. Judith Roizen, "Issues in the Epidemiology of Alcohol and Violence," Kai Pernanen, "Alcohol-Related Violence: Conceptual Models," Alan R. Lang, "Alcohol-Related Violence: Psychological Perspectives," and Philip J. Cook and Michael J. Moore, "Economic Perspectives," in *Alcohol and Interpersonal Violence: Fostering Multidisciplinary Perspectives,* ed. Susan E. Martin, NIAAA Research Monograph no. 24 (Rockville, Md.: National Institutes of Health, 1993), 3–36; 37–69; 121–147; 193-218.

14. James J. Collins, "Alcohol Use and Expressive Interpersonal Violence," David Levinson, "Social Setting, Cultural Factors, and Alcohol-Related Aggression," and Richard E. Boyatzis, "Who Should Drink What, When, and Where if Looking for a Fight," in *Alcohol, Drug Abuse and Aggression,* ed. Edward Gottheil et al. (Springfield, Ill.: Charles C. Thomas, 1983), 5–25; 41–58; 314–329; Klaus A. Miczek, Elise M. Weerts, and Joseph F. DeBold, "Alcohol, Aggression, and Violence: Biobehavioral Determinants," in *Alcohol and Interpersonal Violence,* ed. Martin, 83–119; Mark A. R. Kleiman, *Against Excess: Drug Policy for Results* (New York: Basic Books, 1992), 215–216.

15. Allan Kulikoff, *Tobacco and Slaves: The Development of Southern Cultures in the Chesapeake, 1680–1800* (Chapel Hill: U. of North Carolina Press, 1986), 223; Robert M. Utley, *High Noon in Lincoln: Violence on the Western Frontier* (Albuquerque: U. of New Mexico Press, 1987), 176; Elliott West, *The Saloon on the Rocky Mountain Mining Frontier* (Lincoln: University of Nebraska Press, 1979), 19–21.

16. Levinson, "Social Setting," 43; Erdoes, *Saloons,* 206; Richard W. Slatta, "Comparative Frontier Social Life: Western Saloons and Argentine Pulperias," *Great Plains Quarterly* 7 (1987): 155–165.

17. See Philip Greven, *The Protestant Temperament: Patterns of Child-Rearing, Religious Experience, and the Self in Early America* (New York: Meridian, 1977), esp. pts. 1–2.

18. Philip Greven, *Spare the Child: The Religious Roots of Punishment and the Psychological Impact of Physical Abuse* (New York: Knopf, 1991), pt. 3.

19. Ellison, "Are Religious People Nice People? Evidence from the National Survey of Black Americans," *Social Forces* 72 (1992): 411–430.

20. Jon Butler, *Awash in a Sea of Faith: Christianizing the American People* (Cambridge, Mass.: Harvard U. Press, 1990), 270.

21. E.g., Mary Maples Dunn, "Saints and Sisters: Congregational and

Quaker Women in the Early Colonial Period," 27, 35–37, 46, and
Gerald F. Moran, "Sisters in Christ: Women and the Church in Sev-
enteenth-Century New England," 48–53, 56–57, 63, both in *Women in
American Religion,* ed. Janet James Wilson (Philadelphia: U. of Pennsylvania Press, 1980); Ownby, *Subduing Satan,* 129–133; Roger Finke
and Rodney Stark, *The Churching of America, 1776–1900: Winners and
Losers in Our Religious Economy* (New Brunswick: Rutgers U. Press,
1992), 33–35, 66–71. Quotations: *Land of Their Choice: The Immigrants
Write Home,* ed. Theodore C. Blegen (Minneapolis: U. of Minnesota
Press, 1955), 382–383; "A Trader in the Rocky Mountains: Don Maguire's 1877 Diary," ed. Gary Topping, *Idaho Yesterdays* 27 (Summer
1983): 12; E. C. "Teddy Blue" Abbott, *We Pointed Them North: Recollections of a Cowpuncher* (New York: Farrar and Rinehart, 1939), 33.

22. *The Carolina Backcountry on the Eve of the Revolution: The Journal and
Other Writings of Charles Woodmason, Anglican Itinerant,* ed. Richard J.
Hooker (Chapel Hill: U. of North Carolina Press, 1953), xxvi–xxvii,
16–17, 45; *Autobiography of Peter Cartwright, the Backwoods Preacher,* ed.
W. P. Strickland (New York, 1856), 50–51, 90–92, 132–133, 376–381.

23. Rhys Isaac, "Evangelical Revolt," *WMQ* 31 (1974): 345–368; Greven,
Protestant Temperament, pts. 1, 2, and 4; Ownby, *Subduing Satan,* pt. 3;
Paul E. Johnson, *A Shopkeeper's Millennium: Society and Revivals in Roches-
ter, New York, 1815–1837* (New York: Hill and Wang, 1978), chs. 2, 5, and
afterword; Roger Lane, *Violent Death in the City: Suicide, Accident, and
Murder in Nineteenth-Century Philadelphia* (Cambridge, Mass.: Harvard
U. Press, 1979), 103–104; Lender and Martin, *Drinking in America* (New
York: Free Press, 1982), chs. 2–3; John C. Burnham, *Bad Habits: Drink-
ing, Smoking, Taking Drugs, Gambling, Sexual Misbehavior, and Swearing in
American History* (New York: New York U. Press, 1993), chs. 1, 3.

24. E.g., Kenneth A. Lockridge, *A New England Town: The First Hundred
Years: Dedham, Massachusetts, 1636–1736,* exp. ed. (New York: Norton,
1985), pt. 1.

25. Robert V. Hine, *Community on the American Frontier* (Norman: U. of
Oklahoma Press, 1980), 212–216; Horace Greeley, *Recollections of a
Busy Life,* vol. 2 (rpt. Port Washington, N.Y.: Kennikat Press, 1971),
373; Augustus L. Chetlain, *Recollections of Seventy Years* (Galena, Ill.,
1899), 22, 24; Algeline Jackson Ashley diary entry, 23 June 1852 (TS
copy of original in San Diego Public Library), Ayer Collection no. 32,
Newberry; Jules Remy and Julius Brenchley, *A Journey to Great-Salt-
Lake City,* vol. 2 (London, 1861), 170.

26. "If neglected there," Webster prophetically continued, "it will hardly
exist in society." "On the Education of Youth in America," in *A
Collection of Essays and Fugitiv[e] Writings* (Boston, 1790), 16.

27. Ross W. Beales Jr., "The Reverend Ebenezer Parkman's Farm Workers, Westborough, Massachusetts, 1726–82," *Proceedings of the American Antiquarian Society* 99, pt. 1 (1989): 121–149; Johnson, *Shopkeeper's Millennium,* 38–48, 139–140; W. J. Rorabaugh, *The Craft Apprentice: From Franklin to the Machine Age in America* (New York: Oxford U. Press, 1986), 209; Allan Stanley Horlick, *Country Boys and Merchant Princes: The Social Control of Young Men in New York* (Lewisburg: Bucknell U. Press, 1975), ch. 9.

28. See, e.g., Margaret K. Bacon, Irvin L. Child, and Herbert Barry III, "A Cross-Cultural Study of the Correlates of Crime," *J. of Abnormal and Social Psychology* 66 (1963): 291–300; Isidor Chein et al., *The Road to H: Narcotics, Delinquency, and Social Policy* (New York: Basic Books, 1964), 271–275; Jerald G. Bachman, Patrick M. O'Malley, and Jerome Johnston, *Youth in Transition,* vol. 4 (Ann Arbor: Institute for Social Research, 1978), 26; James Q. Wilson and Richard J. Herrnstein, *Crime and Human Nature* (New York: Simon and Schuster, 1985), chs. 8, 9; Michael R. Gottfredson and Travis Hirschi, *A General Theory of Crime* (Stanford: Stanford U. Press, 1990), 97–105; Deborah A. Dawson, "Family Structure and Children's Health and Well-Being," *JMF* 53 (1991): 573–584; *Gangs, Crime and Violence in Los Angeles,* 18–21; Barbara Dafoe Whitehead, "Dan Quayle Was Right," *Atlantic Monthly* 27 (April 1993): 66, 70, 72, 77, 82; David W. Murray, "Poor Suffering Bastards," *Policy Review* 68 (1994): 9–15; David Blankenhorn, *Fatherless America* (New York: Basic Books, 1995), ch. 2.

29. Frances E. Kobrin and Linda J. Waite, "Effects of Childhood Family Structure on the Transition to Marriage," *JMF* 46 (1984): 807–816; Durkheim, *Suicide, A Study in Sociology,* trans. John A. Spaulding and George Simpson (New York: Free Press, 1951), 270–271.

30. Burlend, *A True Picture of Emigration; or Fourteen Years in the Interior of North America . . .* (London, 1848), 27–28; Abbott, *We Pointed Them North,* 219–225, 240–245; quotation 221.

31. Lévy-Strauss, "The Family," in *Man, Culture, and Society,* ed. Harry L. Shapiro (New York: Oxford U. Press, 1960), 269; Esmond Wright, *Franklin of Philadelphia* (Cambridge, Mass.: Harvard U. Press, 1986), 43.

32. The dead: e.g., *Diary, 1843–1852, of James Hadley, Tutor and Professor of Greek in Yale College, 1845–1872,* ed. Laura Hadley Moseley (New Haven: Yale U. Press, 1951), 255. Segregation: Emily P. Burke, *Reminiscences of Georgia* (Oberlin, 1850), 63–64; Andrew F. Rolle, *The Immigrant Upraised: Italian Adventurers and Colonists in an Expanding America* (Norman: U. of Oklahoma Press, 1968), 175–176; Sherlock Bristol, *The Pioneer Preacher: An Autobiography* (New York, 1887), 291;

Robert Louis Stevenson, *Across the Plains, With Other Memoirs and Essays* (New York, 1892), 26–27. Medicine: Shana Alexander, "They Decide Who Lives, Who Dies," *Life* 53 (9 Nov. 1962): 102–127; Martin S. Pernick, *A Calculus of Suffering: Pain, Professionalism and Anesthesia in Nineteenth-Century America* (New York: Columbia U. Press, 1985), 181, 191–195.

33. Robert F. Schoeni, "The Earnings Effects of Marital Status," Research Report no. 90–172, Population Studies Center, U. of Michigan (March 1990); William Moraley, *The Infortunate: The Voyage and Adventures of William Moraley, an Indentured Servant*, ed. Susan E. Klepp and Billy G. Smith (1743; rpt. University Park: Pennsylvania State U. Press, 1992), 103; "Bypaths of Kansas History," *Kansas Historical Quarterly* 9 (1940): 100; George Gilder, *Naked Nomads: Unmarried Men in America* (New York: Quadrangle, 1974), 152; Sidney L. Harring, "Class Conflict and the Suppression of Tramps in Buffalo, 1892–1894," *Law and Society Review* 11 (1977): 903; Martin Cherniack, *The Hawk's Nest Incident: America's Worst Industrial Disaster* (New Haven: Yale U. Press, 1986), 67; John J. McCook, "The Tramp Problem," *Lend a Hand* 15 (1895): 170; Cartwright, *Autobiography*, 18.

34. Cowboy: Nannie T. Alderson and Helena Huntington Smith, *A Bride Goes West* (rpt. Lincoln: U. of Nebraska Press, 1969), 55–56; Internalizing: Gilder, *Naked Nomads*, 151–152.

35. U.S. Census Office, *Report on Crime, Pauperism, and Benevolence in the United States at the Eleventh Census: 1890*, pt. 2 (1895), 350 (based on 73,362 prisoners of known marital status); U.S. Dept. of Justice, *Historical Corrections Statistics . . . 1850–1984* (Rockville, Md.: Westat, 1986), 98; Donald J. Bogue et al., *The Population of the United States: Historical Trends and Future Projections*, rev. ed. (New York: Free Press, 1985), 148.

36. "State Lunatic Hospital at Worcester, Mass.," *Boston Medical and Surgical J.* 12 (1835): 78; [Edward Jarvis,] "Matrimonial Statistics," *Botanico-Medical Recorder* 11 (1842–43): 74; Durkheim, *Suicide*, 260–268; Dewey Shurtleff, "Mortality among the Married," *J. of the American Geriatrics Society* 4 (1956): 654–666; Walter R. Gove, "The Relationship between Sex Roles, Marital Status and Mental Illness," *Social Forces* 51 (1972): 34–45, and idem, "Sex, Marital Status, and Mortality," *AJS* 79 (1973): 45–67; Bachman, O'Malley, and Johnston, *Youth in Transition*, 195–197; George I. Bliss, "The Influence of Marriage on the Death-Rate of Men and Women," *Publications of the American Statistical Association* 14 (March 1914): 54, 57.

37. See Walter R. Gove, Carolyn Briggs Style, and Michael Hughes, "The Effect of Marriage on the Well-Being of Adults," *J. of Family Issues* 11 (1990): 4–35.

38. U.S. Bureau of Alcohol, Tobacco, and Firearms, "Guns for Sale in U.S.," *ATF Facts* (Washington, Nov. 1994), A3.

39. Bruce L. Benson, "Guns for Protection and Other Private Sector Responses to the Fear of Rising Crime," and Don B. Kates Jr., "Conclusion," both in *Firearms and Violence: Issues of Public Policy*, ed. Don B. Kates Jr. (Cambridge, Mass.: Ballinger, 1984), 351; 529–531.

40. Eugene W. Hollon, *Frontier Violence* (New York: Oxford U. Press, 1974), 109, 115–116; Robert M. Ireland, "Homicide in Kentucky," *Register of the Kentucky Historical Society* 81 (1983): 137; Frederick L. Hoffman, *The Homicide Problem* (Newark: Prudential Press, 1925), 4, 79; H. C. Brearley, *Homicide in the United States* (Chapel Hill: U. of North Carolina Press, 1932), 74.

41. Hoffman, *Homicide Problem*, 60–61; Brearley, *Homicide in the United States*, 70–71.

42. Mark Twain, *Roughing It* (New York: Library of America, 1984), 781; Julian Ralph, "A Talk with a Cowboy," *Harper's Weekly* 36 (16 April 1892): 376; Erdoes, *Saloons*, 72, 76–77, 87.

43. Bell I. Wiley, *The Life of Billy Yank: The Common Soldier of the Union* (rpt. Baton Rouge: Louisiana State U. Press, 1978), ch. 10, quotation 247; Burnham, *Bad Habits*, 25, 185, 188–190, 216, 263; Allan M. Brandt, *No Magic Bullet: A Social History of Venereal Disease in the United States since 1880* (New York: Oxford U. Press, 1985), 54–55.

44. Stephen E. Ambrose, *Nixon: The Education of a Politician* (New York: Simon and Schuster, 1987), 105–116; idem, *Nixon: Ruin and Recovery, 1973–1990* (New York: Simon and Schuster, 1991), 328–329. Nixon excelled at poker but not profanity. His cursing was never as brazen or unselfconscious as that of Dwight Eisenhower, John Kennedy, or Lyndon Johnson—career soldier, man-about-town, and native Texan, respectively.

45. R. Wayne Eisenhart, "You Can't Hack It Little Girl: A Discussion of the Covert Psychological Agenda of Modern Combat Training," *J. of Social Issues* 31 (1975): 18.

46. Elizabeth Bacon Custer, *Tenting on the Plains or General Custer in Kansas and Texas* (1895 rev. ed., rpt. Williamstown, Mass.: Corner House, 1973), 250–255; Richard Slotkin, *The Fatal Environment: The Myth of the Frontier in the Age of Industrialization, 1800–1890* (New York: Atheneum, 1985), 431.

47. Washington to Alexander Hamilton, 22 April 1783, in *The Writings of George Washington*, vol. 26, ed. John C. Fitzpatrick (rpt. Westport, Conn.: Greenwood Press, 1970), 350–351; James M. Denham, "'Some Prefer the Seminoles': Violence and Disorder among Soldiers and Settlers in the Second Seminole War, 1835–1842," *Florida Historical*

   Quarterly 70 (1991): 39–44, 51, 54; *The News from Brownsville: Helen Chapman's Letters from the Texas Military Frontier*, ed. Caleb Coker (Austin: Texas State Historical Association, 1992), 55; Lee quoted in Robert Wooster, *Soldiers, Sutlers, and Settlers: Garrison Life on the Texas Frontier* (College Station: Texas A&M U. Press, 1987), 58.

48. Quotation: "Police Commissioners' Report," *NYT*, 5 Jan. 1866, 4. Edith Abbot, "Crime and the War," and Betty B. Rosenbaum, "The Relationship between War and Crime in the United States," in *J. of the American Institute of Criminal Law and Criminology* 9 (1918–1919): 41–43 and 30 (1939–1940): 725; Michael Stephen Hindus, "The Contours of Crime and Justice in Massachusetts and South Carolina, 1767–1878," *American J. of Legal History* 21 (1977): 224; Eric Foner, *Reconstruction: America's Unfinished Business, 1863–1877* (New York: Harper and Row, 1984), 119–123. Postwar crime waves are not simply the result of returning veterans. Wars also legitimate violence in the general civilian population, as argued in Dane Archer and Rosemary Gartner, *Violence and Crime in Cross-National Perspective* (New Haven: Yale U. Press, 1984), ch. 4.

3. The Geography of Gender

1. Recall that this ratio is conventionally given as the number of males per 100 females. Also known as the sex ratio, this measure is now commonly (though not universally) referred to as the gender ratio.

2. J. H. Benton Jr., *Early Census Making in Massachusetts, 1643–1765* (Boston: Charles E. Goodspeed, 1905); letter to [Thomas A.] Merrill, *The Writings and Speeches of Daniel Webster: Private Correspondence*, vol. 1 (Boston: Little, Brown, 1903), 116; Commonwealth of Massachusetts, Joint Special Committee of the House and Senate, *Emigration of Young Women*, Senate Report no. 156 (29 March 1865), 3.

3. *The Frontier in American History* (rpt. Tucson: U. of Arizona Press, 1986), 259–260, 275.

4. Charles Miner, *History of Wyoming, in a Series of Letters . . .* (Philadelphia, 1845), 135, 138, 164, 208.

5. George R. Carroll, *Pioneer Life in and around Cedar Rapids, Iowa, from 1839 to 1849* (Cedar Rapids, 1895), 13; Memoirs of Joshua Lacy Wilson (MS, n.d.), Box 4, Folder 1, Joshua Lacy Wilson Papers, Durrett Collection, U. of Chicago Library, 4–5; Christian Cackler, *Recollections of an Old Settler* (Kent, Ohio, 1874), 15–16, 24–25; Everett Dick, *The Sod-House Frontier, 1854–1890* (rpt. Lincoln, Neb.: Johnsen Publishing, 1954), 232.

6. E. Gould Buffum, *Six Months in the Gold Mines . . .* (Philadelphia, 1850), 132; Journal of Richard Ness, 29 July 1849, 33, WAC, Bein-

ecke; Rodman W. Paul, *The Far West and the Great Plains in Transition, 1859–1900* (New York: Harper and Row, 1988), 123–124.

7. Walter Prescott Webb, *The Great Plains* (rpt. Lincoln: U. of Nebraska Press, 1981), 505–506; John Mack Faragher, *Women and Men on the Oregon Trail* (New Haven: Yale U. Press, 1979), 183–186; Craig Miner, *West of Wichita: Settling the High Plains of Kansas, 1865–1890* (Lawrence: U. Press of Kansas, 1986), 150–154. Parenthetical quotation: letter from H. S. Herriet to Eclecta Herriet, 5 June 1851, WAC, Beinecke, referring to the trip across the Isthmus of Panama. A typical memoir: Miriam Davis Colt, *Went to Kansas; Being a Thrilling Account of an Ill-Fated Expedition to that Fairy Land, and Its Sad Results . . .* (Watertown, N.Y., 1862). Helper: *The Land of Gold: Reality versus Fiction* (Baltimore, 1855), 21–22. Napheys: *The Physical Life of Woman: Advice to the Maiden, Wife, and Mother,* 5th ed. (Philadelphia, 1870), 127.

8. *Diary of David How* (Cambridge, Mass., 1865), xi; "Diary of Mrs. Elizabeth Dixon Smith Geer," *Transactions of the Oregon Pioneer Association* (1907): 165–166; Julia Etta Parkerson, *Etta's Journal, Jan. 2, 1874–July 25, 1875,* ed. Ellen Payne Paullin (Canton, Conn.: Lithographics, 1981), 13n8.

9. Elizabeth Bacon Custer, *Tenting on the Plains or General Custer in Kansas and Texas* (rpt. Williamstown, Mass.: Corner House, 1973), 391–393.

10. "American Women and the American Character," in *History and American Society: Essays of David M. Potter,* ed. Don E. Fehrenbacher (New York: Oxford U. Press, 1973), 284; Warren S. Thompson and P. K. Whelpton, *Population Trends in the United States* (rpt. New York: Gordon and Breach, 1969), 186–192.

11. *What Shall We Do with Our Daughters? Superfluous Women and Other Lectures* (Boston, 1883), 138–139.

12. Steven Mintz and Susan Kellogg, *Domestic Revolutions: A Social History of American Family Life* (New York: Free Press, 1988), 78, 83; Hans von Hentig, "The Criminality of the Negro," *J. of the American Institute of Criminal Law and Criminology* 30 (1939–1940): 670–671; Joel Williamson, *The Crucible of Race: Black-White Relations in the American South since Emancipation* (New York: Oxford U. Press, 1984), 58–59, 212–213.

13. Constant: David Herlihy and Christiane Klapisch-Zuber, *Tuscans and Their Families: A Study of the Florentine Catasto of 1427* (New Haven: Yale U. Press, 1985), 157, 217. Cities and towns: Joan M. Jensen and Darlis A. Miller, "The Gentle Tamers Revisited: New Approaches to the History of Women in the American West," *PacHR* 49 (1980): 193, 196, 211.

14. E. A. Hammel, Sheila R. Johansson, and Caren A. Ginsberg, "The Value of Children during Industrialization: Sex Ratios in Childhood in

Nineteenth-Century America," *JFH* 8 (1983): 346–366; idem, "The Value of Children during Industrialization: Childhood Sex Ratios in Nineteenth Century America," Program in Population Research Working Paper no. 8, U. of California at Berkeley (Aug. 1982); Caren Anne Ginsberg, "Sex-Specific Child Mortality and the Economic Value of Children in Nineteenth Century Massachusetts" (Ph.D. diss., U. of California, Berkeley, 1984).

15. E.g., John Snow, "On the Comparative Mortality of Large Towns and Rural Districts and the Causes by Which It Is Influenced," *Transactions of the Epidemiological Society of London* 1 (1855): 24; Mary Anne Warren, *Gendercide: The Implications of Sex Selection* (Totowa, N.J.: Rowman and Allanheld, 1985), ch. 2.

16. *Land of Their Choice: The Immigrants Write Home* (Minneapolis: U. of Minnesota Press, 1955), ed. Theodore C. Blegen, 337. See also David T. Courtwright, "The Neglect of Female Children and Childhood Sex Ratios in Nineteenth-Century America," *JFH* 15 (1990): 313–323.

17. Edward O. Wilson, *Sociobiology: The New Synthesis* (Cambridge, Mass.: Harvard U. Press, 1975), 317–318; Robert G. Edwards, *Conception in the Human Female* (London: Academic Press, 1980), 9; Michael S. Teitelbaum, "Factors Associated with the Sex Ratio in Human Populations," in *The Structure of Human Populations,* ed. G. A. Harrison and A. J. Boyce (Oxford: Clarendon Press, 1972), 90–109.

18. C. O. Carter, "Sex Differences in the Distribution of Physical Illness in Children," *Social Science and Medicine* 12B (1978): 163–166; Walter F. Willcox, "The Distribution of the Sexes in the United States in 1890," *AJS* 1 (1896): 736–737.

19. William Forrest Sprague, *Women and the West: A Short Social History* (New York: Arno Press, 1972), 66.

20. Marilyn Irvin Holt, *The Orphan Trains: Placing Out in America* (Lincoln: U. of Nebraska Press, 1992), 2–3, 64–65.

21. Michael Zuckerman, "Pilgrims in the Wilderness: Community, Modernity, and the Maypole at Merry Mount," *New England Quarterly* 50 (1977): 255–277; T. H. Breen and Stephen Foster, "Moving to the New World," *WMQ* 30 (1973): 194; idem, "The Puritans' Greatest Achievement," *JAH* 60 (1973): 5–22; Edmund S. Morgan, *American Slavery, American Freedom: The Ordeal of Colonial Virginia* (New York: Norton, 1975), 235, 407–408; R. Thompson, "Seventeenth-Century English and Colonial Sex Ratios," *Population Studies* 28 (1974): 155–161.

22. Richardson and Wells Counties: Federal Writers' Project American Guide Series, *Nebraska: A Guide to the Cornhusker State* (New York: Viking, 1939), 9, 56, 276, and *North Dakota: A Guide to the Northern Prairie State* (Fargo: Knight Printing Co., 1938), 6–7, 69, 273. Robert

Dykstra, *The Cattle Towns* (New York: Knopf, 1968), 247–248; Odie B. Faulk, *Dodge City: The Most Western Town of All* (New York: Oxford U. Press, 1977), vii–viii, ch. 2; Carroll D. Clark and Roy L. Roberts, *People of Kansas: A Demographic and Social Study* (Topeka: Kansas State Planning Board, 1936), 111–112.

23. Paul, *Far West*, 24; Walter Nugent, "Frontiers and Empires in the Late Nineteenth Century," *Western Historical Quarterly* 20 (1989): 393–408; *Compendium of the Ninth Census* (1872), 546; James E. Davis, *Frontier America, 1800–1840: A Comparative Demographic Analysis of the Settlement Process* (Glendale, Ca.: Arthur H. Clark, 1977), 58–59.

24. C. Vann Woodward, *Origins of the New South, 1877–1913* (Baton Rouge: Louisiana State U. Press, 1971), 299.

25. Hope T. Eldridge and Dorothy Swaine Thomas, *Population Growth and Redistribution in the United States, 1870–1950* (Philadelphia: American Philosophical Society, 1964); Edward L. Ayers, *The Promise of the New South: Life after Reconstruction* (New York: Oxford U. Press, 1992), 24; Michael Wallis, *Route 66: The Mother Road* (New York: St. Martin's Press, 1990), 9, 19; Jack Temple Kirby, "The Southern Exodus," *JSH* 49 (1983): 595–596.

26. George A. Devlin, *South Carolina and Black Migration, 1865–1940* (New York: Garland Studies in Historical Demography, 1989), ch. 10, letters at 392–394; Eldridge and Thomas, *Population*, 90–93, 107, 125; Ayer, *Promise*, 149–151; Nicholas Lemann, *The Promised Land: The Great Black Migration and How It Changed America* (New York: Knopf, 1991), 3–7; Wells, *Revolutions*, 3–7; Sarah Deutsch, "Landscape of Enclaves: Race Relations in the West, 1865–1990," in *Under an Open Sky: Rethinking America's Western Past*, ed. William Cronon et al. (New York: Norton, 1992), 132.

27. Sheldon Hackney, "Southern Violence," in *The History of Violence in America*, ed. Hugh Davis Graham and Ted Robert Gurr (New York: Bantam, 1969), 505–527.

28. Jess Spirer, "Negro Crime," *Comparative Psychology Monographs* 16 (1940): 44; Keith D. Harries, *The Geography of Crime and Justice* (New York: McGraw-Hill, 1974), 34–35; Steven F. Messner, "Regional and Racial Effects on the Urban Homicide Rate," *AJS* 88 (1983): 997–1007; Lin Huff-Corzine, Jay Corzine, and David C. Moore, "Southern Exposure: Deciphering the South's Influence on Homicide Rates," *Social Forces* 64 (1986): 906–924; Richard E. Nisbett, "Violence and U.S. Regional Culture," *American Psychologist* 48 (1993): 441–449.

29. Sherman L. Ricards and George R. Blackburn, "The Sydney Ducks: A Demographic Analysis," *PacHR* 42 (1973): 24–25.

30. Ibid.; Richard A. Bartlett, *The New Country: A Social History of the*

American Frontier (New York: Oxford U. Press, 1974), 439; E. C. "Teddy Blue" Abbott, *We Pointed Them North: Recollections of a Cowpuncher* (New York: Farrar and Rinehart, 1939), 42.

31. *The Life of John Wesley Hardin as Written by Himself,* intro. Robert G. McCubbin (Norman: U. of Oklahoma Press, 1961), 12–14; Dan L. Thrapp, "Billy the Kid," *Encyclopedia of Frontier Biography,* vol. 1 (Lincoln: U. of Nebraska Press, 1988), 113; Bill O'Neal, *Encyclopedia of Western Gunfighters* (Norman: U. of Oklahoma Press, 1979), 60–61; Custer, *Tenting on the Plains,* 387. Some think McCarty may have been closer to twenty-six when he died.

32. Barnes F. Lathrop, "Migration into East Texas, 1835–1860," *Southwestern Historical Quarterly* 52 (1948): 331; Ralph Mann, "The Decade after the Gold Rush: Social Structure in Grass Valley and Nevada City, California, 1850–1860," *PacHR* 41 (1972): 489; James C. Malin, *The Grassland of North America* (rpt. Gloucester, Mass.: Peter Smith, 1967), 289; Blegen, ed., *Land of Their Choice,* 189–190.

33. Quotation: Blegen, ed., *Land of Their Choice,* 245. Charnel house: *The California Diary of General E. D. Townsend,* ed. Malcolm Edwards (Los Angeles: Ward Ritchie Press, 1970), 44.

34. Carl F. Reuss, "The Pioneers of Lincoln County, Washington: A Study in Migration," *Pacific Northwest Quarterly* 30 (1939): 60–62; Mann, "Decade after the Gold Rush," 488.

35. Catlin, *Letters and Notes on the North American Indians,* ed. Michael MacDonald Mooney (New York: Clarkson N. Potter, 1975), 165.

36. E.g., Robert L. Meriwether, *The Expansion of South Carolina, 1729–1765,* (rpt. Philadelphia: Porcupine Press, 1974), 15; Terry G. Jordan and Matti Kaups, *The American Backwoods Frontier* (Baltimore: Johns Hopkins U. Press, 1989), 87–89; Fernando Henriques, *Children of Conflict: A Study of Interracial Sex and Marriage* (New York: Dutton, 1975), 44–45, 56–62. Quotation from Mountain Bill Rhodes in *South Pass, 1868: James Chisholm's Journal of the Wyoming Gold Rush,* ed. Lola M. Homsher (Lincoln: U. of Nebraska Press, 1960), 125.

37. Rolfe: letter to Sir Thomas Dale, *Narratives of Early Virginia, 1606–1625,* ed. Lyon Gardiner Tyler (rpt. New York: Barnes and Noble, 1966), 240. Johnson: Bernard Bailyn with Barbara DeWolfe, *Voyagers to the West: A Passage in the Peopling of America on the Eve of the Revolution* (New York: Knopf, 1986), 576–582. Stuart: Abbott, *We Pointed Them North,* 160.

38. Gary B. Nash, *Red, White, and Black: The Peoples of Early America,* 3rd ed. (Englewood Cliffs, N.J.: Prentice Hall, 1992), 105–107, 280–284; Richard White, *The Middle Ground: Indians, Empires, and Republics in the Great Lakes Region, 1650–1815* (Cambridge: Cambridge U. Press, 1991),

60–75, 339–351, 368–396; Virgil J. Vogel, "Indian-White Intermarriage on the Frontier," in *Transactions of the Illinois Historical Society*, ed. Mary Ellen McElligott (Springfield: Illinois State Historical Society, 1989), 1; Horace Greeley, *An Overland Journey from New York to San Francisco in the Summer of 1859*, ed. Charles T. Duncan (New York: Knopf, 1964), 104, 132.

39. James M. McReynolds, "Family Life in a Borderland Community: Nacogdoches, Texas, 1779–1861" (Ph.D. diss., Texas Tech U., 1978), 117–128, 291.

4. The Altar of the Golden Calf

1. Winfred Blevins assisted by Ruth Valsing, *Dictionary of the American West* (New York: Facts on File, 1993), 148.
2. "Reminiscences of Joseph H. Boyd: An Argonaut of 1857," ed. William S. Lewis, *Washington Historical Quarterly* 15 (1924): 257.
3. J. S. Holliday, *The World Rushed In: The California Gold Rush Experience* (New York: Simon and Schuster, 1981), 297, 354; Julius H. Pratt, "To California by Panama in '49," *Century Magazine*, n.s. 19 (1891): 914; J. Ross Browne and James W. Taylor, *Reports upon the Mineral Resources of the United States* (1867), 38; Mildred F. Stone, *Since 1845: A History of the Mutual Benefit Life Insurance Company* (New Brunswick: Rutgers U. Press, 1957), 36–38; Shepard B. Clough, *A Century of American Life Insurance* (rpt. Westport, Conn.: Greenwood Press, 1970), 84–85.
4. Holliday, *World Rushed In*, 115, 372–373, 407; Charles Ross Parke, *Dreams to Dust: A Diary of the California Gold Rush, 1849–1850*, ed. James E. Davis (Lincoln: U. of Nebraska Press, 1989); John Duffy, "Medicine in the West: An Historical Overview," *J. of the West* 21 (1982): 8–10.
5. "A Woman's Trip Across the Plains in 1849," in *Women's Diaries of the Westward Journey*, ed. Lillian Schlissel (New York: Schocken Books, 1982), 171.
6. Joseph R. Conlin, *Bacon, Beans, and Galantines: Food and Foodways on the Western Mining Frontier* (Reno: U. of Nevada Press, 1986), 69–87, 113–115; Anthony J. Lorenz, "Scurvy in the Gold Rush," *J. of the History of Medicine and Allied Sciences* 12 (1957): 473–510.
7. *Diary of a Physician in California* (New York, 1850), 9; Lorenz, "Scurvy," 492–493; Conlin, *Bacon*, 91.
8. Sherman, letter to Lt. E.O.C. Ord, 28 Oct. 1848, WAC, Beinecke; George Groh, "Doctors of the Frontier," *American Heritage* 14 (April 1963): 90. Wife: [Louise Clappe,] *The Shirley Letters from the California Mines, 1851–1852*, ed. Carl I. Wheat (New York: Knopf, 1970), 161. Observer: E. Gould Buffum, *Six Months in the Gold Mines: From a Journal*

of Three Years' Residence in Upper and Lower California, 1847–8–9 (Philadelphia, 1850), 138.

9. J. F. B. Marshall, "Three Gold Dust Stories," *Century Magazine*, n.s. 19 (1891): 786; Frank Soule, John H. Gihon, and James Nisbet, *Annals of San Francisco*, intro. Richard H. Dillon (rpt. Palo Alto: Lewis Osborne, 1966), 495; Hinton Helper, *The Land of Gold: Reality versus Fiction* (Baltimore, 1855), 64.

10. Holliday, *World Rushed In*, 364; John Williamson Palmer, "Pioneer Days in San Francisco," *Century Magazine*, n.s. 21 (1892): 552; Hubert Howe Bancroft, *California Inter Pocula* (San Francisco, 1888), ch. 22; letters from Mrs. Jerusha (Deming) Merrill to Mr. and Mrs. Selden Deming, 28 Oct. 1849 and 8 Jan. 1851, WAC, Beinecke; Elliott West, *The Saloon on the Rocky Mountain Mining Frontier* (Lincoln: U. of Nebraska Press, 1979), 23.

11. Holliday, *World Rushed In*, 413; Mary Lee Spence, "Waitresses in the Trans-Mississippi West," in *The Women's West*, ed. Susan Armitage and Elizabeth Jameson (Norman: U. of Oklahoma Press, 1987), 222; Donald Dale Jackson, *Gold Dust* (New York: Knopf, 1980), 137; Jacqueline Baker Barnhardt, *The Fair but Frail: Prostitution in San Francisco, 1849–1900* (Reno: U. of Nevada Press, 1986), 25–39.

12. Holliday, *World Rushed In*, 303, 355; Joann Levy, *They Saw the Elephant: Women in the California Gold Rush* (Hamden, Conn.: Archon Books, 1990), 155.

13. *The Journals of Alfred Doten, 1849–1903*, vol. 1, ed. Walter Van Tilburg Clark (Reno: U. of Nevada Press, 1973), 52; *Personal Memoirs of U. S. Grant*, vol. 1 (New York, 1885), 208; Richard Dunlop, *Doctors of the American Frontier* (Garden City, N.Y.: Doubleday, 1965), 115.

14. William H. McFarlin to Margaret McFarlin, 1 Jan. 1852, WAC, Beinecke. I have regularized some of the spelling.

15. Quoted in Holliday, *World Rushed In*, 373.

16. Bennett, *The First Baby in Camp: A Full Account of the Scene and Adventures during the Pioneer Days of '49* (Salt Lake City, 1893), 37; [Clappe,] *Shirley Letters*, 102–105, 136–137; Charles B. Gillespie, "A Miner's Sunday in Coloma," *Century Magazine*, n.s. 20 (1891): 260, 262; Richard Erdoes, *Saloons of the Old West* (New York: Knopf, 1979), 147.

17. Gillespie, "Miner's Sunday," 260; Bennett, *First Baby in Camp*, 4; J. H. Post to Reverend H. Winslow, 5 Jan. 1853, WAC, Beinecke.

18. *Land of Gold*, 43, 44; Hugh C. Bailey, *Hinton Rowan Helper: Abolitionist-Racist* (University, Alabama: U. of Alabama Press, 1965).

19. Gary G. Hamilton, "The Structural Sources of Adventurism: The Case of the California Gold Rush," *AJS* 83 (1978): 1469–1473; *To the Land of Gold And Wickedness: The 1848–59 Diary of Lorena L. Hays*, ed. Jeanne

Hamilton Watson (St. Louis: Patrice Press, 1988), 233; Journal of Dr. George McCowen of Mining Experiences and Conditions in California in the Early Sixties (TS of original in private ownership, n.d.), Ayer Collection no. 541, Newberry, 22–23; [Clappe], *Shirley Letters,* 49; *Journals of Alfred Doten,* vol. 1, 322–323; Palmer, "Pioneer Days in San Francisco," 550.

20. Swain: Holliday, *World Rushed In.* L. M. Wolcott to B[eman] Gates, 20 Feb. 1851, in the appendix of *Gold Rush Diary: Being the Journal of Elisha Douglass Perkins on the Overland Trail in the Spring and Summer of 1849,* ed. Thomas D. Clark (Lexington: U. of Kentucky Press, 1967), 195.

21. *The Diary of a Forty-Niner,* ed. Chauncey L. Canfield (Boston: Houghton Mifflin, 1920), 112.

22. *Land of Gold,* 29, 36–37, 63–68, 153–154, 157, 170–171, 238–239; Soule, Gihon, and Nisbet, *Annals,* 256–257, 399; Robert H. Tillman, "The Prosecution of Homicide in Sacramento County, California, 1853–1900," *Southern California Quarterly* 68 (1986): 170–171.

23. Erwin G. Gudde, *California Gold Camps: A Geographical and Historical Dictionary* . . . (Berkeley: U. of California Press, 1975); Andrew F. Rolle, *California: A History,* 2nd ed. (New York: Crowell, 1969), 252; William Mead Muhler, "Religion and Social Problems in Gold Rush California: 1849–1869" (Ph.D. diss., Graduate Theological Union, 1989), 344–358; Richard Ness journal, WAC, Beinecke, 20, 28; letter from Mary B. Ballou to Selden Ballou, 30 Oct. 1852, WAC, Beinecke, 9–10; Buffum, *Six Months in the Gold Mines,* 83; *Journals of Alfred Doten,* vol. 1, 52; [Clappe,] *Shirley Letters,* 96–97, 166–167.

24. Ness journal, 18–19; Harry Laurenz Wells, *History of Nevada County, California* (Oakland, 1880), 106; David A. Johnson, "Vigilance and the Law: The Moral Authority of Popular Justice in the Far West," *American Quarterly* 33 (1988): 575.

25. Johnson, "Vigilance and the Law," 562; Browne and Taylor, *Reports,* 20–21; Jackson, *Gold Dust,* 313–315, 327–328; [Rodman W. Paul], "Gold and Silver Rushes," *Reader's Encyclopedia of the American West,* ed. Howard R. Lamar (New York: Thomas Crowell, 1977), 445–451.

26. *An Overland Journey from New York to San Francisco in the Summer of 1859,* ed. Charles T. Duncan (New York: Knopf, 1964), 105–106, 127–133; quotation 133.

27. *Roughing It* (New York: Library of America, 1984), chs. 29–31. Not every story told in *Roughing It* should be taken at face value, but this one is corroborated by correspondence. Margaret Sanborn, *Mark Twain: The Bachelor Years* (New York: Doubleday, 1990), 167, 464.

28. *Roughing It,* 839–840.

29. George F. Willison, *Here They Dug for Gold* (New York: Reynal and

Hitchcock, 1946), 173–174, 182; West, *Saloon*, 74, 121–122; U.S. Census Office, *Report on the Defective, Dependent, and Delinquent Classes . . . as Returned at the Tenth Census* (1888), 568; Duane A. Smith, *Rocky Mountain Mining Camps* (Blooming: Indiana U. Press, 1967), 223. In computing these rates I have used a population figure of 20,000, which West argues is more realistic than the census count of 14,820.

30. [Michael A. Leeson,] *History of Montana, 1739–1885* (Chicago, 1885), 296–297.

31. "A Trader in the Rocky Mountains: Don Maguire's 1877 Diary," ed. Gary Topping, *Idaho Yesterdays* 27 (Summer 1983): 7. I have inserted periods where indicated by Maguire's capitalization and corrected one misspelling.

32. Dunlop, *Doctors of the American Frontier*, 118.

33. Generosity: John H. Brown, *Reminiscences and Incidents, of "The Early Days" of San Francisco . . . from 1845 to 1850* (San Francisco, 1886), chs. 3–4, 6; E. G. Waite, "Pioneer Mining in California," *Century Magazine*, n.s. 20 (1891): 133; Twain, *Roughing It*, 773–774. Resident quoted in Roger D. McGrath, "Violence and Lawlessness on the Western Frontier," in *Violence in America*, vol. 1: *The History of Crime*, ed. Ted Robert Gurr (Newbury Park, Ca.: Sage, 1989), 132.

34. Twain, *Roughing It*, 840; Johnson, "Vigilance and the Law," 563; Smith, *Rocky Mountain Mining Camps*, 47; Turner, "Contributions of the West to American Democracy," in *The Frontier in American History* (rpt. Tucson: U. of Arizona Press, 1986), 266.

35. Faro dealer quoted in Erdoes, *Saloons*, 126; Ray A. Billington, *America's Frontier Culture* (College Station: Texas A&M U. Press, 1977), 92.

36. McCowen TS journal, 19; Tocqueville, *Democracy in America*, ed. Richard D. Heffner (New York: New American Library, 1956), 194; Hale, *Log of a Forty-Niner*, 120; [Leeson], *History of Montana*, 226, 266. In Owen Wister's classic western novel, *The Virginian*, the reader never learns the protagonist's name.

37. John Myers Myers, *Doc Holliday* (Boston: Little, Brown, 1955), 17–19, 39.

38. The Nevada County total of 98 murders includes 18 committed by Indians. Leadville: West, *Saloon*, 20, reports 14 homicides in the eight months' worth of newspapers he studied, which, by extrapolation, yields an annual total of 21. I am following West (121 and personal communication) in using a population denominator of 20,000. The Boston arrests were reported in such a way that it was not possible to distinguish between negligent (not intentionally criminal) and non-negligent manslaughter. The true homicide rate for Boston for 1860–

1882 is therefore lower than 5.8, likely somewhere in the range of 4 to 5 per 100,000.

39. James L. Tyson, *Diary of a Physician in California* (New York, 1850), 62–63; Roger D. McGrath, *Gunfighters, Highwaymen, and Vigilantes: Violence on the Frontier* (Berkeley: U. of California Press, 1984), 54, 258; James J. Rawls, *Indians of California: The Changing Image* (Norman: U. of Oklahoma Press, 1984), 126–130, 171–201; Richard White, *"It's Your Misfortune and None of My Own": A History of the American West* (Norman: U. of Oklahoma Press, 1991), 337–340.

40. McGrath, "Violence and Lawlessness."

41. "Rail Road Towns" (MS, n.d.), Box 1, Dodge Papers, Newberry; James McCague, *Moguls and Iron Men: The Story of the First Transcontinental Railroad* (New York: Harper and Row, 1964), 187–189.

42. James Chisholm, *South Pass, 1868: James Chisholm's Journal of the Wyoming Gold Rush*, ed. Lola M. Homsher (Lincoln: U. of Nebraska Press, 1960), 15–36, 100–101; Emmett D. Chisum, "Boom Towns on the Union Pacific: Laramie, Benton and Bear River City," *Annals of Wyoming* 53 (1981): 4, 7–9.

43. McGrath, *Gunfighters*, 261–271, is a balanced overview of the debate.

44. Orderville: Robert V. Hine, *Community on the American Frontier: Separate but Not Alone* (Norman: U. of Oklahoma Press, 1980), 212–216.

45. "'Poor Men with Rude Machinery': The Formative Years of the Gold Hill Mining District, 1842–1853," and "The Miners World: Life and Labor at Gold Hill," *North Carolina Historical Review* 61 (1984): 1–35 and 62 (1985): 420–447.

5. The Cowboy Subculture

1. Nannie T. Alderson and Helena Huntington Smith, *A Bride Goes West* (rpt. Lincoln: U. of Nebraska Press, 1969), 73; *A Compilation of the Messages and Papers of the Presidents*, vol. 11, ed. James D. Richardson (New York: Bureau of National Literature, n.d.), 4640–4641; "The Cow-Boys of the Western Plains and Their Horses," *Cheyenne Daily Leader*, 3 Oct. 1882, rpt. in *Trailing the Cowboy: His Life and Lore as Told by Frontier Journalists*, ed. Clifford P. Westermeier (Caldwell, Idaho: Caxton Printers, 1955), 50.

2. Siberts with Walker D. Wyman, *Nothing but Prairie and Sky: Life on the Dakota Range in the Early Days* (Norman: U. of Oklahoma Press, 1954), 100–101; Wallace Stegner, "Who Are the Westerners?" *American Heritage* 38 (Dec. 1987): 36.

3. David Dary, *Cowboy Culture: A Saga of Five Centuries* (Lawrence: U. Press of Kansas, 1989), 276. My brief and much simplified description of the

range cattle industry draws on Dary's work and on J. Frank Dobie, *The Longhorns* (rpt. Boston: Little, Brown, 1950); Joe B. Frantz and Julian Ernest Choate Jr., *The American Cowboy* (Norman: U. of Oklahoma Press, 1955); Edward Everett Dale, *The Range Cattle Industry*, rev. ed. (Norman: U. of Oklahoma Press, 1960); [Joe A. Stout], "Cowboy," *Reader's Encyclopedia of the American West*, ed. Howard R. Lamar (New York: Thomas Y. Crowell, 1977), 268–270; Richard W. Slatta, *Cowboys of the Americas* (New Haven: Yale U. Press, 1990); Richard White, *"It's Your Misfortune and None of My Own": A History of the American West* (Norman: U. of Oklahoma Press, 1991); Terry G. Jordan, *North American Cattle-Ranching Frontiers* (Albuquerque: U. of New Mexico Press, 1993).

4. E. C. "Teddy Blue" Abbott, *We Pointed Them North: Recollections of a Cowpuncher* (New York: Farrar and Rinehart, 1939), 42.

5. TNT: *Workin' on the Railroad: Reminiscences from the Age of Steam*, ed. Richard Reinhardt (Palo Alto: American West Publishing, 1970), 95; [Stout], "Cowboy," 268; Philip Durham and Everett L. Jones, *The Negro Cowboys* (New York: Dodd, Mead, 1965), chs. 1–4. The one-seventh estimate for blacks may have been true in southeastern Texas in the years immediately after the Civil War, but if so the proportion shrank substantially during the 1870s. Cf. Jordan, *North American Cattle-Ranching Frontiers*, 214–215. Texas rate: Robert M. Ireland, "Homicide in Nineteenth Century Kentucky," *Register of the Kentucky Historical Society* 81 (1983): 134.

6. Dary, *Cowboy Culture*, 107, 209; Abbott, *We Pointed Them North*, 33.

7. Augustus L. Chetlain, *Recollections of Seventy Years* (Galena, Ill., 1899), 130–131; John E. Baur, "Cowboys and Skypilots," in *The American West and the Religious Experience*, ed. William Kramer (Los Angeles: Will Kramer, 1974), 41–70.

8. Charles Askins, *Texans, Guns and History* (New York: Winchester Press, 1970), 3, 7; *Trailing the Cowboy*, ed. Westermeier, 70–71, 72; George E. Goodfellow, "Cases of Gunshot Wound of the Abdomen Treated by Operation," *Southern California Practitioner* 4 (1889): 209–217; "The Fatal Six-Shooter Again," *Caldwell Post*, 20 July 1882, cited in *Trailing the Cowboy*, ed. Westermeier, 117; Donald Curtis Brown, "The Great Gun-Toting Controversy, 1865–1910" (Ph.D. diss., Tulane U., 1983), 19, 89–91, 130, 152–153.

9. *We Pointed Them North*, 247, 31–32.

10. *Workin' on the Railroad*, ed. Reinhardt, 96.

11. *We Pointed Them North*, 251; Marvin E. Wolfgang, *Patterns in Criminal Homicide* (Philadelphia: U. of Pennsylvania Press, 1958), 188–192, 196–197.

12. *Trailing the Cowboy*, ed. Westermeier, 25, 54; *Cowboy Life: Reconstructing*

An American Myth, ed. William W. Savage Jr. (Norman: U. of Oklahoma Press, 1975), 158.

13. Joseph G. McCoy, *Historic Sketches of the Cattle Trade of the West and Southwest* (Kansas City, 1874), 138–142; Abbott, *We Pointed Them North*, 256–257; *Trailing the Cowboy*, ed. Westermeier, ch. 5; W. C. Holden, "Law and Lawlessness on the Texas Frontier, 1875–1890," *SHQ* 44 (1940): 190–191; Dary, *Cowboy Culture*, 209.

14. Love quoted in John McPhee, *Rising from the Plains* (New York: Farrar, Straus, Giroux, 1986), 89. Food: Joseph R. Conlin, "Grub and Chow," in *The American West, as seen by Europeans and Americans*, ed. Rob Kroes (Amsterdam: Free University Press, 1989), 131; McCoy, *Cattle Trade*, 137. Coffee: Winfred Blevins assisted by Ruth Valsing, *Dictionary of the American West* (New York: Facts on File, 1993), 9.

15. Abbott, *We Pointed Them North*, 145–146; Richard Erdoes, *Saloons of the Old West* (New York: Knopf, 1979), 87, 89, 150–151.

16. Dary, *Cowboy Culture*, 217; Richard F. Selcer, "Fort Worth and the Fraternity of Strange Women," *SHQ* 96 (1992): 74; Neil Larry Shumsky, "Tacit Acceptance: Respectable Americans and Segregated Prostitution, 1870–1910," *J. of Social History* 19 (1986): 673–674.

17. Allan M. Brandt, *No Magic Bullet: A Social History of Venereal Disease in the United States since 1880* (New York: Oxford U. Press, 1985), 31; Mark Thomas Connelly, *The Response to Prostitution in the Progressive Era* (Chapel Hill: U. of North Carolina Press, 1980), 68, 180nn5,6; Howard B. Woolston, *Prostitution in the United States* (rpt. Montclair, N.J.: Patterson Smith, 1980), 180, 187; Lewis Thomas, *The Youngest Science: Notes of a Medicine Watcher* (New York: Viking, 1983), 32–34, 45–46.

18. *Trailing the Cowboy*, ed. Westermeier, 33; Dary, *Cowboy Culture*, 258, 284.

19. Loaded dice: Philip D. Jordan, *Frontier Law and Order* (Lincoln: U. of Nebraska Press, 1970), 54–55. Compulsive gambling: e.g., John Brown, *Twenty-Five Years a Parson in the Wild West: Being the Experience of Parson Ralph Riley* (Fall River, Mass., 1896), 55–56. Became gamblers: Julian Ralph, "A Talk with a Cowboy," *Harper's Weekly* 36 (16 April 1892): 375–376.

20. [Robert Schick], "Prostitution," *Reader's Encyclopedia of the American West*, 973; Anne M. Butler, *Daughters of Joy, Sisters of Misery: Prostitutes in the American West, 1865–90* (Urbana: U. of Illinois Press, 1985), 67–68; C. Robert Haywood, *Victorian West: Class and Culture in Kansas Cattle Towns* (Lawrence: U. Press of Kansas, 1991), 29–30.

21. Dykstra, *The Cattle Towns* (New York: Knopf, 1968), 113, 142–148; Roger D. McGrath, "Violence and Lawlessness on the Western Frontier," in *Violence in America*, vol. 1: *The History of Crime*, ed. Ted Robert Gurr (Newbury Park, Ca.: Sage, 1989), 134–135; Robert Tyrus Cashion,

"An Examination of Frontier Violence at Fort Griffin, Texas" (master's thesis, U. of Texas at Arlington, 1989), 17, 55. The most commonly cited source, Don H. Biggers, *Shackelford County Sketches,* ed. Joan Farmer (Albany and Fort Griffin: Clear Fork Press, 1974), 41, reports at least fifty-five killings, including twelve lynchings, at Fort Griffin over a period of twelve years. Cashion reports "a population of approximately one-thousand and almost as many transients." I have combined the two and rounded upward to two thousand for purposes of computing the rate. A work commonly cited to deny that the trail towns were especially violent is Frank Prassel, *The Western Peace Officer: A Legacy of Law and Order* (Norman: U. of Oklahoma Press, 1972). Prassel in turn cites statistics from U.S. Census Office, *Report on the Defective, Dependent, and Delinquent Classes . . . as Returned at the Tenth Census* (1888), 566-574, to substantiate his claim that New York and other eastern cities were more violent than western towns (17). However, these data are either biased or simply wrong. Leadville officially reported no homicides in 1880, but Elliott West, as noted in Chapter 4, found fourteen in just eight months. Moreover, Prassel's table (260) contains a significant transcription error: 9,067 murders for New York in 1880 rather than 37, which is what the Census report shows.

22. Dary, *Cowboy Culture,* 201; Dykstra, *Cattle Towns,* 89–90.
23. Dykstra, *Cattle Towns,* 116–124, 131–132, 143; Cashion, "Frontier Violence," 36.
24. Butler, *Daughters of Joy,* 102–103; Selcer, "Strange Women," 65–67; Carol Leonard and Isidor Wallimann, "Prostitution and Changing Morality in the Frontier Cattle Towns of Kansas," *Kansas History* 2 (Spring 1979): 41.
25. [Alfred T. Andreas,] *History of the State of Kansas* (Chicago, 1883), 1574; Dykstra, *Cattle Towns,* 127–128, 257–259; Leonard and Wallimann, "Prostitution," 39–40.
26. Dykstra, *Cattle Towns,* 128–131; C. Robert Haywood, "Cowtown Courts: Dodge City Courts, 1876–1886," *Kansas History* 11 (1988): 24, 31–32; Abbott, *We Pointed Them North,* 31.
27. Robert M. Utley, *High Noon in Lincoln: Violence on the Western Frontier* (Albuquerque: U. of New Mexico Press, 1987), 172–173; C. C. Rister, "Outlaws and Vigilantes on the Southern Plains," *Mississippi Valley Historical Review* 19 (1933): 544.
28. Richard Maxwell Brown, "The American Vigilante Tradition," in *Violence in America: Historical and Comparative Perspectives,* ed. Hugh Davis Graham and Ted Robert Gurr (New York: Bantam, 1969); Joe B. Frantz, "The Frontier Tradition: An Invitation to Violence," ibid., 140–143.

29. Cashion, "Frontier Violence," 63; Richard Maxwell Brown, *Strain of Violence: Historical Studies of American Violence and Vigilantism* (New York: Oxford U. Press, 1975), 246–251.

30. David H. Breen, *The Canadian Prairie West and the Ranching Frontier, 1874–1924* (Toronto: U. of Toronto Press, 1983), 85–86; Carlos A. Schwantes, "Perceptions of Violence on the Wageworkers' Frontier: An American-Canadian Comparison," *Pacific Northwest Quarterly* 77 (1986): 54–56.

31. Brown, "Gun-Toting Controversy," 17; Clark C. Spence, "The Livery Stable in the American West," *Montana* 36 (1986): 39.

32. Yankee marshals: Abbott, *We Pointed Them North*, 28.

33. Brown, "Gun-Toting Controversy," 152–164, quotations 163–164.

34. Ibid., 435–440.

35. Joseph Nimmo Jr., "The American Cow-Boy," *Harper's New Monthly Magazine* 57 (1886): 880–884; Abbott, *We Pointed Them North*, 231.

36. Don Russell, *The Lives and Legends of Buffalo Bill* (Norman: U. of Oklahoma Press, 1960), 21–32; John G. Blair, "Buffalo Bill and Sitting Bull: The Wild West as Media Event," in *The American West, as seen by Europeans and Americans*, ed. Rob Kroes (Amsterdam: Free U. Press, 1989), 262–281; Richard Slotkin, *Gunfighter Nation: The Myth of the Frontier in Twentieth-Century America* (New York: Atheneum, 1992), ch. 2; Dary, *Cowboy Culture*, 333.

37. George N. Fenin and William K. Everson, *The Western: From Silents to the Seventies*, expanded ed. (New York: Grossman, 1973); Thomas Schatz, *Hollywood Genres* (New York: Random House, 1981), 46–47; Slotkin, *Gunfighter Nation*, chs. 7–9.

38. Garth S. Jowett, "The Concept of History in American Produced Films," *J. of Popular Culture* 3 (1970): 813; Fenin and Everson, *The Western*, ch. 16; Robert G. Athearn, *The Mythic West in Twentieth-Century America* (Lawrence: U. Press of Kansas, 1986), 183; Elliott West, "Shots in the Dark: Television and the Western Myth," *Montana* 38 (1988): 72–73; Dary, *Cowboy Culture*, 335.

39. John H. Lenihan, *Showdown: Confronting Modern America in the Western Film* (Urbana: U. of Illinois Press, 1980), ch. 7; Schatz, *Hollywood Genres*, 53–54, 58–63; Michael Wood, *America in the Movies or "Santa Maria, It Had Slipped My Mind"* (New York: Delta, 1975), 42–43.

40. See James Q. Wilson and Richard J. Herrnstein, *Crime and Human Nature* (New York: Simon and Schuster, 1985), ch. 13.

41. John L. Caughey, *Imaginary Social Worlds: A Cultural Approach* (Lincoln: U. of Nebraska Press, 1984); Stegner, "Who Are the Westerners?" 39.

42. The John Wayne cult is discussed in Slotkin, *Gunfighter Nation*, 512ff.

43. Paraphrasing Michael Herr, *Dispatches* (New York: Knopf, 1977), 209.

Language from Herr and Charles Mohr, "U.S. Special Forces: Real and on Film," *New York Times*, 20 June 1968, 49; S. L. A. Marshall, *Crimsoned Prairie: The Wars between the United States and the Plains Indians during the Winning of the West* (New York: Charles Scribner's Sons, 1972), 155; Philip D. Beidler, *American Literature and the Experience of Vietnam* (Athens: U. of Georgia Press, 1982); *Dictionary of the Vietnam War*, ed. James S. Olson (Westport, Conn.: Greenwood Press, 1988); Gregory R. Clark, *Words of the Vietnam War* (Jefferson, N.C.: McFarland, 1990); Christopher Robbins, *The Ravens: The Men Who Flew in America's Secret War in Laos* (New York: Crown, 1987); and personal communication with John Olson, Lydia Fish, and Larry Wright.

44. "Festive Cowboy," in *Trailing the Cowboy*, ed. Westermeier, 53.
45. Odie B. Faulk, *Dodge City: The Most Western Town of All* (New York: Oxford U. Press, 1977), 85.

6. The Ecology of Frontier Violence

1. *The Human Condition: An Ecological and Historical View* (Princeton: Princeton University Press, 1980), 6–8.
2. *The Native Population of the Americas in 1492*, 2nd ed., ed. William M. Denevan (Madison: U. of Wisconsin Press, 1992), xvii–xxix; David E. Stannard, *American Holocaust: Columbus and the Conquest of the New World* (New York: Oxford U. Press, 1992), 261–268; John D. Daniels, "The Indian Population of North America in 1492," *WMQ* 49 (1992): 298–320.
3. James H. Merrell, *The Indians' New World: Catawbas and Their Neighbors from European Contact through the Era of Removal* (Chapel Hill: U. of North Carolina Press, 1989), 18–23, 192–195; Michael A. Leeson, *History of Montana, 1739–1885* (Chicago, 1885), 117; George Catlin, *Letters and Notes on the North American Indians*, ed. Michael MacDonald Mooney (New York: Clarkson N. Potter, 1975), chs. 11, 23; Donald R. Hopkins, *Princes and Peasants: Smallpox in History* (Chicago: U. of Chicago Press, 1983), 271–274.
4. Richard A. Bartlett, *The New Country: A Social History of the American Frontier, 1776–1890* (New York: Oxford U. Press, 1974), 17–18; Frederick Jackson Turner, *The Frontier in American History* (rpt. Tucson: U. of Arizona Press, 1986), 16–17; Harold S. Bender and C. Henry Smith, *Mennonites and Their Heritage*, rev. ed. (Scottdale, Pa.: Herald Press, 1964), 93; Robert M. Utley, *The Indian Frontier of the American West, 1846–1890* (Albuquerque: U. of New Mexico Press, 1984), 79; Everett Dick, *The Sod-House Frontier, 1854–1890* (Lincoln: Johnsen Publishing, 1954), 173.
5. John G. Bourke, "General Crook in the Indian Country," *Century*

Magazine, n.s. 19 (1891): 652; Frank Gilbert Roe, *The Indian and the Horse* (Norman: U. of Oklahoma Press, 1955), 192–195.

6. Attack villages: e.g., Colin G. Calloway, *The American Revolution in Indian Country* (Cambridge: Cambridge U. Press, 1995). Wounded Knee: Robert M. Utley and Wilcomb E. Washburn, *Indian Wars* (Boston: Houghton Mifflin, 1977), 299; S. L. A. Marshall, *Crimsoned Prairie: The Wars between the United States and the Plains Indians during the Winning of the West* (New York: Charles Scribner's Sons, 1972), 243.

7. Sherburne F. Cook, *The Conflict between the California Indian and White Civilization* (Berkeley: U. of California Press, 1976), combining tables 4 and 5, 357, 361; James J. Rawls, *Indians of California: The Changing Image* (Norman: U. of Oklahoma Press, 1984), chs. 6–7; Lou Conway Roberts, *A Woman's Reminiscences of Six Years in Camp with Texas Rangers* (Austin: Von Boeckmann-Jones, 1928), 27; James B. Gillett, *Six Years with the Texas Rangers,* ed. M. M. Quaife (rpt. Lincoln: U. of Nebraska Press, 1976), 19.

8. Joseph Nimmo Jr., "The American Cow-Boy," *Harper's New Monthly Magazine* 57 (1886): 881; Baylis John Fletcher, *Up the Trail in '79,* ed. Wayne Gard (rpt. Norman: U. of Oklahoma Press, 1968), 50–54.

9. Robert M. Utley, *Frontier Regulars: The United States Army and the Indian, 1866–1891* (New York: Macmillan, 1973), 23–28; Robert Wooster, *Soldiers, Sutlers, and Settlers: Garrison Life on the Texas Frontier* (College Station: Texas A&M U. Press, 1987), 59; D. Alexander Brown, *The Galvanized Yankees* (Urbana: U. of Illinois Press, 1963); Philip Weeks, *Farewell, My Nation: The American Indian and the United States, 1820–1890* (Arlington Heights, Ill.: Harlan Davidson, 1990), 92.

10. Elizabeth Burt, *Indians, Infants and Infantry: Andrew and Elizabeth Burt on the Frontier,* ed. Merrill J. Mattes (rpt. Lincoln: U. of Nebraska Press, 1988); E. S. Topping, *The Chronicles of the Yellowstone,* ed. Robert A. Murray (rpt. Minneapolis: Ross and Haines, 1968), 7–8; James Axtell, *The European and the Indian: Essays in the Ethnohistory of Colonial America* (Oxford: Oxford U. Press, 1981), 217–218; Richard White, "The Winning of the West: The Expansion of the Western Sioux in the Eighteenth and Nineteenth Centuries," *JAH* 65 (1978): 321–322; Dan Flores, "Bison Ecology and Bison Diplomacy: The Southern Plains from 1800 to 1850," *JAH* 78 (1991): 475.

11. Reginald Horsman, *Race and Manifest Destiny: The Origins of American Racial Anglo-Saxonism* (Cambridge, Mass.: Harvard U. Press, 1981), ch. 10.

12. On atrocities see, e.g., John H. Brown, *Reminiscences and Incidents, of "The Early Days" of San Francisco, Actual Experience of an Eye-Witness, from 1845 to 1850* (San Francisco, 1886), ch. 1; J. C. Long, *Lord Jeffrey Amherst: A Soldier of the King* (New York: Macmillan, 1933), 186–187;

Topping, *Chronicles of the Yellowstone,* 69, 111, 116, 119; *Land of Their Choice: The Immigrants Write Home,* ed. Theodore Blegen (Minneapolis: U. of Minnesota Press, 1955), 226; James L. Tyson, *Diary of a Physician in California* (New York, 1850), 62–63; report of Lt. Charles G. Hubbard, 20 June 1862, in *The War of the Rebellion: A Compilation of the Official Records of the Union and Confederate Armies,* ser. 1, vol. 50, pt. 1 (1897), 74. Venisse, letter of 20 June 1856, in *Documents of California Catholic History (1784–1963),* ed. Francis J. Weber (Los Angeles: Dawson's Book Shop, 1965), 72.

13. E.g., Richard White, *The Middle Ground: Indians, Empires, and Republics in the Great Lakes Region, 1650–1815* (Cambridge: Cambridge U. Press, 1991), 376–377, 388; Virginia Bergman Peters, *The Florida Wars* (Hamden, Conn.: Archon, 1979), 150–151; Duane Schultz, *Month of the Freezing Moon: The Sand Creek Massacre, November 1864* (New York: St. Martin's, 1990), 134–135; Raphael Pumpelly, *Across America and Asia* (New York, 1870), 16–17, 34; Richard Dodge's Black Hills MS diary, 1 June 1875, Dodge Papers, Newberry; *A Cannoneer in Navajo Country: Journal of Private Josiah M. Rice, 1851,* ed. Richard H. Dillon (Denver: Denver Public Library, 1970), 38–39; Evan S. Connell, *Son of the Morning Star* (San Francisco: North Point Press, 1984), 19, 254–255, 333.

14. On Indian atrocities and desecrations see, e.g., Samuel J. Crawford, *Kansas in the Sixties* (Chicago, 1911), 265–272; Craig Miner, *West of Wichita: Settling the High Plains of Kansas* (Lawrence: U. Press of Kansas, 1986), chs. 2, 9; Mary A. Maverick and George Madison Maverick, *Memoirs of Mary A. Maverick* (rpt. Lincoln: U. of Nebraska Press, 1989), 30–31, 38, 42; Charles H. Springer, *Soldiering in Sioux Country: 1865,* ed. Benjamin Franklin Cooling III (San Diego: Frontier Heritage Press, 1971), 46, 50, 52; *Narratives of Captivity among the Indians of North America . . .* (Chicago: Newberry Library, 1912). Rumor: e.g., *Land of Their Choice,* ed. Blegen, 426.

15. Robert M. Utley, *High Noon in Lincoln: Violence on the Western Frontier* (Albuquerque: U. of New Mexico Press, 1987), 173–174; Greeley, *An Overland Journey from New York to San Francisco in the Summer of 1859,* ed. Charles T. Duncan (New York: Knopf, 1964), 99.

16. Pranksters: *Mollie: The Journal of Mollie Dorsey Sanford in Nebraska and Colorado Territories, 1857–1866,* ed. Donald F. Danker (Lincoln: U. of Nebraska Press, 1959), 151–152; Dick, *Sod-House Frontier,* 170–171; C. C. Rister, "Outlaws and Vigilantes on the Southern Plains," *Mississippi Valley Historical Review* 19 (1933): 541.

17. Edwin Capron to Amelia Capron, 28 May 1865, Capron letters, Graff collection no. 579, Newberry. I have made a few minor changes in punctuation and one in spelling.

18. Cited in Connell, *Son of the Morning Star*, except for redskined Deavels, which is in "The Letters of John Ferguson, Early Resident of Western Washington County," *Kansas Historical Quarterly* 12 (1943): 345.

19. Frantz, "The Frontier Tradition: An Invitation to Violence," in *The History of Violence in America*, ed. Hugh Davis Graham and Ted Robert Gurr (New York: Bantam, 1969), 147; Connell, *Son of the Morning Star*, 258–259.

20. Axtell, *The European and the Indian*, chs. 2, 8; Dodge, *Our Wild Indians: Thirty-three Years' Personal Experience among the Red Men of the Great West* (Hartford, 1883), 517; E. C. "Teddy Blue" Abbott, *We Pointed Them North: Recollections of a Cowpuncher* (New York: Farrar and Rinehart, 1939), 204.

21. Letter of 17 March 1865 to Amelia Capron, Newberry.

22. John Mack Faragher, *Daniel Boone: The Life and Legend of an American Pioneer* (New York: Henry Holt, 1992), 22. By war: Agnes Wright Spring, *Caspar Collins: The Life and Exploits of an Indian Fighter in the Sixties* (rpt. Lincoln: U. of Nebraska Press, 1969), 167. No sense: Homer W. Wheeler, *Buffalo Days* (rpt. Lincoln: U. of Nebraska Press, 1990) 143. Suicide boys: Bill O'Neal, *Fighting Men of the Indian Wars* (Stillwater, Ok.: Barbed Wire Press, 1991), 108.

23. Laurel Thatcher Ulrich, *Good Wives: Image and Reality in the Lives of Women in Northern New England, 1650–1750* (New York: Oxford U. Press, 1983), 167–168.

24. Sandra L. Myres, *Westering Women and the Frontier Experience* (Albuquerque: U. of New Mexico Press, 1982), 64; Glenda Riley, *Frontierswomen: The Iowa Experience* (Ames: Iowa State U. Press, 1981), 179–180. Savage Other: e.g., Anne Ellis, *The Life of an Ordinary Woman* (rpt. New York: Arno Press, 1974), 11–12. Friendships: Glenda Riley, *Women and Indians on the Frontier, 1825–1915* (Albuquerque: U. of New Mexico Press, 1984), esp. ch. 5.

25. "Recollections of Benjamin Franklin Bonney," ed. Fred Lockley, *Oregon Historical Society Quarterly* 24 (1923): 50–51.

26. *In a Different Voice: Psychological Theory and Women's Development* (Cambridge, Mass.: Harvard U. Press, 1982).

27. Richard White, *"It's Your Misfortune and None of My Own": A History of the American West* (Norman: U. of Oklahoma Press, 1991), 340.

28. Sherman Day, *Historical Collections of the State of Pennsylvania* . . . (Philadelphia, 1843), 274, 277–281, 398–400; Solon J. Buck and Elizabeth Hawthorn Buck, *The Planting of Civilization in Western Pennsylvania* (Pittsburgh: U. of Pittsburgh Press, 1939), 111–113.

29. *The Writings of George Washington from the Original Manuscript Sources, 1745–1799*, vol. 34, ed. John C. Fitzpatrick (Washington: G.P.O.,

1940), 391; John C. Miller, *The Federalist Era, 1789–1801* (New York: Harper and Row, 1960), 183.

30. Francis Paul Prucha, *American Indian Policy in the Formative Years: The Indian Trade and Intercourse Acts, 1790–1834* (Lincoln: U. of Nebraska Press, 1962), 49–50, 190–203, 275–277; Robert F. Berkhofer Jr., *The White Man's Indian: Images of the American Indian from Columbus to the Present* (New York: Knopf, 1978), 147–148.

31. See Gregory H. Nobles, "Breaking into the Backcountry: New Approaches to the Early American Frontier, 1750–1800," *WMQ* 46 (1989): 659–664, 668–669.

32. Edmund S. Morgan, *American Slavery, American Freedom* (New York: Norton, 1975), bks. 3–4.

33. Alexander Hamilton, "Report . . . relative to the inexecution of the Excise Law in certain Counties of Pennsylvania," in *Proceedings of the Executive of the United States, Respecting the Insurgents, 1794* (Philadelphia, 1795), 99–124; Bartlett, *New Country,* 139.

34. Edmund S. Morgan, *The Challenge of the American Revolution* (New York: Norton, 1976), 192–193.

35. "Letters of John Ferguson," 339, 342–345; Rodman W. Paul, *The Far West and the Great Plains in Transition* (New York: Harper and Row, 1988), 154.

36. Faragher, *Daniel Boone,* 20.

37. William Cronon, *Changes in the Land: Indians, Colonists, and the Ecology of New England* (New York: Hill and Wang, 1983), 99–100, 168–169; Peter C. Mancall, "Drinking and Sobriety in Indian Villages in Colonial America" (paper presented at the annual meeting of the Organization of American Historians, Chicago, April 1992), 4, 12–14; Winfred Blevins assisted by Ruth Valsing, *Dictionary of the American West* (New York: Facts on File, 1993), 133.

38. Catlin, *Letters and Notes,* 253–254.

39. Clyde N. Dollar, "The High Plains Smallpox Epidemic of 1837–38," *Western Historical Quarterly* 8 (1977): 27.

40. Flores, "Bison Ecology," 483, 485; Roosevelt, *Hunting Trips of a Ranchman: Sketches of Sport on the Northern Cattle Plains* (New York, 1886), 260.

41. Sheridan quoted in John R. Cook, *The Border and the Buffalo: An Untold Story of the Southwest Plains* (rpt. New York: Citadel Press, 1967), 163–164; Paul, *Far West and Great Plains,* 196–197, 209, 212, 223.

42. Dick, *Sod-House Frontier,* 155, 157; Flores, "Bison Ecology," 481–482.

43. Crawford, *Kansas in the Sixties,* 9, 13–14.

44. Richard Erdoes, *Saloons of the Old West* (New York: Knopf, 1979), 50; *The White House: An Historic Guide,* 17th ed. (Washington: National Geographic Society, 1991), 58, 142.

45. Percy G. Ebbutt, "Emigrant Life in Kansas," in *The Heritage of Kansas*, ed. Everett Rich (Lawrence: U. Press of Kansas, 1960), 113; John S. Collins, *Across the Plains in '64* (Omaha, 1904), 120; Don Russell, *The Lives and Legends of Buffalo Bill* (Norman: U. of Oklahoma Press, 1960), 295–296; A. W. Schorger, *The Passenger Pigeon: Its Natural History and Extinction* (Norman: U. of Oklahoma Press, 1973).

46. Connell, *Son of the Morning Star*, 159; Springer, *Soldiering in Sioux Country*, 67–70.

47. *The Memoirs of Henry Heth*, ed. James L. Morrison Jr. (Westport, Conn.: Greenwood Press, 1974), 84.

48. O'Neal, *Fighting Men*, 97; Collins, *Across the Plains in '64*, 117–118.

49. *Dictionary of the American West*, 147.

50. Craig MacAndrew and Robert B. Edgerton, *Drunken Comportment: A Social Explanation* (Chicago: Aldine, 1969), 88, 130–134, 140–147.

51. Cook, *Conflict*, 268–273, 336–339; Albert L. Hurtado, *Indian Survival on the California Frontier* (New Haven: Yale U. Press, 1988), ch. 9.

52. Cook, *Conflict*, 85–90.

53. Harry Laurenz Wells, *History of Nevada County, California* (Oakland, 1880), 105–106.

54. Ronald C. Woolsey, "Crime and Punishment: Los Angeles County, 1850–56," *Southern California Quarterly* 61 (1979): 82–84, 91–92; Hurtado, *Indian Survival*, 160–161.

55. Turner, *Frontier in American History*, 4; Robert Bachman, *Death and Violence on the Reservation: Homicide, Family Violence, and Suicide in American Indian Populations* (New York: Auburn House, 1992), 7, 23–24; Thomas Young, "Alcohol Use and Misuse among Native Americans," *Social Pharmacology* 3 (1989): 272–275. I do not mean to suggest that all contemporary Indian problems are echoes of frontier contact. The high rates of homicide, suicide, and alcoholism are affected by poverty and unemployment as well as social disorganization, local customs, and other factors that vary between and even within tribes. Stephen J. Kunitz, *Disease and Social Diversity: The European Impact on the Health of Non-Europeans* (New York: Oxford U. Press, 1994), 137–140, 163–168.

56. William H. McNeill, *The Great Frontier: Freedom and Hierarchy in Modern Times* (Princeton: Princeton U. Press, 1983), 16; Kunitz, *Disease and Social Diversity*, 178.

7. Women and Families

1. Sally McMillen, "Pregnancy and Childbirth on the Southern Frontier" (paper presented at the annual meeting of the Organization of American Historians, Washington, March 1990), 5.

2. Richard Dodge MS diary, 21 July 1875, Richard Irving Dodge Papers, Newberry.

3. Quoted in John Mack Faragher, *Women and Men on the Overland Trail* (New Haven: Yale U. Press, 1979), 184.

4. Typed transcription of a letter from Mary B. Ballou to Selden Ballou, 30 Oct. 1852, WAC, Beinecke, 8; *The Journal of Mollie Dorsey Sanford in Nebraska and Colorado Territories, 1857–1866,* ed. Donald F. Danker (Lincoln: U. of Nebraska Press, 1959), 135; Joseph R. Conlin, *Bacon, Beans, and Galantines: Food and Foodways on the Western Mining Frontier* (Reno: U. of Nevada Press, 1986), 156.

5. E. S. Topping, *The Chronicles of the Yellowstone,* ed. Robert A. Murray (rpt. Minneapolis: Ross and Haines, 1968), 28; E. C. "Teddy Blue" Abbott, *We Pointed Them North: Recollections of a Cowpuncher* (New York: Farrar and Rinehart, 1939), 222; John McPhee, *Rising from the Plains* (New York: Farrar, Straus, Giroux, 1986), 86.

6. *The Records of the Virginia Company of London,* vol. 3, ed. Susan Myra Kingsbury (Washington: G.P.O., 1933), 493–494; Mildred Campbell, "Social Origins of Some Early Americans," in *Seventeenth-Century America,* ed. James Morton Smith (Chapel Hill: U. of North Carolina Press, 1959), 74; Herbert Moller, "Sex Composition and Correlated Culture Patterns of Colonial America," *WMQ* 2 (1945): 140–141; David Galenson, *White Servitude in Colonial America: An Economic Analysis* (Cambridge: Cambridge U. Press, 1984), 24–25, 234n4.

7. *Etta's Journal, Jan. 2, 1874–July 25, 1875,* ed. Ellen Payne Paullin (Canton, Conn.: Lithographics, 1981), 32. Gender ratio from 1870 census data for Riley County, Kansas.

8. Eugene Albertson helped me extract this data from manuscript census returns for Fort Larned (1870) and Forts Sisseton and Russell (1880).

9. Oliver Knight, *Life and Manners in the Frontier Army* (Norman: U. of Oklahoma Press, 1978); Larry A. Toll, "The Military Community on the Western Frontier, 1866–1898" (Ph.D. diss., Ball State U., 1990), chs. 2–4; *The News from Brownsville: Helen Chapman's Letters from the Texas Military Frontier, 1848–1852,* ed. Caleb Coker (Austin: Texas State Historical Association, 1992), 27; Holman Hamilton, *Zachary Taylor* (Indianapolis: Bobbs-Merrill, 1951), 25–26, 136.

10. *The Colonel's Lady on the Western Frontier: The Correspondence of Alice Kirk Grierson,* ed. Shirley A. Leckie (Lincoln: U. of Nebraska Press, 1989), 75–76, 80, 96–97; Knight, *Life and Manners in the Frontier Army,* 40, 67–68, 222; Edward M. Coffman, *The Old Army: A Portrait of the American Army in Peacetime, 1784–1898* (New York: Oxford U. Press, 1986), 105, 311–314; Jerry L. Nixon, "Women on the Kansas Military Frontier" (Ph.D. diss., U. of Notre Dame, 1989), ch. 6.

11. *Crockett at Two Hundred: New Perspectives on the Man and the Myth,* ed. Michael A. Lofaro and Joe Cummings (Knoxville: U. of Tennessee Press, 1989), xxi; David Crockett, *A Narrative of The Life of David Crockett of the State of Tennessee,* ed. James A. Shackford and Stanley J. Folmsbee (Knoxville: U. of Tennessee Press, 1973 facsimile ed.), 52–55; Blaine T. Williams, "The Frontier Family," in *Essays on the American West,* ed. Harold M. Hollingsworth and Sandra L. Myres (Austin: U. of Texas Press, 1969), 53.

12. Edmund S. Morgan, *American Slavery, American Freedom* (New York: Norton, 1975), 165–170.

13. Alexander Keyssar, "Widowhood in Eighteenth-Century Massachusetts," *Perspectives in American History* 8 (1974): 89–116; John Carr, *Early Times in Middle Tennessee* (Nashville, 1857), 231.

14. *T*-tests show all relationships to be significant at $p \leq .01$. Data from Robert V. Wells, *The Population of the British Colonies in America before 1776: A Survey of Census Data* (Princeton: Princeton U. Press, 1975), 74–76, 93–95.

15. Scott J. South and Katherine Trent, "Sex Ratios and Women's Roles: A Cross-National Analysis," *AJS* 93 (1988): 1096–1115.

16. Virginia Bernhard, "'Men, Women, and Children' at Jamestown: Population and Gender in Early Virginia, 1607–1610," *JSH* 58 (1992): 603, 616; Lois G. Carr and Lorena S. Walsh, "The Planter's Wife: The Experience of White Women in Seventeenth-Century Maryland," in *Colonial America,* 3rd ed., ed. Stanley N. Katz and John M. Murrin (New York: Knopf, 1983), 115; Evan S. Connell, *Son of the Morning Star* (San Francisco: North Star Press, 1984), 191; Keith Burgess-Jackson, "Violence on the Michigan Frontier," *Detroit in Perspective* 7 (1983): 56; Martineau, *Society in America,* vol. 3 (London, 1837), 120; Percy G. Ebbutt, "Emigrant Life in Kansas," in *The Heritage of Kansas: Selected Commentaries on Past Times,* ed. Everett Rich (Lawrence: U. Press of Kansas, 1960), 115.

17. Carr and Walsh, "Planter's Wife," 115; Williams, "Frontier Family," 57.

18. Comment appended to abstract of 1731 census, *The Documentary History of the State of New-York,* vol. 1, ed. E. B. O'Callaghan (Albany, 1850), 471. I do not mean to imply that fertility was simply a function of the age of women at marriage. Religious and ethnocultural factors also played a role, e.g., the hostility of the Puritan immigrants to contraception. Nevertheless, there is broad agreement among historical demographers that, other things being equal, early female marriages tended to increase fertility and later marriages to decrease it. See, e.g., Jim Potter, "Demographic Development and Family Struc-

ture," in *Colonial British America: Essays in the New History of the Early Modern Era,* ed. Jack P. Greene and J. R. Pole (Baltimore: Johns Hopkins U. Press, 1984), 149.

19. Margaret Van Horn Dwight, *A Journey to Ohio in 1810,* ed. Max Farrand (New Haven: Yale U. Press, 1920 printing), v–vi.

20. Steven Patterson, "Settling the Frontier in Washington County, Kansas" (research paper, University of North Florida, 1992).

21. Galenson, *White Servitude,* 30; Allan Kulikoff, *Tobacco and Slaves: The Development of Southern Cultures in the Chesapeake, 1680–1800* (Chapel Hill: U. of North Carolina Press, 1986), 5, 13, 33–34, 42; Darrett B. Rutman and Anita H. Rutman, "Of Agues and Fevers: Malaria in the Early Chesapeake," *WMQ* 33 (1976): 52–53, 55.

22. *A Woman's Reminiscences of Six Years in Camp with Texas Rangers* (Austin: Von Boeckmann-Jones, 1928), 47–48.

23. "Bypaths of Kansas History," *Kansas Historical Quarterly* 9 (1940): 99–101.

24. Sarah Peairs her Pamphlet James Peairs her Brother and Ann Peairs her Sister (MS, n.d.), 8–13, Ayer collection no. 691, Newberry.

25. [Louise Clappe,] *The Shirley Letters from the California Mines, 1851–1852,* ed. Carl I. Wheat (New York: Knopf, 1970), 23–24, 96–97; Mary B. Ballou to Selden Ballou, 30 Oct. 1852, WAC, Beinecke, 9–12; Robert V. Hine, *Josiah Royce: From Grass Valley to Harvard* (Norman: U. of Oklahoma Press, 1992), 29–31.

26. David C. Humphrey, "Prostitution and Public Policy in Austin, Texas, 1870–1915," *SHQ* 96 (1983): 477, 480; Neil Larry Shumsky, "Tacit Acceptance: Respectable Americans and Segregated Prostitution, 1870–1910," *J. of Social History* 19 (1986): 670.

27. Alice Cowan Cochran, *Miners, Merchants, and Missionaries: The Roles of Missionaries and Pioneer Churches in the Colorado Gold Rush and Its Aftermath, 1858–1870* (Methuen, N.J.: Scarecrow Press, 1980), 102–131, 188–189; C. Robert Haywood, *Victorian West: Class and Culture in Kansas Cattle Towns* (Lawrence: U. Press of Kansas, 1991), 109–110. Newton church: *Workin' on the Railroad: Reminiscences from the Age of Steam,* ed. Richard Reinhardt (Palo Alto: American West Publishing, 1970), 90.

28. James Joseph Poth, "A History of Crime and Violence in Washington Territory, 1851–1860" (Master's thesis, U. of Washington, 1969), 5.

29. Mary Floyd Williams, *History of the San Francisco Committee of Vigilance of 1851* (rpt. New York: Da Capo Press, 1969), 197; Roger W. Lotchin, *San Francisco, 1846–1856: From Hamlet to City* (New York: Oxford U. Press, 1974), ch. 13; James Andrew Baumohl, "Dashaways and Doctors: The Treatment of Habitual Drunkards in San Francisco from the

Gold Rush to Prohibition" (Ph.D. diss., U. of California, Berkeley, 1986), 36–42.

30. Peggy Pascoe, *Relations of Rescue: The Search for Female Moral Authority in the American West, 1874–1939* (New York: Oxford U. Press, 1990), ch. 1; Barbara Leslie Epstein, *The Politics of Domesticity: Women, Evangelism, and Temperance in Nineteenth-Century America* (Middletown: Wesleyan U. Press, 1981), ch. 5; Ruth Bordin, *Woman and Temperance: The Quest for Power and Liberty, 1873–1900* (Philadelphia: Temple U. Press, 1981), ch. 9; Jack S. Blocker Jr., *American Temperance Movements: Cycles of Reform* (Boston: Twayne, 1989), 83–85.

31. Robert R. Dykstra, *The Cattle Towns* (New York: Knopf, 1968), 260.

32. Stuart Henry, *Conquering Our Great American Plains* (New York: E. P. Dutton, 1930), 85.

33. Joseph G. McCoy, *Historic Sketches of the Cattle Trade of the West and Southwest* (Kansas City, 1874), 231; Dykstra, *Cattle Towns*, 257–263, 294–307, quotation 304.

34. Johanna Nel, "A Territory Is Founded: Political, Social, Economic and Educational Conditions in Wyoming, 1850–1890," *Annals of Wyoming* 61, no. 2 (1989): 8; Carol Leonard and Isidor Wallimann, "Prostitution and Changing Morality in the Frontier Cattle Towns of Kansas," *Kansas History* 2 (Spring 1979): 45–46; Richard Erdoes, *Saloons of the Old West* (New York: Knopf, 1979), 246; W. C. Holder, "Law and Lawlessness on the Texas Frontier, 1875–1890," *SHQ* 44 (1940): 201.

35. Shumsky, "Tacit Acceptance," 665–679; Humphrey, "Prostitution and Public Policy," 505–515; Richard White, *"It's Your Misfortune and None of My Own": A History of the American West* (Norman: U. of Oklahoma Press, 1991), 355–362.

36. "The Letters of John Ferguson, Early Resident of Western Washington County," *Kansas Historical Quarterly* 12 (1943): 346.

37. Chapman, *News from Brownsville*, 97, 111–112, 202–203.

38. Elliott West, *Growing Up with the Country: Childhood on the Far Western Frontier* (Albuquerque: U. of New Mexico Press, 1989), 186; Roger Lane, *Violent Death in the City: Suicide, Accident, and Murder in Nineteenth-Century Philadelphia* (Cambridge, Mass.: Harvard U. Press, 1979), 122–123; Richard A. Bartlett, *The New Country: A Social History of the American Frontier, 1776–1890* (New York: Oxford U. Press, 1974), 390–391; Haywood, *Victorian West*, 122.

39. Elliott West, *The Saloon on the Rocky Mountain Mining Frontier* (Lincoln: U. of Nebraska Press, 1979), 134; Blocker, *American Temperance Movements*, 68–69; Jim Baumohl, "On Asylums, Homes, and Moral Treatment: The Case of the San Francisco Home for the Care of the Inebriate, 1859–1870," *Contemporary Drug Problems* 13 (1986): 406–

407; Julie Roy Jeffrey, *Frontier Women: The Trans-Mississippi West, 1840–1880* (New York: Hill and Wang, 1979), 139; Haywood, *Victorian West,* 184–187.

40. Frank R. Rossiter, *Charles Ives and His America* (New York: Liveright, 1975), 26–53, 320–323; Leon Edel, *Henry James, the Master: 1901–1916* (Philadelphia: J. B. Lippincott, 1972), 279.

41. Sherman L. Ricards and George R. Blackburn, "The Sydney Ducks: A Demographic Analysis," *PacHR* 42 (1973): 20–23, 31; *Sydney in Ferment: Crime, Dissent, and Official Reaction, 1788 to 1973* (Canberra: Australian National U. Press, 1977), 4–43, 165–176.

8. Chinatown

1. Stanford M. Lyman, *Chinese Americans* (New York: Random House, 1974), 88–90; U.S. Senate, *Report of the Joint Special Committee to Investigate Chinese Immigration* [hereafter *JSC*], Senate Report no. 689, 44th Cong., 2nd sess. (1877), 489; Gunther Barth, *Bitter Strength: A History of the Chinese in the United States, 1850–1870* (Cambridge, Mass.: Harvard U. Press, 1964), ch. 1; Victor G. and Brett de Bary Nee, *Longtime Californ': A Documentary Study of an American Chinatown* (New York: Pantheon, 1973), 17–18, 411; Stan Steiner, *Fusang: The Chinese Who Built America* (New York: Harper and Row, 1979), 68.

2. June Mei, "Socioeconomic Origins of Emigration: Guangdong to California, 1850 to 1882," in *Labor Immigration under Capitalism: Asian Workers in the United States before World War II,* ed. Lucie Cheng and Edna Bonacich (Berkeley: U. of California Press, 1984), 240; Jack Chen, *The Chinese of America* (San Francisco: Harper and Row, 1980), 62.

3. California Senate, Special Committee on Chinese Immigration, *Chinese Immigration: Its Social, Moral, and Political Effect* (Sacramento, 1878), 221; Shih-Shan Henry Tsai, *The Chinese Experience in America* (Bloomington: Indiana U. Press, 1986), 1–10; Alexander Saxton, *The Indispensable Enemy: Labor and the Anti-Chinese Movement in California* (Berkeley: U. of California Press, 1971), 8; Barth, *Bitter Strength,* 99–100.

4. Mary R. Coolidge, *Chinese Immigration* (New York: Henry Holt, 1909), 21–25, 498; Nee and Nee, *Longtime Californ',* 33, 36; Daniel Cleveland to J. Ross Browne, 27 July 1868, doc. 1, *American Diplomatic and Public Papers: The United States and China.* Series II: *The United States, China, and Imperial Rivalries, 1861–1893* [hereafter *ADPP: China*], vol. 13, ed. Jules Davids (Wilmington, Del.: Scholarly Resources, 1979).

5. "Reminiscences of Joseph H. Boyd: An Argonaut of 1857," ed. William S. Lewis, *Washington Historical Quarterly* 15 (1924): 259.

6. William Speer, *An Humble Plea, Addressed to the Legislature of California in Behalf of the Immigrants of the Empire of China to This State* (San Francisco, 1856), 35; *ADPP: China,* doc. 1: 3, 10–11.

7. *ADPP: China,* doc. 1: 3–4, 10–11; Stephen Williams, "The Chinese in the California Mines" (M.A. thesis, Stanford U., 1930), 66–67; Chen, *Chinese of America,* 45–46.

8. Clipping from the *San Francisco Morning Call,* month and day not noted, Loren L. Williams MS Journals, 1851–1880, vol. 1., Graff collection, Newberry.

9. Coolidge, *Chinese Immigration,* 498; Tsai, *Chinese Experience,* 16–17; Crocker to Cornelius Cole, 12 April 1865, in Catherine Coffin Phillips, *Cornelius Cole: California Pioneer and United States Senator* (San Francisco: John Henry Nash, 1929), 138. There is every indication that their work was superior to, not "nearly equal to," that of the white workers. Nee and Nee, *Longtime Californ',* 40; George Kraus, *High Road to Promontory* (Palo Alto: American West Publishing, 1969), 111.

10. *JSC,* 27–28.

11. Christian G. Fritz, "Due Process, Treaty Rights, and Chinese Exclusion, 1882–1891," in *Entry Denied: Exclusion and the Chinese Community in America, 1882–1943,* ed. Sucheng Chan (Philadelphia: Temple U. Press, 1991), 25.

12. Sucheng Chan, "The Exclusion of Chinese Women, 1870–1943," in *Entry Denied,* 94–146.

13. Lucie Cheng, "Free, Indentured, Enslaved: Chinese Prostitutes in Nineteenth-Century America," in *Labor Immigration under Capitalism,* ed. Cheng and Bonacich, 417; Joann Levy, *They Saw the Elephant: Women in the California Gold Rush* (Hamden, Conn.: Archon Books, 1990), 153–154. Percentage of prostitutes: Judy Yung, *Chinese Women of America: A Pictorial History* (Seattle: U. of Washington Press, 1986), 18; Tsai, *Chinese Experience,* 41.

14. Chan, "Exclusion of Chinese Women," 105–107; Mei, "Socioeconomic Origins," 225.

15. "Rock Springs Massacre, 1885," in *American Violence: A Documentary History,* ed. Richard Hofstadter and Michael Wallace (New York: Knopf, 1970), 331; *ADPP: China,* vol 12, docs. 30–54: 173–239; Paul Crane and Alfred Larson, "The Chinese Massacre," *Annals of Wyoming* 12 (1940): 47–55, 153–161.

16. Steiner, *Fusang,* 173–174, quotation at 174; Hubert Howe Bancroft, *California Inter Pocula* (San Francisco, 1888), 563–568; Nee and Nee, *Longtime Californ',* 55.

17. Betty Lee Sung, *Mountain of Gold: The Story of the Chinese in America* (New York: Macmillan, 1967), 253–259, 320; "New York Notes" (TS,

n.d.), 2–3, Box 43, Records of the United States Delegation to the International Opium Commission and Conference, 1908–1913, National Archives; Lyman, *Chinese Americans,* 94.

18. Ching Chao Wu, "Chinese Immigration in the Pacific Area" (rpt. San Francisco: R & E Research Associates, 1974), 16–17.

19. I. E. Cohn, "The Chinese and Their Peculiar Medical Ideas," *Medical Record* 42 (1892): 477–478; Lyman, *Chinese Americans,* 89, 152–153; Sung, *Mountain of Gold,* 85–89; U.S. Bureau of the Census, *1990 Census of Population: Asians and Pacific Islanders in the United States* (1993), 6.

20. Nee and Nee, *Longtime Californ',* 69–70; Tsai, *Chinese Experience,* 38.

21. Nee and Nee, *Longtime Californ',* 24.

22. Tsai, *Chinese Experience,* 10, 38–39; Mei, "Socioeconomic Origins," 238; Lyman, *Chinese Americans,* 96–97; Ramon D. Chacon, "The Beginning of Racial Segregation: The Chinese in West Fresno and Chinatown's Role as Red Light District, 1870s–1920s," *Southern California Quarterly* 70 (1988): 382–384.

23. Cheng, "Chinese Prostitutes," 411.

24. Marlon K. Hom, *Songs of Gold Mountain: Cantonese Rhymes from San Francisco Chinatown* (Berkeley: U. of California Press, 1987), 294.

25. David Courtwright, *Dark Paradise: Opiate Addiction in America before 1940* (Cambridge, Mass.: Harvard U. Press, 1982), 9–34, 65–70; Tsai, *Chinese Experience,* 39–40.

26. David Courtwright, Herman Joseph, and Don Des Jarlais, *Addicts Who Survived: An Oral History of Narcotic Use in America, 1923–1965* (Knoxville: U. of Tennessee Press, 1989), 83.

27. Ira M. Condit, *The Chinaman as We See Him and Fifty Years of Work for Him* (Chicago, 1900), 60; Hawaii, Legislature, Special Commission on Opium, *Report* (Honolulu, 1892), 6–11; Hom, *Songs of Gold Mountain,* 302; Lawrence M. Friedman and Robert V. Percival, *The Roots of Justice: Crime and Punishment in Alameda County, California, 1870–1910* (Chapel Hill: U. of North Carolina Press, 1981), 300, 303.

28. Friedman and Percival, *Roots of Justice,* 89–91, 106–107; Lyle A. Dale, "Rough Justice: Criminal Justice in San Luis Obispo County, California, 1880–1910" (Master's thesis, California State U., Fullerton, 1990), 49–52; Charles A. Tracy, "Race, Crime and Social Policy: The Chinese in Oregon, 1871–1885," *Crime and Social Justice* 11 (Winter 1980): 21.

29. "Negro education not a source of crime" (TS, probably 1904), 3, container 38, Willcox Papers, LC; Lyman, *Chinese Americans,* ch. 5. Newspaper headlines: *Rocky Mountain News,* 17 Oct. 1875, 4; *New York Tribune,* 19 June 1881, 7; Yung, *Chinese Women,* 19.

30. Peggy Pascoe, *Relations of Rescue: The Search for Female Moral Authority*

in the American West, 1874–1939 (New York: Oxford U. Press, 1990), 16; Frederick J. Masters, "Opium and Its Votaries," *California Illustrated Magazine* 1 (1892): 641; Dale, "Rough Justice," 50; Riis, *How the Other Half Lives: Studies among the Tenements of New York* (rpt. New York: Hill and Wang, 1957), 76.

31. Kiichi Kanzaki, *California and the Japanese* (rpt. San Francisco: R & E Research Associates, 1971), 8–9; U.S. Bureau of the Census, *Chinese and Japanese in the United States, 1910* (1914), 26.

32. Yuji Ichioka, "*Amerika Nadeshiko:* Japanese Immigrant Women in the United States, 1900–1924," *PacHR* 49 (1980): 339–357; idem, *The Issei: The World of the First Generation Japanese Immigrants, 1885–1924* (New York: Free Press, 1988), 51–56, 71–72, 244; Azusa Tsuneyoshi, "Meiji Pioneers: The Early Japanese Immigrants to the American Far West and Southwest, 1880–1930" (Ph.D. diss., Northern Arizona U., 1989), 30.

33. Paul S. Taylor, "Crime and the Foreign Born: San Francisco," in National Commission on Law Observance and Enforcement, *Report on Crime and the Foreign Born* (1931), 352–354, 385–389.

34. Condit, *Chinaman as We See Him,* 60; H. H. Kane, *Opium Smoking in America and China* (New York, 1882), 13. Used strictly the word "tong" refers to any Chinese secret society, including those that served legal and benevolent purposes. By the late 1880s, however, the term had acquired strong criminal connotations and, for simplicity's sake, I use it in this sense.

35. Richard H. Dillon, *The Hatchet Men: The Story of the Tong Wars in San Francisco's Chinatown* (New York: Coward-McCann, 1962), ch. 3; Roger D. McGrath, *Gunfighters, Highwaymen, and Vigilantes: Violence on the Frontier* (Berkeley: U. of California Press, 1984), 133; Cheng, "Chinese Prostitutes," 416–418; Barth, *Bitter Strength,* 103.

36. Nee and Nee, *Longtime Californ',* 92, 82.

37. Tsai, "Chinese Experience," 53–54; Ivan H. Light, *Ethnic Enterprise in America: Business and Welfare Among Chinese, Japanese, and Blacks* (Berkeley: U. of California Press, 1972), 96–97 and fig. 13.

38. June Mei, "Socioeconomic Developments among the Chinese in San Francisco, 1848–1906," in *Labor Immigration under Capitalism,* ed. Cheng and Bonacich, 383; Chen, *Chinese in America,* 184–185.

39. C. N. Reynolds, "The Chinese Tongs," *AJS* 40 (1935): 622; Lyman, *Chinese Americans,* 105; Nee and Nee, *Longtime Californ',* 80–81.

40. Julia Cherry Spruill, *Women's Life and Work in the Southern Colonies* (Chapel Hill: U. of North Carolina Press, 1938), 15–19.

41. Perceval, letter of 4 May 1769 to James Grant, quoted in Daniel L. Schafer, "'Yellow Silk Ferret Tied round Their Wrists': African Americans in British East Florida, 1763–1784," in *The Black Heritage of*

Florida, ed. David R. Colburn and Jane L. Landers (Gainesville: U. Press of Florida, 1995), 90; Herbert G. Gutman, *The Black Family in Slavery and Freedom, 1750–1925* (New York: Vintage, 1977), 79; *Advice among Masters: The Ideal in Slave Management in the Old South,* ed. James O. Breeden (Westport, Conn.: Greenwood Press, 1980), 239–245.

9. The Floating Army

1. E.g., Patricia Limerick, *The Legacy of Conquest: The Unbroken Past of the American West* (New York: Norton, 1987), 17–32.
2. Warren S. Thompson and P. K. Whelpton, *Population Trends in the United States* (rpt. New York: Gordon and Breach, 1969), 173.
3. Bruce Catton, *The Civil War* (New York: American Heritage Press, 1971), 1–2, 149–152; James M. McPherson, *Battle Cry of Freedom: The Civil War Era* (New York: Oxford U. Press, 1988), 608.
4. U.S. Bureau of the Census, *Historical Statistics of the United States: Colonial Times to 1970,* pt. 2 (1975), 728, 731; Sam H. Schurr and Bruce C. Netschert, *Energy in the American Economy, 1850–1975* (Baltimore: Johns Hopkins U. Press, 1960), 511–512.
5. Eric H. Monkkonen, "Introduction," in *Walking to Work: Tramps in America, 1790–1935,* ed. Monkkonen (Lincoln: U. of Nebraska Press, 1984), 8, 16n8; John C. Schneider, "Tramping Workers, 1890–1920: A Subcultural View," ibid., 213–215; Eric H. Monkkonen, *The Dangerous Class: Crime and Poverty in Columbus, Ohio, 1860–1885* (Cambridge, Mass.: Harvard U. Press, 1975), 160. Many migrant workers preferred to describe themselves as hobos, "tramps" referring more specifically and derogatorily to wandering men who shunned work and supported themselves by begging or stealing. But this distinction was ignored or blurred by those outside (and sometimes inside) the subculture, who often used "tramps" as a general descriptive term.
6. "Chicago: Hobo Capital of America," *Survey* 50 (1923): 287–290, 303–305; Schneider, "Tramping Workers," 223–225; Roger Bruns, *Knights of the Road: A Hobo History* (New York: Methuen, 1980), ch. 7.
7. Eric H. Monkkonen, "Regional Dimensions of Tramping, North and South, 1880–1910," in *Walking to Work,* 189–211; Josiah Flynt [Willard], *Tramping with Tramps: Studies and Sketches of Vagabond Life* (rpt. College Park, Md.: McGrath, 1969), 110 (quotation); Jeffrey A. Drobney, "Where Palm and Pine Are Blowing: Convict Labor in the North Florida Turpentine Industry," *Florida Historical Quarterly* 72 (1994): 420–421, 428–429 (death rates).
8. Edward L. Ayers, *The Promise of the New South: Life after Reconstruction* (New York: Oxford U. Press, 1992), 151–159.

9. John C. Schneider, "Omaha Vagrants and the Character of Western Hobo Labor, 1887–1913," *Nebraska History* 63 (1982): 262–264; idem, "Tramping Workers," 213–217; Priscilla Ferguson Clement, "The Transformation of the Wandering Poor in Nineteenth-Century Philadelphia," in *Walking to Work*, 64–65, 73; Alexander Keyssar, *Out of Work: The First Century of Unemployment in Massachusetts* (Cambridge: Cambridge U. Press, 1986), 130–142.

10. Schneider, "Tramping Workers," 212–213, 226–229; Bruns, *Knights of the Road*, 9.

11. *Arrowsmith* (New York: P. F. Collier and Son, 1925), 97.

12. [John James McCook,] "Tramp," *New International Encyclopedia*, 2nd ed., vol. 22 (New York: Dodd, Mead, 1922), 413; Nels Anderson, *The Hobo: The Sociology of the Homeless Man* (rpt. Chicago: U. of Chicago Press, 1961), 66; Bruns, *Knights of the Road*, 26–60, 91; Gregory R. Woirol, *In the Floating Army: F. C. Mills on Itinerant Life in California, 1914* (Urbana: U. of Illinois Press, 1992), 101.

13. *"The Shanty Boy," or Life in a Lumber Camp* (rpt. Berrien Springs, Mich.: Hardscrabble Books, 1979), 102–103; Harold M. Hyman, *Soldiers and Spruce: Origins of the Loyal Legion of Loggers and Lumbermen* (Los Angeles: Institute of Industrial Relations, 1963), 109.

14. Frank A. Crampton, *Deep Enough: A Working Stiff in the Western Mine Camps* (Denver: Sage Books, 1956), 101–117; Rodman W. Paul, *The Far West and the Great Plains in Transition* (New York: Harper and Row, 1988), 278–281.

15. Martin Cherniack, *The Hawk's Nest Incident: America's Worst Industrial Disaster* (New Haven: Yale U. Press, 1986).

16. Yuji Ichioka, *The Issei: The World of the First Generation Japanese Immigrants, 1885–1924* (New York: Free Press, 1988), 84–85, reports 3,410 adult deaths for 1906–1913. According to U.S. Bureau of the Census, *Chinese and Japanese in the United States, 1910* (1914), 26, there were 37,822 adult Japanese in California in 1910. The estimated annual adult death rate is thus 3,410 divided by 37,822 divided by 8 times 1,000 equals 11.3. National mortality figures: *Historical Statistics of the United States*, pt. 1, 61.

17. Ichioka, *Issei*, 84–85; I. E. Cohn, "The Chinese and Their Peculiar Medical Ideas," *Medical Record* 42 (1892): 477–478; Bruns, *Knights of the Road*, 165; Crampton, *Deep Enough*, 220–222; Richard A. Bartlett, *The New Country: A Social History of the American Frontier, 1776–1890* (New York: Oxford U. Press, 1974), 348; Robert H. Coombs, "Marital Status and Personal Well-Being: A Literature Review," *Family Relations* 40 (Jan. 1991): 97–98.

18. Bruns, *Knights of the Road*, 46–47.

19. "Chicago: Hobo Capital," 303; Bruns, *Knights of the Road*, 49, 84–85; Kenneth Allsop, *Hard Travellin': The Hobo and His History* (rpt. New York: New American Library, 1970), 141.

20. [Willard], *Tramping with Tramps*, 291–314; Bruns, *Knights of the Road*, 42–45; Monkkonen, "Introduction," *Walking to Work*, 9–10.

21. Jacob Riis, *How the Other Half Lives* (rpt. New York: Hill and Wang, 1957), 59; Monkkonen, *Police in Urban America, 1860–1920* (Cambridge: Cambridge U. Press, 1981), 86–109; idem, "The Organized Response to Crime in Nineteenth- and Twentieth-Century America," *J. of Interdisciplinary History* 14 (1983): 127–128.

22. Lyle A. Dale, "Rough Justice: Criminal Justice in San Luis Obispo County, California, 1880–1910" (Master's thesis, California State U., Fullerton, 1990), 59–62, 78–79, 128.

23. Woirol, *Floating Army*, ch. 4; Bruns, *Knights of the Road*, 133–134; Bruce Siberts with Walker D. Wyman, *Nothing but Prairie and Sky: Life on the Dakota Range in the Early Days* (Norman: U. of Oklahoma Press, 1954), 130–131.

24. Paul T. Ringenbach, *Tramps and Reformers, 1873–1916: The Discovery of Unemployment in New York* (Westport, Conn.: Greenwood Press, 1973), 43–45; Carlos A. Schwantes, *Coxey's Army: An American Odyssey* (Lincoln: U. of Nebraska Press, 1985).

25. *Bill Haywood's Book: The Autobiography of William D. Haywood* (New York: International Publishers, 1929); Allsop, *Hard Travellin'*, 304; Bruns, *Knights of the Road*, 145–161; Woirol, *Floating Army*, ch. 7; John S. Gambs, *The Decline of the I.W.W.* (New York: Columbia U. Press, 1932), 165–166.

26. Joseph Robert Conlin, *Bread and Roses Too: Studies of the Wobblies* (Westport, Conn.: Greenwood Press, 1969), 111; *Rebel Voices: An I.W.W. Anthology*, ed. Joyce L. Kornbluh (Ann Arbor: U. of Michigan Press, 1964), ch. 2.

27. Michael Lesy, *Wisconsin Death Trip* (New York: Random House, 1973), entries for 21 Sept. 1893, 4 June 1894, and 25 Feb. 1897; Woirol, *Floating Army*, 103, 113.

28. Waldo L. Cook, "Murders in Massachusetts," *Journal of the American Statistical Association* 3 (1893): 373; Larry V. Bishop and Robert A. Harvie, "Major Crime in Three Rural Counties of Montana, 1895–1915," *J. of Police Science and Administration* 10 (1982): 84, 86, 90–91; *Workin' on the Railroad: Reminiscences from the Age of Steam*, ed. Richard Reinhardt (Palo Alto: American West Publishing Company, 1970), 74; Siberts, *Nothing but Prairie and Sky*, 140.

29. Lawrence R. Friedman and Robert V. Percival, *The Roots of Justice: Crime and Punishment in Alameda County, California, 1870–1910* (Chapel Hill:

U. of North Carolina, 1981), 317; [Willard], *Tramping with Tramps*, 100.

30. Bruns, *Knights of the Road*, 32, 200, 202–203; *Rebel Voices*, ed. Kornbluh, 86.

31. Monkkonen, "Afterword," in *Walking to Work*, 239; Stephan Thernstrom and Peter Knights, "Men in Motion: Some Data and Speculations about Urban Population Mobility," in *Anonymous Americans: Explorations in Nineteenth-Century Social History* (Englewood Cliffs, N.J.: Prentice-Hall, 1971), 17–47, esp. 39.

32. *We Pointed Them North: Recollections of a Cowpuncher* (New York: Farrar and Rinehart, 1939), 223.

33. Anderson, *The Hobo*, ch. 10; John Paul McKinsey, "Transient Men in Missouri" (Ph.D. diss., University of Missouri, 1940), 156–159; Allsop, *Hard Travellin'*, ch. 18; Edwin H. Sutherland and Harvey J. Locke, *Twenty Thousand Homeless Men: A Study of Unemployed Men in the Chicago Shelters* (rpt. New York: Arno Press, 1971), 128–132.

34. Letter from William Aspinwall quoted in John James McCook, "Leaves from the Diary of a Tramp, VIII," *Independent* 54 (1902): 874.

35. "How I Became a Socialist," in *Jack London: Novels and Social Writings* (New York: Library of America, 1982), 1117–1120; Bruns, *Knights of the Road*, 16; Journal of F. M. Hutchinson (MS, 1871–1873), 15, WAC, Beinecke.

36. Hutchinson journal.

37. Siberts, *Nothing but Prairie and Sky*, 9–45, 206–207.

38. Peter Way, "Evil Humors and Ardent Spirits: The Rough Culture of Canal Construction Laborers," *JAH* 79 (1993): 1407–1413; Lawrence J. McCaffrey, *Textures of Irish America* (Syracuse: Syracuse U. Press, 1992), 30; Mike Royko, *Boss: Richard J. Daley of Chicago* (New York: Dutton, 1971), 27.

39. Ted Robert Gurr, "Historical Trends in Violent Crime," and Roger Lane, "On the Social Meaning of Homicide Trends in America," in *Violence in America*, vol. 1: *The History of Crime*, ed. Ted Robert Gurr (Newbury Park, Ca.: Sage, 1989), 21–54, 55–79.

40. Aspinwall's letters: SRP, roll 12.

41. John J. McCook, "The Tramp Problem," *Lend a Hand* 15 (1895): 171–172.

42. SRP, roll 12, frame 871; McCook, "Leaves from the Diary of a Tramp, IX," *Independent* 54 (1902): 1542.

43. [John J. McCook,] *Report of the Special Committee on Outdoor Alms of the Town of Hartford A.D. 1891* (Hartford), xlv–xlvi; David McCullough, *Truman* (New York: Simon and Schuster, 1992), 67–68; McCook, *The*

Drink Business: What It Is; What It Does; What to Do with It (Hartford, 1895), 2. Eric Monkkonen, "Regional Dimensions," in *Walking to Work*, 193, doubts McCook's findings. He believes the information about intemperance was "the ideology of the person making the record. The hurried notations of busy police desk clerks answering McCook's queries reflect in no way an informed evaluation." This is too sweeping a dismissal. The forms were structured in such a way that the person filling them out had to ask detailed questions of the tramps themselves. There are, moreover, vignettes and quotations that unmistakably come from the subjects, e.g., "drinking man— 'would have a dollar in pocket but for this'" (SRP, roll 2, frames 104, 290, 295). While bias may have inflated the percentage, binge drinking was undoubtedly widespread among tramps.

44. McCook, "Tramp Problem," 169–170.
45. Quoted in Bruns, *Knights of the Road*, 141.
46. Anderson, *The Hobo*, 67.
47. Jeremy W. Kilar, "Great Lakes Lumber Towns and Frontier Violence," *Journal of Forest History* 31 (1987): 73–77; Ramon D. Chacon, "The Beginning of Racial Segregation: The Chinese in West Fresno and Chinatown's Role as Red Light District, 1870s–1920s," *Southern California Quarterly* 70 (1988): 389–390.
48. Carl Wittke, *The Irish in America* (rpt. New York: Russell and Russell, 1970), 36–37; W. J. Rorabaugh, *The Alcoholic Republic: An American Tradition* (New York: Oxford U. Press, 1979), 144; Way, "Evil Humors and Ardent Spirits," 1412–1413; Andrew F. Rolle, *The Immigrant Upraised: Italian Adventurers and Colonists in an Expanding America* (Norman: U. of Oklahoma Press, 1968), 154.
49. Haywood quoted in Page Smith, *America Enters the World: A People's History of the Progressive Era and World War I* (New York: McGraw-Hill, 1985), 113. Dickson: Charles W. Collins and John Day, "Dope, the New Vice," *Everyday Life*, 4 (July 1909): 5.
50. Quoted in Norman H. Clark, *Deliver Us from Evil: An Interpretation of American Prohibition* (New York: Norton, 1976), 4.
51. James H. Timberlake, *Prohibition and the Progressive Movement, 1900– 1920* (Cambridge, Mass.: Harvard U. Press, 1966), chs. 2–4; Paul Boyer, *Urban Masses and Moral Order in America, 1820–1920* (Cambridge, Mass.: Harvard U. Press, 1978), ch. 13; John J. Rumbarger, *Profits, Power, and Prohibition: Alcohol Reform and the Industrializing of America, 1800–1930* (Albany: State U. of New York Press, 1989).
52. Richard Erdoes, *Saloons of the Old West* (New York: Knopf, 1979), 60, 82; John C. Burnham, *Bad Habits: Drinking, Smoking, Taking Drugs, Gambling, Sexual Misbehavior, and Swearing in American History* (New

York: New York U. Press, 1993), 57; Boyer, *Urban Masses and Moral Order*, 193; Anderson, *The Hobo*, 27.

53. Burnham, *Bad Habits*, 28; Mark Edward Lender and James Kirby Martin, *Drinking in America: A History* (New York: Free Press, 1982), 136–139.

54. Anderson, *The Hobo*, 135.

55. McKinsey, "Transient Men in Missouri," 160.

56. *The Hobo*, xxi.

57. James F. Rooney, "Societal Forces and the Unattached Male," in *Disaffiliated Man: Essays and Bibliography on Skid Row, Vagrancy, and Outsiders*, ed. Howard M. Bahr (Toronto: U. of Toronto Press, 1970), 18–21; Schneider, "Omaha Vagrants," 269–270; Carlos A. Schwantes, "The Concept of the Wageworkers' Frontier," *Western Historical Quarterly* 18 (1987): 44, 54.

58. Thomas Minehan, *Boy and Girl Tramps of America* (rpt. Seattle: U. of Washington Press, 1976), xiv–xv; McKinsey, "Transient Men in Missouri," 43.

59. Walter J. Stein, *California and the Dust Bowl Migration* (Westport, Conn.: Greenwood Press, 1973), 44, 50, 55.

60. Samuel E. Wallace, *Skid Row as a Way of Life* (Totowa, N.J.: Bedminster Press, 1965), 22–25; James P. Spradley, *You Owe Yourself a Drunk: An Ethnography of Urban Nomads* (Boston: Little, Brown, 1970), 120–121, 179, 254, 258.

61. "The Prejudice against Men," *Nation* 253 (8 July 1991): 46.

10. Marriage Boom, Urban Bust

1. Warren S. Thompson and P. K. Whelpton, *Population Trends in the United States* (rpt. New York: Gordon and Breach, 1969), 172–175; Donald J. Bogue et al., *The Population of the United States: Historical Trends and Future Prospects*, rev. ed. (New York: Free Press, 1985), 349.

2. Rowe, letter of 8 March 1918, *Letters from a World War I Aviator*, ed. Genevieve Bailey Rowe and Diana Rowe Doran (Boston: Sinclaire Press, 1986), 59; Thompson and Whelpton, *Population Trends in the United States*, 174–175.

3. John Higham, *Strangers in the Land: Patterns of American Nativism, 1860–1925* (New York: Atheneum, 1975).

4. Marion F. Houstoun, Roger G. Kramer, and Joan Macklin Barrett, "Female Predominance in Immigration in the United States Since 1930: A First Look," *International Migration Review* 18 (1984): 908–963.

5. "Another Stereotype Upset," *NYT*, 15 Sept. 1985, 4E.

6. Robert V. Wells, *Revolutions in Americans' Lives: A Demographic Perspec-*

tive on the History of Americans, Their Families, and Their Societies (West-port, Conn.: Greenwood Press, 1982), 221.

7. Bogue et al., *Population of the United States,* 42, 234; U.S. Bureau of the Census, *Statistical Abstract of the United States, 1995* (1995), 14.

8. Bogue et al., *Population of the United States,* 150; Deborah L. Wingard, "The Sex Differential in Morbidity, Mortality, and Lifestyle," *Annual Review of Public Health* 5 (1984): 453.

9. Willard Waller, *The Veteran Comes Back* (New York: Dryden Press, 1944), 138; Steven Mintz and Susan Kellogg, *Domestic Revolutions: A Social History of American Family Life* (New York: Free Press, 1988), 153–154.

10. Bogue et al., *Population of the United States,* 166.

11. U.S. Bureau of the Census, *Historical Statistics of the United States: Colonial Times to 1970,* pt. 1 (1975), 224; Mintz and Kellogg, *Domestic Revolutions,* 152; John Patrick Diggins, *The Proud Decades: America in War and in Peace, 1941–1960* (New York: Norton, 1988), 180; John Hajnal, "The Marriage Boom," *Population Index* 19 (1953): 85.

12. Bogue et al., *Population of the United States,* 147; Sidonie M. Gruenberg, "Why They Are Marrying Younger," *New York Times Magazine,* 30 Jan. 1955, 38.

13. Keith W. Olson, *The G.I. Bill, the Veterans, and the Colleges* (Lexington: U. Press of Kentucky, 1974), 25 (quotation), 33–34, 44; "GI Bill Saluted on 50th Birthday," *Florida Times-Union,* 23 June 1994, A1, A8.

14. Olson, *G.I. Bill,* 75–76.

15. Mintz and Kellogg, *Domestic Revolutions,* 180; Douglas T. Miller and Marion Nowak, *The Fifties: The Way We Really Were* (New York: Doubleday, 1977), ch. 6; J. Ronald Oakley, *God's Country: America in the Fifties* (New York: Dembner Books, 1986), 118, 293–294; Brett Harvey, *The Fifties: A Women's Oral History* (New York: HarperCollins, 1993), 68–70.

16. Stephanie Coontz, *The Way We Never Were: American Families and the Nostalgia Trap* (New York: Basic Books, 1992), 25–26, 183.

17. Kenneth T. Jackson, *Crabgrass Frontier: The Suburbanization of the United States* (New York: Oxford U. Press, 1985), 232. Wanted-to-rent, e.g., *Florida Times-Union,* 9 Dec. 1945, 26; 16 Dec. 1945, 26.

18. Jackson, *Crabgrass Frontier,* 236; Oakley, *God's Country,* 112; David Halberstam, *The Fifties* (New York: Villard Books, 1993), ch. 9.

19. Quoted in Studs Terkel, *The Good War: An Oral History of World War Two* (New York: Ballantine Books, 1984), 134.

20. Jackson, *Crabgrass Frontier,* 248–249; Mark H. Rose, *Interstate: Express Highway Politics, 1939–1989,* rev. ed. (Knoxville: U. of Tennessee Press, 1990), 1–2, 92–93.

21. Terkel, *Good War*, 139.

22. Jackson, *Crabgrass Frontier*, 290; Nicholas Lemann, *The Promised Land: The Great Black Migration and How It Changed America* (New York: Knopf, 1991), 70; Wells, *Revolutions*, 220.

23. Rates are also available for accidental deaths not involving motor vehicles, but the data for the past thirty to forty years are falsely low because of changes in federal classification and hence are not used here. See Paul C. Holinger, *Violent Deaths in the United States: An Epidemiologic Study of Suicide, Homicide, and Accidents* (New York: Guilford Press, 1987), 102.

24. "Wilson Blames Speeders," *New York Times*, 28 Feb. 1906, 3. Problems with pre-1933 data: H. C. Brearley, *Homicide in the United States* (Chapel Hill: U. of North Carolina Press, 1932), 15-18; Roger Lane, "On the Social Meaning of Homicide Trends in America," in *Violence in America*, vol. 1: *The History of Crime*, ed. Ted Robert Gurr (Newbury Park, Ca.: Sage, 1989), 64-74. Other articles in this anthology, Gurr's "Historical Trends in Violent Crime," 37-41, and Neil Alan Weiner and Margaret A. Zahn, "Violent Arrests in the City," esp. 113, are also germane. Highway safety: Bob Minzesheimer, "National Speed Limits Losing Some Steam," *USA Today*, 11 May 1995, 3A. Emergency medical services: David Simon, *Homicide: A Year on the Killing Streets* (New York: Houghton Mifflin, 1991), 161; William G. Doerner and John C. Speir, "Stitch and Sew: The Impact of Medical Resources on Criminally Induced Lethality," *Criminology* 24 (1986): 319–330.

25. Holinger, *Violent Deaths in the United States*; William Wilbanks, *Murder in Miami* (Lanham, Md.: U. Press of America, 1984), 11–12.

26. William L. O'Neill, *A Democracy at War: America's Fight at Home and Abroad in World War II* (New York: Free Press, 1993), 250.

27. E. B. Sledge, *With the Old Breed at Peleliu and Okinawa* (rpt. Novato, Cal.: Presidio Press, 1981); John W. Dower, *War Without Mercy: Race and Power in the Pacific War* (New York: Pantheon, 1986); William H. Sullivan, *Obbligato, 1939–1979: Notes on a Foreign Service Career* (New York: Norton, 1984), 70.

28. Winthrop S. Hudson, *Religion in America* (New York: Scribner, 1965), 396; William Martin, *A Prophet with Honor: The Billy Graham Story* (New York: William Morrow, 1991), 106; James Hudnut-Beumler, *Looking for God in the Suburbs: The Religion of the American Dream and Its Critics, 1945–1965* (New Brunswick: Rutgers U. Press, 1994), ch. 2; Blanshard, *American Freedom and Catholic Power*, 2nd rev. and enl. ed. (Boston: Beacon Press, 1958), viii.

29. Wade Clark Roof and William McKinney, *American Mainline Religion* (New Brunswick: Rutgers U. Press, 1987), ch. 1; Hazel Gaudet Er-

skine, "The Polls: Church Attendance," *Public Opinion Quarterly* 28 (1964): 676, 679; Jackson W. Carroll et al., *Religion in America: 1950 to the Present* (New York: Harper and Row, 1979), 20–21.

30. Alexander Keyssar, *Out of Work: The First Century of Unemployment in Massachusetts* (Cambridge: Cambridge U. Press, 1986), 171–172.

31. Bogue et al., *Population of the United States,* 14; Marvin Wolfgang, *Youth and Violence* (Washington: G.P.O., 1970), 35–39; Landon Y. Jones, *Great Expectations: America and the Baby Boom Generation* (New York: Coward, McCann and Geoghegan, 1980), ch. 11.

32. Samuel H. Preston and Alan Thomas Richards, "The Influence of Women's Work Opportunities on Marriage Rates," *Demography* 12 (1975): 209–222; David M. Heer and Amyra Grossbard-Shectman, "The Impact of the Female Marriage Squeeze and the Contraceptive Revolution on Sex Roles and the Women's Liberation Movement in the United States, 1960 to 1975," *JMF* 43 (1981): 54.

33. Susan Cotts Watkins, Jane A. Menken, and John Bongaarts, "Demographic Foundations of Family Change," *ASR* 52 (1987): 354; Popenoe, "Cultural Changes and the Family," paper prepared for the Children's Roundtable Retreat, Boca Raton, Florida, 11–14 Feb. 1994, 10.

34. Mark Edward Lender and James Kirby Martin, *Drinking in America: A History* (New York: Free Press, 1982), 197; Philip J. Cook and Michael J. Moore, "Economic Perspectives on Reducing Alcohol-Related Violence," in *Alcohol and Interpersonal Violence,* ed. Susan E. Martin (Rockville, Md.: National Institutes of Health, 1993), 193–212; David F. Musto, *The American Disease: Origins of Narcotic Control,* exp. ed. (New York: Oxford U. Press, 1987), ch. 12.

35. Holinger, *Violent Deaths in the United States,* 210.

36. Keith D. Harries, *The Geography of Crime and Justice* (New York: McGraw-Hill, 1974), 62.

37. Lemann, *Promised Land,* 41.

38. Robert W. Pearson, "Economy, Culture, Public Policy, and the Urban Underclass," *Items* 43 (June 1989): 25–27; Roger Lane, "Black Philadelphia, Then and Now," *Public Interest,* no. 108 (Summer 1992): 50–51.

39. John Koren, *Economic Aspects of the Liquor Problem* (Boston, 1899), ch. 6; Muriel W. Sterne, "Drinking Patterns and Alcoholism among American Negroes," in *Alcoholism,* ed. David J. Pittman (New York: Harper and Row, 1967), 66–99; "State Reports to NIAA Show Alcoholism Rate in the U.S. at 9.3 Million," *Report on Alcoholism* 33 (1975): 8–9; David Courtwright, Herman Joseph, and Don Des Jarlais, *Addicts Who Survived: An Oral History of Narcotic Use in America, 1923–1965* (Knoxville: U. of Tennessee Press, 1989), 14–19.

40. Lewis Yablonsky, *The Violent Gang* (rpt. Baltimore: Penguin Books, 1967), 18–19.
41. Courtwright, Joseph, and Des Jarlais, *Addicts Who Survived*, 313.
42. William Julius Wilson, *The Truly Disadvantaged: The Inner City, the Underclass, and Public Policy* (Chicago: U. of Chicago Press, 1987); Loïc J. D. Wacquant and William Julius Wilson, "The Cost of Racial and Class Exclusion in the Inner City," *AAAPSS* 501 (1989): 8–25; Elijah Anderson, "The Story of John Turner," *Public Interest,* no. 108 (Summer 1992): 23 (quotation), 31–34.
43. Courtwright, Joseph, and Des Jarlais, *Addicts Who Survived*, 254.
44. Norman B. Rushforth et al., "Violent Death in a Metropolitan County: Changing Patterns in Homicide (1958–74)," *NEJM* 297 (1977): 531; Kurt Gorwitz and Ruth Dennis, "On the Decrease in the Life Expectancy of Black Males in Michigan," *PHR* 91 (1976): 145; "Homicide among Black Males," *PHR* 95 (1980): 549.
44. Colin McCord and Harold P. Freeman, "Excess Mortality in Harlem," *NEJM* 322 (1990): 174, 176; Donna M. Shai, "Mortality Associated with Drug Misuse among Blacks in New York City, 1979–1981," *IJA* 27 (1992): 1433–1443.
46. Wolfgang, *Patterns in Criminal Homicide* (Philadelphia: U. of Pennsylvania Press, 1958), 365; Ralph Blumenthal, "Life and Death in a New York Homicide Precinct," *NYT,* nat. ed., 16 April 1990, A1, A16.
47. "Night as Frontier," *ASR* 43 (1978): 6.
48. Melbin, "Night as Frontier," 7–8, 10–12; idem, *Night as Frontier* (New York: Free Press, 1987), 33–35.
49. *Accident Facts, 1983 Edition* (Chicago: National Safety Council, 1983), 50; William L. Carlson, "Age, Exposure, and Alcohol Involvement in Night Crashes," *Journal of Safety Research* 5 (1973): 252, 257; H. M. Simpson, D. R. Mayhew, and R. A. Warren, "Epidemiology of Road Accidents Involving Young Adults: Alcohol, Drugs and Other Factors," *Drug and Alcohol Dependence* 10 (1982): 47; Jacksonville, Fl., Office of the Sheriff, "Report of Offense Type by Hour of Day, 1992," data furnished by Chuck Alsobrook.
50. James A. Inciardi and Juliet L. Dee, "From the Keystone Cops to *Miami Vice:* Images of Policing in American Popular Culture," *J. of Popular Culture* 21 (1987): 88.
51. "The '50s," *Newsweek* 123 (3 Jan. 1994): 36.

11. Ghetto Violence

1. Morton Owen Schapiro and Dennis A. Ahlburg, "Why Crime Is Down," *American Demographics* 8 (1986): 56–57.

2. Thomas Byrne Edsall, "Black vs. White in Chicago," *NYRB* 36 (13 April 1989): 22.

3. U.S. National Center for Health Statistics, *Health, United States, 1993* (Hyattsville, Md.: Public Health Service, 1994), 130; U.S. Senate Judiciary Committee, "Fighting Crime in America: An Agenda for the 1990's" (Washington, D.C.: majority staff report, 12 March 1991), 1–12; Paul Kennedy, *Preparing for the Twenty-First Century* (New York: Random House, 1993), 304; Peter Reuter, Mathea Falco, and Robert MacCoun, *Comparing Western European and North American Drug Policies: An International Conference Report* (Santa Monica: RAND Drug Policy Research Center, 1993), 6.

4. "Homicide," *Newsweek* 124 (15 Aug. 1994): 22–23; F. Landis MacKellar and Machiko Yanagishita, "Homicide in the United States," *Population Trends and Public Policy,* no. 21 (Feb. 1995): 4–19.

5. Kenneth Tardiff et al., "Homicide in New York City," *JAMA* 272 (1994): 44; Jeffrey A. Roth, "Firearms and Violence," *National Institute of Justice: Research in Brief* (Feb. 1994): 1.

6. "Homicide," 23; MacKellar and Yanagishita, "Homicide in the United States," 4.

7. David Simon, *Homicide: A Year on the Killing Streets* (New York: Houghton Mifflin, 1991).

8. Marc Mauer and Tracy Huling, *Young Black Americans and the Criminal Justice System* (Washington: The Sentencing Project, 1995); David J. Rothman, "The Crime of Punishment," *NYRB* 41 (17 Feb. 1994): 34–35.

9. William A. Darity Jr. and Samuel L. Myers Jr., "Does Welfare Dependency Cause Female Hardship? The Case of the Black Family," and Frances E. Kobrin and Linda J. Waite, "Effects of Childhood Family Structure on the Transition to Marriage," both in *JMF* 46 (1984): 775–776 and 807–816; David W. Murray, "Poor Suffering Bastards," *Policy Review,* no. 68 (Spring 1994): 9–15; James Q. Wilson, "Culture, Incentives, and the Underclass," in *Values and Public Policy,* ed. Henry J. Aaron, Thomas E. Mann, and Timothy Taylor (Washington: Brookings Institution, 1994), 62–63.

10. M. Belinda Tucker and Claudia Mitchell-Kernan, "Trends in African American Family Formation: A Theoretical and Statistical Overview," in *The Decline in Marriage among African Americans,* ed. idem (New York: Russell Sage Foundation, 1995), 3–26; U.S. Bureau of the Census, *Statistical Abstract of the United States, 1993* (1993), 53.

11. U.S. Department of Labor, Office of Planning and Research, *The Negro Family: The Case for National Action* (1965), 59; *Statistical Abstract, 1993,* 78; Stacy Furukawa, *The Diverse Living Arrangements of Children: Summer 1991,* Current Population Reports P70–38 (1994), 3.

12. Moynihan, "How the Great Society 'Destroyed the American Family,'" *Public Interest* (Summer 1992): 56–57; *The Negro Family*, 13, 93.

13. Lee Rainwater and William L. Yancey, *The Moynihan Report and the Politics of Controversy* (Cambridge, Mass.: MIT Press, 1967); Nicholas Lemann, *The Promised Land: The Great Black Migration and How It Changed America* (New York: Knopf, 1991), 172–177; Michael Katz, *The Undeserving Poor: From the War on Poverty to the War on Welfare* (New York: Pantheon, 1989), 25–29, 44–50.

14. Kim A. Winpisinger et al., "Risk Factors for Childhood Homicides in Ohio," *AJPH* 81 (1991): 1052–1054. Steven F. Messner, "Regional and Racial Effects on the Urban Homicide Rate," *AJS* 88 (1983): 1001, also reports a strong correlation (+.71) between the percentages of one-parent children and homicide rates for 204 SMSAs.

15. *Losing Ground: American Social Policy, 1950–1980* (New York: Basic Books, 1984), 212.

16. Katz, *Undeserving Poor*, 153; George James, "Job Is Picking Up Garbage: 100,000 New Yorkers Want It," *NYT*, nat. ed., 21 Sept. 1990, A14.

17. Allen J. Matusow, *The Unraveling of America: A History of Liberalism in the 1960s* (New York: Random House, 1984), 238–239; Paul A. Jargowsky and Mary Jo Bane, "Ghetto Poverty in the United States, 1970–1980," in *The Urban Underclass*, ed. Christopher Jencks and Paul E. Peterson (Washington: Brookings Institution, 1991), 246–247.

18. Lewis, "The Culture of Poverty," *Scientific American* 215 (Oct. 1966): 19–25; Katz, *Undeserving Poor*, ch. 1.

19. Richard J. Herrnstein, *IQ in the Meritocracy* (Boston: Atlantic–Little, Brown, 1973); James Q. Wilson and Richard J. Herrnstein, *Crime and Human Nature* (New York: Simon and Schuster, 1985); R. J. Herrnstein, "Still an American Dilemma," *Public Interest* 98 (1990): 3–17; Richard J. Herrnstein and Charles J. Murray, *The Bell Curve: Intelligence and Class Structure in American Life* (New York: Free Press, 1994).

20. Carl N. Degler, *In Search of Human Nature: The Decline and Revival of Darwinism in American Social Thought* (New York: Oxford U. Press, 1991).

21. Moynihan, *Negro Family*, 36.

22. "Neighborhood Effects on Teenage Pregnancy," in *The Urban Underclass*, ed. Jencks and Peterson, 383. See also Anderson's "Sex Codes and Family Life among Poor Inner-City Youths," *Annals of the American Academy of Political and Social Sciences* 501 (1989): 59–78; "The Story of John Turner," *Public Interest*, no. 108 (Summer 1992): 3–34; and "The Code of the Streets," *Atlantic Monthly* 273 (May 1994): 81–94.

23. *Tales Out of School,* ed. Dan Morgan (New York: Elisabeth Sifton/Penguin Books, 1988), 51–52.
24. Greg Donaldson, *The Ville: Cops and Kids in Urban America* (New York: Ticknor and Fields, 1993), 26–27.
25. Carl S. Taylor, *Dangerous Society* (East Lansing: Michigan State U. Press, 1989), 60; Terry Williams and William Kornblum, *The Uptown Kids* (New York: Putnam, 1994), 129, 134.
26. William Finnegan, "Out There, I" *New Yorker* 66 (10 Sept. 1990): 66, 84, and "Out There, II" (17 Sept. 1990): 73, 84.
27. Sanyika Shakur, *Monster: The Autobiography of an L.A. Gang Member* (New York: Atlantic Monthly Press, 1993), 102.
28. Taylor, *Dangerous Society,* 56; Anderson, "Code of the Streets," 94; Terry Williams, *The Cocaine Kids: The Inside Story of a Teenage Drug Ring* (New York: Addison Wesley, 1989), 81.
29. *Makes Me Wanna Holler: A Young Black Man in America* (New York: Random House, 1994), 114–118.
30. Anderson, "Code of the Streets."
31. Steve Patterson, "The Lure of Gangs," *Florida Times-Union,* 8 May 1994, A6; Donaldson, *The Ville,* 27.
32. Léon Bing, *Do or Die* (New York: HarperCollins, 1991), 49.
33. David Hackett Fischer, *Albion's Seed: Four British Folkways in America* (New York: Oxford U. Press, 1989), 756, 768; Bing, *Do or Die,* 152–153. Interestingly, no one can remember the name of the girl over whom the dispute began; this particular Helen has been lost to history. Episodes of the war, which featured kidnapping, rape, and mutilation as well as murder, are described in Shakur, *Monster.*
34. *Gangs, Crime and Violence in Los Angeles* (Los Angeles: District Attorney's Office, 1992).
35. Shakur, *Monster,* 138; Patterson, "Lure of Gangs," A6; Bing, *Do or Die,* 214.
36. Willard W. Waller, *On the Family, Education, and War: Selected Writings,* ed. William J. Goode, Frank F. Furstenberg Jr., and Larry R. Mitchell (Chicago: U. of Chicago Press, 1970), 177–178, 197–198.
37. *Too Many Women? The Sex Ratio Question* (Beverly Hills: Sage, 1983), ch. 1.
38. John W. Briggs, "Fertility and Cultural Change among Families in Italy and America," *AHR* 91 (1986): 1142–1143.
39. Scott J. South and Katherine Trent, "Sex Ratios and Women's Roles: A Cross-National Analysis," *AJS* 94 (1988): 1096–1115.
40. *Statistical Abstract of the United States, 1994,* 20.
41. Douglas J. Besharov and Timothy S. Sullivan, "One Flesh: America Is

Experiencing an Unprecedented Increase in Black-White Intermarriage," *New Democrat* 8 (July/Aug. 1996): 19–21.

42. Panel on High-Risk Youth, Commission on Behavioral and Social Sciences and Education, National Research Council, *Losing Generations: Adolescents in High-Risk Settings* (Washington: National Academy Press, 1993), 34; McCall, *Makes Me Wanna Holler*, 271.

43. Graham B. Spanier and Paul C. Glick, "Mate Selection Differentials between Whites and Blacks in the United States," *Social Forces* 58 (1980): 707–725; Guttentag and Secord, *Too Many Women?* 227–229; *The Decline in Marriage among African Americans*, ed. Tucker and Mitchell-Kernan, chs. 5, 6, and 11.

44. Messner and Sampson, "The Sex Ratio, Family Disruption, and Rates of Violent Crime: The Paradox of Demographic Structure," *Social Forces* 69 (1991): 693–713.

45. Alex Kotlowitz, *There Are No Children Here: The Story of Two Boys Growing Up in the Other America* (New York: Doubleday, 1991), 10; Jewelle Taylor Gibbs, "Young Black Males in America: Endangered, Embittered, and Embattled," in *Young, Black, and Male in America: An Endangered Species*, ed. idem (Dover, Mass.: Auburn House, 1988), 4; *Statistical Abstract, 1993*, 23.

46. Robert Tillman, "The Size of the 'Criminal Population': The Prevalence and Incidence of Adult Arrest," *Criminology* 25 (1987): 567–569; Andrew Hacker, *Two Nations: Black and White, Separate, Hostile, Unequal* (New York: Ballantine, 1992), ch. 11; Christopher Lasch, *The Revolt of the Elites and the Betrayal of Democracy* (New York: Norton, 1995); Marvin Wolfgang, "Real and Perceived Changes of Crime and Punishment," *Daedalus* 107 (Winter 1994): 146.

47. "Hanging Out," *NYRB* 42 (25 May 1995), 36.

48. *Gangs, Crime and Violence in Los Angeles*, 19–20; *Juba to Jive: A Dictionary of African-American Slang*, ed. Clarence Major (New York: Penguin, 1994).

49. And only if poorly socialized inner-city men actually took the jobs and kept at them. There is skepticism on this point, e.g., Michael R. Gottfredson and Travis Hirschi, *A General Theory of Crime* (Stanford: Stanford U. Press, 1990), 163–165.

12. The Crack Era

1. See John C. Burnham, *Bad Habits: Drinking, Smoking, Taking Drugs, Gambling, Sexual Misbehavior, and Swearing in American History* (New York: New York U. Press, 1993), ch. 7.

2. Herbert G. Gutman, *The Black Family in Slavery and Freedom, 1750–1925* (New York: Pantheon, 1976); Christopher Jencks, "Deadly Neighborhoods," *New Republic* 198 (13 June 1988): 28–30.

3. William Finnegan, "Out There, II," *New Yorker* 66 (17 Sept. 1990): 74.

4. Brown, *Die, Nigger, Die* (New York: Dial Press, 1969), 18–19; Morris Janowitz, "Patterns of Collective Racial Violence," in *The History of Violence in America,* ed. Hugh Davis Graham and Ted Robert Gurr (New York: Bantam, 1969), 412–444.

5. Peter Plagen et al., "Violence in Our Culture," *Newsweek* 117 (1 April 1991): 51; Richard Brunelli, "Study Measures Changes in Black Household TV Viewing," *Mediaweek* 3 (15 April 1993): 4.

6. Steven F. Messner, "Television Violence and Violent Crime: An Aggregate Analysis," *Social Problems* 33 (1986): 230; James Patterson and Peter Kim, *The Day America Told the Truth: What People* Really *Believe about Everything that Really Matters* (New York: Prentice Hall, 1991), 123; Alexander Cockburn, "Rituals in the Dark," *American Film* 16 (Aug. 1991): 27.

7. Jerrold Ladd, *Out of the Madness* (New York: Warner Books, 1994), 114–115.

8. E.g., Deborah Prothrow-Stith with Michaele Weissman, *Deadly Consequences: How Violence Is Destroying Our Teenage Population and a Plan to Begin Solving the Problem* (New York: HarperCollins, 1991), 36–38; Brandon Centerwall, "Television and Violence," *JAMA* 267 (1992): 3059-3063.

9. West, *Race Matters* (Boston: Beacon Press, 1993), 16–17, 29–30, 36–37, 56.

10. Homework data: Sanford M. Dornbusch, personal communication, 12 Feb. 1990. See also Fox Butterfield, "Why Asians Are Going to the Head of the Class," *NYT,* 3 Aug. 1986, sec. 12, 18–23; John H. Bunzel, "Minority Faculty Hiring: Problems and Prospects," *American Scholar* 59 (Winter 1990): 51.

11. Jeff Cohen and Norman Solomon, "Crime Time," *Folio Weekly,* 23 Aug. 1994, 9. See also Catherine S. Manegold, "A Grim Wasteland on News at Six," *NYT,* 14 June 1992, metro sec., 41, 50; Michael Freeman, "Networks Doubled Crime Coverage in '93, Despite Flat Violence Levels in U.S. Society," *Mediaweek* 4 (14 March 1994): 4.

12. Garland Williams, New York District Supervisor of the Bureau of Narcotics, to Harry Anslinger, Commissioner of Narcotics, 9 Feb. 1940, U.S. Treasury Department File 0120–9, Drug Enforcement Administration, Washington; David T. Courtwright, "The Rise and Fall and Rise of Cocaine in the United States," in *Consuming Habits: Drugs in History and Anthropology,* ed. Jordan Goodman, Paul E. Lovejoy, and

Andrew Sherratt (London: Routledge, 1995), 206–228. Portions of the latter are incorporated into this chapter.

13. Gerald T. McLaughlin, "Cocaine: The History and Regulation of a Dangerous Drug," *Cornell Law Review* 58 (1973): 555–556.

14. Joseph L. Zentner, "Cocaine and the Criminal Sanction," *J. of Drug Issues* 7 (1977): 98; Scott E. Lukas, *Amphetamines* (New York: Chelsea House, 1985); Edward Brecher, *Licit and Illicit Drugs* (Boston: Little, Brown, 1972), 267–305.

15. Todd Gitlin, *The Sixties: Years of Hope, Days of Rage* (New York: Bantam, 1987), ch. 8.

16. Thomas L. Dezelsky, Jack V. Toohey, and Robert Kush, "A Ten-Year Analysis of Non-Medical Drug Use Behavior at Five American Universities," *J. of School Health* 51 (1981): 52–53; Joseph Kennedy, *Coca Exotica: The Illustrated Story of Cocaine* (Rutherford, N.J., and New York: Fairleigh Dickinson University Press and Cornwall Books, 1985), 117–122.

17. Guy Gugliotta and Jeff Leen, *Kings of Cocaine: Inside the Medellín Cartel* (New York: Simon and Schuster, 1989).

18. Rensselaer W. Lee III, *The White Labyrinth: Cocaine and Political Power* (New Brunswick, N.J.: Transaction Publishers, 1989), 100; *Price and Purity of Cocaine* (Washington: Office of National Drug Control Policy, 1992), 5–6.

19. Dan Waldorf, Craig Reinarman, and Sheigla Murphy, *Cocaine Changes: The Experience of Using and Quitting* (Philadelphia: Temple U. Press, 1991), 103–139; U.S. House of Representatives, Select Committee on Narcotics Abuse and Control, *Cocaine: A Major Drug Issue of the Seventies: Hearings*, 96th Cong., 1st sess. (1980), 91, 120–121, 125; Gordon Witkin et al., "The Men Who Invented Crack," *U.S. News and World Report* 111 (19 Aug. 1991): 44–53; Douglas McDonnell, Jeanette Irwin, and Marsha Rosenbaum, "'Hop and Hubbas': A Tough New Mix," *Contemporary Drug Problems* 17 (1990): 147–151; Beatrice A. Rouse, "Trends in Cocaine Use in the General Population," in *The Epidemiology of Cocaine Use and Abuse*, ed. Susan Schober and Charles Schade, National Institute on Drug Abuse Research Monograph 110 (Washington: G.P.O., 1991), 14.

20. Terry Williams, *Crackhouse: Notes from the End of the Line* (Reading, Mass.: Addison-Wesley, 1992), 3, 8–10; Lewis Cole, *Never Too Young to Die: The Death of Len Bias* (New York: Pantheon, 1989), 150–151; Elliott Currie, *Reckoning: Drugs, the Cities, and the American Future* (New York: Hill and Wang, 1993).

21. Peter Reuter, Robert MacCoun, and Patrick Murphy, *Money from Crime: A Study of the Economics of Drug Dealing in Washington, D.C.* (Santa

Monica: RAND Corporation, 1990), 56, 66; Carl S. Taylor, *Dangerous Society* (East Lansing: Michigan State U. Press, 1990), 45, 70; Philippe Bourgois, "In Search of Horatio Alger: Culture and Ideology in the Crack Economy," *Contemporary Drug Problems* 16 (1989): 619–649, and idem, "Growing Up," *American Enterprise* 2 (May/June 1991): 30–34.

22. A. James Giannini et al., "Cocaine-Associated Violence and Relationship to Route of Administration," *J. of Substance Abuse Treatment* 10 (1993): 67. See also Norman S. Miller, Mark S. Gold, and John C. Mahler, "Violent Behaviors Associated with Cocaine Use: Possible Pharmacological Mechanisms," *IJA* 26 (1991): 1077–1088.

23. Peter M. Marzuk et al., "Cocaine Use, Risk Taking, and Fatal Russian Roulette," *JAMA* 267 (1992): 2635–2637.

24. Kenneth Tardiff et al., "Homicide in New York City," *JAMA* 272 (1994): 43–46.

25. Terry M. Williams and William Kornblum, *Growing Up Poor* (Lexington, Mass.: Lexington Books, 1985), 50, 127; Bruce D. Johnson et al., *Taking Care of Business: The Economics of Crime by Heroin Abusers* (Lexington, Mass.: Lexington Books, 1985), 175; Paul J. Goldstein, "Drugs and Violence," in U.S. National Institute of Justice, *Questions and Answers in Lethal and Non-Lethal Violence*, ed. Carolyn Rebecca Block and Richard L. Block (1993), 11.

26. Reuter, MacCoun, and Murphy, *Money from Crime*, 96–98.

27. Witkin et al., "Men Who Invented Crack," 52–53; Nicholas Lemann, *The Promised Land: The Great Black Migration and How It Changed America* (New York: Knopf, 1991), 336–337; Jerome H. Skolnick, Ricky Bluthenthal, and Theodore Correl, "Gang Organization and Migration," in *Gangs: The Origins and Impact of Contemporary Youth Gangs in the United States*, ed. Scott Cummings and Daniel J. Monti (Albany: State University of New York Press, 1993): 203.

28. Léon Bing, *Do or Die* (New York: HarperCollins, 1991), 223–224 (quotation); Sanyika Shakur, *Monster: The Autobiography of an L.A. Gang Member* (New York: Atlantic Monthly Press, 1993), 25; Craig Wolff, "In New York, the Brazenness Of Illegal Gun Dealers Grows," *NYT*, nat. ed., 6 Nov. 1990, A1, B12.

29. Prothrow-Stith with Weissman, *Deadly Consequences*, 121; Joseph B. Treaster and Mary B. W. Tabor, "Teen-Age Gunslinging Is on Rise," *NYT*, nat. ed., 17 Feb. 1992, A1, A12.

30. "Homicide," *Newsweek* 124 (15 Aug. 1994): 25; Michael deCourcy Hinds, "Number of Killings Soars in Big Cities across U.S.," *NYT*, nat. ed., 18 July 1990, 10.

31. *Gangs, Crime and Violence in Los Angeles* (Los Angeles: District Attorney's

Office, 1992), 86–88, 106–107; Prothrow-Stith with Weissman, *Deadly Consequences,* ch. 8.

32. Alfred Blumstein, "Youth Violence, Guns, and the Illicit-Drug Industry," Carnegie Mellon U., Heinz School of Public Policy and Management, working paper 94–29 (July 1994), 18; Treaster and Tabor, "Teen-Age Gunslinging," A12.

33. "1990 and the Promised Land," New York State Division of Substance Abuse Services *Outlook* (Jan./Feb. 1991), 21.

34. Isabel Wilkerson, "'Crack House' Fire: Justice or Vigilantism?" *NYT,* 22 Oct. 1988, 1, 6; Tucker Carlson, "Smoking Them Out," *Policy Review,* no. 71 (Winter 1995): 60, 61.

35. McDonnell, Irwin, and Rosenbaum, "'Hop and Hubbas,'" 154; Taylor, *Dangerous Society,* 70–71.

36. Norman S. Miller and Mark S. Gold, "Criminal Activity and Crack Addiction," *IJA* 29 (1994): 1069–1078; Edward Walsh, "Image of Parks Tall Again: Draws Attention to Crime Plague," *Buffalo News,* 2 Sept. 1994, A13; Barbara Reynolds, "If Civil Rights Legend Rosa Parks Isn't Safe, Who Is?" *USA Today,* 2 Sept. 1994, 11A.

37. U.S. General Accounting Office, *Drug Abuse: The Crack Cocaine Epidemic: Health Consequences and Treatment* (1991), 17; Ladd, *Out of the Madness,* 116; McDonnell, Irwin, and Rosenbaum, "'Hop and Hubbas,'" 154; Gina Kolata, "New Picture of Who Will Get AIDS Is Dominated by Addicts," *NYT,* 28 Feb. 1995, C3.

38. Herman Joseph and Karla Damus, "Prenatal Cocaine/Crack Exposure in New York City," and Daniel R. Neuspiel and Sara C. Hamel, "Cocaine and Infant Behavior," in *Cocaine/Crack Research Working Group Newsletter,* no. 2 (Oct. 1991), 4–6, 14–25.

39. Mercel L. Sullivan, "Absent Fathers in the Inner City," *AAAPSS* 501 (1989): 54–56; Jerald G. Bachman, Patrick M. O'Malley, and Jerome Johnston, *Youth in Transition,* vol. 6: *Adolescence to Adulthood—Change and Stability in the Lives of Young Men* (Ann Arbor: Institute for Social Research, 1978), 195–197.

40. Patrick Biernacki, *Pathways from Heroin Addiction: Recovery without Treatment* (Philadelphia: Temple U. Press, 1986), 76–77.

41. George E. Peterson and Adele V. Harrell, "Introduction: Inner-City Isolation and Opportunity," in *Drugs, Crime, and Social Isolation,* ed. Harrell and Peterson (Washington: Urban Institute, 1992), 23.

42. Hamid, "Drugs and Patterns of Opportunity in the Inner City," in *Drugs, Crime, and Social Isolation,* ed. Harrell and Peterson, 238; Alan Burdick, "Looking for the High Life," *The Sciences* 31 (June 1991), 17.

43. Burdick, "Looking for the High Life," 15; Eric D. Wish, "U.S. Drug

Policy in the 1990s," *IJA* 25 (1990–1991): 377–409; Susan S. Evering-
ham and C. Peter Rydell, *Modeling the Demand for Cocaine* (Santa
Monica: RAND Drug Policy Research Center, 1994), ch. 7.

44. Sam Vincent Meddis, "Is the Drug War Racist?" *U.S.A. Today,* 23–25
July 1993, 26 July 1993, 27 July 1993. Racial disparity was also built
into the sentencing provisions of the 1986 federal antidrug law. That
statute specified a mandatory minimum sentence of ten years for a
violation involving 50 grams of crack cocaine but required a full 5
kilograms—100 times the weight of crack—to warrant a comparable
sentence for a powder cocaine violation. The U.S. Sentencing Commission concluded that the harmful effects of crack did not justify the
100-to-1 ratio. Congress kept it anyway. Richard B. Conaboy et al.,
Cocaine and Federal Sentencing Policy (N.c.: U.S. Sentencing Commission,
1995).

45. James Q. Wilson, "Culture, Incentives, and the Underclass," in *Values
and Public Policy,* ed. Henry J. Aaron, Thomas E. Mann, and Timothy
Taylor (Washington, D.C.: Brookings Institution, 1994), 59–60; Larry
Reibstein et al., "Back to the Chain Gang?" *Newsweek* 124 (17 Oct.
1994): 87.

46. Roberts quoted in Jack Anderson's column, "Sentence Reform Good
Penal Policy, but Bad Politics," *Florida Times-Union,* 20 Aug. 1993,
A13; Stuntz, "Crime Talk and Law Talk," *Reviews in American History*
23 (1995): 157.

47. Mark A. R. Kleiman and Kerry D. Smith, "State and Local Drug
Enforcement: In Search of a Strategy," in *Drugs and Crime,* ed.
Michael Tonry and James Q. Wilson, vol. 13 of *Crime and Justice*
(Chicago: U. of Chicago Press, 1990), 87; Daniel Patrick Moyni-
han, "Defining Deviancy Down," *American Scholar* 62 (Winter
1993): 28.

48. McGrath, "Treat Them to a Good Dose of Lead," *Chronicles* 18 (Jan.
1994): 18–19.

49. Benjamin Mark Cole, "Bank Deposits Getting High on Drug Money
Flooding L.A.'s Underground Economy," *Los Angeles Business Journal,*
3 June 1991, 13.

50. Adam Walinsky, "The Crisis of Public Order," *Atlantic Monthly* 276
(July 1995): 46; Joe Lambe and Glenn E. Rice, "A Young Life Abruptly
Ended, but Who Has Paid?" *Kansas City Star,* 28 May 1995, A1.

51. A. Alvarez, *Night: Night Life, Night Language, Sleep, and Dreams* (New
York: Norton, 1995), 244.

52. Simon, *Homicide: A Year on the Killing Streets* (New York: Houghton
Mifflin, 1991).

53. Elijah Anderson, "The Code of the Streets," *Atlantic Monthly* 273

(May 1994): 94; Taylor, *Dangerous Society*, 71–72; Shakur, *Monster*, 163.

Conclusion: Life in the New Frontier Society

1. Buford, *Among the Thugs* (New York: Norton, 1992), 248–249.
2. Thomas J. Bouchard Jr. et al., "Sources of Human Psychological Differences: The Minnesota Study of Twins Reared Apart," *Science* 250 (1990): 228.
3. Sanyika Shakur, *Monster: The Autobiography of an L.A. Gang Member* (New York: Atlantic Monthly Press, 1993), 36, 55; Cheryl W. Thompson, "HUD Chief, Aide Rough It on City's Poverty 'Frontier,'" *Chicago Tribune* 20 June 1993, sec. 2, 3; Loïc J. D. Wacquant and William Julius Wilson, "The Cost of Racial and Class Exclusion in the Inner City," *AAAPSS* 501 (1989): 15; Gordon Witkin et al., "The Men Who Invented Crack," *U.S. News and World Report* 111 (19 Aug. 1991): 52; Mary B. W. Tabor, "Brooklyn Youths Taking Drugs as Trade to Buffalo," *NYT*, nat. ed., 26 Feb. 1992, A1, B12.
4. *Gangs, Crime and Violence in Los Angeles* (Los Angeles: District Attorney's Office, 1992), 31–32; Léon Bing, *Do or Die* (New York: HarperCollins, 1991).
5. Roger D. McGrath, "Violence and Lawlessness on the Western Frontier," in *Violence in America*, vol. 1: *The History of Crime*, ed. Ted Robert Gurr (Newbury Park, Ca.: Sage, 1989), 140–141.
6. Dan Keating and Charles Strouse, "Living Dangerously: We're Capital of Crime," *Miami Herald*, 4 Dec. 1994, 1A, 22A.
7. Laurie Cassaday, "Man Guilty in 2 Slayings," *Florida Times-Union*, 10 March 1995, B1, B3.
8. Jacksonville Sheriff's Office, "Fourth Quarter 1994 SHO Summary" (Jan. 12, 1995). I am indebted to Gus Carlson for assistance in obtaining this document.
9. "Early 1995 Murder Rate Takes Dramatic Drop," *Florida Times-Union*, 18 Dec. 1995, A7; Jim Newton, "The NYPD: Bigger, Bolder—and Better?" *Los Angeles Times*, 24 Dec. 1995, A1, A18-19; Michael Massing, "Crime and Drugs: The New Myths," *NYRB* 43 (11 Feb. 1996): 16–20.
10. James Alan Fox and Glenn Pierce, "American Killers Are Getting Younger," *USA Today* (magazine) 122 (Jan. 1994): 24–26; Alfred Blumstèin, "Youth Violence, Guns, and the Illicit-Drug Industry," Carnegie Mellon U., Heinz School of Public Policy and Management, working paper 94–29 (July 1994), 22–23; Adam Walinsky, "The Crisis of Public Order," *Atlantic Monthly* 276 (July 1995): 49, 52.

11. As pointed out in a paper by David Popenoe, "Cultural Changes and the Family" (1994), kindly furnished to me by the author.

12. The erosion of parental authority and the disruption of families by external market, bureaucratic, and professional forces is explored by Christopher Lasch in *Haven in a Heartless World* (New York: Basic Books, 1977); *The Culture of Narcissism* (New York: Norton, 1979); *The Minimal Self* (New York: Norton, 1984); and *The Revolt of the Elites and the Betrayal of Democracy* (New York: Norton, 1995).

13. Blankenhorn, *Fatherless America: Confronting Our Most Urgent Social Problem* (New York: Basic Books, 1995), 35, 32; David Popenoe, *Life without Father* (New York: Free Press, 1996), 52–53, 153–157; Gottfredson and Hirschi, *A General Theory of Crime* (Stanford: Stanford U. Press, 1990), 272–273.

14. Lykken, *The Antisocial Personalities* (Hillsdale, N.J.: Erlbaum, 1995), chs. 14–15, quotation at 22.

15. Hubert Howe Bancroft, *California Inter Pocula* (San Francisco, 1888), 311; Gary G. Hamilton, "The Structural Sources of Adventurism: The Case of the California Gold Rush," *AJS* 83 (1978): 1469–1473.

16. U.S. Centers for Disease Control, "Physical Violence during the 12 Months Preceding Childbirth—Alaska, Maine, Oklahoma, and West Virginia, 1990–1991," *MMWR: Morbidity and Mortality Weekly Report* 43 (4 March 1994): 135. See also Blankenhorn, *Fatherless America*, 34–35; Walter R. Gove, Carolyn Briggs Style, and Michael Hughes, "The Effect of Marriage on the Well-Being of Adults," *J. of Family Issues* 11 (1990): 21–25.

INDEX

Abilene, Kansas, 96, 98, 146–147
Abortion, 5, 245, 248. *See also* Contraception; Infanticide
Accidents: and gender, 10, 11; and age, 13, 214; and family status, 38, 40, 68; among miners, 69, 76, 77, 85; among cowboys, 88, 89–90, 91, 94; among tramps, 175–177, 185; statistics, 208–212; at night, 222, 223
Age: and violence or disorder, 2, 5, 9, 13–15, 20–21, 27, 67, 79–80, 84, 88, 91–92, 93, 117–118, 150, 202, 220, 223, 225, 226, 244, 250, 255–256, 257, 259–260, 261, 270–271, 272, 274, 275, 280; and testosterone, 18–20; of U.S. population, 22, 61, 210; and religion, 35–36; and frontier, 49, 61–62, 65, 111, 170; of prostitutes, 94; at marriage, 137–139, 204, 205, 215; and nighttime, 222, 223, 239. *See also* Accidents; Cowboys
Aggression: defined, 15; male, 15–18, 27, 237–238; and testosterone, 18–20; and alcohol, 33, 128; female, 237; and cocaine, 256
Alcohol use: and violence or disorder, 3, 6, 32–34, 36, 52, 66, 67, 74, 76, 78, 85, 91–92, 97, 102, 105, 108, 121, 128, 129, 145, 165, 170, 181, 184, 185, 192, 211, 218–219, 222, 239, 256, 257, 262, 271, 272, 278, 279; prohibition of, 5, 36, 147, 191–194, 268; and gender, 10, 43, 134; and age, 13, 214; and steroids, 20; by Irish, 36, 166, 191; and marriage, 39, 142, 219; in military, 44, 45;

by miners, 70, 73; by cowboys, 87, 88, 94; as legal defense, 99–100; by Indians, 123–124, 128, 129–130; by Chinese, 161; by tramps, 177, 189–191, 193–194; extent of, 193, 215; by blacks, 218, 255. *See also* Alcoholism; Mortality
Alcoholism: and gender, 11, 150; and marital status, 41, 177; Indian, 129–130; of prostitutes, 133; of tramps, 188, 189, 196, 330n43; black, 218, 219, 221; recovery from, 263
American Revolution, 23, 24, 45, 121, 136
Amphetamines, 252–253
Arizona, 50, 75, 133
Arson, 13, 178, 181, 260
Arthur, Chester A., 87, 156
Aspinwall, William, 184, 187–189
Assault: and gender, 10; and age, 21; and honor, 29; and alcohol, 34; by cowboys, 99; by Chinese, 163; at night, 221, 222; statistics, 225; failure to punish, 266
Atlanta, Georgia, 59, 263
Aurora, Nevada, 81–83
Australia, 150–151, 278
Automobiles: and family-based commuting, 5, 194–195; and suburbs, 206–207, 216–217, 245; and homicide rate, 209; and nighttime, 222; theft of, 225, 267. *See also* Accidents

Baby boom, 5, 225, 226, 272, 275
Bachelors: shorter lives, 18, 39, 40,